PARTICIPATION

RESEARCH

RETHINKING
HIGHER EDUCATION

George Fallis   **AND**

DIFFERENTIATION

Queen's Policy Studies Series
School of Policy Studies, Queen's University
McGill-Queen's University Press
Montreal & Kingston • London • Ithaca

SCHOOL OF
Policy Studies

Publications Unit
Robert Sutherland Hall
138 Union Street
Kingston, ON, Canada
K7L 3N6
www.queensu.ca/sps/

The preferred citation for this book is:
Fallis, G. 2013. *Rethinking Higher Education: Participation, Research, and Differentiation.* Montreal and Kingston: Queen's Policy Studies Series, McGill-Queen's University Press.

Library and Archives Canada Cataloguing in Publication

Fallis, George, 1947-, author
    Rethinking higher education : participation, research, and differentiation / George Fallis.

(Queen's policy studies series / School of Policy Studies, Queen's University)
Includes bibliographical references and index.
Issued in print and electronic formats.
ISBN 978-1-55339-333-7 (pbk.).—ISBN 978-1-55339-334-4 (ebook).—
ISBN 978-1-55339-342-9 (pdf)

    1. Education, Higher—Ontario. 2. Universities and colleges—Ontario.
I. Queen's University (Kingston, Ont.). School of Policy Studies, issuing body
II. Title. III. Series: Queen's policy studies series

LA418.O6F35 2013   378.713   C2013-905296-8
                                                      C2013-905297-6

TABLE OF CONTENTS

ACKNOWLEDGEMENTS

The idea for this book originated as I read and participated in the very active discussion of Ontario's system of higher education; much of the discussion stimulated by the work of the Higher Education Quality Council of Ontario (HEQCO). The first outlines of my thinking were presented at a seminar at HEQCO. Sections of the analysis were presented at symposia organized by the Higher Education Group at the Ontario Institute for Studies in Education (OISE). Ontario has been well served by the leadership of HEQCO and OISE in the development and discussion of public policy on higher education. I would like to thank participants in the seminars at both HEQCO and OISE for their helpful comments and suggestions.

The comments and suggestions of colleagues as my thinking developed have been very helpful, especially those of Glen Jones, Ian Clark, Michael Skolnik, David Trick, Ken Norrie, Didier Pomerleau, and Dan Lang. Michael Wayne, Peter Victor, Avi Cohen, Bryan Massam, Bob Gibbs, and Ross Rudolph were always thoughtful conversationalists about teaching and learning and universities.

I am grateful for the financial support from the SSHRC Small Grants Program and from the Faculty of Liberal Arts and Professional Studies at York University.

And as always, my greatest debt is to Sheila, my companion on the (longish) journey to publication.

INTRODUCTION

It is time to rethink higher education in Ontario.

The basic structures of Ontario's higher education system—the types of institutions, their mandates, and the system of finance—were put in place in the mid-1960s. These structures have served Ontario well, but it is time to undertake the reforms needed for the decades ahead.

Any system of higher education has two basic missions: teaching and research. The teaching mission can be subdivided into two levels. First-level higher education requires a secondary school diploma for entry, and awards bachelor's degrees, diplomas, and certificates. Upper-level higher education requires a bachelor's degree for entry, and is made up of graduate education, awarding master's and doctoral degrees, and certain professional programs such as medicine or law. Thus the system of higher education can be conceptualized around three activities: first-level higher education, upper-level higher education, and research. As we rethink our system of higher education, asking whether we have the best system in place to serve the needs of Ontarians for the next twenty years, the question should be asked about each activity: do we have the best system to provide first-level higher education, the best system to provide upper-level higher education, and the best system to support research?

Since the mid-1960s, Ontario has had a binary system of higher education—universities and Colleges of Applied Arts and Technology (CAATs).[1] There is a separate policy framework for each sector: operating grants are different; tuition is different; and the governance, quality assurance, and accountability structures differ.

Both sectors provide first-level higher education and each sector has a distinct mandate: universities offer bachelor's degree programs with an academic orientation; CAATs offer diploma and certificate programs with a career orientation. Colleges also offer the in-class components of apprenticeships.

Rethinking Higher Education: Participation, Research, and Differentiation, G. Fallis. Kingston: School of Policy Studies, Queen's University. © 2013 The School of Policy Studies, Queen's University at Kingston. All rights reserved.

Only the university sector has the mandate for upper-level higher education: universities are responsible for graduate education and for professional education that requires a bachelor's degree for admission.

And the university sector has an explicit research mandate: all full-time professors have the responsibility to teach and to conduct research.

The money to pay for the annual operation of the system comes from three main sources: for both colleges and universities the revenue comes from (i) formula operating grants, based on enrolments, from the Ontario government; and (ii) tuition fees paid by students. Universities have an additional major source of funds: (iii) sponsored research income, especially research grants from the national granting councils of the federal government.

Thus, the institutions of higher education in Ontario are divided into two groups. The differentiation arises because of the mandate given by government to each sector, supported by the separate government policy framework for each sector. Within each sector, there is differentiation among institutions, but particularly in the university sector, universities have tended to become more similar over time through their own institutional decision making. As we rethink higher education for the decades ahead, we must also ask whether Ontario would be better served by a more differentiated system. The approach of this book asserts that the question cannot be addressed without, first, undertaking a comprehensive analysis of each component of the system, i.e., first-level higher education, upper-level higher education, and research.

One central thesis of this book is that Ontario's system of higher education has been designed almost entirely around the provision of first-level higher education. And further, the focus has been accessibility and expanding the number of places.

The rethinking of this book concludes that the first-level system is now large enough and therefore policy should stop its focus on expansion. Attention should shift to improving existing programs and providing a more diverse array of first-level programs for Ontario's students.

Rethinking higher education for the next twenty years will require more attention paid to how the system should be designed for graduate education, particularly doctoral education, and for research. The biggest gap in provincial higher education policy relates to research. Provincial policy for the design of the university system has had little to say explicitly about the research mission of universities.

The basic structures, put in place in the 1960s, have been used during the enormous expansion of the system since then. The expansion has been especially rapid since the late 1990s—at a pace and scale that most observers do not realize.

For example, full-time undergraduate enrolment at Ontario universities rose nearly 75 percent from 1998 to 2008; the universities added 150,000 undergraduates, which are 60,000 more than were added in the baby boom decade of 1965 to 1975. College enrolments grew by 14 percent from 1998 to 2008. Participation rates have increased significantly. Today, by the time Ontarians have reached the age of 21, almost 75 percent have entered university or college.

At the same time that first-level higher education grew, there was also an enormous expansion of graduate education: enrolments in master's programs rose by nearly 60 percent and enrolment in doctoral programs rose more than 70 percent. This was the greatest expansion in graduate education in Ontario's history.

Research support grew even more rapidly. Federal government support for university research across Canada rose from $733 million to $2.9 billion, a fourfold increase from 1997/98 to 2007/08. Ontario's support rose as well. Total sponsored research income at Ontario universities tripled from 1998 to 2008. Sponsored research income is now a larger source of income for universities than tuition fees. And much of this increased support was different than in the past; there was a "new research agenda" at both the federal and provincial levels. The research support grew out of concern with economic growth during a time of globalization and rapid technological change. The analysis concluded that research and innovation were crucial to economic prosperity and saw higher education institutions as crucial in the national innovation system. The additional research support emphasized the commercialization of the findings and was concentrated in certain fields, especially science, engineering, technology, and medicine.

The extraordinary expansion of Ontario's higher education system over the last fifteen years reflects the cross-party consensus that higher education is more important than ever before: to achieve our goal of equality of opportunity in a knowledge-based society, to support cultural flourishing, to support effective public policy, to improve our health, and to sustain economic prosperity during this era of globalization and rapid technological change. So what lies ahead?

There is little doubt that higher education will be just as important in the years ahead. After such expansion across all the components of higher education, using the same basic structures, it is appropriate to pause and to ask a fundamental question: do we have the best system in place to serve the needs of Ontarians for the next twenty years?

As we assess our current system and plan for the future, we should benchmark ourselves against the best in the world. Too often the policy debate about Ontario higher education has been inward looking. We must look outward and assess ourselves against international standards and aspire to excellence. Through such a process, Ontario can achieve the higher education system it needs and deserves.

This introduction has spoken of the "system" of higher education. Often when we talk about the system of higher education, we think it is the result of conscious design by government. But we should be cautious about how to interpret this idea of system. The analysis of this book, like much analysis of Ontario higher education, asserts that "Ontario has never had a higher education *system* [italics added], in a holistic organizational sense, or a master-plan" (Jones 1997, 157). Rather Ontario established the binary structure, accompanied by an often-evolving network of regulatory policies and funding arrangements. Universities, in particular, have enjoyed tremendous autonomy within their broad mandate. Certainly government policies have great influence, but the higher education system we actually observe is the result of both government policy and of institutional choices, and importantly also the result of student choices about which institutions to attend and which programs to enrol in.

Very often, and this has been the case in Ontario, this complex dynamic leads institutions to become more similar, a process called isomorphism. Ontario universities are becoming more similar, as all aspire to the same goals particularly to grow at the graduate level and to increase their level of research. Colleges are becoming more similar to universities as they offer bachelor's degrees and expand their research role. If we are to realize a more differentiated system, and this book concludes Ontario needs greater institutional differentiation, it is important to understand institutional decision making and the forces of isomorphism. Greater institutional differentiation can only be realized if there is a stronger government vision for the entire system. Institutional mandates will have to change, and the financial and accountability arrangements revised, to create the more differentiated system. This book recommends a series of key policy directions that government should follow to shape the future evolution of the system.

AN OPPORTUNE TIME

It is an opportune time to rethink higher education because the Government of Ontario has indicated it wishes to consider alternatives in the design of the system.[2]

In 2010, the deputy minister of Training, Colleges, and Universities asked the Higher Education Quality Council of Ontario (HEQCO) to explore "whether a more strongly differentiated set of universities would help improve the overall performance and sustainability of the system, and help Ontario compete internationally…[and]…how to operationalize a differentiation policy, should government be interested in pursuing this as a strategic objective" (Weingarten and Deller 2010, 6).

In early 2012, the Ministry of Training, Colleges, and Universities (MTCU) issued a discussion paper—*Strengthening Ontario's Centres of Creativity, Innovation, and Knowledge: A discussion paper on innovation to make our university and college system stronger*—and invited universities and colleges to respond, as well as student groups, staff and faculty associations (Ontario. MTCU 2012). The discussion paper focused on first-level higher education and invited particular discussion around expanded credential options, improved credit transfer and student mobility, year-round learning, improving teaching and learning outcomes, technology-enabled learning, and creating a tuition framework.

Later in 2012, MTCU asked each university and college to submit a draft Strategic Mandate Agreement; these are now public documents. HEQCO, at MTCU's request, established an expert review panel to evaluate the submissions in terms of their "ability to achieve significant improvements in productivity, quality, and affordability through innovation and differentiation." The panel will identify those universities and colleges "whose submissions demonstrate the greatest ability to serve as lead institutions ... those that provide the most compelling and promising visions, mandate statements and plans that advance government policies, objectives and goals ... The lead institutions selected through this exercise would be the first to receive funding to pursue their mandates as early as 2013–14" (HEQCO 2013b). The Expert Panel has now reported. The panel felt it could not, on the basis of this exercise, identify lead institutions. It concluded that "system-level planning will require the government to be more active and assertive. Bottom-up processes like that used with this SMA exercise will not produce the system changes we believe are necessary." Further, analysis and evidence are required to support "institutional claims of primacy, quality, distinctiveness or excellence. Self-proclamations of these attributes are entirely inadequate to drive decision making" (HEQCO 2013b, 7).

This book is a contribution to this policy dynamic.

It is also an opportune time for rethinking because over the last fifteen years a great deal of excellent research has been published about higher education in Canada and in Ontario. The Canada Millennium Scholarship Foundation and HEQCO have been important supporters of this research, especially around questions of access. The research allows the development of evidence-based policy recommendations and this book draws heavily upon the research. The book, *Academic Transformation: The Forces Reshaping Higher Education in Ontario* (Clark et al. 2009), funded by HEQCO, is an excellent analysis of the history and current state of higher education in Ontario. That book and its follow-on, *Academic Reform: Policy Options for Improving the Quality and Cost-Effectiveness of Undergraduate Education in Ontario* (Clark, Trick, and Van Loon 2011) frame subsequent discussions about higher education policy in Ontario. In contrast to the latter book, the analysis here examines doctoral education and research, as well as first-level higher education.

The book deals with "higher education," that is, with the universities and colleges. Higher education is by far the largest component of postsecondary education, but the two are not synonymous. Postsecondary education also includes apprenticeships and adult education, neither of which is dealt with here. While the analysis deals with both colleges and universities, in the later chapters, the analysis deals more with universities. This reflects both the experience and knowledge of the author, and also the state of the available literature.

Like many books about higher education, the analysis rests upon careful reading of the literature, long observation of the system, and personal experience within it. In this case, I draw significantly upon my previous writing about universities—*Multiversities, Ideas, and Democracy* (Fallis 2007)—and my experience in academic administration as a chair and dean of arts at York University and my recent experience in the classroom, particularly teaching large undergraduate classes.

This book contributes to the Ontario policy discussion—it is hoped in a timely manner. But policy discussions and priorities often change rapidly, and one risks being left behind by events. Nonetheless, there is much analysis and many recommendations that are not tied to the policy cycle and can contribute to policy development in the longer run. In this vein, the book also hopes to contribute to policy development in other jurisdictions, because the questions it explores—How high can the participation rate be? How best to support research across the higher education system? Should there be more differentiation of institutions and greater diversity of programs?—are crucial questions in higher education across Canada, the United States and Europe, and indeed across the world.

Finally, it is a critical time to rethink higher education because of the difficult economic and fiscal circumstances in Ontario. After the financial crisis and recession, economic growth is modest and there remains great uncertainty about the future direction of the world economy, and in particular the economy of the United States, our largest trading partner. The Province of Ontario and the federal government have large deficits. Even with robust growth, there will have to be some blend of tax increases and expenditure restraint in the years ahead. Every policy area will be scrutinized intensely and there will be difficult choices about priorities. We will need a well-thought-out higher education system for the years ahead.

OVERVIEW

The core principle in designing Ontario's system was to provide a place in first-level higher education for every qualified student who wished to attend. The expansion of higher education helped to ensure the equality of opportunity so valued in a democratic society. And in a happy coincidence of democratic needs and economic needs, the graduates were required by the postindustrial economy. The institutions of each sector—the universities and colleges—are geographically distributed across all regions of the province and offer a comprehensive range of programming, and within each sector there is the same government funding, and approximately the same fees charged, for the same activities, so that within each sector with respect to first-level higher education, institutions provide programs of roughly similar quality. This framework for providing first-level higher education is the foundation of Ontario's system; it has served us very well and should be retained.

The beginning of any comprehensive study of Ontario's system of higher education—and this book is no exception—has been to analyze first-level higher education, especially the demand for first-level higher education and to ask how many places do we need? This analysis was done in the late 1950s, when the province began planning for the arrival of the baby boom at the postsecondary level. This was the question when the baby boom arrived and moved through the system; it was the question when the double cohort arrived, and has been the question over the last fifteen years. And it is the first question we face today: do we have enough capacity for the years ahead in the existing system?

The usual analysis, to answer how many new places we need, begins with a demographic projection, a projection of the number of 18–24 year olds in the coming years, i.e., the size of the group who would be eligible for higher education. In most of the major planning episodes, the 18–24 age group was projected to grow. Next in the planning is a forecast of the participation rate—the share of the 18–24 year olds who will attend higher education. Over the last sixty years, overall participation rates have been rising, especially among women; today the participation rate of women is higher than of men. Also, the participation rate of immigrants is higher than of native-born Ontarians. In every planning exercise, the participation rate was forecast to increase. These forecasts of rising participation rates proved correct. And therefore with a growing 18–24 group and rising participation rates, the number of needed places grew. And, the system was expanded; sometimes by creating new institutions, but since the 1970s, mainly by expanding existing institutions.

Many recent policy analyses have assumed the continuing need for more places and have recommended the creation of new types of institutions to meet the still-increasing demand. This analysis comes to a very different conclusion. The size of the 18–24-year-old age cohort will decline by almost 8 percent over the next decade. Participation rates are now very high. For the first time in Ontario, we must think carefully about how high participation rates can go and also think carefully about the labour market demand for the graduates. I believe that participation rates cannot, and should not as a matter of public policy, go much higher.

The analysis of demography and participation rates leads to the conclusion that the system of first-level higher education in Ontario is now large enough. This is a tremendous accomplishment that should be recognized and celebrated. However, with this recognition, a radically new mindset is required in planning higher education.

In first-level higher education, we should stop the focus on adding new places that has dominated policy since the 1960s. We do not need any new types of institutions. (There is one exception. Ontario students would benefit greatly from an open university/college.) We should shift the focus to assessing and improving the programs we have in place, and to filling gaps in the types of programs available and the means of delivery. The question for the future becomes: how can first-level higher education be improved?

And amid consideration of reform proposals, we must also confront the fact that there is a substantial minority of students attending university today who are disengaged: they have little sense of why they are at university and little willingness to undertake the demanding program of reading, writing, and analytical thought that constitutes an undergraduate education. These students are benefitting little from their time at university (except for receiving a credential) and likely will not realize the predicted gains in the labour market upon graduation.

How well are we doing in first-level higher education and how can we improve? A number of key directions are recommended. Over the last decades, universities have tended to place less emphasis on undergraduate education and more on graduate education and research. This should change; we need to make undergraduate education a higher priority and to focus on improving teaching and learning. Also, there is also need for more liberal education programs and more honours undergraduate degree programs at universities for high-engagement, high-ability students.

There are several gaps in the range of programs available to Ontario students. The greatest need is for more career-oriented programs at the bachelor's degree level. Many students at the university are taking degrees in the arts and sciences despite little engagement with the academic discipline and are struggling after they graduate to make the transition to the labour force. Bachelor-level degrees that combine academic study with more career-oriented study would better suit their interests and needs. These more career-oriented programs can be provided through better structured college-university collaborations, but mainly they should be provided by the colleges by expanding their degree offerings, including three-year degrees.

At the same time that first-level higher education grew so rapidly from 1998 to 2008, there was an equally large expansion of graduate education. And we should ask: have we been implementing the best system possible for graduate education?

The policy logic of graduate education and the policy logic of first-level higher education are very different. First-level higher education is built upon the fundamental principle that there should be a place for every qualified student who wishes to attend. Accessibility is paramount. This has meant that universities and colleges have been established in all regions of the province and that the different institutions in each sector offer a comprehensive range of quite similar programs.

In contrast, upper-level higher education has no such commitment to universal access. Most students will not go on from their bachelor's degree to do a master's degree. And still fewer students will go on from a master's degree to a doctoral degree. Given that each graduate degree program needs to have a critical mass of students and of faculty members, there will be a limited number of graduate degree programs. The difference in policy logic is especially compelling at the doctoral level.

Given this very different policy logic, the questions for public policy regarding doctoral education are different. The first policy question is the same—how many places should there be? Then the questions change: how many programs to have, how large should they be, and at which universities should they be located? Doctoral programs are very expensive with relatively little of the cost covered by tuition. Ontario students have excellent opportunities to study abroad (in fact we encourage our students to go to the best universities in the world) and our doctoral programs seek to attract top students from abroad. The design of our system of doctoral education can only be undertaken with careful awareness and comparison to the best programs available abroad. Given the demand, there can be relatively few doctoral programs in each field in order to ensure the critical mass of students and of faculty necessary for high quality programs.

And where should these programs be located? The analysis of this book concludes universities should be differentiated: all universities should offer bachelor's and master's degrees but doctoral programs should be offered at only a subset of universities.

At the same time as undergraduate education and graduate education expanded, research support expanded even more. The university sector has a clear research mandate. Yet if we ask—as Ontario designed and built and expanded its university system—what has been Ontario's policy with respect to university-based research? We have to pause and ponder, and then we realize that Ontario didn't really have a policy. It is not so much that we need to *rethink* Ontario's system of supporting university-based research, as it is that we need to *start thinking* about how to design the university system for supporting university-based research.[3]

The research mission has been layered on top of a system designed to provide undergraduate education. Given the needs at the undergraduate level, new universities were created and individual universities expanded. This meant more professors were hired, and given their joint responsibilities for teaching and research, more research was done. The professors were hired across all fields in order to provide comprehensive undergraduate degree programming, and so the research was comprehensive across all fields. The professors also applied for research grants, especially from the national granting councils, and so more research could be supported. The costs for faculty time on research and the indirect costs of research were covered from the operating fund, that is, from the operating grant and tuition, which are a function of enrolment. The university-based research endeavour in Ontario has been largely driven by the expansion of the system at the undergraduate level and by the availability of federal research funds. Provincial policy for the design of the university system has had little to say explicitly about the research mission of universities.

Consider the two major examinations of Ontario's system of higher education over the last twenty years: the Smith Commission (Ontario. Ministry of Education and Training 1996) and the Rae Review (Rae 2005). Neither was given a mandate to examine the research function of the system. The ministry responsible for Ontario's higher education system—the Ministry of Training, Colleges, and Universities—has no programs directed toward research. Ontario does have provincial programs to support research; but they were all developed for the economic innovation agenda—the new research agenda of the past twenty years—and delivered by ministries other than the ministry responsible for universities and colleges. First, they were delivered by the Ministry of Energy, Science and Technology, then by the Ministry of Enterprise, Opportunity and Innovation, next by the Ministry of Economic Development and Trade, then by the Ministry of Research and Innovation, and recently folded back into the Ministry of Economic Development and Innovation. Just as the Ontario policy on higher education has had little to say about the research mission of universities, so, too, the provincial programs that support university research have had little to say about the design of the university system. Ontario's approach lacks coherence and transparency.

The new role of research in the colleges is similarly disconnected from design, operation, and funding of the college system. The colleges, as part of their purpose to support the economic and social development of their communities, were given the authority to conduct "applied research" in the *Ontario Colleges of Applied Arts and Technology Act,* 2002. But there was no change in the operating funding to reflect this new role and the workload of faculty members remains focused exclusively on teaching.

Throughout, there has been a curious disconnect between these innovation-linked programs supporting university and college research and the provincial policy on higher education. The first step in *starting to think* whether we have the best system for supporting research is to end this disconnect. Ontario should establish a provincial policy regarding research at universities and colleges and integrate this into the design of the system.

The ad hoc nature of Ontario's policy toward research at universities becomes still clearer when we compare the systems of assessment and accountability between those for teaching programs and research. Ontario has very thorough and well-developed systems for evaluating undergraduate degree programs, graduate, and professional programs.

These systems are designed to ensure that all universities assess their degree programs and have the mechanisms to identify areas for improvement. In glaring contrast, the Ontario university system has no similar mechanisms for research assessment and accountability. The second step in establishing the best system for supporting research is to initiate a research documentation and assessment system in the university sector. This assessment is especially important because the expansion of support for university-based research over the last fifteen years has emphasized that the research must be at world class levels. We cannot design a system of support for university research without rigorous international comparison of how well we are doing.

As we begin to analyze research within the context of the entire university system, some fundamental questions get raised. Ontario has ignored them during the expansion but they must be addressed. Two are paramount. Should all professors devote the same share of their workload to research? Should universities be differentiated according to their relative focus on research? Over the last thirty years, Ontario universities have become more similar in that the teaching loads of professors have declined in order that more time can be spent on research. And the teaching loads for professors have moved toward the loads at research-intensive universities. All our universities aspire to be equally research intensive.

Our universities all have the same mandate, aspire to the same goals, and are becoming more similar. This comes at a cost.

Institutions are more effective when they are more focused and specialized. As institutions focus and specialize, they become more efficient— deliver the same service at lower cost. With focus and specialization, they can deliver higher quality services, are more likely to innovate, and more likely to develop a culture of excellence. With a more limited range of activities and purposes, the institutions can better report their activities and be better held accountable to governments and the public. Without some focus, institutions tend to suffer from mission stretch, or mission overload; they do many things adequately rather than fewer things excellently.

Ontario would be well served by differentiating the university system as two distinct groups.

All our universities have large undergraduate student bodies and offer a full range of programs. Their undergraduate activity is far larger than their graduate activities. Undergraduate education is their primary task. This is as it should be. In this sense, all our universities are and will remain primarily undergraduate universities. And all professors have the responsibility to teach and to conduct research. Again, this is as it should be. In this sense, all our universities are and will remain research universities.

However, one group should be designated as doctoral/research universities. Like all universities, this group would offer bachelor's and master's degrees, but doctoral education would be provided only by this group. All universities have, and should continue to have, a research mandate. However, the doctoral/research universities should have a special mandate to be more research intensive. This group of universities would be the focus for major research initiatives under the new research agenda. Also, this group would be the focus of province-wide planning of doctoral education.

While the university system has been becoming more similar, the college system has been differentiating. Certain colleges have taken on the designation of Institute of Technology and Advanced Learning (ITAL), allowing up to 15 percent of programming in bachelor's degrees. All these degrees have been four-year degrees. Also, colleges have been taking on a role in applied research as part of the new research agenda. Several recent federal programs have been directed toward colleges and most Ontario programs allow applications from the college sector. This evolving differentiation should be formalized.

Given the gaps in current Ontario first-level higher education and the need for more career-oriented bachelor's degrees, the ITALs (or a larger group should other colleges take the designation) should be allowed to expand applied bachelor's programming (including three-year degrees) to 30 percent. Also, ITALs should be given an enhanced research mandate and a lead role in applied research. The enhanced research mandate will require changes in the college funding and in the agreements governing responsibilities and workload of faculty members.

Thus, Ontario's binary system should be further differentiated. The university sector should be differentiated as two groups and the college sector should be differentiated as two groups. This differentiation could be started relatively easily through government-determined mandates articulated in Mandate and Accountability Agreements. All universities and all colleges should remain subject to the same policy framework (operating grants, tuition policy, quality assurance, and accountability) when they engage in the same activity. However, over time, the differentiation will have to be supported by a separate policy, funding, and accountability framework for each group with respect to that group's special mandate.

In discussions with colleagues, I have described this as a "short policy-focused book." It begins by examining Ontario's existing system of higher education. Then it explores why institutional differentiation is desirable in a system of higher education; and analyzes how our current system is the outcome of both government policy and institutional decision making. Against this background, the three components of our current system—first-level higher education, upper-level higher education, and research—are analyzed. The book makes a number of recommendations, both specific proposals and policy directions to be pursued. In some ways, the policy directions are more important; detailed proposals for implementation will of necessity be worked out by governments, universities, colleges, faculty members, staff, and students through the policy process. The main policy directions are brought together, with a discussion of implementation, in the concluding chapter.

NOTES

1. What follows is a general description of each sector, focusing on the essential characteristics. Colleges can now offer some bachelor's degrees, they have some academically oriented instruction, and are becoming engaged in research. Universities actually offer many career-oriented degrees, and many diplomas and certificates. Some universities have permanent full-time professors with teaching responsibilities but not research responsibilities. A more detailed description of the sectors is provided in the following chapters.
2. The official opposition party has also indicated a desire for change, issuing An Ontario PC Caucus White Paper—*Paths to Prosperity: Higher Learning for Better Jobs* (Ontario PC Caucus 2013).
3. Colleges have been expanding their research activities and have been given the authority to undertake applied research. As discussed below, it is recommended that a group of colleges be given an enhanced mandate in applied research.

Chapter 1

ONTARIO'S SYSTEM OF HIGHER EDUCATION

The starting point for rethinking higher education must be a thorough understanding of our current system. Ontario has a binary system, made up of a college sector and a university sector. This chapter distills the essential features of our current system.

As a very broad statement, it may be said that the colleges are quite similar to one another and the universities are quite similar to one another. However, there are some differences among the colleges, as well as among the universities, particularly with respect to graduate education and professional education, and research. These differences allow the institutions to be classified into groups; the chapter concludes by classifying the institutions into groups according to the Statistics Canada classification system.

Two questions are central to rethinking higher education: does Ontario need greater institutional differentiation and does Ontario need greater program diversity? This chapter serves as a prelude to analyzing these questions by documenting the existing level of institutional differentiation and program diversity.

THE ENTIRE EDUCATION SYSTEM

Before we begin our examination of Ontario's system of higher education, let us situate it within the entire education system. Broadly speaking, an entire educational system has three levels: primary education, secondary education, and postsecondary education.

The entire Ontario system, in slightly more detail, is represented schematically in Figure 1.1 (in Ontario, primary education is referred to

Rethinking Higher Education: Participation, Research, and Differentiation, G. Fallis. Kingston: School of Policy Studies, Queen's University. © 2013 The School of Policy Studies, Queen's University at Kingston. All rights reserved.

as elementary education). Children enter the pre-elementary level; then proceed to the elementary level; then to the secondary level; and finally through to postsecondary education.

It all seems rather obvious.

However, this simple schema is useful because it highlights a number of fundamental themes regarding how one should think about higher education; themes that are woven into the argument of this book.

First, it highlights that the educational system should be conceptualized as people moving through different levels as they get older. Again, this seems rather obvious. This is how we live our lives. This is how people think of their own educational experience and how they think about

FIGURE 1.1
The Entire Education System

EARLIEST CHILDHOOD

PRE-ELEMENTARY

ELEMENTARY

SECONDARY

POSTSECONDARY

- Universities
- Colleges of Applied Arts and Technology
- Apprenticeships
- Private career colleges
- Adult education/retraining

ADULTHOOD

- employment and career
- community membership/citizenship
- personal life
- knowledge for its own sake

Source: Author's compilation.

the education of their children. However, as we shall see, this is not how most data for analysis of higher education are collected. The schema of Figure 1.1 conceptualizes education using a life course, or longitudinal, approach. The best method for empirical study would be to follow a cohort of people of the same age as they grow up and move through the system. However, only recently have cohort data become available. Most analyses of higher education use data taken as a snapshot at one point in time, i.e., cross-section analysis. Analysts try to convert cross-section pictures into a longitudinal analysis, but this is difficult; sometimes, looking only at a cross-section picture can lead to misunderstanding. It is fundamental in the analysis of higher education to use a longitudinal approach, as in Figure 1.1. This book uses such an approach.[1]

A life course approach emphasizes that people move through the system at different rates, that people move out of the system and back in, and that some do not complete all three levels. Using this longitudinal approach, key characteristics of the entire system can be expressed as four percentages: the percentage of an age cohort that does not finish secondary school; the percentage that finishes secondary school, but does not go further; the percentage that enters postsecondary education; and the percentage that attains a postsecondary qualification. It takes time for the full outcome to be realized and, therefore, the way the current system is functioning can best be determined by looking at people's educational participation and attainment in their late twenties. They have moved through the system and their choices have been made. (Of course, educational participation and attainment for some will still increase if they return to education later.) These percentages for Ontario will be discussed in Chapter 4. (A little quiz for the reader: before reading Chapter 4, what do you think the first three percentages are? For example, are they 25/25/50, or 20/20/60, or something else?)

Figure 1.1 shows that postsecondary education in Ontario is made up of five components:

- Universities
- Colleges of Applied Arts and Technology (CAATs)
- Apprenticeships
- Private career colleges
- Adult education/retraining.

In Canada, the terms "postsecondary education" and "higher education" are often used synonymously. In this book, the terms refer to different things—higher education, comprising colleges and universities, is a component of postsecondary education (PSE). This book deals with higher education—with universities and colleges—and thus does not analyze the whole of postsecondary education. However, it is important always to remember that universities and colleges are only a portion of postsecondary education. Some students finish secondary school and take an apprenticeship, or attend a private career college, or postpone further education until later in life.

Second, Figure 1.1 situates the entire education system as part of the process of development from earliest childhood to adulthood. The entire educational system is part of the process of preparing people for independent and responsible adulthood—to prepare individuals for three domains: for employment, for membership in the community, and for personal life.[2]

After an individual has completed his or her time in the educational system, whether it be after secondary school or after postsecondary education, he or she becomes responsible for themselves. Thus, for all its other purposes, education is always—in part—preparation for a job. This is inescapable and fundamental. Preparation for a job is fundamental to students (and their families), and it is fundamental to the society that finances the entire education system. Thus a constant theme in designing an entire system of education is the balance between academic education and vocational education. Should students begin to focus on vocational education at some level in the system? Should there be institutions that focus on one or the other? How can students move between one and the other? What sorts of skills learned in academic education are transferable to a job?

Membership in the community involves many things including, very importantly, being a citizen in our democracy. Thus education is always in part a preparation for active democratic citizenship. Preparation for community membership also involves learning about our country's geography, history, and culture; and developing a sense of commitment to our fellow citizens balanced by the fundamental responsibility of individuals to take care of themselves and their families. Preparation for community membership also means cultivating certain values such as tolerance, truthfulness, respect for law, a predisposition to non-violence, and commitment to equality of opportunity and to full equality for women. It also means developing one's moral reasoning, developing a critique of what is and a vision of what might be, and understanding the means to make it better. Community membership brings both rights and responsibilities.

Higher education has a special role in preparation for employment and for democratic citizenship; and therefore an assessment of the system of higher education must examine how well it achieves both purposes. Too often today, the purpose of higher education is reduced to preparation for a job. This book recognizes the several purposes of higher education and evaluates the system against each.[3]

Under the heading of personal life, we could include, for example, marriage, raising a family, recreation and hobbies, keeping fit and healthy, managing one's personal finances, and saving for retirement. Education helps prepare us for these. Elementary education and secondary education have the lead role with respect to these purposes; postsecondary education has a much smaller role.

So far, this discussion of the purpose of education takes an instrumental orientation—education is the means to some end. But the purposes of education are broader than this. Knowledge gained though education helps us to understand the natural world and the human condition, and we as humans want this understanding. Cardinal Newman said it best: "Knowledge is capable of being its own end. Such is the constitution of the human mind, that any kind of knowledge, if it be really such, is its own reward" (Newman in Turner 1996, 78). A fundamental purpose of all education, and of higher education in particular, is knowledge for its own sake.

Of course, the educational system is not responsible alone for the preparation for adulthood; the family and individuals themselves have a responsibility. Religious institutions are important for many people, and the entire community has a role—as captured in the African proverb: it takes a village to raise a child.

And there will always be debate about which level of education should be responsible for which domain: for example, should both secondary and postsecondary be concerned with education for democratic citizenship? And there will be debate about the relative importance of the domains of adulthood: for example what should be the balance between education for a job and education for citizenship? And there will be debate about the balance between the role of the school and the role of the family: for example should there be sex education in the secondary schools or is this the job of the family? Whatever the debates, the issue is one of the right balance, because formal education at every level is vital in preparation for all of these domains.

And finally, Figure 1.1 emphasizes that higher education is part of the entire education system, and that all three levels of the system share the same fundamental purposes. Many educators believe that the most important stages in the entire education system are the pre-elementary and elementary levels. Over the last few years in Ontario, pre-elementary and elementary education have been top priorities. Ontario has embarked upon a major reform of pre-elementary education by committing to providing all-day kindergarten across the province and it has provided extra money to reduce class sizes in the early grades of elementary education.

In recent years, the Government of Ontario has announced fundamental goals for each level of the entire education system. The goal at the elementary level is to increase the number of Grade 3 and Grade 6 students meeting Ontario's standards in reading, writing, and math to 75 percent. At the secondary level, the goal is to increase graduation rates to 75 percent. And the goal at the postsecondary level is to have 70 percent of the population aged 25–64 achieve a postsecondary qualification.[4]

In a study of higher education like this, it is particularly important to understand the nature of secondary education: only those who have completed the secondary level can enter higher education. Figure 1.1 emphasizes the obvious fact that higher education is preceded by secondary education. The design and success of any system of higher education will be dependent upon the design and success of the secondary level.

At the secondary level in Ontario, attendance is compulsory (to age 18) and the education is publicly provided and free. Elementary education is intended to provide a common experience for everyone and thus there is a common curriculum for all; in contrast, secondary education is designed to allow many paths for students, recognizing the great diversity of their interests, motivations, and abilities. In Ontario, as in many jurisdictions, a shift toward vocational education becomes possible at the secondary level. In the 1950s, Ontario had two distinct types of secondary school; one academically oriented and the other vocationally oriented. The Colleges of Applied Arts and Technology (CAATs) did not exist then, so the vocationally oriented students would go straight into the workforce after secondary school (perhaps through an apprenticeship). Gradually, Ontario shifted so that secondary schools were not separated into the two types, but within each high school there is a different curriculum available depending on the student's interests and goals. One curriculum prepares students for university, another prepares students for CAAT destinations, and another prepares students for the workforce. Not all schools have the full offerings for the three curricula; most have the university-bound and college-bound curriculum (these two share many courses, especially in the lower levels). Taking university-bound courses allows entrance to the college system; but taking only college-bound courses does not allow entrance to university.[5] Student diversity is also accommodated through specialized institutions. In many large public school boards, there are a few specialized secondary schools, for example oriented more towards the arts, or toward science, or toward students who need a more alternative/flexible schooling.

In 1980, Ontario introduced a province-wide program of special education for both the elementary and secondary levels. The *Education Act* requires that school boards provide, or purchase from another board, special education programs and services for their exceptional pupils. The act defines an exceptional pupil as "a pupil whose behavioural, communicational, intellectual, physical or multiple exceptionalities are such that he or she is considered to need placement in a special education program." Students are identified according to the categories and definitions of exceptionalities provided by the Ministry of Education. An Identification, Placement, and Review Committee (IPRC) in each school identifies a pupil as "exceptional," develops their Individual Education Plan (IEP) and arranges for their placement. Parents attend the IPRC meetings, are involved in the design of the IEP, and may appeal the designation of their child. There are two broad categories of exceptional pupils: the academically exceptional or "gifted" students, and those with special needs, for example with physical disabilities or learning disabilities.[6] In 2007–2008, more than 192,000 students were identified by an IPRC as exceptional pupils; and a further 96,600 students who were not formally identified were provided with special education programs and services. Together these represent over 25 percent of pupils in the elementary and secondary levels.

While the vast majority of institutions at the secondary level are public, there are many private (or as they prefer to be called, independent) schools, allowing a diversity of educational approaches, but they still must offer the provincially established curriculum. Some private schools offer a greater emphasis on the development of the whole person and on extracurricular activities than is available in the public system; some offer a more academically demanding program; some offer the International Baccalaureate (IB) program as well as the Ontario curriculum. The Ontario public system offers Catholic schools. But families with other religious beliefs, especially many Jewish and more evangelical protestant families, want an educational program suffused with their religious values and traditions and thus have established private schools. The private schools receive no operating support from the government and charge fees.

The secondary system in Ontario is very diverse, with curricula, pathways, and schools designed to meet the diverse abilities, interests, and aspirations of students. No doubt, this is a major part of the explanation for why secondary school completion rates have risen so much.

Now let us proceed to higher education. If, having received an Ontario Secondary School Diploma (OSSD), a student wants to go on to higher education, then she/he has two choices: to enter a university or to enter a college. Universities offer bachelor's degree programs with academically-oriented curricula; the programs typically require four years of full-time study, although many universities offer three-year degrees. Universities also offer many career-oriented bachelor's degrees, for example in engineering, education, nursing, and business, as well as many diplomas and certificates, often with a vocational orientation. Colleges offer diplomas and certificates and curricula that emphasize preparation for the labour market in their region; the diploma programs vary in length, requiring one, two, or three years of full-time study. Colleges also offer graduate certificates of one or two years, to students who already have a bachelor's degree. Some colleges also offer four-year bachelor's degrees, mainly with an applied orientation. A distinguishing feature of the CAATs is that each program has a Program Advisory Committee that links the programs to employers of graduates of the program as well as to the relevant professional associations. Both sectors offer both full-time and part-time programs.

Many students use both sectors of the higher education system, combining academic and vocationally oriented study, obtaining two credentials. Some proceed from college to university obtaining a bachelor's degree; and others from university to college, obtaining a graduate certificate. The pathways between the two sectors are an important characteristic of the overall system.

Higher education is not compulsory and it is not free, although it is publicly supported. Students must pay tuition and buy their books and supplies when they attend higher education. Many students, out of necessity or preference, will live away from home and thus also face rent, living, and transportation expenses. Certainly from a student perspective, a full description of the higher education system must include not just the institutions but also the tuition/student assistance policy. In Ontario, tuition fees are regulated and have been rising at about 5 percent a year over the last fifteen years. Basic university tuition (with ancillary fees) in arts and science is about $6,000 per year; college tuition (with fees) is about $3,400 (there is considerable variation by program). There is a complicated system of student assistance in Ontario. The core program is the Ontario Student Assistance Program (OSAP). There are also Registered Education Savings Plans (RESPs); tuition and living costs are deductible under the personal income tax system (with a portion transferable to a parent); and each university has a whole range of merit-based and needs-based assistance. As well, each university implements the Ontario Student Access Guarantee, as mandated by the government.[7] In 2012–2013, Ontario instituted a 30 percent off tuition grant for full-time college and university students whose parents' gross income (before taxes) was $160,000 or less. For many students, the improvements in student assistance have offset the increase in tuition fees.

This completes the description of the entire education system in Ontario. The big question for education policy is: have we provided the best possible education system to help each student proceed from earliest childhood to adulthood? And the more focused question in this book is: have we provided the best possible higher education system to help each student proceed from secondary school to adulthood?

However, before taking up this question, we should note two important gaps in this discussion of the higher education system. As noted in the Introduction, higher education has three components: first-level higher education, second-level higher education, and research. The discussion above and the schema of Figure 1.1 have dealt only with the first level.

After completing a bachelor's degree, a student may go on to complete a master's degree or doctoral degree, what is called graduate education. Or, a student may go on to a professional degree program—for example, law or medicine—that requires a bachelor's degree for entrance. In Ontario, this upper level is entirely within the university sector.

The other gap in the discussion so far is that it has focused entirely upon the education of students. This is of course *the* fundamental purpose of educational institutions. However, the institutions of higher education have other purposes, most importantly, to conduct research. In Ontario, this has been the responsibility of the university sector.[8]

The design of the system of higher education in Ontario has been dominated by concerns about the education of students to the first level of higher education. Part of rethinking higher education in Ontario will be to focus more on the design of the system to best meet the responsibility of higher education institutions to provide graduate education and to conduct research.

FIRST-LEVEL HIGHER EDUCATION: ESSENTIAL FEATURES

Now let us focus on Ontario's current system of higher education, identifying its essential characteristics. This section examines first-level education; subsequent sections examine upper-level education and research.

TABLE 1.1
First-level Enrolments at Universities and Colleges, 2009–2010

UNIVERSITIES	Full-time Undergraduates	COLLEGES	FTE Enrolments
Toronto	56,800	Seneca	20,481
York	41,500	George Brown	19,125
Ottawa	28,100	Humber	18,878
Western	22,100	Algonquin	16,236
Waterloo	22,000	Sheridan	16,024
McMaster	21,500	Fanshawe	13,851
Guelph	20,600	Mohawk	11,617
Ryerson	18,600	Centennial	10,851
Carleton	18,200	Conestoga	8,755
Queen's	15,100	Georgian	8,468
Brock	14,200	St. Clair	8,184
Laurier	13,900	Durham	7,869
Windsor	11,600	Niagara	7,609
Lakehead	6,500	Fleming	6,297
UOIT	6,500	St. Lawrence	5,698
Trent	6,300	La Cité Collégiale	4,009
Laurentian	6,200	Cambrian	3,658
Nipissing	3,900	Loyalist	3,518
OCAD	3,100	Confederation	3,294
Algoma	900	Canadore	2,905
		Lambton	2,713
		Sault	2,189
		Collège Boréal	1,586
		Northern	1,384
TOTAL	**327,600** (367,615 FTE)		**205,199 FTE**

Source: AUCC (2011a), Colleges Ontario (2011a), and COU (2011a).

This book analyzes the twenty-four colleges that are members of Colleges Ontario (CO) and the twenty universities that are members of the Council of Ontario Universities (COU). The universities and colleges are listed in Table 1.1, ordered by their number of full-time students in first-level education. These colleges and universities are created by public statute (although the statutory framework is quite different for colleges and for universities) and receive operating grants (and capital grants) from the government. There are a number of small private universities (with religious affiliation) and many private career colleges which do not receive public operating support. There is one private college, the Michener Institute formed by a consortium of hospitals to train people for the health sector, which receives operating support from the Ministry of Health, but it will not be included here.

The first essential feature of Ontario's higher education system is the commitment that there shall be a place in first-level higher education for every qualified student who wishes to attend. This has been Ontario's commitment since the 1950s when the government began to plan for the arrival of the baby boom generation.

With a growing population aged 18–24 and rising participation rates, the higher education system grew dramatically over the last sixty years. Total enrolments and participation rates by sector are provided in Figures 1.2 and 1.3. Participation rates are measured as total full-time equivalent (FTE) enrolment, as a share of the population aged 18–24.

However, we should be careful to recognize that the commitment is to provide a place for every "qualified" student. To enter a college or a university, a student must have obtained an Ontario Secondary School Diploma (OSSD) and a certain average on their upper-level courses.

To enter college, the admission standard is an OSSD, including six upper-level courses from the college-bound (or the university-bound) curriculum. Different diploma programs require different minimum averages on these six courses.

To enter university, the admission standard is an OSSD, including six upper-level courses from the university-bound curriculum. Most university programs rely on the average grade on these six courses to determine admission. Roughly speaking, about one half of students who graduate from high school through the university-bound curriculum have an average of 80 percent or above; about 18 percent have averages below 70 (Finnie, Childs, and Wismer 2011, 37). The "cutoff" (the minimum acceptable average) for admission to university in Ontario is about 70 percent (although some students are admitted with averages in the high 60s). Many individual programs require much higher averages for admission. And some universities have a cutoff of 80 percent, or above, for most of their programs. Across the university system, cutoffs are generally higher in business, science, and engineering than in humanities and social sciences.

Each year, there are always more applicants to Ontario universities than admissions. Many applicants do not have the high school grades to enter university. Also, many applicants do not have the average to enter their first choice of degree program or their first choice of university.

The second essential feature of higher education in Ontario is that it is a binary system—divided clearly into the university sector and the college sector, each with distinct mandates, and each with a distinct statutory framework. The college system operates under a single statute whereas each university is established by its own statute.

In 1950, the binary system was not yet in place. Ontario had five publicly supported universities—Toronto, Queen's, Western, McMaster, and Ottawa—and there was no college system. The participation rate (as defined above) in higher education was about 5 percent—this was elite higher education. The higher education system first began to expand in the 1950s with the establishment of three new universities—Carleton, Waterloo, and York. The movement to mass higher education occurred during the 1960s with the arrival of the baby boom generation and the transition to a post-industrial economy. Seven universities were established and the college sector was created: twenty colleges were established in 1966. Statistics Canada defines the baby boom as those born in the years 1946–1965 (the peak, the year with the largest number of births, was 1959). Assuming students enter higher education at age 18, baby boomers would be entering higher education from 1964–1983. By the time the boomers

FIGURE 1.2
University and College Participation Rates

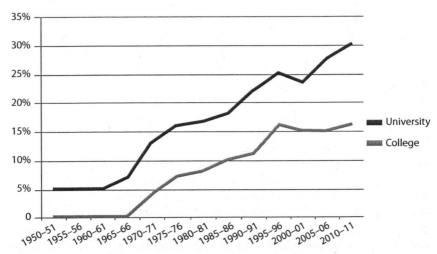

Participation rate: enrolment as the percentage of the population aged 18–24.

Source: Clark et al. (2009) with extensions.

FIGURE 1.3
University and College Enrolments, FTE

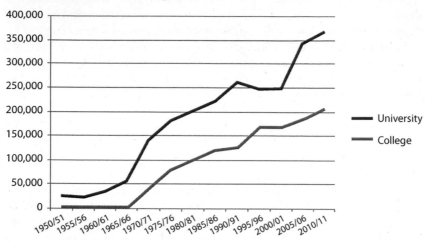

Source: Clark et al. (2009) with extensions.

left the system in 1987, the participation rate was 30 percent; 20 percent in universities and 10 percent in colleges. Participation rates, especially in university, rose again over the last ten years; so that the current participation rate is 45 percent, 30 percent in universities and 15 percent in colleges. The postwar expansion of Ontario's higher education system is often described as moving from elite, to mass, to near-universal higher education.

The binary system in the late 1960s had fifteen universities and twenty colleges. Since then five universities have joined the Council of Ontario Universities, but four were previously either colleges federated with another university (Algoma and Nipissing) or were higher education institutions that became universities (Ryerson and Ontario College of Art and Design). Only one truly new university was created—University of Ontario Institute of Technology (UOIT). Four more colleges were established, all with special mandates to serve the north and/or franco-Ontarians—Collège Boréal, Canadore College, La Cité Collégiale, and Sault College.

None of these additions altered the basic binary structure of the higher education system and thus the system we have today is little changed from 1966. And almost all enrolment growth from that time has been accommodated by institutions in existence. Thus not only has there been enormous growth of the entire system, but also enormous growth of individual institutions.

For many years after the college system was established, enrolments at universities and colleges grew roughly in tandem. But since the late 1990s, student choices have shifted strongly toward universities; the university system has expanded much more than the college system (Figure 1.3).

Most jurisdictions have a binary system of higher education, but Ontario's binary system is of a particular type. In many jurisdictions, colleges have a transfer function, as well as providing diploma programs; that is, the colleges provide the first two years of study toward a baccalaureate degree. After completing two years at a college, a student can transfer to a university to complete their baccalaureate degree. This has never been part of the design of Ontario's system.

Another essential feature of Ontario's system is that institutions of each sector are geographically distributed across the province. Table 1.2 shows the distribution of colleges and universities across the regions of the province. The boundaries of the regions are those used in the Ontario demographic forecasts. Ontario has made a special commitment to provide higher education in the north, although population densities are very low. This distribution of institutions across the province, in part, follows from the overarching commitment that there should be a place for every qualified student who wishes to attend. Of course, there cannot be an institution in every city and town, but students should not have to leave their region. And recent research has confirmed that participation in higher education is influenced by the proximity of an institution.

TABLE 1.2
Institutions of Higher Education by Region

COLLEGES				
Southwest	*Central*	*GTA*	*East*	*Northern*
Fanshawe	Conestoga	Centennial	Algonquin	Collège Boréal
Lambton	Georgian	Durham	Fleming	Cambrian
Niagara	Mohawk	George Brown	La Cité Collégiale	Canadore
St. Clair		Humber	Loyalist	Confederation
		Seneca	St. Lawrence	Northern
		Sheridan		Sault

UNIVERSITIES				
Southwest	*Central*	*GTA*	*East*	*Northern*
Brock	Guelph	OCAD	Carleton	Algoma
Western	Laurier	Ryerson	Ottawa	Lakehead
Windsor	McMaster	Toronto	Queen's	Laurentian
	Waterloo	UOIT	Trent	Nipissing
		York		

Source: Author's compilation.

Within each sector of the Ontario system, the institutions are funded in the same way—there is similar funding for similar activity. Institutions are funded by tuition fees and government operating grants (and capital grants). Tuition fees are regulated and differ very little between institutions. Government operating grants are calculated by formulae based on enrolments at each institution. The operating grant varies depending on the type of program, for example a science student has a larger grant than a social science student, reflecting the higher costs of providing science education; but each institution receives the same grant per science student. And because similar activities are funded in the same way across institutions, the first-level higher education programs tend to be of similar quality across institutions.

To sum up, Ontario's current system of first-level higher education has four essential features:

- A place for every qualified student who wishes to attend
- A binary system: the vocationally oriented college (CAAT) sector offers diplomas (no transfer function) and the academically oriented university sector offers bachelor's degrees
- Geographical distribution of institutions of both sectors across the province
- The same government funding and fees for the same activity: within each sector institutions provide first-level higher education of roughly similar quality.

In Ontario, whether you live in Thunder Bay, or Windsor, or Kingston, or Toronto, you will have access to a college or a university, offering the core programs of first-level higher education, and of similar quality. This system of higher education embodies an extraordinary commitment to equality of opportunity that Ontarians regard with justifiable pride. It serves our people and our economy very well.

A fundamental question in any rethinking of higher education will be: do we want to retain these essential features of first-level higher education? I believe that they should be retained. We should remain committed to a public system with a place for every qualified student; we should retain the binary system, with institutions spread across the province providing first-level higher education of similar quality, receiving similar funding when they do similar things. It is these features, I believe, that are the core of Ontario's system.

DIFFERENTIATION IN FIRST-LEVEL HIGHER EDUCATION

Overall, the institutions within each sector are quite similar with respect to first-level higher education. Ontario does not have as much institutional differentiation as in many jurisdictions. However, there are dimensions of differentiation in Ontario, discussed below, and identifying these differences is part of describing our current system of higher education. But the basic design principle has been one of similarity within each sector. A central question in rethinking higher education in Ontario is whether the system should be designed for greater institutional differentiation.

Each college has the same mandate: to deliver certificate and diploma programs suited to the regional labour market, to deliver the in-class components of apprenticeship programs, and more broadly to contribute to the social and economic development of their community. The diplomas (and some certificates) are directed to those with a secondary school diploma; while the graduate certificates are directed to those who have completed a bachelor's degree. The specific certificate and diploma programs available at each college will differ somewhat, but the purpose is the same; and there are many commonalities, for example all have programs in business and in information technology. However, recent changes have led the colleges to be more differentiated.

In 2000, under the *Postsecondary Education Choice and Excellence Act*, and then formalized in the *Ontario Colleges of Applied Arts and Technology Act, 2002*, the colleges obtained the authority to award bachelor's degrees in applied fields. To offer such a degree, the college makes a proposal to the Postsecondary Education Quality Assessment Board (PEQAB), which in turn makes a recommendation to the minister of Training, Colleges, and Universities. With ministerial consent, the college can offer the applied bachelor's degree program. These have all been four-year degrees. The uptake of this new opportunity by the colleges and the uptake of offered applied degree programs by students have been slower than anticipated. But, this new authority does represent a fundamental change in the binary system of Ontario's higher education. In 2009, PEQAB revised the nomenclature for college degrees, eliminating the requirement that they be called "applied" degrees.[9]

Colleges may now obtain the designation of Institute of Technology and Advanced Learning (ITAL) which allows them to offer up to 15 percent of their programming in bachelor's degree programs (the limit for other colleges is 5 percent). There are now five ITALS in Ontario—Conestoga, George Brown, Humber, Seneca, and Sheridan College. There are many who support this differentiation of the colleges, arguing that the degrees provided by colleges are needed in our system and that, by identifying certain colleges as having a larger role, the programs will be more effectively created and delivered. Others are less supportive, worrying that this differentiation will lead the ITALs to pay less attention to their core mandate of providing diplomas and the in-class instruction for apprenticeships.

The number of each type of credential awarded by each college is presented in Table 1.3. The first five listed colleges are the ITALs. At present, no college offers more than 5 percent of their programming in bachelor's degrees; but the ITALs have the highest percentages. The ITALs also generally have the higher percentages in graduate certificates, all having over 10 percent (Georgian, Centennial, and Durham also have more than 10 percent, and Niagara has almost 10 percent). The ITAL group, with this extension, has a significant share of their programming in bachelor's degrees or graduate diplomas. For the other colleges, well over 90 percent of programming is 1- to 3-year certificates and diplomas.

TABLE 1.3
Credentials Awarded in the College Sector, 2010–2011

	4-Year Degree		1–2 Year Graduate Certificate		1–3 Year Certificate/ Diploma	
	(#)	(%)	(#)	(%)	(#)	(%)
Sheridan	212	3.8	607	10.9	4,752	85.3
Seneca	191	3.1	652	10.6	5,317	86.3
Humber	195	2.9	1,448	21.2	5,199	76.0
Conestoga	75	2.2	395	11.7	2,917	86.1
George Brown	116	1.7	1,124	16.8	5,444	81.4
Georgian	48	1.6	314	10.4	2,663	88.0
Niagara	54	1.6	326	9.6	3,020	88.8
St. Lawrence	28	1.3	83	3.9	2,001	94.7
La Cité Collégiale	17	1.1	19	1.3	1,465	97.6
Algonquin	47	0.8	406	7.1	5,298	92.1
Centennial	20	0.3	998	17.4	4,733	82.3
Fanshawe	18	0.3	373	6.5	5,354	93.2
Loyalist	3	0.2	69	4.6	1,444	95.3
Durham	0	0.0	372	11.7	2,814	88.3
Mohawk	0	0.0	332	7.7	3,980	92.3
Lambton	0	0.0	52	4.9	1,004	95.1
Fleming	0	0.0	121	4.5	2,579	95.5
Cambrian	0	0.0	80	4.4	1,738	95.6
Sault	0	0.0	30	3.5	832	96.5
St. Clair	1	0.0	64	2.1	3,025	97.9
Canadore	0	0.0	18	1.3	1,332	98.7
Confederation	0	0.0	16	1.2	1,335	98.8
Northern	0	0.0	8	1.0	786	99.0
Collège Boréal	0	0.0	4	0.6	683	99.4

Source: HEQCO (2013b).

Likewise, universities are quite similar, having the same mandate and able to offer degree programs in all branches of learning at all levels of study.[10] At the undergraduate level there is great similarity in the programs offered. The universities all offer the "core" undergraduate programs in science, humanities, and social sciences. For example, every university offers degrees in biology, English, and political science; and the nature of the degree programs is very similar.[11] There is significant difference among universities in the amount of graduate education and professional education and in the amount of research (discussed in sections below), but at the undergraduate level they are very similar. There are some differences in the length of degree offered. Some universities offer only four-year degrees while others offer a three-year degree as well.

On closer examination, the differentiation between universities as "academically oriented" and colleges as "vocationally oriented" is not as sharp as characterized. In fact, universities offer many vocationally-oriented degree programs as part of our first-level higher education system; in particular, they offer undergraduate professional degrees.

There are many ways to define a professional degree program, but a strict definition would include the following components. A professional degree program prepares students for employment in a specific job—a specific profession. Examples are engineering, nursing, and education. In order to practice in this profession, you need both the study of a well-defined body of theoretical knowledge and practical experience under the supervision of an established professional. The study of theoretical knowledge is done inside the university (and is certified by a bachelor's degree); the practical experience is gained outside the university. In Ontario, the professions have been granted the right of self-regulation. The professional body (for example, the Professional Engineers Ontario or the Ontario College of Teachers), not the university, establishes the requirements for entering the profession and grants the license to practice. The professional body accredits the university degree program as meeting their requirements, and can be very influential in shaping the curriculum and determining the qualifications needed by professors to teach the courses.[12]

There are many other degree programs—for example in business, information technology, journalism, or public administration—that have most of the characteristics of professional programs (except the right of self-regulation) and are often referred to as "professional" programs by people within the university. There is no outside body accrediting the curriculum, but usually there is some council of advisers who are practicing professionals. Often outside professionals teach courses. And the purpose of the degree is to prepare students for work in a certain domain.

The professional degree programs are in stark contrast to the degree programs in the arts and sciences: the humanities, social sciences, and natural sciences. These degrees are not designed to prepare students for a specific job; they are designed for learning an academic discipline, for example, English literature, political science, or chemistry. There is no outside body involved in designing or accrediting the curriculum. Of course, it is recognized that some of the knowledge acquired and many of the skills will be "transferrable" to a job, but the fundamental purpose is very definitely not preparation for a specific profession. Until the middle of the nineteenth century, almost all of the university's degree programs were in the arts and sciences; only since then have professional degrees been added. But, the study in the arts and sciences, and research in these fields, is still the core of the university. Its values and orientation determine the essential character of the university.

If we examine the undergraduate degree programs and enrolments in Ontario universities, we find that only 50 percent are in the core arts and science. The other 50 percent are professional or vocationally oriented. The universities and the colleges are not so different in this respect.[13]

It was noted above that each university offered the core arts and science degrees. It also turns out that almost all the universities also offer engineering, nursing, education, and business programs—what I shall call the core first-level professional programs. This is an important refinement: Ontario's university system has universities across the province offering both the core arts and science and the core professional programs. Thus at the first level of higher education, the universities are not very differentiated. But this is a good thing. This feature is necessary to ensure equality of opportunity in Ontario.

This system of first-level higher education is the foundation for the entire higher education system. This is understandable and appropriate, because the central task of the entire system is first-level higher education. *In Ontario, 92 percent of the students in our higher education system are in first-level studies.* (See Table 1.4.) Upper-level higher education and research are layered on top of this foundation structure.

TABLE 1.4
Higher Education Enrolments, FTE, 2009

UNIVERSITIES	FTE Enrolments	COLLEGES	FTE Enrolments
First-level		*First-level*	
Bachelor's	367,615	Diplomas, certificates, degrees	202,000
Upper-level		*Upper-level*	
Graduate	51,041		
TOTAL	418,656	**TOTAL**	202,000

Source: COU (2011a) and Colleges Ontario (2011a).

UPPER-LEVEL HIGHER EDUCATION: GRADUATE EDUCATION

In the Ontario system, graduate education—the awarding of master's and doctoral degrees—is solely the responsibility of the university sector. (This contrasts with the systems in some other jurisdictions, especially with many European countries, where the vocationally oriented sector can offer some upper-level degrees, especially of an applied nature.)

Graduate programs require a bachelor's degree for admission and therefore, until recently, all students entering graduate programs came from the university sector. Now that colleges can offer bachelor's degrees, it is possible that students can enter graduate programs from the college sector. There has been some controversy about whether such students have adequate preparation, and for a time some universities would not accept such applicants; now, their applications are handled on a case-by-case basis. Over time, as graduate programs at universities have more experience with students who have college-awarded bachelor's degrees, the possibilities of this pathway in the Ontario system will be clarified.

The previous section indicated that all universities were quite similar, as in principle, all could award degrees at all levels, in all fields of study. And certainly they are very similar at the undergraduate level in terms of degree programs offered, although the size of the undergraduate student body differs greatly across institutions. However, there is significant differentiation of universities according to the amount and level of graduate education.

Table 1.5 provides several measures of the graduate education at each university.

TABLE 1.5
University Differentiation by Graduate Education

	Doctoral Students 2009	Average Annual Doctorates Awarded 2007–09	Master's Students 2009	Total Graduate Students 2009
Toronto	5,841	724	8,817	14,658
Western	1,833	222	3,201	5,034
York	1,800	156	4,245	6,045
Waterloo	1,671	213	2,535	4,206
Ottawa	1,518	185	3,904	5,422
McMaster	1,320	184	2,373	3,693
Queen's	1,230	158	2,607	3,837
Carleton	945	108	2,517	3,462
Guelph	834	116	1,593	2,427
Windsor	378	44	1,335	1,713
Ryerson*	198	7	1,767	1,965
Laurier	159	16	1,290	1,449
Laurentian	114	4	597	711
Trent	111	10	294	405
Brock	108	8	1,434	1,542
Lakehead	90	5	525	615
UOIT	27	—	315	342
Nipissing			372	372
OCAD			63	63
Algoma				

*Ryerson student data are for 2008.

Source: Canadian Association of Graduate Studies (2012).

Column 5 reports the total number of graduate students (master's and doctoral). Every Ontario university had some graduate education in 2009, with the exception of Algoma. In this basic sense, there is no difference between the universities—and all of them aspire to increase their graduate enrolments. Since 2002–2003, under the government's *Reaching Higher* plan, the Ontario system has added 15,000 new graduate spaces, an increase of about 50 percent, and all universities participated in this expansion (except Algoma). In the 2012 exercise of submitting draft Strategic Mandate Agreements, the Expert Panel noted "almost all of the universities intend to sustain and expand research and graduate studies" (HEQCO 2013b, 11).

Although all universities provide graduate education, there are differences in the absolute size of the graduate programming at the various universities as shown by column 5. University of Toronto is the largest by far with 14,658 graduate students. Next is York, with 6,045 graduate students, in a group of twelve universities whose numbers fall without a significant percentage gap between them, ending with Laurier that has 1,449 graduate students. There is a 50 percent drop to the next university, Laurentian, with 711 graduate students.

Column 4 reports the number of master's students at each Ontario university. Again, all universities except Algoma, provide master's education, and most universities have significant numbers of master's students.

The significant differentiation occurs at the doctoral level.

In thinking about university differentiation, it is important to distinguish master's education from doctoral education. Master's programs are one or two years long and the majority of the study is course work. Many are course-work-only degrees. Some master's programs require a thesis, but there is not the general expectation that the thesis constitutes an original piece of work of publishable quality. Many master's programs have an applied or professional orientation. Doctoral programs take four years (and usually much longer), involve course work, but most significantly require a major thesis, or dissertation, that is expected to be original work of publishable quality—it should be a contribution to knowledge of interest to others working on the topic. Doctoral education has a very academic orientation, and is the training ground for the future advanced researchers. A doctorate is a requisite for appointment as a professor at a university, and for many positions in the research groups and labs of governments, NGOs, and the private sector.

Doctoral education is interconnected with the research function of a university in a fundamental way that master's education and bachelor's education are not. Doctoral students work on their dissertation with a professor, their supervisor, who is a specialist in the field, and an active researcher. Many doctoral students choose which university to attend in order to work with a specific professor. In the sciences, doctoral students usually work closely with their supervisor, often on the same project. The doctoral students are crucial members of the team carrying forward a research program. The publications that come from doctoral dissertations are an important part of the research output of the university.

Column 2 of Table 1.5 reports the number of doctoral students at each university in 2009; the universities in Table 1.5 are ordered by this number. The universities are very differentiated. One might ask whether they fall into distinct groups. One way to determine the separation between groups would be to locate it where there is a very large percentage drop from one university to the next. Going down the column, University of Toronto is the largest centre of doctoral education by a considerable margin. It is a group on its own. Its relative role in Ontario's doctoral education is much larger than its role in undergraduate education (although it is also, by a good margin, the largest centre of undergraduate education). Next is Western in a group of eight universities, whose doctoral enrolments decline by modest percentages, to Guelph. Then, there is a more than 50 percent drop from Guelph to Windsor, and another almost 50 percent drop from Windsor to Ryerson. Beginning with Ryerson, there is a group of seven universities with smaller doctoral enrolments. Finally, there are three universities with no doctoral students.

Column 3 reports the average annual number of doctorates awarded from 2007 to 2009 at each university. The ordering changes, but the broad pattern is the same: Toronto awards the most doctorates by a very large margin; the next group of eight universities differ relatively little between each other in percentage terms as one goes down the column. There is a large drop from this group to Windsor, and a very large drop from Windsor to the next group.

Combining the data on doctoral education in columns 2 and 3, the data support the identification of four groups: group I is U of T alone; group II, from Western to Guelph, has eight universities (those in this group have at least 800 doctoral students and award at least 100 doctorates annually); group III, from Windsor to UOIT, has eight universities with some doctoral education; and group IV has three universities with no doctoral education. This categorization into groups is quite robust, in the sense that no university could conceivably move between groups over the next five years.

This characterization of universities has examined data on the number of graduate students. In thinking about system design, this is relevant because it identifies concentrations of graduate education. One could also examine data on the share of total enrolments in graduate education; that is, the relative size of first-level versus upper-level higher education in each university. This share may affect the university's sense of itself and how it assigns priorities to its activities.

UPPER-LEVEL HIGHER EDUCATION: PROFESSIONAL PROGRAMS

There are many professional programs that require some prior university study, usually a bachelor's degree. The information site for Ontario degree programs defines these professional programs as "a program of advanced learning that leads to an occupation governed by a mandatory regulatory body. Practicing members of the profession must complete a licensing exam before they can actively practice and must keep their credentials current, through additional education mandated by the regulatory body" (OUAC 2011). These upper-level programs are only in the university sector and there is considerable differentiation across universities in their offerings.

The most familiar and prestigious of the upper-level professional programs are medicine and law. Until recently, there were five medical schools in Ontario and six law schools.

The medical schools were at the five oldest universities in Ontario—Toronto, Ottawa, Western, McMaster, and Queen's—and were spread across the western, central, and eastern regions of the province. Although the medical schools have relatively few students compared to their university, such is their prestige, level of research, and influence on other disciplines at the university, that the presence of a medical school is often seen as a defining characteristic of a university. In 2005, the Northern Ontario School of Medicine (NOSM) began admitting students, the first new medical school in Canada in over thirty years. The school is a joint initiative of Lakehead University and Laurentian University with main campuses in Thunder Bay and Sudbury, and multiple teaching and research sites distributed across Northern Ontario. NOSM is the only Canadian medical school to be established as a stand-alone, not-for-profit corporation, with its own Board of Directors and corporate bylaws. Both because Lakehead and Laurentian do not have large doctoral programs, and because NOSM is a stand-alone non-profit organization, this medical school is not likely to shape their character in the same way.

The six law schools were at Toronto, Ottawa, Western, Queen's, York, and Windsor. Again, most, but not all, are at the old universities. Again, a law school is an important differentiating feature of a university. Following the pattern of choosing the North for a new medical school, Ontario has announced a new law school at Lakehead University to open in 2013.

The other upper-level professional programs have many fewer programs: dentistry (Toronto, Western), optometry (Waterloo), pharmacy (Toronto, Waterloo), occupational therapy (Toronto, Queen's, McMaster, Western), and physiotherapy (McMaster, Queen's, Toronto, Western), physician's assistant (Toronto), primary health care nurse practitioner (Lakehead, McMaster, Queen's, Windsor), speech-language pathology/

audiology (Toronto, Western), veterinary medicine (Guelph). Most of these programs are in health-related areas and tend to be at universities with a medical school. There clearly is a cluster of professional programs that grow up around a medical school; part of the reason why a medical school is such a defining feature of a university.

Overall, there are three features of differentiation by upper-level professional programs in Ontario: in each occupation, there are many fewer programs than universities so that most universities have no upper-level professional programs; the professional programs (with the exception of the two recent northern initiatives), are all at the universities with substantial doctoral education. Thus professional education further differentiates the entire system and re-enforces the differentiation based upon doctoral education.

UNIVERSITY DIFFERENTIATION BY RESEARCH

An important function of the higher education system is to conduct research. This function was assigned to the university sector alone. Recently, a role for colleges has emerged; this will be discussed in a brief following section and taken up again later in Chapters 7 and 8 dealing with research.

Differentiating universities according to the research published by their professors (and graduate students) is far more complicated—and controversial—than any of the other categories. Some of the complexity and some of the controversy—though by no means all—arises because research activity is difficult to measure. Research results are disseminated in many diverse ways, making it hard to document all the research done at a university. Also, any thoughtful assessment of research at a university must consider not just the quantity of the published work, but also its quality. Research results vary widely in quality—judging quality by the originality of the work and by how substantial its contribution is to knowledge in its field. It is even harder to assess the quality of the work than to document the quantity.

Much writing about universities defines certain universities as "research" universities, or "research-intensive" universities. Most people around the university sector have a strong intuitive sense that more research is conducted at some universities than others. But, universities are very sensitive about the category into which they fall. And perhaps such categories mislead us about the activities of universities. To label a university as a research university seems to imply that this is its main activity, but in fact most of the students at a research university are undergraduates and the primary activity of a "research" university is still undergraduate education. Also professors at all universities— including primarily undergraduate universities—conduct research. One of the defining characteristics of a university is that its permanent professors are engaged in both teaching and research and its students are taught by active researchers.[14] In this sense, all universities are research universities.

Research is an important responsibility of the university, and this responsibility has become much more important over the last fifteen years. Most professors spend more than 30 percent of their time on research (for many the share is over 50 percent), and the share has been rising over the past twenty years. Clark et al. (2009) estimate that, on average, professors spend 40 percent of their time on research, 40 percent on teaching, and 20 percent on service. Despite all the complexities and controversies, the university community should be able to report upon the research done at each university and to analyze whether universities are differentiated by research.

Unfortunately, there is no requirement that universities report on their research publications and there is no collection of data on a comparable basis to report on the entire system. This is a glaring gap in the accountability framework in Ontario. In a basic research accountability system, the research published by professors at each university would be reported. The fundamental purpose of academic research in any field is to contribute to knowledge in that field. The standard process in all fields is that after the research work has been completed, it is written for dissemination to others working in the field. There are four main dissemination routes: articles in academic journals, books, chapters in books, and conference presentations. The importance of each varies considerably by field, and we should recognize that there are many other means of dissemination. Nonetheless, there is broad consensus among academics that the most important routes are journals, chapters, and books.[15] In order to be selected for publication in these, the work must first be reviewed by peers in the field to determine the quality of the work and that it is a sufficient contribution to merit publication. Thus, the core research output of professors is published through peer-reviewed channels, most importantly journals, chapters, and books. In principle, this should be easy to report; it is documented on the curriculum vitae (CV) of each professor. Some jurisdictions, for example Australia, do ask for such reports from each university. Unfortunately, in Ontario, we do not.

Another way to document research, rather than looking at the CVs of professors, would be to look at academic publications—the journals and books published—and then count the items that came from each university. This is the approach used by university ranking systems, and is fraught with its own limitations and controversies. This bibliometric approach will be discussed in Chapter 8, when the differentiation of universities according to ranking systems is discussed. Recently, Higher Education Strategy Associates (HESA) published measures of research strength at Canadian universities based upon the number of publications and how often they have been cited (Jarvey and Usher 2012). These will also be discussed in Chapter 8.

In the absence of reports from universities on research publications, or bibliometric studies, analysts must rely on proxy measures. The most commonly used is sponsored research income; this is the income from grants and contracts received by the university that is intended to pay for research. A firm, Re$earch Infosource, regularly publishes a list of "Canada's Top 50 Research Universities" and uses sponsored research income as a measure of research (Re$earch Infosource 2012). The sponsored research income at each Ontario university is listed in Table 1.6; the universities are rank ordered by this income.

If one is interested in academic research, a better proxy measure is one component of sponsored research income: research grants from the national granting councils—the Canadian Institutes of Health Research (CIHR), the Natural Sciences and Engineering Research Council (NSERC), and the Social Sciences and Humanities Research Council (SSHRC).

These data measure an input into research, but do not measure research output. Nonetheless, there is some justification for these proxies, especially using the national granting council data, beyond the fact that these data are available. The justification runs as follows. We can assume that all professors would like to have an external research grant—the grants provide money above what the university itself can provide to support the costs of doing the research and most grants provide support for graduate students. The majority of the grants from the councils support projects suggested by the applicant, rather than projects in targeted areas. Research grant applications are adjudicated by peers and are judged by the feasibility and promise of the research proposal and by the research track record of the applicant. In some fields, especially in the CIHR and NSERC fields, an external research grant is necessary to conduct research. Thus, it is reasonable to conclude that universities with more grants and/ or more sponsored research income are doing more research. However, there are severe problems with this conclusion.

The most obvious is that, in fact, much research gets done without a research grant. The granting councils receive many applications, and routinely judge applications as worthy, but do not have the funds to support them. Many professors do not bother to apply and can do their research using the university's libraries, computers, labs, and internal small research grants.

Furthermore, the use of data on grants and sponsored research income to measure research is heavily biased against research in the SSHRC fields. Research in the SSHRC fields is much less likely to require external support than in the CIHR and NSERC fields. Also, there is much more support available for NSERC work and for CIHR work, especially in medical fields, both scientific and clinical, than for SSHRC-type work. It is no surprise that the top five Ontario universities, ranked by sponsored research income, are the five universities with a medical school.

The best way to mitigate the bias against SSHRC research is, when universities are compared, to disaggregate the research income into SSHRC, NSERC, and CIHR comparisons. This way the analysis can identify the top SSHRC universities, the top NSERC universities, and so on.

Table 1.6 provides data on grants from the three national granting councils, and then the granting council data are disaggregated into the SSHRC, NSERC, and CIHR categories.

TABLE 1.6
University Differentiation by Research

	Sponsored Research Income ($ 000, annual average 2009–11)	Total Canada Research Chairs (CRCs) (2012 allocation)	SSHRC CRCs	NSERC CRCs	CIHR CRCs
Toronto	884,189	248	37	77	134
McMaster	366,347	70	8	29	33
Ottawa	262,158	76	16	25	35
Western	227,222	66	12	26	28
Queen's	179,492	52	10	29	13
Guelph	152,274	36	6	26	4
Waterloo	149,410	62	9	49	4
York	67,635	34	19	11	4
Carleton	67,516	23	7	15	1
Windsor	31,737	14	3	10	1
Ryerson	24,627	14	5	8	1
Laurentian	22,946	5	1	3	1
Lakehead	19,223	7	3	3	1
Brock	14,464	8	5	3	
Trent	13,798	7	2	4	1
Laurier	10,597	7	4	3	
UOIT	9,042	5	1	4	
Nipissing		1	1		
OCAD					
Algoma					

Source: Canada Research Chairs (2013), Re$earch Infosource (2011, 2012).

In Table 1.6, the granting council awards to each university are not measured directly, but rather by the Canada Research Chairs (CRCs) allocated to each university. The Canada Research Chairs program of the federal government provides funds for professorships. There are 1,880 regular CRCs funded across Canada—45 percent in NSERC fields, 35 percent in CIHR fields, and 20 percent in SSHRC fields. In each of these categories, universities are awarded a share of the CRCs equal to their share of a three-year total of funds awarded by that granting council. Therefore, a university's number of CRCs is an index for the value of grants that it received from the granting council over the three-year period, and these indices are comparable across universities. In order to receive a regular CRC, a university had to have an annual grant income of at least $100,000. There was an additional allocation of CRCs for small universities, and there have been a number of special CRCs. Neither of these is included in Table 1.6. The table reports regular CRCs according to the 2012 allocation data.

Using the total number of CRCs as the index, eighteen universities received significant funds from the granting councils. University of Toronto received the largest amount by a considerable margin, over three times higher than the next university. After U of T, the number declines, with small percentage declines until a large percentage decline from Carleton to Windsor (64 percent). Two universities received no CRCs. Using this index, universities are differentiated by research and fall into four groups: Toronto is a group on its own; then a group of eight universities from Ottawa to Carleton; then Windsor and Ryerson; then a group of six universities from Ryerson to Nipissing; and a group of two universities. (The data on total sponsored research give approximately the same picture.)

All these data deal with total research dollars; they are thus a measure of differentiation by total research activity. For the purposes of designing a system of higher education, the total data are most important. The important idea is to identify concentrations of research activity. However of course, larger universities will have larger amounts of total research. What about a measure of research per faculty member? This could be calculated (that is, proxied) by grants per faculty member, or total sponsored research income per faculty member. It turns out that the differentiation of universities is not affected much by looking at research support per faculty member (Re$earch Infosource 2012). The universities are ordered in roughly the same way according to total research and according to research per faculty member, and the lists divide into roughly the same groups. University of Toronto leads both lists by a considerable margin; its dominance overall is a result of being the largest university *and* having the highest research per faculty member. There is a second group according to research per faculty member, and it is roughly the same as the second group according to total research. The same holds true for the third group.

Universities can also be differentiated by their relative concentration in each of the granting council areas. The percentage of total CRCs in SSHRC, NSERC, and CIHR are 20, 45, and 35. A university's research is balanced across the areas if its individual percentages of CRCs in each area are relatively close to the overall percentages. It can be said to be relatively concentrated in one area if its individual percentage is well above the overall. Table 1.6 also reports the CRC data for each granting council area. By this measure, among the top nine universities, Toronto is a CIHR-focused university; Waterloo and Guelph are NSERC-focused universities; and York is a SSHRC-focused university.

University of Toronto has the largest number of CRCs in each area and is the largest centre of research in all areas: CIHR, NSERC, and SSHRC. Its dominance is largest by far in the health area (CIHR). The orderings of the universities within each area are quite different from the orderings by total CRCs or by sponsored research income. For example, the top five SSHRC universities are Toronto, York, Ottawa, Western, and Queen's; the top five NSERC universities are Toronto, Waterloo, McMaster/Queen's, and Western/Guelph; and the top five CIHR universities are Toronto, Ottawa, McMaster, Western, and Queen's (of course, these are the universities with medical schools).

COLLEGES AND RESEARCH

Historically, the colleges had no role in research, but this is now changing as they have been given the authority to conduct applied research. The level of research so far is modest; a 2004 report from the colleges stated about 2 percent of full-time faculty engaged in applied research and about 20 percent hold research-based master's or doctoral degrees (ACAATO 2004). But, the colleges will certainly have a larger role in the years ahead. The Ontario Ministry of Research and Innovation included colleges along with universities as key academic institutions in Ontario's Innovation Strategy, and colleges are now eligible to apply under many of the Ministry's programs. The Ministry encourages the colleges to work with businesses in their region on applied research projects. Reflecting their move into applied research, the colleges have formed the Colleges Ontario Network for Industry Innovation (CONII), which receives ongoing support from the Ontario government. After a pilot program begun in 2004, the federal government, through the Natural Sciences and Engineering Research Council (NSERC), established a permanent program in 2008, the College and Community Innovation (CCI) program, as a component of the new research agenda. The CCI program offers six types of grants to colleges and institutes of technology to support applied research and to enhance collaborations between colleges and companies (NSERC 2013). Recent federal budgets have increased the funding for college-based applied research. For example, the March 2011 federal budget made further major commitments to applied research at colleges. It proposed $80 million in new funding over three years through the Industrial Research Assistance Program to help small- and medium-sized businesses accelerate their adoption of key information and communications technologies through collaboration and projects with colleges. It proposed thirty new

Industrial Research Chairs at colleges ($5 million per year) and an alloca-
tion of $12 million over five years for the Ideas to Innovation program
to support joint college-university commercialization projects (Canada.
Ministry of Finance 2011).

Colleges Ontario, in their paper *A New Vision for Higher Education in
Ontario*, recommends an increased role in applied research (Colleges
Ontario 2011b, 14).

Polytechnics Canada is a recently formed organization of a small group
of colleges across Canada and represents itself as "a national alliance
of Canada's leading research-intensive, publicly-funded colleges and
institutes of technology" (Polytechnics Canada 2010). Of the ten current
members, six are Ontario colleges: Conestoga, Sheridan, Humber, George
Brown, Seneca, and Algonquin. This membership constitutes a certain
level of differentiation among Ontario colleges with respect to research.

It is too early to have a comprehensive picture of the emerging role
of colleges in research. The annual publication of Re$earch Infosource
(2012) regularly includes a section on college research, but does not report
total sponsored research income at each institution. HEQCO (2013, 21)
reports on NSERC grants at colleges, but such grants are only a portion
of total research income. However, the college role is certainly growing
and some dimensions are clear: this new role is more a part of economic
policy than higher education policy, and it will be research with commercial application. And the research will be mainly in the domains of
science, engineering, and technology.

OTHER ASPECTS OF DIFFERENTIATION

A noteworthy feature of Ontario's higher education system is that the
universities differ significantly by size. The colleges, on the other hand,
are relatively similar in size. (Table 1.1 listed universities ordered by the
total number of full-time undergraduate students and listed the colleges by FTE enrolments; and Table 1.4 showed the number of graduate
students at each university.) The great variation in the size of Ontario
universities was not a principle of system design; it was a response to
where students live.

Universities range from Toronto with 69,900 total students to Algoma
with 900. Both Toronto and York are extremely large by international
standards. U of T is as large as the largest US university (Arizona State)
and York is comparable in size to the top 10 percent of the largest US
universities. Toronto and York are much larger than universities in the
United Kingdom, Australia, and Europe.

However, each individual university should not be regarded as a
homogeneous entity. University of Toronto contains within itself several
federated universities and colleges, and operates on three campuses
each of which is larger than most universities. Several universities have

small colleges/universities federated within them—for example, Huron College is federated with Western, University of Sudbury is federated with Laurentian, Université Saint-Paul is federated with Ottawa. Many of these federated components are relatively old and began as religiously sponsored institutions. Most universities now have satellite campuses. For example, York's Glendon College is located on a separate campus in midtown Toronto, and Guelph has a campus in Kemptville offering agriculturally oriented programs. From the perspective of a student, their educational experience will be greatly shaped by which part of the heterogeneous whole they attend.

General arguments for institutional differentiation (see Chapter 2) do not offer much guidance about the appropriate differentiation by size. It can be argued that the student experience differs across universities according to their size and that students differ in whether they would prefer the experience of a large university rather than that at a small university. Larger universities will offer more program choice, but less sense of community and cohesion, than smaller universities. Thus students will be better served by having institutions differing by size to choose from. It might be that universities can be too large—their programs and activities are too many and diverse to be effective institutions. Perhaps University of Toronto and York are too large, although U of T has mitigated the difficulty somewhat using a three-campus model. It might be that universities can be too small—they cannot offer a sufficient range of programs for students and the activities are more costly because there are not enough activities spread across the fixed facilities. Algoma is likely too small by this argument. However, these arguments neglect location issues. Algoma has a special mandate to provide education in the North and to provide a supportive educational setting for Anishinabe (First Nations, Metis, and Inuit) students. U of T and York are in Toronto where there are a huge number of students and where there is a good transportation system that allows students to live at home while attending university.

On balance, there does not seem to be an argument that Ontario needs greater differentiation by size. However, it does seem a reasonable policy goal that University of Toronto (especially on the St. George campus) and York not grow any larger. (If these institutions were smaller, they would very likely be more effective, but it does not seem a reasonable goal to have them shrink.)

There is a related feature of Ontario's system that will be very important in later chapters as we take up the question of how to improve undergraduate education. In Ontario, although there are twenty universities, much of the undergraduate education is provided by a few large universities. University of Toronto and York provide 30 percent; the five largest universities provide 52 percent, and the ten largest provide over 80 percent. Therefore, although the smaller universities may be more focused on undergraduate education, reforms to undergraduate education cannot focus on small universities. Undergraduate education is important at all universities, and indeed to significantly improve undergraduate education, it will have to be improved in the largest universities. These largest universities are also where most graduate education and research take place. So paradoxically, to improve undergraduate education, it must be addressed in institutions with concentrations of graduate education and research.

The CAATs in Ontario are much smaller than most universities and vary less in size. By international standards, they are relatively small; many jurisdictions have very large, multi-campus institutions to provide career-focused diplomas like Ontario's colleges. However, there does not seem to be any rationale for greater differentiation of colleges by size in Ontario.

Ontario's institutions of higher education are differentiated according to language of instruction; it has been an important principle in the design of the system to provide higher education in both of Canada's official languages. There is a subgroup of colleges with a special mandate to provide instruction in French. Collège Boréal and La Cité Collégiale have this mandate. Similarly, there is a subgroup of universities (or one of their components). The Association of Universities of the Canadian Francophonie includes in Ontario: Université de Hearst (federated with Laurentian), Université laurentienne, Université de Sudbury (federated with Laurentian), Collège universitaire Glendon (a Faculty of York University), Université d'Ottawa, and Université Saint-Paul (federated with Ottawa).

Universities and colleges are differentiated by their location, their character, their setting, their student body, and their reputation. There is little doubt that students and their parents see such differences between institutions and that these differences influence the student's choice of which institution to attend, although sometimes these characteristics are very hard to define and quantify. The character of an institution, especially of a university, is certainly likely shaped by its age. There are the five old universities established in the nineteenth century; ten were established between 1950 and 1970, and five after 1990. Twenty CAATs were established at the outset in 1966, and four have been established since. Character has other aspects: some institutions are seen as "party schools," others as places of rah rah spirit, and still others as austere places where you could get lost and no one would know. Some institutions are in large cities, some in small; in large cities, some are in the suburbs while others are downtown. Some institutions have many students living on campus and in a nearby "student ghetto"; in other institutions, most students live further away and commute to campus. The student body differs by institution: some institutions have more academically oriented students, some are more ethnically diverse, some have more international students, and so on.

And perhaps most elusive of all is the reputation and prestige of an institution. No doubt people differ in how they assess the reputation of each institution and no consensus ranking would exist, but there is also no doubt that reputation and prestige matters. Among the many possible factors, reputation certainly seems to depend upon the reputation of the faculty members and the selectivity of the entry criteria for students. Many analysts argue that the best summary of what the leadership of universities is trying to accomplish is to increase the reputation and prestige of their university.

CLASSIFICATION OF COLLEGES AND UNIVERSITIES

If there are differences among institutions of higher education, this should allow a classification system to be developed, which would help us to better understand the full nature of the Ontario system and allow better policy analysis. With a classification system, it would ensure that when institutions in Ontario (or between jurisdictions) are being compared, the comparison is like-with-like. This section completes the description of Ontario's system of higher education by classifying the institutions into groups, using Statistics Canada's classification system for postsecondary institutions (Orton 2009).

With a classification system, if it is used internationally, we would be able to compare Ontario with other jurisdictions and ask whether Ontario lacks certain types of institutions that other jurisdictions have developed successfully. The most well-known classification system, internationally, is the Carnegie Classification System of Institutions of Higher Education, developed by the Carnegie Commission on Higher Education in the early '70s for American institutions, and since revised several times. The Carnegie system is widely studied internationally and often used as a reference in designing other classification systems. Closely related to the issue of institutional classification is the issue of institutional ranking. There is now widespread ranking of universities, including world university rankings. The issues of international classification systems, and how the Ontario system fits within them, are taken up in the next chapter; how Ontario places in world university rankings is taken up in Chapter 8.

Statistics Canada created a "Register of Postsecondary and Adult Education Institutions" that divides the institutions into types and subtypes. The register is, of course, designed to incorporate the sometimes very different systems in the provinces and territories of Canada. There are six types of institution in the register: 1. university and degree granting, 2. colleges and institutes, 3. career colleges, 4. school board and adult education, 5. government—direct, and 6. consortia.

The first two types correspond to the two components of the Ontario binary higher education system described above: universities and colleges of applied arts and technology. Thus, the Statistics Canada system classifies institutions in the same way as has been done so far in this book.

The precise definitions of the remaining four types need not concern us too much here. The school board type is included to recognize that many school boards responsible for primary and secondary education also offer a range of programs directed at adults; type 5, the government—direct category includes apprenticeships. It should be noted how this register highlights (as does Figure 1.1 and the discussion earlier in this chapter) that postsecondary education includes more than just colleges and universities.

The first type of institution—universities—is divided by Statistics Canada into four sub-types: primarily undergraduate, comprehensive, medical doctoral, and special purpose. The register notes that the definitions of the sub-types are rather general and that more precise definitions are needed. The definitions of medical doctoral and comprehensive categories mention research, but do not address it in any systematic way. The definitions "borrow from *Maclean's* which in turn borrowed from the Carnegie Classification which has been in common use in the United States and in academic research since the mid-1970s" (Orton 2009). The first three sub-types classify universities according to the level of degrees awarded and by the presence of a medical school. This classification of Ontario universities is presented in Table 1.7.

This classification and the assignment of universities to each group has been used by Statistics Canada and by *Maclean's* for many years and is now widely accepted and used as a frame for understanding Ontario's university system. However, this book, after analyses of undergraduate education, graduate education, and research, concludes that a better classification of universities would be that of doctoral/research and master's/bachelor's universities.

The fourth sub-type—special purpose universities—is a broad category. *Maclean's* annual *Guide to Canadian Universities* (*Maclean's*, various years) refers to such universities as specialty universities or niche institutions. In Ontario, Algoma University and Ontario College of Art and Design University fall into this category (as in Table 1.7).

The register also divides colleges into sub-types: degree granting, multi-purpose, and special purpose. Degree-granting colleges have the normal range of diploma programs and also award bachelor's degrees; Ontario's Institutes of Technology and Advanced Learning (ITALs) are of this sub-type. Multi-purpose colleges offer a broad range of one-, two-, and three-year programs; the remainder of Ontario colleges is of this sub-type. Special purpose colleges are those whose mandates identify a specific field of study. Ontario does not have such colleges within Colleges Ontario. (The Michener Institute is a special purpose college, created to train health care workers, but it does not belong to Colleges Ontario.) The classification of Ontario's colleges is presented in Table 1.7.

TABLE 1.7
Ontario's Institutions of Higher Education
Statistics Canada Classification

UNIVERSITIES	COLLEGES
Medical Doctoral	**Degree-granting**
Toronto	Seneca
Western	George Brown
Ottawa	Humber
McMaster	Sheridan
Queen's	Conestoga
Comprehensive	**Multi-purpose**
York	Algonquin
Waterloo	Fanshawe
Carleton	Mohawk
Guelph	Centennial
Windsor	Georgian
	St. Clair
Primarily Undergraduate	Durham
Ryerson	Niagara
Brock	Fleming
Laurier	St. Lawrence
Lakehead	La Cité Collégiale
UOIT	Cambrian
Trent	Loyalist
Laurentian	Confederation
Nipissing	Canadore
	Lambton
Special Purpose	Sault
OCAD	Collège Boréal
Algoma	Northern

Source: Author's compilation.

The description of Ontario's system of higher education is now complete. It has been situated in the entire educational system; its essential features at first-level higher education have been identified; the differentiation by graduate education, professional education, and research have been documented; and the institutions of the university and colleges sectors have been classified into groups.

The question is: do we have the system that will best serve Ontarians in the years ahead?

NOTES

1. The February 2011 issue of the journal *Canadian Public Policy* is devoted to examining the use of life course analysis in public policy. The lead article, McDaniel and Bernard (2011), provides an overview.

2. The Council of Europe, cited in Bergan (2011), recommends that the purposes and missions of higher education are threefold: preparation for the labour market; preparation for life as active citizens in democratic societies; and personal development. See also endnote 8.

3. Fallis (2007) examines the role of undergraduate education in preparation for citizenship. The analysis is situated in a wider conception of the university: the university itself is a fundamental institution of democracy and should be held accountable for its contributions to democratic life. These contributions go much beyond undergraduate education for citizenship, to include, for example, the responsibility of professors to be public intellectuals.

4. Ontario (2011) provides an overview of Ontario's educational policies and progress towards announced goals.

5. Ontario. Ministry of Education (1999) and Ontario. Ministry of Education (2010) outline the Ontario secondary school curriculum.

6. Ontario. Ministry of Education (1999) and Ontario. Ministry of Education (2010) outline the Ontario policies for exceptional students.

7. Norrie and Lennon (2011) provide a detailed overview of Ontario's tuition and student assistance policies. Usher and Duncan (2008) look at the net effect of tuition increases and increased assistance.

8. The Council of Europe, cited in Bergan (2011), includes a fourth purpose/ mission for higher education: the development and maintenance of a broad, advanced knowledge base. See endnote 2.

9. The colleges wish to expand their degree-granting still further, recommending that they be allowed to offer certain professional bachelor's programs, such as nursing, on their own, rather than jointly with universities as is the case currently. (In many jurisdictions, the college-type sector delivers degree programs like nursing and education.)

10. Ryerson, UOIT, and OCAD are slight exceptions, which will be discussed later. Technically, Algoma does not at present have the authority to offer doctoral education. See Jones and Skolnick (2009, 4-6).

11. The degree programs offered at each university are listed on the e-Info website (OUAC 2011).

12. This same definition of a professional program is used later in this chapter. There however, the discussion is of upper-level higher education and the professional programs require a bachelor's degree for entry.

13. The distinction between academically oriented universities and vocationally oriented colleges is further blurred because two universities have defined themselves as having a career focus. Ryerson University declares itself to be "a leader in innovative, career-focused education." University of Ontario Institute of Technology (UOIT) states: "each of our programs is innovative and responsive to students' needs and the market-driven requirements of employers."

14. Most universities have part-time professors, and full-time professors on limited-term contracts, who have only teaching responsibilities. And some

universities now have teaching-only, full-time, permanent professors. But the great majority of permanent professors have both teaching and research responsibilities.

15. University-based research is intended to contribute, not just to academic knowledge, but also to public policy and to cultural life. Much of this research is disseminated through means other than journal articles, chapters, and books. This research cannot be measured and assessed in the same way as academic research.

Chapter 2

INSTITUTIONAL DIFFERENTIATION:
MANDATE AND PROGRAMS

Chapter 1 described the essential features of Ontario's current system of higher education and how the colleges and universities are currently differentiated. The purpose of this chapter is to explore why institutional differentiation is desirable in a system of higher education and to begin our assessment of the current Ontario system. This chapter makes one recommendation for a new type of institution in the Ontario system—an open university/college. But, the main purpose of the chapter is to develop the analytical framework and identify the different types of institutions that might be part of a system of higher education.

In the analysis of a system of higher education, the concept of institutional differentiation has two distinct components. One component relates to mandate. The overall mandates of the institutions are different, as for example when one type of institution offers academically oriented programs and another offers vocationally oriented programs; or when one type of institution offers only undergraduate programs and another offers both undergraduate and graduate programs. Institutional differentiation by mandate arises through government policy: the legislation establishing the institution, or a government agreement with the institution, specifies its mandate, and usually there is a separate government funding structure and governance and accountability framework for each type of institution. The focus of this chapter is institutional differentiation by mandate.

For the most part, the literature on diversity in higher education has emphasized this differentiation by mandate. A widely used general definition was offered by Martin Trow in 1995 and cited in a recent survey of diversity in higher education systems (Codling and Meek 2006, 35): diversity is "the existence of distinct forms of post-secondary institutions and groups of institutions within a state or nation that have different and distinct missions, educate and train for different lives and careers, have different styles of instruction, are organized and funded and operate under different laws and relationships to government."

The second component of institutional differentiation arises because institutions with the same mandate choose to offer different degree and diploma programs. Also, institutions can be differentiated by the research programs they choose to pursue. This sort of diversity had received much less attention in the literature, but is given attention here because of its particular relevance to the Ontario policy context. This component of institutional differentiation arises through institutional decision making. For example, one university might offer a degree in art history, or in environmental biology, or a co-op degree option that other universities do not offer. Or one college may offer a diploma in tourism management, while another college a diploma in health informatics. Similarly for example, one university might specialize in diabetes research while another in space science. Institutional differentiation by program can be influenced by government policies, but it is fundamentally determined by the choices of each institution. The focus of the next chapter is on how this interaction of government policy and institutional decision making leads to institutional differentiation by program. But also, the next chapter takes up how this interaction between government policy and institutional choice can lead to institutions with the same mandate (and even with different mandates) becoming more similar, a process of isomorphism.

Broadly speaking in Ontario higher education, institutions are differentiated both by mandate and by choice of program. They are differentiated by mandate as two types: universities and colleges. These mandates are specified by legislation, and carried out under different funding, governance, and accountability structures. Within the university sector, all have the same mandate, but universities are differentiated by their choice of programs offered. Similarly, all colleges have the same mandate, but they are differentiated by choice of programs offered too.

Before one can finally make recommendations about how greater institutional differentiation might improve Ontario's system, one should first carefully assess how well the Ontario system is doing in first-level higher education (this assessment is done in Chapter 4 and Chapter 5), and assess how well the Ontario system is doing in upper-level higher education, that is in graduate education and professional education (this assessment is done in Chapter 6), and how well it is doing in research (this assessment is done in Chapter 7 and Chapter 8). The three activities must fit together coherently within each institution and within the system.

After analyzing the three components of Ontario's system, I conclude that greater institutional differentiation by mandate is called for, and in addition, greater program diversity. Overall, such recommendations require a greater government role in system design than at present.

Recommendations for redesign of the system are contained in Chapter 9 and Chapter 10.

The first third of this chapter presents the two-part theoretical argument as to why institutional differentiation by mandate is desirable in a system of higher education.

In the middle third of the chapter, this two-part rationale is applied to the Ontario system. First, it shows how the rationale forms the basis of Ontario's binary system. Next, the rationale is used to explore institutional diversity by field of study, an option that has not been part of the Ontario debate. Then, it identifies one area where further institutional diversity by mandate would be beneficial in first-level higher education: the creation an open university/college.

The final third of the chapter explores several classification systems for the institutions of higher education used in other countries, in particular the Carnegie Classification. These other classification systems identify other possible ways that colleges and universities might be differentiated. One way of classifying universities under the Carnegie system is according to the intensity of their orientation to research and doctoral education, which suggests the possibility that universities might be differentiated on this basis.

There are several world universities rankings that have considerable influence on higher education policy in many countries; these countries have identified as a policy goal that their university system should contain a certain number of highly ranked universities. The rankings are discussed, and the many problems of methodology and interpretation, are explored in Chapter 8. The world rankings of universities are mentioned here because the design of Ontario's system for higher education must take cognizance of international competition, and because in Ontario we should consider whether to have such a policy objective. Also, the issue of rankings is mentioned because I want to assert at the outset that in designing a system of higher education in Ontario we should set high standards for ourselves, and we should benchmark ourselves against other countries and their institutions: Ontario should aspire to have a system of higher education comparable to the best in the world.

The possibility of having more institutional differentiation in their system of higher education is being raised in many countries, often creating controversy. Running through the differentiation debates in most countries are two subtexts, which, though often not clearly explained, are nonetheless fundamental to understanding the controversy. One involves undergraduate education at universities. Until the early 1950s, undergraduate education was elite education, but since then most systems have moved from elite, to mass, to near-universal higher education. The overall system grew enormously and most individual universities grew enormously as well. And this system can be expensive, especially as it often tries to preserve many aspects of the elite system. The first subtext in the differentiation debates is the desire to find a less expensive means to provide undergraduate education: perhaps by differentiating institutions, there could be some universities that provide undergraduate education at lower cost. The often unaddressed question is whether the lower cost alternative will be lower quality. The other subtext concerns graduate education and research. It is argued that university systems of large jurisdictions need a few universities that can compete at the highest level internationally, in terms of the graduate education offered and the quality of the research conducted. These institutions would need a higher level of funding to allow them to compete internationally. Both of these subtexts will be critically examined in more detail later in the book; here the purpose is make sure these subtexts are recognized as we begin the analysis.

Amidst all the writing in favour of greater differentiation, there are writers who take a more cautionary tone. Diversity is not necessarily desirable particularly if, in the name of differentiation, resources are unevenly distributed across institutions, and this policy "lets slide into penury those institutions which bear the brunt of mass teaching and learning whilst creating poles of excellence for a fortunate few." (Neave 2000, 19) This cautionary view will be especially important in Ontario because an essential feature of our current system is that universities offer undergraduate degree programs of similar quality and colleges offer diploma and degree programs of similar quality across the province. I believe any policy to achieve greater differentiation should not compromise this essential feature of Ontario's system.

WHY INSTITUTIONAL DIFFERENTIATION BY MANDATE IS DESIRABLE

The general argument that institutional differentiation by mandate is desirable in a system of higher education has two parts.[1]

The first part asserts that higher education involves diverse activities and purposes. For example, the students attending higher education are very diverse and therefore a diverse array of degree and diploma programs is needed to meet their different interests, aspirations, and capabilities. Also, as knowledge advances, new fields emerge and new approaches to existing fields open up new areas of study, requiring new degree or diploma programs. And higher educational institutions are expected to contribute to society in a wide range of ways—from graduating well-educated students across many fields with different degrees and diplomas in order to meet the needs of the economy, to conducting research not only for its own sake but also to address specific social issues, and to contribute to national and regional economic development. This part of the argument usually asserts that the activities and purposes of higher education have multiplied and become more diverse over the last fifty years. As countries moved from elite to mass higher education, the need for more diverse degree and diploma programs is obvious. Similarly, with the coming of the knowledge-based society and with a higher and higher percentage of jobs requiring a higher education qualification, there is need for more diverse programs. Also, over the last twenty years especially, society has asked higher education institutions to contribute in more and more ways, asking for more economic benefits from research, asking for more knowledge mobilization to address social problems, asking for more community engagement. Thus the activities and purposes of higher education have become more and more diverse.

This first part of the argument is an argument for *program/activity* diversity. However, this first part of the argument does not require institutional diversity by *mandate*: all these diverse activities and purposes could be carried out in a system with many similar institutions. There could be *program/activity* diversity within each institution and all institutions could have the same mandate.

The second part of the argument rests on a certain view of institutional behaviour: it is argued that institutions are more effective when they are more focused and specialized. As institutions focus and specialize, it is argued, they become more efficient—delivery of the same service at lower cost. With focus and specialization, they can deliver higher quality services and are more likely to be innovative. With a more limited range of activities and purposes, the institutions can better report their activities and be better held accountable to governments and the public. Without some focus, institutions tend to suffer from mission stretch, or mission overload; they do many things adequately rather than fewer things excellently.

Taking the two parts together, the argument is that diverse programs are better delivered by institutions mandated to focus on only a subset of this range of programs.

This second part of the argument rests upon a theory of institutional behaviour and decision making; to understand and assess the argument will require understanding of the literature on institutional behaviour. Why do institutions behave in a certain way? How do they make decisions? What objectives are they pursuing? These questions are especially difficult to answer for non-profit, publicly assisted institutions like universities and colleges. But answers will be needed both to understand the current level of institutional and program diversity and to develop realistic proposals for greater institutional and program diversity. The analysis of institutional decision making is developed in the next chapter. Lying in the background of the two-part argument is the belief that institutions will not naturally, or through competition and co-operation, differentiate themselves sufficiently. Rather they will tend to become more similar, a process called isomorphism. This is taken up in the next chapter.

On its face, the two-part argument would seem to call for highly specialized institutions, that is, for highly differentiated higher education institutions, each focused on a narrow range of programs and activities. However, the problems of diverse activities can be mitigated within an institution by dividing the institution into sub units—at universities, for example, this is done by creating faculties: the Faculty of Science, the Faculty of Engineering, the Faculty of Arts and so on. The university combines heterogeneous programs, but each faculty is specialized and can make decisions effectively.

Also, a complete analysis must also recognize that there can be advantages to combining apparently very different programs in the same institution. First, there are many advantages for students in having diverse bachelor's degree or diploma programs in the same institution. Many students do not yet know which program is best suited to them and use their first year to explore several programs; others enter a program, find it is not for them, and wish to change. It is always easier to change programs within an institution than to change programs by changing institution. In a system with highly differentiated institutions, it becomes more difficult for students to change programs. Also students benefit from being in a diverse student body, getting to know others with very different interests who have come to the institution for the very different programs. Second, there are many apparently diverse activities which in fact can actually be complementary. For example, undergraduate education and research many seem to be distinct and competing activities, but the undergraduate curriculum might be improved by having the courses designed and taught by professors actively engaged in research. Or another example, research in neuroscience and English literature may seem poles apart, but each can complement the other as researchers try to understand such fundamental motivations of human behaviour as greed or pride. And finally, diverse activities can share facilities so that the average cost of each activity is lower if it is in a large heterogeneous institution than if it were on its own. For example, diverse higher education programs can share libraries and computer labs, not to mention parking lots, residences, and communications professionals. The average costs for each different activity will be lower if combined into one larger institution compared to each activity being in a separate small institution.

The subtle and difficult question is what level of diversity within a university or college is compatible with ensuring that the institution remains focused and effective?

And finally, the arguments about how much institutional differentiation is desirable must confront the complex nexus of concepts dealing with critical mass, peer group effects, and institutional culture. The ideas are illusive, very difficult to define and measure, but lie at the heart of the rationale for differentiation. To begin to explore the ideas, let us consider some examples.

Suppose the universities in the higher education system were quite undifferentiated, and each had a small doctoral program in South Asian Studies and a small group of faculty members researching the history, culture, and economy of South Asia. The doctoral program and the research program at each institution might be below the critical mass, of both students and faculty, needed to achieve high quality. Of course, there is a trade-off to confront. There are some benefits to having small programs at each institution across the province, but it might be that Ontario would be better served by having only a few institutions with doctoral and research programs in South Asian issues.

One means to characterize the differences between institutions is by the differences in their student body. Many countries have a small group of highly selective universities within a system of near-universal higher education. This is not the case in Ontario. Peer group effects are controversial, indeed so controversial that in Ontario we do not want to talk about them or analyze them. We prefer to believe that all students are the same—after all, they have all met the entry standard. But in reality, students differ in their abilities, their interests, and their aspirations. Ontario universities mix students of widely different abilities. The top students lose out: the high-ability, high-interest, high-aspiration students lose the peer group effect of being surrounded by equally talented students and being stimulated to higher achievement. Of course, again, there is a complex trade-off to confront; there are some benefits to having students of differing abilities in the same program, but also again, Ontario students might benefit from giving high-ability, high-engagement, high-aspiration students more opportunities. In many countries, this is done through institutional differentiation—a small subset of universities has highly selective admissions. Given Ontario's current system, this could be done more fruitfully through more diversity of degree programs within an institution.

Another means to characterize the differences among institutions is by the differences in their professoriate. We prefer to believe that all professors are the same, and many faculty associations assert it vociferously—after all, everyone has met the criteria for appointment and the permanent faculty members have all met the standards for tenure and promotion. But professors, like students, are different. Professors, as both teachers and researchers, differ in their abilities, interests, and aspirations. Some professors are better teachers than others. Should all spend the same amount of time on teaching versus research? Some professors are better researchers than others—they have higher ability, higher interest, and higher aspiration. Should all professors spend the same share of their time on research? In Ontario, the workload of faculty members is quite similar and has become less differentiated over time. And there are peer effects among professors. Would Ontario benefit from a clustering of high-ability, high-interest, high-aspiration teachers in some institutions and a clustering of high-ability, high-interest, high-aspiration researchers in a few other institutions? Should Ontario universities be more differentiated in terms of workload of faculty—i.e., in the balance of faculty time devoted to teaching versus research? The Ontario system does some sorting of professors across institutions according to research, especially through the initial hiring process; as any recent doctoral graduate seeking a university position or member of a departmental hiring committee can attest. For example in recruiting new faculty, University of Toronto competes against a few Canadian universities and the major US universities to attract the top researchers. The recruitment at smaller universities is very different—the candidates are different and the university has different competitors, and also somewhat different hiring criteria.

Together this mix of the student body and the mix of professors in each institution, and in a complex interaction with the history and current strategic direction of the institution, determine the institutional culture of a university. Many countries have a few universities that combine two characteristics: they are highly selective in terms of students and they focus on hiring faculty members with high-ability, high-interest, high-aspiration in research. Ontario does not have such institutions and it would require a massive restructuring to create them. The practical policy question is whether Ontario would be well served if some institutions evolved in this direction.

Having explored the arguments for institutional differentiation by mandate, let us examine further the institutional differentiation of the current Ontario system and apply the analysis.

DIFFERENTIATION BY ACADEMIC ORIENTATION VERSUS VOCATIONAL ORIENTATION

The two-part argument for institutional differentiation is very clear in the justification for Ontario's binary system of higher education. The binary system arose out of analysis about providing the best system of first-level higher education. In 1950, Ontario had five universities and no colleges. As Ontario moved from elite to mass higher education, it was recognized that, for first-level higher education, responding to the greater diversity of students, there should not only be academically-oriented bachelor's degrees but also vocationally-oriented diplomas. Rather than accommodating all the expansion in the university sector alone, which would have meant greatly widening the previous mandate of universities, it was decided that a binary diversification of higher education institutions was desirable. A similar sort of differentiation occurred in many countries as they moved toward mass higher education in the 1960s and 1970s (Codling and Meek 2006). Universities would have a certain focus and mandate; colleges would have a separate focus and mandate. Each sector would be more efficient, more accountable, and deliver programs of higher quality, than if all these activities were combined in one sort of institution. This argument was widely accepted then and continues to be. The value of a basic differentiation into academically-oriented institutions and vocationally-oriented institutions is agreed. No one today would argue that rethinking higher education in Ontario should lead to merging universities and colleges into one all-purpose type of institution.

DIFFERENTIATION BY FIELD OF STUDY

After the differentiation of the institutions of higher education into academically-oriented universities and vocationally-oriented colleges, the two-part general argument would seem to recommend that institutions be differentiated further by general field of study. Let us explore the issue of differentiation by field of study, using the university sector for our examples. A similar analysis would hold for the college sector.

It could be argued that, for example, there should be science and technology universities, universities focused upon medically related fields, or social science universities. And there exist many such specialized universities in the world. For example, the California Institute of Technology (Caltech) is a science and technology university; University of California (UC) San Francisco is a health sciences university, and the London School of Economics and Political Science (LSE) is a university focused on the social sciences. These universities are acknowledged world leaders in these fields, and it is certainly a credible argument that their focus, in part, explains their success. Should Ontario move to have its universities become more differentiated according to general fields of study?

And of course, the specialization by field of study could be pushed further to argue for universities specialized in single fields; for example universities specialized in psychology, or history, or biology. Specialization pushed to this level seems problematic, but it does clearly illustrate that there could be too much differentiation by field of study. In the past in many countries, there were university-like institutes of this highly specialized sort, but most have been incorporated into universities. However, some free-standing university-type institutions still exist, for example the French grandes écoles, the elite subsystem of the university system in France, that are highly specialized institutions by field of study.

As we think about differentiation by field of study, let us consider the primary mission of a university: to provide undergraduate education. Would Ontario students be well served if a guiding principle in the design of Ontario's system was that universities should be differentiated according to fields of study? I believe Ontario students would be poorly served, and I think most would agree. The current system design does not differentiate much in terms of undergraduate programs available at each university. This is to ensure equality of opportunity for students regardless of where they live.

However, it may be sound system design to have a few specialized institutions amidst an overall system with little differentiation at the undergraduate level. Indeed, this is the case for Caltech, UC San Francisco, and LSE—they should be seen as components of a system in which most universities are not differentiated by fields of study. But because Ontario does not need another university, this possibility is moot.[2] Nonetheless the general point remains: universities specialized by field of study have a place in a system where most universities are similar. In Ontario, OCAD and UOIT are examples of such universities.

AN OPEN UNIVERSITY/OPEN COLLEGE

One of the most important aspects of a system of higher education is the provision of both full-time and part-time education. Program diversity of this sort is vital to meeting the needs of diverse students. Let us first consider the university sector, but the same analysis applies to the college sector.

All universities offer courses in the late afternoon and evening, and on the weekend, to better accommodate part-time students, many of whom are older and hold full-time jobs. (In recent years, the distinction of full-time students attending daytime courses and part-time students attending late afternoon and evening courses has broken down. Now, both types of students attend throughout the day.) Ontario universities have large numbers of part-time students averaging about 25 percent of the number of full-time students. The northern universities are higher, ranging up to 38 percent, which is understandable given the vast spaces they serve. Ryerson is significantly different from all other universities, with part-time students being 70 percent of the full-time total. Ryerson defines itself as an "innovative career-focused university," "offering a professionally relevant curriculum," and designs a number of programs to accommodate part-time students.

However, these part-time programs are a small portion of total university activity in Ontario and tend not to be given high priority at most universities or by the government in system design. Would Ontario's diverse students be better served by the creation of an institution differentiated by mandate to provide part-time degree programs?

There is one particular type of part-time education that Jones and Skolnik (2009) identified as a gap in the Ontario system: an open university. Open universities significantly improve access, especially for working adults, non-traditional populations, and those living far from existing institutions. Although strictly speaking, not defined as institutions for part-time learning, the vast majority of open university students are part-time. An open university does not have its own campus, instead, offering education at a distance. Increasingly this means offering courses online and through other electronic means (sometimes combined with short intense periods of study in one location). As Jones and Skolnik point out, an open university is not simply defined by being part-time or by the technology used in instruction; rather it is defined by an educational philosophy. "A key element of that philosophy is open admissions, i.e., admissions to programs and courses is not [entirely] based upon prior academic achievement, but on learners' needs and aspirations. Further, an open university provides the flexibility to enable learners to utilize its resources and infrastructure in whatever way will best meet the learner's needs. ...Other features of an open university are continuous admission, 24 hour learning, and affordability" (Jones and Skolnik 2009, 7). All universities offer courses online and courses for part-time students, but Ontario does not have an open university. Greater institutional differentiation to establish one seems warranted.

Open universities have become specialized in delivering education via the web and in using the new information and communications technologies as part of their pedagogy. There is growing evidence that these new information and communications technologies could enhance education if combined with traditional on-campus instruction. So called "mixed-mode pedagogy" or "blended learning" is better than traditional on-campus lecture/tutorial/lab instruction; traditional pedagogy can be significantly enhanced through the use of new technologies. Yet, universities have been very slow to innovate in this area—most of the instruction occurs in the traditional way. Another benefit of an open university in Ontario would be that it would develop specialized components—in the parlance of this field these components are called learning objects—that could be blended into the traditional instruction at universities.

These same arguments apply to colleges. Each offers a great deal of part-time and online programming, and in contrast to universities, the colleges already have an institution for collaboration. "OntarioLearn.com is a consortium of 24 Ontario Community Colleges that have partnered to develop and deliver online courses. Each partner college selects courses from the OntarioLearn.com course inventory that will complement its existing distance education offerings. This partnership approach has allowed member colleges to optimize resource use, avoid duplication and, more importantly, increase the availability of online learning opportunities for their students" (OntarioLearn n.d.). Single online courses are available as well as over fifty certificates that are entirely online.

The 2010 Speech from the Throne in Ontario announced the establishment of the Ontario Online Institute which would bring together colleges, universities and training networks to increase postsecondary online learning opportunities for students in Ontario. It would also work to enhance the quality of online courses. However, although this initiative continues to be mentioned by the relevant minister, few details are available about how it will function, despite the government being in receipt of a full feasibility study.

Whatever shape the initiative finally takes a number of general points are clear.

Both online education and a full open university/open college are very important for improving access of currently underrepresented groups. I believe that such initiatives are the most important way to improve accessibility to higher education in Ontario.

There is much evidence that students would be well served by creating better pathways and means to combine university courses and college courses in their postsecondary study. A conclusion of this book is that Ontario needs more options for students to have career-oriented education (Chapter 5). Therefore, the Ontario Online Institute should encompass both university courses and college courses in the same organization. Over time such an organization would help to enhance the pathways and collaborations between universities and colleges. Across its degree and diploma programs, the Institute would focus upon career-oriented education.

The central dilemma in taking this initiative is whether it becomes a full open university/open college with its own degree and diploma granting authority or whether it is a coordinating consortium of the existing universities and colleges. The feasibility report recommended the latter: a consortium approach.[3] This has the benefit of being less costly, easier to establish quickly, and of not arousing the worries and perhaps opposition of the existing institutions. However, the drawback of the consortium approach is that it would not be able to fully implement an "open" educational philosophy and this is the innovation that would truly improve access. Also, the part-time and online courses at each university would remain a low priority—a consortium would be less likely to stimulate creative design of new courses and improvements in online education. Only the creation of an open university/open college can realize all the benefits of differentiation by mandate.

The broad policy direction is clear: Ontario needs a province-wide organization, encompassing both universities and colleges, to coordinate and enhance online higher education and to truly offer "open higher education."

At the outset, a consortium approach is most feasible, but in the longer run the development of a full open university/open college is the more important initiative. This is a case where a new type of institution, differentiated by mandate, would improve Ontario's system of higher education.[4]

A FURTHER LOOK AT CLASSIFICATION SYSTEMS

Classification systems can be helpful in analyzing whether Ontario has the right mix of institutions in its system of higher education. This is particularly the case for classification systems used in other countries because these can help to define institutional types used in other systems of higher education that might be beneficially developed in Ontario.

Chapter 1 classified the Ontario institutions of higher education using the Statistics Canada system. This system used two criteria to classify institutions: (i) the types and level of degrees/diplomas awarded and (ii) the presence of a medical school. Using these criteria, the institutions were first divided into universities and colleges, and then each into subcategories. The colleges were classified as degree-granting or multi-purpose. The universities were classified as medical doctoral, comprehensive, primarily undergraduate, and special purpose.

With this classification system in mind, one could ask: do we have the right mix of institutions or would a different mix be better? Would Ontario be better served by more medical doctoral universities and fewer primarily undergraduate, or by more comprehensive universities and fewer primarily undergraduate? Also, we could ask: should Ontario have more degree-granting colleges (ITALs) and fewer multi-purpose colleges?

The most widely studied system of classifying institutions of higher education is the Carnegie Classification of Institutions of Higher Education in the United States, originally developed in the 1970s by the Carnegie Commission on Higher Education to support its program of research and policy analysis (Carnegie Foundation for the Advancement of Teaching 2012). Its influence is widespread. For example, the Statistics Canada system drew heavily on the Carnegie approach, and there is a European Classification of Higher Education Institutions being developed that also uses the Carnegie work as a starting point. The Carnegie system has been revised several times but the basic classification structure has remained constant. The system divides institutions into five types.

1. Doctorate-granting Universities
    *   RU/VH: Research Universities (very high research activity)
    *   RU/H: Research Universities (high research activity)
    *   DRU: Doctoral/Research Universities

2. Master's Colleges and Universities

3. Baccalaureate Colleges and Universities
    *   Bac/A&S: Baccalaureate Colleges—Arts & Sciences
    *   Bac/Diverse: Baccalaureate Colleges—Diverse Fields
    *   Bac/Assoc: Baccalaureate Colleges/Associate's Colleges

4.   Associate's Colleges

5.   Special Focus Institutions.

The first three types are universities, divided according to the highest degree awarded—into doctorate-granting universities, master's universities, and baccalaureate colleges. The definitions make clear that all three types offer a wide range of baccalaureate programs. The fourth type, called Associate's Colleges, award one-year certificates and two-year, often vocationally focused, Associate's degrees. (This type is most analogous to Ontario's Colleges of Applied Arts and Technology.) Many colleges also have a transfer function, providing the first two years of study of a baccalaureate degree. The fifth type is special focus institutions which includes faith-related institutions, institutions specializing in one field such as engineering, agriculture, or education, and also tribal colleges.

This Carnegie system highlights a number of ways of conceptualizing institutional diversity that might be of interest in assessing the Ontario system of higher education. In Ontario, as was documented in Chapter 1, all our universities have the majority of their students in baccalaureate education, and virtually all our universities have significant master's education, but there is significant differentiation in the amount of doctoral education. Using the Carnegie approach, Ontario would seem to divide into Master's/Bachelor's universities and Doctorate-granting universities.

If we look more closely at the definition of the Doctorate-granting category in the Carnegie Classification, it is defined *both* by the awarding of doctorates (at least twenty per year) and by the amount of research activity (measured mainly, although not entirely, by research grant income). This Carnegie approach is sound because of the intimate interconnections between doctoral education and research. It clearly is a defining characteristic of a university—even recognizing that the majority of its students are undergraduates—that there is a substantial amount of doctoral education and a substantial amount of research. And this characteristic differentiates it from other universities.

Over the various revisions of the Carnegie Classification, the subtypes of Doctorate-granting Universities have been labelled differently but the principles for the subtypes have been the same. The universities are divided according to the number of doctorates awarded and by the research activity as measured by the amount of research support (mainly from the federal granting agencies). In the most recent version, they are divided into Research Universities (very high research activity); Research Universities (high research activity); and Doctoral/Research Universities. To make clear the two-part definition within the Doctorate-granting University category, I think the overall category is perhaps better labelled as Doctoral/Research universities.

In Ontario, as documented in Chapter 1, universities are differentiated by research, as measured by research income, and the group with the greater research income is essentially the group with the greater doctoral education. This reinforces the notion that Ontario universities are differentiated into Doctoral/Research universities and Master's/Bachelor's universities.

Under our current policies, Ontario universities all have the same mandate, but are in reality differentiated according to doctoral education and research. The issue for public policy is whether Ontario would be better served by mandating the system as two groups: the Doctoral/Research universities and the Master's/Bachelor's universities. This could imply, for example, the limiting of all future growth of doctoral programs to the Doctoral/Research group and limiting the share of graduate education in the Master's/Bachelor's group. With this mandated differentiation, would each group be more focused and deliver programs more efficiently, more creatively, and with greater accountability? Would such mandated differentiation better ensure critical mass and strong peer group effects and help to shape institutional culture? These questions are analyzed in later chapters; the purpose of this chapter is to set the analytical framework and raise the questions.

The Carnegie Classification identifies, as an institutional type, universities that award only bachelor's degrees—an institutional type not found in Ontario. Although not formally part of the classification, such universities may be presumed to place a special emphasis on teaching and undergraduate student learning. Jones and Skolnik's examination of institutional diversity in Ontario concluded: "the greatest gap in institutional types in Ontario postsecondary education may be that of a university level institution that concentrates on undergraduate education and the teaching function (Jones and Skolnik 2009, 6). Clark et al. (2009) made the creation of such teaching-focused institutions the centrepiece of their analysis of higher education in Ontario, driven by the need to find a less expensive, but good quality, means of providing undergraduate education. Clark, Trick, and Van Loon (2011) provided a detailed blueprint of how such universities might be established. My analysis in Chapter 4 concludes that Ontario's system of first-level higher education is now large enough and therefore that the possibility of creating a group of bachelor's/teaching universities is moot.

The Carnegie Classification was significantly revised in 2005, but retained the basic principles discussed above. The revision developed further ways to classify institutions, including an "elective" classification called "community engagement." Institutions may elect to classify themselves, for example as "community engagement universities," supplying data and information about their activities to substantiate this characterization.

The European Commission, following the creation of the European Higher Education Area and the European Research Area, supported the development of a classification system, now called U-Map The European Classification of Higher Education Institutions (European Commission 2012). One of its components is similar to the revised Carnegie system and identifies community engagement as a means to classify institutions. The European system also indentifies "international orientation" as a means to classify institutions.

Of course, all institutions have community engagement and international orientation; the issue is relative priority and strategic commitment. Some universities in Ontario are making significant strategic commitments to each. These recent developments in classification systems highlight the range of roles of institutions of higher education and the diversity of ways to classify institutions. These elective classifications are clearly those which differentiate universities by program, i.e., by institutional decision making rather than by government mandate. The issues for public policy are several: whether Ontario would benefit from having all universities engage more in these activities, whether Ontario would benefit from having a group of universities focused upon community engagement or on international orientation, and finally whether new government incentives are needed to achieve the desired results.

NOTES

1. The classic analysis of the value of institutional diversity is Birnbaum (1983). He offers more extensive, and somewhat different, arguments in favour of institutional diversity.
2. Chapter 1 showed that there is some differentiation of Ontario universities by field of study in research. It might be the case that Ontario would benefit if some of its existing universities were to develop further their focus in certain broad fields of study, in graduate education and research, while retaining their similarity at the undergraduate level.
3. For a discussion of the feasibility report, see Bates (2011).
4. Many jurisdictions have tried a consortium approach, usually with modest success. A recent re-imagining of the California system called for an end to the consortium approach and the establishment a stand-alone California Open University (Douglass 2010, 9).

Chapter 3

GOVERNMENT POLICY, INSTITUTIONAL DECISION MAKING, AND ISOMORPHISM

As we rethink higher education in Ontario, we are asking ourselves whether a more differentiated system—both in terms of institutional differentiation and diversity of programs—would achieve better results. In order to answer this question, we must understand what determines the current extent of institutional differentiation and program diversity in the system. Too often when we think of the "system" of higher education, we think that it is the result of conscious design by government. Certainly government policies have great influence, and indeed have the pre-eminent influence, but the higher education system and its outcomes are better conceived as being shaped by the interaction of government policy and institutional decisions. And within the institutions, the decisions are primarily shaped by the senior administration of the institutions (presidents, vice-presidents, and deans), the faculty members, and the students. All four actors and how they interact should be recognized as influential in creating the current system.

Broadly speaking, the government first establishes the various classes of higher education institutions specifying their mandate, funding, and governance and accountability structures. Then within each sector, the government sets the framework and provides much of the funding; the senior administration (after consultation) charts the strategic direction of their institution, including which new degree programs to offer, and seeks more resources to support their institution. The faculty members choose whom to hire and to promote, and they design the curriculum, teach the courses, and conduct the research. Students choose which institution to attend (and so which sector to enter), which program to enrol in, and bring their abilities, interests, and aspirations to the learning

Rethinking Higher Education: Participation, Research, and Differentiation, G. Fallis. Kingston: School of Policy Studies, Queen's University. © 2013 The School of Policy Studies, Queen's University at Kingston. All rights reserved.

process. Government policy is important—but so is the decision making that goes on within institutions. As noted in Chapter 2, the argument for institutional differentiation is based on a theory of institutional behaviour: institutions will be more effective if they have a focused mandate. Understanding institutional decision making will be crucial if we are to understand what creates the system and its outcomes and if we are to realize a more differentiated system and better results.

The detailed discussion in this chapter deals with only with universities. The situation for colleges is roughly, although by no means entirely, similar.[1]

GOVERNMENT

The first role for government in higher education in Ontario is to establish the binary system by mandate and to establish the institutions (universities and colleges) in each sector. Then, the government sets the framework and funding within which institutions operate. In the university sector, it is crucial to realize that universities are autonomous institutions, independent of government, able to pursue their mission as they see fit, within the broad framework set by the government.

The government framework and the funding arrangements for universities in Ontario are very complicated but the key components can be identified:

- Operating grants (enrolment based)
- Special purpose operating grants (usually enrolment based)
- Tuition policy
- Student assistance policy
- Research grants and contracts (provincial/federal)
- Key performance indicators
- Quality assurance (approval of new programs/review of existing programs)
- Multi year accountability agreements (MYAAs) [strategic mandate agreements (SMAs)].

The first five components of the government framework determine the revenues available to universities for annual operations. (There is a separate structure for capital funding—for construction of new buildings and renovation of existing buildings—that will be discussed briefly below.)

The last three components are the quality assurance and accountability arrangements established by the government, which are designed to influence institutional behaviour and thus steer the system and its outcomes.[2] (The boards of governors of universities have special responsibilities for other forms of accountability that are not discussed here.)

The last item—the multi year accountability agreement—is particularly important for this analysis. The MYAA is a relatively new device for managing the interaction of government policy and institutional choice. The MYAAs were begun following the Rae Review of 2005. It appears that these have now been discontinued and are being replaced by strategic mandate agreements (SMAs). During the Fall of 2012, universities submitted SMAs to the government, but the final implementation of the SMA framework has not been completed. Despite the different labels and some differences in emphasis, both are examples of a new device for managing the interaction of government policy and institutional choice. And both provide the government with a new instrument to shape and steer the university system. The discussion below deals only with MYAAs, but the principles apply to the emerging SMAs.

The MYAA is an agreement signed between the ministry and an individual university. The ministry establishes the policy goal and the institution sets out how it will work to achieve that goal. The MYAA formalizes the institution's commitment to the government. For example, the government announced that it wished particular attention should be placed on accessibility to university for certain designated groups, including students whose parents did not attend higher education, aboriginal students, and students with disabilities. Each university through its MYAA set out how it would approach improving accessibility for the designated groups. The MYAA is a public document. After a certain interval, the university reports to government on its activities under the MYAA. This report is also a public document. To date, the government had not made a public response to the MYAA reports, nor has it tied resources to how well the university has achieved the announced goals. (The SMAs provide more scope for universities to articulate their own strategic goals. The SMA then formalizes this commitment to the government, and opens the possibility that progress toward goals would be reported and perhaps that future funding be tied to progress toward goals.) Most discussion about how to increase institutional diversity in the Ontario system of universities has suggested that the MYAA (or some variant) would be the vehicle to accomplish this.[3]

There are complex arrangements for each component of the government framework, but for this analysis, the details are not the crux of the matter. The crux of the matter is to identify the features of the government framework which steer the system and influence its outcomes.

Let us first look at the revenue available to universities for their core functions of teaching and research, what I shall call comprehensive operations.

The Canadian Association of University Business Officers (CAUBO) reports the total revenues and expenditures of universities using the principles of fund accounting. For details see CAUBO (2009). Fund accounting is an accounting system, widely used by non-profit organizations, designed to demonstrate accountability rather than to measure profitability. In this system, a fund is a self-balancing set of accounts, segregated for specific purposes in accordance with laws and regulations or special restrictions. Usually funds are received for certain purposes; fund accounting insures that funds are spent for the intended purposes. The funds used by CAUBO are general operating, special purpose and trust, sponsored research, ancillary, capital, and endowment. Most analyses of annual university operations focus on the operating fund. However, this is too limited a view. For the purposes of understanding university activities, we want to identify the funding available for what I am calling comprehensive operations—for teaching *and* research. To identify comprehensive operating revenue (COR), we begin from the total revenues in all funds and then deduct the revenues from the ancillary fund. These are revenues from such activities as residences, parking, bookstores, and food services—activities that are outside the strictly defined educational realm and usually intended to be self-supporting. We also deduct revenues from the capital fund; these are revenues that come to the university to be used for new buildings and for renovation, not for operating purposes. And we deduct the endowment fund; these are capital inflows to the university. Thus, COR comes from three funds: the general operating, special purpose and trust, and the sponsored research income funds.[4]

The comprehensive operating revenue for Ontario universities in 2008 came from three main sources (CAUBO 2009):

- Operating grants from the province (34 percent)
- Tuition (24 percent)
- Sponsored research income (26 percent).

The remainder of the revenue comes from many small sources.

There are three things to note about this simple description of comprehensive operating revenue. The first is the importance of sponsored research income; this revenue is now greater than tuition. Too often when people look at university annual operations, they look only at the general operating fund and its main components: government operating grants and tuition fees. When analysis of university revenues looks only at the general operating fund, it misses this huge role of research revenue. The second point of note is what is absent from this list of main sources: revenues earned from endowments. In Ontario, revenues from endowments are a tiny percentage of total revenue. University presidents spend a significant share of their time seeking external donations, but to date in Ontario, although total endowments have grown, earnings from these funds have had little effect on comprehensive operating revenue (although at the margin having a significant effect on certain activities).

This is in marked contrast to the funding of many universities in the United States, both public and private. And the third thing to note is that these shares of revenues will vary significantly among universities. For example, universities without a medical school or large science and engineering faculties will have a lower share of sponsored research income and will be more reliant on tuition and government grants.

A crucial feature of the government-determined revenue framework is that the operating grants for universities are based solely upon enrolments (with different payments for students in different fields). This is entirely consistent with the fact that higher education policy in Ontario has been dominated by concern with access and with expanding the number of places. Our funding system has been designed with this in mind. The operating grant is often made up of two parts, one for undergraduate students and the other for graduate students. Each year, the government makes "arrangements" with universities and specifies the number of funded places and the funding per student.[5] Each university commits to a certain number of enrolments. These operating grants are not connected to performance (except that if students do not enrol at the institution, there is no operating grant for those students). The crucial aspect of these arrangements is that, effectively, there is a cap on the number of students at each university that will be eligible for operating grants.

Within the commitments to certain enrolment levels in undergraduate and graduate programs, the university decides on which programs to offer and on how many to admit to each program.

When universities make their decisions about admission of students, they do not want to admit more students than will be eligible for an operating grant—they need both the grant and the tuition to pay for the costs of providing the program. (From time to time, institutions overshoot and have "unfunded" students, and receive only tuition. But then next year, they approach the government and seek to have these unfunded students included in their operating grant. Over time, these unfunded students usually get folded in.) Although institutions do not want to overshoot the number of available funded places, they do not want to undershoot either. When governments have made available operating grants for enrolment growth, the system always expands to utilize the increased number of funded places. Universities expand when growth funding is available, both because the government obviously wants them to and because universities hope to provide the extra places at a cost less than the revenue from the grant plus tuition. This difference between the revenue from growth and the cost of growth is used to pay for other things, most importantly for salary increases of existing senior administration, faculty, and staff.

There are, from time to time, special purpose operating grants; for example, there are grants to help cover the extra costs of northern institutions, and there have been grants to expand computer science programs, nursing programs, and education programs. Universities have always expanded to take up these special purpose grants. Clearly, government does influence the type and size of programs offered by universities through these grants, but the enrolments involved are a very small share of total enrolments. And like regular operating grants, they are based on enrolments with no other measure of performance required to receive the funds.

It is a three-actor dynamic that determines the size and growth of the system of higher education and thus accessibility of the system (how many attend and who attends): government makes available operating grants for new university places, the universities plan to expand and make more offers of admission to the pool of applying students, and the students decide whether to apply and whether to take up the offers. Fundamentally, the accessibility of the system is determined by the number of places the government is willing to fund (not by the level of tuition). It is possible that after the government makes available operating grants for more places and after universities have made plans to expand and set their target for new admissions, that individual universities are unable to achieve their new admission targets. The pool of applicants is only so big. To attract more students a university may have to reduce its cutoff (the minimum secondary school grade average for admission). But, reducing the cutoff often means admitting students who are less capable of university-level study. At some point, despite the fact that there are still applicants, universities will not reduce their cutoff further and will fall short of their new admission targets. In recent years universities in northern Ontario have struggled to achieve their new admission targets. Very likely with the decline in the 18–21-year-old group over the next decade and with level participation rates, this will be a problem for more universities especially outside the GTA.

The tuition charged by universities for each degree program is a decision of that university within the framework set by government. Broadly, the government framework divides programs into those with regulated tuition and those with "formerly unregulated" tuition. For a full description of recent policy, see Norrie and Lennon (2011). All programs entered directly from secondary school have regulated tuition. Roughly, their tuition could be raised about 4 percent per year. The formerly unregulated programs include graduate programs, professional programs, and a few undergraduate programs entered after first year. As a legacy of their unregulated past, these programs currently have much higher tuition than the regulated programs. These formerly unregulated programs are now subject to regulation; tuition can rise for an entering group up to 8 percent, and for all other years up to 4 percent per year. As a rough summary, although governments have set the framework and let institutions set tuition up to a maximum, most institutions have raised tuition the maximum allowable. Thus, over the last few years in Ontario, university tuition has been rising at about 4 to 5 percent per year. Tuition charged to international students is not subject to regulation. In March 2013, the Ontario government announced a new four-year tuition framework that caps tuition increases, on average, at 3 percent per year (Ontario 2013).

The sum of the operating grant per student and the tuition charged per student is the total revenue per student, often expressed as revenue per full-time equivalent (FTE) student. Clark et al. (2009) provide an exceptionally valuable and clear analysis of the changes in real FTE funding at Ontario universities and colleges over the last twenty years. The picture is startling and rather at odds with the common preconceptions. It is widely reported that in undergraduate education class sizes have been going up, the student-faculty ratio has been going up, and the share of all teaching done by part-time faculty and graduate students has been going up. All these are generally taken as proxy measures for the quality of education—and all show quality has been declining. Also, anyone in the university sector can tell you that budget cuts have to be made year after year. With these quality indicators falling and with annual budget cuts, one might conclude, and this is the common preconception, that real funding per student has been going down. However, Clark et al. (2009) demonstrate that the real funding per FTE at universities, adjusted for inflation using the consumer price index (CPI), has been *constant* over the last twenty years. For colleges, the funding at first declined and has now risen again, so here too, real funding per FTE has been almost constant.

How can real revenue per student be constant yet classes get larger each year? The simple answer is that costs have been rising faster than the CPI. Real revenue per FTE student, using an index of the prices institutions face, has been declining. Salaries have been rising faster than the CPI, as have the costs of energy, insurance, books and journals for the library, and so on. Also some activities, like communications and fundraising, student assistance and scholarships, and computing and information technology are taking a higher share of the budget, leaving less money for the classroom. Clark et al. (2009) provide a good analysis of these cost increases. Of course, the share of the budget for these activities is not entirely given, but is affected by choices made by the university.

It is important to consider the total revenue per student, including government grants and tuition, and how it has changed over time in real terms, but it is even more important to ask whether this total revenue is sufficient to deliver a high quality program. And of course, there is no easy answer to this question. However, comparison with other jurisdictions is a good start to the analysis. Ontario has the lowest total revenue per student of any province in Canada, and the lowest government grant per student (COU 2012c, 10).[6] There is a strong argument that Ontario's universities are underfunded.

And the years ahead will be especially difficult. Expenditure restraint will slow the growth of, and even freeze, the operating grant per student, and at the same time tuition increases have been limited to 3 percent. Operating revenues will slow more than operating costs—so there will be severe annual budget cuts at Ontario universities.

There is a certain lack of clarity, and often a good deal of confusion, about how the comprehensive annual operations of the university are funded. The focus is usually upon government grants and tuition. But what are these revenues to pay for? These revenues flow in proportion to the number of students taught, and so one tends to think that the revenues are to be used to pay for the degree programs provided to these students. This is of course true—the government grant and tuition revenues are used to pay for the costs of instruction, as well as the annual costs of the buildings, libraries, computer systems, labs, and so on that are needed to provide the degree programs. But the professors are hired not just to teach but also to conduct research. What is usually not recognized is that these grant and tuition revenues are also used to fund research at the university; that is, the revenues are used to pay for the portion of a professor's time spent on research as well as the buildings, libraries, computer systems, labs and so on needed to conduct research. This is obvious when one realizes that even if there were not any sponsored research income at the university, there would still be research undertaken. Indeed, the majority of professors do their research without a research grant. Unfortunately, the Ministry of Training, Colleges and Universities that is responsible for operating grants and tuition policy has virtually no responsibility for research. (The fact that MTCU has no clear role in research is discussed further in Chapter 8.)

The interaction between research funding and funding for the classroom has been recognized to operate in another way. When a university receives a research grant, the grant covers the direct costs of the research. However, the research activities also have indirect costs: operating and maintaining the buildings, labs, computer systems needed for the research, as well as managing the research process including financial accounting, health and safety, ethics review, accountability reports, and managing intellectual property. AUCC reports that every dollar of external research funding also requires at least 40 cents to support the indirect costs (AUCC 2009). These indirect costs must be paid for from the operating grants and tuition revenues. The Ontario government has had a modest program to help cover indirect costs. In 2001, the federal government began a program to help with the indirect costs of federal research grants and the target has been to contribute about 25 cents for each research dollar, leaving significant indirect costs still uncovered. The university is caught in a difficult bind: it pursues external research grants, but each new grant does not cover all of the indirect costs, and so money must be taken from the operating grant and tuition funds. The net result is that increases in research income take money from the classroom—class sizes increase and student-faculty ratios increase.[7]

Capital grants (or ongoing interest support on loans arranged to finance capital expansion) are used to help pay for the new buildings and equipment needed when enrolments expand, and to pay for the renovation of existing buildings. Universities make proposals for capital funding and, from among these, the government chooses which to support, so the government has considerable influence on the strategic direction of universities through the capital allocation process. For example, recently the government has tended to select capital projects to house programs in the science and technology fields. Indeed, the allocation of capital grants is one of the most powerful instruments of government policy shaping the broad directions of the university system.[8] In recent years, governments have provided funds for less than half of the cost of new buildings so that universities have had to borrow money for the new construction. This has meant that loan payments have been a growing item in the operating budget. Phrased differently, enrolment growth, coupled with reduced grant funding for new capital, has meant less money for the classroom.

The student assistance policy of course influences students and their decisions, but it also affects the university's budget. Over the last decade or so, as government policy allowed tuition to increase, there was a parallel improvement in assistance available to students from modest- and low-income families. At first, universities had to set aside 10 percent of the increase in tuition (allowed under the tuition policy) for needs-based student assistance and later 30 percent. Today, universities are responsible for the Student Access Guarantee (SAG). Under the Ontario Student Assistance Program (OSAP) financial need is equal to allowable educational expenses minus expected contributions. If, after receiving OSAP assistance, a student still has unmet financial need, then the university must provide the funds to cover the unmet need. These amounts can be considerable, for example in 2008–2009 York spent $11,637,000 for SAG-related assistance and overall spent $40,324,000 on scholarships, bursaries and prizes (total tuition revenue was $261,933,000) and Toronto spent $32,620,000 for SAG-related assistance and overall spent $94,398,000 on scholarships, bursaries and prizes (total tuition revenue was $458,111,000).[9] Thus, the government's policy on student assistance does influence university spending patterns. The increasing share of the budget allocated to student assistance payments also helps to further explain why, despite constant real revenue per FTE student (deflated at the CPI), average undergraduate class size continues to rise and there are annual budget cuts in the system.

As tuition fees rose, not only did the universities have to set aside more money for student assistance, but the government increased its commitments as well, particularly in recent years. In 2011, MTCU established the Ontario Access Grant that covered between 25 percent and 50 percent of tuition to a maximum of $3,000 per year for students from low- and modest-income families. This is now being phased into the new Ontario

Tuition Grant that reduces tuition by 30 percent for students from families whose income is $160,000 or less.

These improvements to student assistance often go unrecognized, even though the improvements have been more than enough to offset the increase in tuition for many low- and modest-income students. Currently OSAP recipients pay roughly half of the tuition charged by the university (COU 2012d, 5).

The third major source of comprehensive operating revenue is sponsored research income. As noted above, research income is 26 percent of COR in Ontario—larger than tuition income. Sponsored research income comes mainly from government: 47 percent from the federal government especially from the national granting councils and 15 percent from the provincial government. Businesses provide 16 percent and non-profit organizations supply 15 percent (CAUBO 2009). Corporate funding for research is not nearly as large as is often supposed. The amount of research done at an institution will depend in part on the amount of sponsored research income it has. The government can determine how much it allocates in total for research grants and contracts but the allocation to individual institutions will depend on the success of the faculty members in winning research grants and contracts. This competition between universities for research grants significantly affects the nature of the current system. The differentiation of universities by sponsored research income was reported in Table 1.6 in Chapter 1.

Federal government support for university research across Canada has risen dramatically: from $733 million to $2.9 billion, a fourfold increase from 1997/98 to 2007/08 (AUCC 2008, 14). Ontario government support rose significantly as well. Support from other sources also grew. In the decade from 1998 to 2008, sponsored research income at Ontario universities rose from $797 million to $2.4 billion—a threefold increase (CAUBO 1999 and 2009). Research income has grown much faster than government operating grants or tuition income.

The last three items of the government framework are the quality assurance and accountability framework governing universities.

Ontario universities must report three key performance indicators (KPIs) for the entire institution and for the major program areas (for example for education, business, humanities, and so on). The three KPIs are graduation rates (the share of an entering class of students who graduated within seven years), employment rates (after six months and after two years), and OSAP default rates (default rates on the loans of those who graduated two years prior). The university must make these indicators publicly available through their website. There is a very small amount of government operating revenue allocated by the government on the basis of these KPIs. The differences across institutions are modest and these KPIs have not exerted much effect on institutional decision making. The KPIs are, though, an important report about the functioning of the system. And, they are used by some students in making their choice of program.

For many years, Ontario's quality assurance framework has included both procedures for the approval of new programs and procedures for the periodic review of existing programs, at the graduate level and at the undergraduate level. This framework was recently revised through the initiative of the Ontario Council of Academic Vice Presidents (OCAV), which had been responsible for the previous policies. The revised approach (just as the past approach) begins from the premise that each university itself has the fundamental responsibility to ensure the quality of the programs it offers and to work for the improvement of that quality. With the revised approach, a body at arm's length both from the government and from the universities—the Ontario Universities Council on Quality Assurance (the Quality Council)—was established "to guide Ontario's publicly assisted universities in the ongoing quality assurance of their academic programs" (Ontario Universities Council on Quality Assurance 2011).

The Quality Council has published a *Quality Assurance Framework* which sets out the protocols of what should be done for the approval of new degree programs and protocols about what should be done to review regularly (at least every eight years) all existing degree programs. Both proposals for new degree programs and the review of existing programs must involve reviewers from outside the university. Each university must write, and have passed by their senate, their own institutional quality assurance process (IQAP). The IQAP must be consistent with the protocols of the *Quality Assurance Framework* and must be approved by the Quality Council. All new degree programs must be approved by the Quality Council. The Quality Council will audit universities to see that they are correctly following their IQAP when they approve new degrees and when they review existing programs.

Thus, the quality assurance process is not, strictly speaking, mandated or designed by the government. Yet, the government clearly wants a quality assurance process. Universities have established this process of self-regulation, both because they want an internationally credible system for Ontario universities and to elude the possibility that the government would take on the task of quality assurance itself. The government is satisfied with this system of self-regulation.

This quality assurance process, quite understandably, encourages the comparison of similar degree programs at different universities. Universities are encouraged to look at others to ensure comparable quality and to encourage the adoption of best practices. While this process is good for quality assurance and quality improvement, it has the unintended effect of encouraging similarity of degree programs across universities.

The system of multi year accountability agreements (MYAAs), already introduced above, is a relatively new mechanism for steering the university system. They were established after the Rae Review and after tuition fees, having been frozen from 2004–2006, were allowed to rise again. The government sought to insure that universities used the increased revenue for quality improvement (rather than simply for salary increases) and to insure that student access was not comprised especially for the groups identified in the Rae Review as being underrepresented. Each university had to prepare and negotiate a multi year accountability agreement with the government. The MYAA set out what initiatives for quality improvement would be undertaken and how results would be measured. Also the MYAA set out what initiatives for underrepresented groups would be undertaken and how results would be measured. Each university files an MYAA Report-Back and this report must be publicly available. There is little evidence, however, that the development of MYAAs has had any appreciable effect on university decision making. Most faculty members are unaware of their existence. The MYAAs have certainly not affected faculty salaries or led to quality improvements that would not have occurred without them. The MYAAs perhaps have had some slight influence in shifting university resources to improve access for underrepresented groups.

To sum up, the degree of institutional differentiation and program diversity in our system of higher education should be conceived as being shaped by four actors: government, the senior administration of the institutions, faculty members, and students.

The government sets the broad framework and provides most of the money; the main components of the government's role have been articulated and described above. Looking back at this government framework, the remarkable conclusion is that the Ontario government does very little to require, or even to encourage, institutional differentiation or program diversity.

Within this framework, senior administrators, professors, and students play their roles.[10] Let us consider each in turn.

UNIVERSITY GOVERNANCE

In order to understand the internal decision making of the university, we must understand its relationship to the society which supports it. The university has a multi-faceted mission, taking many tasks for society. Universities provide undergraduate education, graduate education and professional education, and they conduct research, both pure and applied. The public, through their governments and through tuition fees, provides huge sums of money to the university and demands accountability about how the money is spent.[11]

How, then, should universities be governed in order to best fulfill these public purposes, and to ensure they are accountable? Should universities be under the direct control of governments? Should their professors be supervised as civil servants? The answer has always been "no." Instead, it has been concluded that to best fulfill its responsibilities to society, the university must be an autonomous institution. Also, professors must have academic freedom in their work. And to protect this institutional autonomy and academic freedom, universities should operate under a system of collegial self-governance. So essential is this institutional arrangement that the very definition of what constitutes a university includes both a specification of its activities *and* of this governance: a university is an autonomous institution, whose professors and students have academic freedom, and which operates on academic matters with a system of collegial self-governance. In order for an institution to become a member of the Association of Universities and Colleges of Canada (AUCC) or of the Council of Ontario Universities (COU) it must pass this test of governance.

The senior administration, unlike senior management in the private sector or the public sector, has relatively little direct authority. The university is not a hierarchical organization. Rather, the university operates through a system of shared governance. In principle, academic policy decisions must be approved by the relevant faculty council and by the Senate of the university, and professors are members (and sometimes a majority) of these decision-making bodies. Thus, the senior administration must work with the faculty members both to develop the strategic direction and to implement it.

Although formally the senior administration only "implements" and "administers" the academic decisions of the Senate and faculty councils; in practice the senior administrators are responsible for the budget, and have authority to allocate resources. Further, most university-wide initiatives, for example on research policy or strategic direction, are originated and driven forward by the senior administration. The senior administration is full time, whereas the faculty members devote only a small portion of their time to administration. The staff of the university report to the senior administration, in the manner of employees in business or government. These staff employees provide analytical support to the president and senior administration. All these reasons combine to provide the president (and by delegation, the vice-presidents and deans) with de facto authority and responsibility for management and leadership of the university, albeit within a complex environment of shared governance.[12]

However, whatever the formal governance structure, and despite the significance of presidential power, the dominating ethos within all universities remains that faculty members should rule supreme on academic matters—there should be collegial self-governance. Faculty supremacy and collegial self-governance are easiest to achieve at the department level within the university. Within their own department, professors do indeed control the requirements for the degree, what is taught in the courses, the assessment of students, who is hired and who is tenured. They prepare academic plans for their departments and determine the evolution of their discipline. Collegial self-governance is realized through department meetings and a committee structure—hiring committees, tenure committees, curriculum committees, etc. Although professors complain fiercely about the time required by committees, they even more fiercely defend their autonomy.

However, collegial self-governance is very hard to achieve, and has little reality, at the university-wide level. Universities are bewildering, complex, and diverse institutions; few professors understand the whole or have the experience and expertise to analyze the tasks at hand. Planning at this level requires a detailed knowledge of not only academic issues, but also the financial structure of the university and the policies of governments and research granting agencies. To acquire the knowledge means foregoing attention to teaching and research. Often decisions must be made quickly, leaving little time for consultation with the Senate. Most key decisions are made by the senior university administration. This creates a tension within the governance of the university: the ethos of collegial self-governance clashes with the reality of governance by the senior administration.

Outsiders sometimes see this governance as "organized anarchy," while rueful insiders have commented that "trying to lead the professors is like trying to herd cats." However we label it, this decision-making process must be recognized if we are to understand how the university operates and why it reaches the decisions it does, and also, therefore, if we are to understand what creates the Ontario system of universities and its current level of differentiation.

With this background about governance, let us consider more explicitly the roles of the senior administration and professors in the university's decision making.

SENIOR ADMINISTRATION

The senior administration (in consultation with faculty members, students, staff, and alumni) charts the strategic direction for the university and seeks resources to help achieve the strategic plan. The question is: what is the senior administration trying to achieve when it charts a strategic direction? What is the objective when the senior administration makes decisions?

These are seemingly simple questions, but questions that scholars of higher education have found hard to answer precisely. In the case of profit-making enterprises, the answer is indeed simple: the senior managers make decisions to maximize the profits for shareholders. But universities are not profit-making enterprises; they are non-profit institutions.

As a non-profit enterprise, we might hypothesize that the senior administration tries to fulfill the mission of the institution in the best way possible, given the resources available. And also, the senior administration seeks to obtain more resources in order to do an even better job in fulfilling the mission.[13] The witty (and wise) observation of Howard Bowen, a distinguished scholar of higher education, was that universities "will raise all the money they can and spend all the money they raise" (Bowen, 1981). The quest for more resources is not just an imperative of less well-funded universities; it is equally an imperative at the best-funded universities in the world. More money can always help you do a better job in fulfilling the mission.

Thus, the senior administration seeks to fulfill the mission of the university: to provide undergraduate education, graduate education, and professional education, and to conduct research, and to be a crucial institution of the economy, and to be a crucial institution of democratic life. This is easier said than done, of course, because the mission is multi-dimensional and vigorously pursuing one dimension may reduce accomplishment in another. Nonetheless, this is probably a fair initial statement of the objective of decision makers. It is very often the case in non-profit institutions that people are drawn to work there because they believe in the mission, often receiving lower pay than they would in other occupations. This is certainly true of universities, and universities place a very high value, when they select their presidents, vice-presidents, and deans, on appointing people who have a deep understanding of, and commitment to, the mission of the university.[14]

The balance that senior administrators strike across the various dimensions of the mission will depend upon the history and character of each university and how it sees its future; often a president will be selected because she or he is felt to be particularly able to lead the university in a particular direction (as well as being particularly able to raise resources for that goal). Nonetheless, all universities will be drawn toward those activities that bring new revenue to the university, and each of the three major sources of revenue listed above offer opportunities for more revenue: universities will grow, both at the undergraduate and the graduate level, if governments provide fully-funded places in the operating grants; universities will raise tuition to the limit allowed under regulation and will want to expand in areas where tuition is high and deregulated; and universities will seek research grants because these will help to expand the research output. Over the last fifteen years, universities have given a higher priority to science, engineering, technology, and medicine because the government has expanded research grants more rapidly in these areas.[15] Also universities have given a lower priority to their role in democracy and a higher priority to their role in the economy because the former is unlikely to help attract new resources while the latter clearly is.

The constant pressure to find new resources—to better fulfill the mission—has led many universities to seek "profits" from their research, for example from patents and licenses on research discoveries. This has lead to a troubling drift away from the values inherent in the mission of the university. Derek Bok (2003) chronicles this well in his book, *Universities and the Marketplace: the Commercialization of Higher Education.*

Another line of analysis of the objective of senior administrators starts from the recognition that it is very hard—indeed perhaps impossible—to observe and measure how well a university is fulfilling its mission. Indeed, this is in the nature of what the university does and is one of the reasons why higher education is largely provided by non-profit, rather than for-profit, institutions. With direct observation of how well you are doing impossible, people fall back on indirect measures. And the indirect measure that seems to explain the behaviour of universities is that universities seek to increase their reputation and prestige.[16] A "strong reputation often shows that the college or university has been successful in pursuit of its mission." Reputation and prestige help attract better students, from both home and abroad, help attract better faculty, and help attract donations and research contracts. Although regardless of how prestige and reputation are defined, it remains true that "critical to success in higher education ... is the perception that the school's primary priority and mission is the welfare of the student and the production and dissemination of knowledge" (Weisbrod, Ballou and Asch 2008, 175).

The pursuit of reputation and prestige helps explain much university decision making. It explains why they spend so much on advertising and communication and why they spend heavily on scholarships, in competition with other universities, to attract better students, despite this being a zero sum game. Research in science and medicine is more prestigious than other fields. Universities often seek to advance in these fields, even when the new initiative will not cover its costs and will drain resources from other activities. And overall it seems that research accomplishments of a university bring more prestige than improvements to undergraduate education and so the senior administration of universities places more emphasis on research.

FACULTY MEMBERS

The third group shaping the university system is faculty members. They design the curriculum, teach the courses, and do the research. As noted, they are members of Senate and the majority on the faculty councils deciding academic policy. Most professors define themselves first as members of a discipline and many professors care more about the "quality of their department" than about their faculty or the whole university.

How then should we analyze the actions of faculty members? Just as with the senior administration, it is a fair initial statement of their objectives that faculty members seek to fulfill the mission of the university: to provide undergraduate education, graduate education, and professional education; to conduct research; to be a crucial institution of the economy; and to be a crucial institution of democratic life. They seek to fulfill this mission in the best way possible, given the resources available (and more resources will always help them to do a better job). And of course, similarly, this is easier said than done because the mission is multi-dimensional and vigorously pursuing one dimension may reduce accomplishment in another. The faculty is a more heterogeneous group than the senior administration and contains a wider range of views about which dimension of the mission to give priority.

All faculty members teach and do research.[17] And, it is also a fair initial statement that all faculty strive to do a good job on both. But there are significant differences. Here the work of scholars, like Joseph Hermanowicz, who study the culture of academic life is helpful. Hermanowicz (2005) interviewed professors and asked how they saw themselves, their work, and their careers and how they characterized their departments. He identified three cultures which can also be used to identify three types of professor. There are those with an elite orientation who place the highest premium on research, in the presence of teaching, especially research that makes a significant original contribution and is influential in the international scholarly literature. There are those with a pluralist orientation who place an equal premium on teaching and research. And there are those with a communitarian orientation who place a premium on teaching, in the presence of research. Communitarians are often especially concerned to provide undergraduate education that will be of greatest assistance to the students in their community.

Nonetheless, it should be emphasized that all professors are committed to research. They see themselves as part of their discipline and have been strongly socialized, especially through the experience of completing a doctorate at graduate school, to the norms of academic life. The doctorate is a research degree and is a prerequisite to holding a permanent position at a university. Professors are drawn to academic life usually because of the joys and challenges of reading the literature in their discipline and of conducting research that will contribute to that literature. The research enterprise is focused upon the creation of new knowledge and new understandings, and it grants recognition to those who have made significant original contributions. The greatest recognition and greatest prestige is given to those professors who are the most outstanding researchers.

At all universities, whether elite, pluralist, or communitarian, the criteria for being hired, for being granted tenure, and for being promoted include the candidate's accomplishments and promise with respect to both teaching and research. The differences among universities is in the balance between the two and the weight given to truly original research contributions. And all universities, regardless of the starting point, have given greater weight to research over the past twenty years.

Thus professors as they allocate their own time, and as they participate in the councils of university decision making, tend to favour research over teaching, and especially over teaching at the undergraduate level.

We must be careful, however, not to overstate this characterization: it is not absolute, rather it is "tend to favour." Most professors care very much about their teaching, including undergraduate teaching, especially the teaching of courses for students who will major in their discipline. Many upper level undergraduate courses become more specialized and deal with topics that are connected to the field of the professor's own research. Professors bring their passion, their sense of the advances of their field, to the classroom. The students benefit greatly from this passion and from directly experiencing the restless dynamism of new knowledge, new understandings, and new interpretations.

STUDENTS

The final actors in shaping the university are students. Although students have representation on most of the decision-making bodies within the university, they have relatively little influence on the overall evolution of the system of higher education through these bodies. The student influence comes from which universities they choose to attend, which degree programs they choose, and the aptitudes, aspirations, and commitment they bring to their studies. Student choices of university shape which institutions grow, how fast each grows, and the makeup of the student body at each university.

Their choices of which degree program strongly influences how resources are allocated within the university—it is not a perfect correlation, but resources do flow to where students are enrolled within the university. And finally, the learning outcomes of those attending university are shaped by students. The learning outcomes are jointly determined by professors and students: half determined by the professors—by the curriculum and how the professors teach the courses, and half determined the students—by what the students bring to the learning process.

Another significant influence of students has come outside the university through public pressure on governments to limit the growth of tuition and even to roll it back. Students have highlighted the worries that rising tuition would limit the access of those from lower income backgrounds and the reality that higher tuition results in many students graduating with significant debt. Student pressure on government has brought results. Despite the rising provincial deficit and debt, and the recognized need for expenditure restraint, the Government of Ontario announced it would provide a tuition rebate of up to 30 percent to students from families earning less than $160,000 per year, beginning in 2012.

ISOMORPHISM

It is the interaction of these four groups—government, the senior administration of each university, professors, and students—that determines the current level of institutional differentiation and program diversity in Ontario's system of higher education. As has already been noted, the framework of government does little to require or even to encourage either institutional differentiation or program diversity.

The universities of Ontario have become more similar, in many dimensions, over the last ten years. All grew at the undergraduate level during the rapid expansion of this time. More significantly, all grew at the graduate level as well. During the second phase of the *Reaching Higher* plan, government grants were made available for new places at the graduate level. Universities were invited to submit their plans for expansion to the Ministry of Training Colleges and Universities (MTCU). Because all universities place a high priority on expansion at the graduate level, all universities submitted plans for expansion (except Algoma, a very small special purpose institution). The submitted plans exceeded the number of available places and difficult negotiations with MTCU followed. The final allocations were spread across all universities, including the primarily undergraduate universities—indeed the primarily undergraduate universities were particularly anxious to expand at the graduate level. At the end of the exercise, the universities had become more similar in terms of the share of total enrolments at the graduate level. The enthusiasm for graduate expansion was so strong that many universities took on new targets that they have had trouble reaching.

All universities have been placing a higher priority on research over the last twenty years. On this, both the senior administration and professors are in agreement so institutional decision making easily followed. The sponsored research income available, much of it from the national granting councils, has risen faster than government grants and faster than tuition, so not surprisingly, all universities shifted in this direction. All universities evolved to have a shift in the workload of professors, moving more of their time to research and less to teaching, especially undergraduate teaching. The workload arrangement for professors is established either through collective bargaining with a faculty union or some other form of collective negotiation with a faculty association. The parties on either side of this negotiation—the senior administration[18] and the professors—have many differences, but both place a high priority on making their university more research intensive and more prestigious. The bargain shifted more of the workload into research. And now many primarily undergraduate universities have a workload split between research and teaching that is the same as the doctoral/research universities.

The range of degree programs and the relative size of the programs are remarkably similar across universities at the undergraduate level. This follows primarily from government policy and from student choices. As discussed in Chapter 1, the government has established universities across the regions of the province and funded each on the same basis. All universities draw heavily from their region. All can offer a full range of undergraduate programs, and the students in each region have relatively similar interests and preferences about the fields they wish to study. Thus all universities[19] offer programs across the sciences, social sciences, and humanities, and in the core undergraduate professional areas (engineering, business, education). And the relative size of various departments will tend to be the same; for example, the English department will be larger than the philosophy department; biology will be larger than the physics; economics will be larger than anthropology and so on.

However, this result is an important part of the explanation of why universities differ so little. All Ontario universities, even the doctoral/research universities, have the great majority of their enrolment at the undergraduate level. Given that the forces at the undergraduate level create such similarity in the range of programs and their relative size, it is very difficult to achieve significant differentiation across universities in graduate education and research that have been layered on top of the undergraduate structure.

And the content of each degree program is also very similar across universities. This is because the content of the curriculum is guided by the norms in that discipline, the professors at different universities often went to the same graduate schools, and the graduate schools often also have similar curricula. In some fields like economics or biology or psychology, the consensus about the required undergraduate curriculum is extraordinarily strong and very similar textbooks and readings will be studied at all universities. The quality assurance process governing the approval of new undergraduate degree programs and the review of existing degree programs is also a powerful force for similarity.[20]

This tendency for institutions to become more similar has been noted and studied by sociologists of organizational behaviour; the constraining process that drives institutions to become more similar is called isomorphism. A justly famous early paper, "The Iron Cage Revisited: Institutional Isomorphism and Collective Rationality in Organizational Fields," by DiMaggio and Powell (1983), analyzes the process. Reading it so many years later in the context of analyzing the institutional differentiation of Ontario universities, the analysis is eerily prescient.

DiMaggio and Powell begin from Max Weber's analysis of the rationalist spirit in modern capitalism that brought bureaucratization and institutional similarity. "For Weber, bureaucratization resulted from three related causes: competition among capitalist firms in the marketplace; competition among states, increasing rulers' needs to control their staff and citizenry; and bourgeois demands for equal protection under the law. Of these three, the most important was the competitive marketplace" (DiMaggio and Powell 1983, 147). The rationalist spirit, and its drive toward bureaucracy and similarity, was so strong that Weber called it an "iron cage."

Weber's analysis focused upon corporations and the state. DiMaggio and Powell argue that a analogous dynamic is making non-government organizations more similar, driven by government and by the evolution of the professions. Universities provide an excellent case study for their analysis, driven by government and the evolution of the professoriate. "Highly structured organizational fields" [the university sector in our case study] "provide a context in which individual efforts to deal with uncertainty and constraint often lead in aggregate, to homogeneity in structure, culture, and output" (DiMaggio and Powell 1983, 147). They identify three mechanisms of institutional isomorphic change and offer a number of hypotheses about predictors of isomorphic change.

The three mechanisms of isomorphic change are: 1) *coercive* isomorphism that follows from the power of the state and the desire of institutions to establish their legitimacy; 2) *mimetic* isomorphism that follows when institutions, dealing with uncertainty, tend to model themselves on similar organizations that they perceive to be more legitimate and successful; and 3) *normative* isomorphism that stems from the emergence and standardization of professions. All three are powerfully at work in the university sector.

Coercive isomorphism operates at many levels, the most basic being that all universities operate within the same framework and funding structure established by government (outlined in the eight-part structure set out above). This is a powerful homogenizing force. Mimetic isomorphism is also extremely strong: universities tend to model themselves and judge themselves by universities they regard as more successful. Here, the model of the research-intensive-university—the Berkeleys, Harvards, and Oxfords—is especially potent. And normative isomorphism is very much at work through the professionalization of all the jobs at the university, whether senior administration, professoriate, or staff. Each occupation tends to have similar conditions of work, to require similar preparation to enter the occupation, and to be bound together across organizations through a professional association. "Such mechanisms create a pool of almost interchangeable individuals who occupy similar positions across a range of organizations and possess a similarity of orientation and disposition that may override variation in tradition and control that might otherwise shape organizational behavior" (DiMaggio and Powell 1983, 152). This obviously applies to senior administration (presidents, vice-presidents and deans), to professors, and to staff—to student services, fundraising, research accounting, and communications professionals.

It is no wonder that universities through their institutional decision making are becoming more similar.

DiMaggio and Powell (1983 154-156) offered a number of hypotheses about when organizations will tend to become more similar. Again, they were prescient. Several of most relevance to universities are repeated below:

- The greater the extent to which organizations in the field transact with agencies of the state, the greater the extent of isomorphism.
- The greater the extent to which an organization in a field is dependent upon a single (or several similar) source of support for vital resources, the higher the level of isomorphism.
- The more ambiguous the goals of an organization, the greater the extent to which the organization will model itself after organizations that it perceives to be successful.
- The more uncertain the relationship between means and ends, the greater the extent to which an organization will model itself after organizations it perceives to be successful.
- The greater the reliance on academic credentials in choosing managerial and staff personnel, the greater the extent to which an organization will become like other organizations in the field.
- The greater the participation of organizational managers in trade and professional associations, the more likely the organization will be, or will become, like other organizations in the field.

In every case, the hypothesis predicts that universities will tend to be very similar.

More recently, Codling and Meek offer a number of propositions about institutional diversity, after reviewing the literature on diversity in higher education, and conclude that the "convergent tendency of institutions will predominate unless very specific environmental and economic conditions prevail, and/or specific policy direction is implemented" (Codling and Meek 2006, 31).

To conclude, there are clearly powerful forces explaining the lack of institutional differentiation and program diversity in the Ontario university system. We should not go overboard in our concern, though; many of the forces which produce similarity are also forces that ensure high quality and keep out poorly thought out or poorly funded alternatives. Nevertheless, if we are to seek some change, we must confront what is causing the current situation.

From the analysis, it is clear that universities will not become significantly more differentiated, operating as they have been, making institutional decisions as they have been, within the current government framework. Change will require a changed government framework, a more intrusive government.

There are great risks however. New government policies designed to steer a system as complex as the university system all too often become clumsy, bureaucratic, and costly interventions with much less impact than thought. And ironically, government itself usually, perhaps inevitably, forces uniformity on the organizations it supports in the broader public sector. The task will be to find a new framework that does steer the system but nonetheless allows significant university autonomy and encourages innovation and difference.

Having now examined the Ontario system of higher education, explored more carefully the rationale for differentiation of institutions and programs, and analyzed the policies and decisions that create the outcomes we observe, let us turn to more carefully rethinking Ontario's higher education, asking ourselves: do we have the best system for the years ahead? Do we have the best system for first-level higher education, the best system for graduate education, and the best system for research?

NOTES

1. Some detail about the framework for the colleges is contained in the references cited through this chapter.
2. Over the last twenty years, governments have implemented more and more accountability measures with which universities must comply. Many scholars identify this as one of the key forces shaping the system. See for example, Clark et al. (2009), Chapter 5, and the discussion of the many accountability requirements for universities.
3. For example, this was the recommendation of the Drummond Report (Commission on the Reform of Ontario's Public Services 2012) and also of the Council of Ontario Universities (COU 2011b).
4. This is the approach to defining annual operating revenue used by Statistics Canada in calculations of total research and development expenditure (Statistics Canada 2010a). See also discussion in Chapter 7.
5. These paragraphs are a highly simplified characterization, intended to identify the key drivers of the system.
6. Ontario total revenue per student is also much below comparable US universities.
7. These issues of research funding are a taken up further in Chapters 7 and 8 which focus on rethinking research in Ontario higher education.
8. There has been a much less systematic process for funding the maintenance of existing buildings and equipment, with the result that most universities have a serious problem of deferred maintenance.
9. See University of Toronto (2012), York University (2012), and CAUBO (2009).
10. This, of course, is too simple; there is actually much interdependence: senior administrators, professors, and students all have influence on the sort of framework that the government adopts.
11. This section draws directly, including slightly rewritten paragraphs, from Fallis (2007) and the discussion of the social contract between university and society.
12. Jones, Shanahan, and Goyan (2004) offer a description and analysis of the role of the academic senate in university governance in Canada.
13. A recent book, *Mission and Money: Understanding the University, (Weisbrod, Ballou, and Asch 2008)* uses economic analysis to analyze the behaviour of US universities using this framework.
14. See Fallis (2007) for a more extensive discussion of the mission of the university, in particular its mission to contribute to democratic life.

15. Government research grants have expanded across all areas, but the greatest expansion has been in these fields. See AUCC (2008).
16. Many scholars of higher education have found that this characterization of the objective of senior administrators is very consistent with observed decisions. See for example Brewer, Gates and Goldman (2002), Ehrenberg (2000), and Weisbrod, Ballou and Asch (2008).
17. This is a broad generalization. All regular tenure-stream faculty have both responsibilities. But most universities now have full-time teaching-only positions, and some universities have research professorships with little or no teaching responsibility.
18. Strictly speaking, the professors bargain with the board of governors of the university, but in fact the senior administration manages the bargaining.
19. There are some small deviations from this pattern, but these are not a significant characteristic of the system.
20. See Skolnik (1989) for an analysis of how academic program review encourages homogeneity.

Chapter 4

PARTICIPATION: UNIVERSAL HIGHER EDUCATION HAS BEEN ACHIEVED

The narrative of higher education in Ontario since the mid-1960s has been of expansion—adding new institutions and expanding existing ones—using the same basic structures. The core principle in designing the system has been to provide a place in first-level higher education for every qualified student who wished to attend.

A higher education system is said to be elite higher education if up to 15 percent of the eligible age group participate; it is mass higher education if the participation rate is between 15 and 50 percent; and described as universal higher education if over 50 percent participate. The postwar expansion of Ontario's higher education system is often described as moving from elite, to mass, to near-universal higher education. But, it is said, the desired goal of universal higher education has not yet been achieved.

Martin Trow (1973) set out the categories of elite, mass, and universal higher education and argued that the problems of higher education in the 1960s and 1970s could be understood as arising from the transition from elite to mass higher education.[1] This chapter argues the transition through the stages is now complete: universal higher education has been achieved. Today, the problem of higher education is how to design a universal system: what range of programs is needed and how differentiated should institutions be?

The usual starting point of any comprehensive study of Ontario's system of higher education has been to analyze the demand for first-level higher education and to ask: how many places do we need? This analysis was done in the late 1950s, when the province began planning for the arrival of the baby boom at the postsecondary level. This was the question when the baby boom arrived and moved through the system, it was

Rethinking Higher Education: Participation, Research, and Differentiation, G. Fallis. Kingston: School of Policy Studies, Queen's University. © 2013 The School of Policy Studies, Queen's University at Kingston. All rights reserved.

the question when the double cohort arrived, and has been the question over the last ten years; indeed it was the question addressed in the 2011 Ontario budget when the government announced plans for 60,000 new student places in colleges and universities. And the starting point of this book in rethinking higher education in Ontario is to ask the same question: how many places do we need for the years ahead?

The usual analysis begins with a demographic projection, a projection of the number of 18–24 year olds in the coming years, i.e., a projection of the size of the group who would be eligible for higher education. Next in the analysis, there is a forecast of the participation rate—the share of the 18–24 year olds who will attend higher education. Together, the size of the eligible group and the participation rate determine the demand for places. Many recent policy analyses have forecast the continuing need for more places—there is a coming boom in enrolments—especially in the Greater Toronto Area (GTA).

The analysis of this chapter reaches a very different conclusion: universal higher education has been achieved. The eligible group is about to shrink. Participation is as high as it can or should be. Ontario's system does not need any more places. The dominant postwar policy of expansion is no longer appropriate. Recognizing this, the planning of higher education will require a radically new mindset.

The chapter first examines the forecast of an increasing demand for higher education. Then, the evidence that universal higher education has been achieved will be presented and the possibilities of still higher participation rates explored. Finally, the required new approach to accessibility will be discussed. But before examining the demographic projections and the participation rate forecasts, let us set the wider context.

THE LABOUR MARKET CONTEXT

The main purposes of first-level higher education are several: the learning is valuable for its own sake, but is also intended to prepare students for a job, and to prepare students for membership in the community, especially their role as a citizen in a democratic society. Access to higher education is vital for equality of opportunity and social inclusion.

Although there are these several purposes, the focus in designing the overall system—that is, in determining the number of first-level places needed—has always been on access and employment. Many groups are still underrepresented in higher education and so there follows the presumption that expanding places would improve their access. This is balanced by an analysis of the economy. What sorts of jobs will there be in the future economy? What sorts of educational qualifications will be needed to hold these jobs? The expansion of higher education over the last fifty years helped to ensure the equality of opportunity so valued in a democratic society, and in a happy coincidence of democratic needs and economic needs, the graduates were required by the postwar postindustrial economy. Using this sort of thinking, the Ontario government has a target to increase the number of adult Ontarians with a postsecondary qualification to 70 percent (from the current 62 percent). Axelrod (1982) argues that, throughout the postwar period, government support for higher education rested primarily on the contributions of its graduates—skilled manpower—to economic prosperity.

It is extraordinarily difficult to forecast the jobs of the future economy and the educational qualifications needed for these jobs. Nonetheless, there seems to be a consensus that future jobs will require higher educational qualifications than do the current mix of jobs. Several studies have predicted that about 70 percent of the future jobs in Ontario will require postsecondary qualifications; these studies form the basis for Ontario's target for the postsecondary system.[2]

The introduction to this chapter spoke of the "demand for higher education." This is the demand from the perspective of students, and higher education institutions are the suppliers of higher education. In the wider context, the labour market is the framework and one examines the supply of graduates from our system and the demand for higher education graduates in the economy. Over the postwar period, roughly speaking, the demand for graduates has risen faster than the supply of graduates, and so the incomes of graduates have risen relative to those without higher education. But, this need not always be the case. In the metaphor of Goldin and Katz (2008), there is a race between education and technology. For example in the United States during the 1970s, supply grew faster than demand and returns to higher education fell. In many developing nations, the supply of higher education graduates has expanded faster than the demand for graduates resulting in high rates of unemployment and underemployment among graduates.

It is possible, although we have not experienced it in Ontario, that the supply of graduates could expand faster than the demand from the economy, in which case the return to education would decline (and there would be many discontented graduates). In the analysis below, it is argued that for the first time, Ontario may be confronting this scenario. Participation rates have now risen so high that the supply of graduates may be greater than the labour force demand—even the demand from the rapidly-changing, knowledge-based, economy. Also, there is likely to be a mismatch between the types of graduates and the types of jobs available. For the first time, Ontario will have to analyze very carefully the complex issues of access, supply of graduates, and labour demand.

As we ask, how many places we need for the decades ahead, we are asking not only about the appropriate system but also about the ideal system, balancing concerns about access and about available jobs.

As a mental experiment, let us be bold and optimistic and envision the ideal Ontario system of higher education: it would have the capacity to allow 80 percent of the arriving age group to have a postsecondary qualification. This 80 percent is well above the Government of Ontario's 70 percent target and above most forecasts of labour demand. Let us further assume that 30 percent achieve a college diploma or degree, and 45 percent a university degree. Thus, 75 percent would complete higher education: this would be universal higher education by any standard. (The remaining 5 percent would complete an apprenticeship.)

To realize this vision, how many places would we need in our colleges and our universities? Later in this chapter, the analysis to answer this question will be developed. For now, let us hold this vision of the ideal system in the background.

THE COMING BOOM IN ENROLMENTS?

The Ministry of Finance in Ontario prepares population projections used by all government departments and widely outside government, and that can be used in analyzing the demand for higher education. The current projection begins from the Ontario population as reported in the 2006 census—its total number, age structure, marital patterns, and so on. Then, the projection makes assumptions about fertility, mortality, immigration and emigration, and interprovincial migration. From the base population, it projects, for the years ahead, total population, its age structure, and its distribution by region. The most recent update was published in spring 2011.

The proper planning horizon for designing a system of higher education cannot be unambiguously set, but certainly a horizon of some length is needed. If expansion is called for, it takes a long time to select which institutions will grow, or to establish new institutions, to construct the required new campus buildings, to hire the new professors, and so on. The horizon should be about fifteen years with an emphasis on the first decade. This is the time frame used here.

In planning for the number of future places over this time horizon, the key issue is the size of the incoming cohorts, the 18- and 19 year olds, in the years ahead. This incoming group is going to decline over the next decade, and then begin to rise, but the incoming cohort in 2026 will still be less than 2011. This uneven pattern of incoming cohorts is going to move through the system; overlaying this are the larger past cohorts still completing their higher education. With this very uneven pattern of incoming cohorts, balancing all the factors, the best population projection for planning the number of future places is a projection of the 18–21-year-old group, rather than the 18–24 group.[3]

The total Ontario population is projected to grow strongly over the next fifteen years. It is projected to be about 13 percent higher by 2021 and 20 percent higher by 2025. But for the purposes of planning higher education, it is not total population that matters, but rather the age group that will attend higher education.

In 2011, there were 745,306 people in the 18–21-year-old group. The Ministry of Finance projections indicate that the 18–21-year-old group reached its maximum size in 2011 and will now begin to decline, falling 8.6 percent over the decade to 2021. This decline is because the baby boom echo (the children of the baby boomers) has been moving through the system and is now about to decline. After 2021, the 18–21-year-old group begins to grow again, but in 2026 it is still 4.5 percent below its 2011 level. See Figure 4.1. (Only by 2031 does it rise above today's level.) It is somewhat puzzling that most analysts assume a coming boom in enrolments, yet the 18–21-year-old group is going to decline significantly over the next decade. It is doubly puzzling because, in the past few years in the secondary schools, declining enrolments have been a major policy problem—requiring the establishment of a Declining Enrolment Working Group by the Ministry of Education. At the very least, the sharp decline in the 18–21-year-old group over the next decade should be a cautionary signal.[4]

The forecasts of a boom in enrolments, therefore, rely on an increase in participation rates, indeed, a very sharp increase in participation. If total enrolments are to grow, there must be an increase in participation first to overcome the 8.6 percent demographic decline and then to generate an increase in demand.

FIGURE 4.1
Ontario Population Aged 18–21

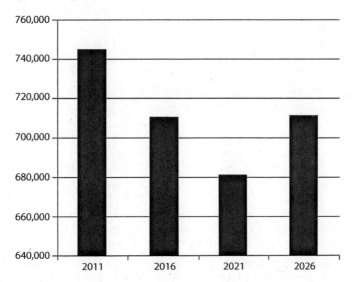

Source: Ontario. Ministry of Finance (2011).

Again, there is something of a puzzle in the analysis. Although the forecasts rely entirely on participation rates, there is little explicit analysis of them. The actual participation rate used in the forecast is not specified. Rather, it is assumed that the participation rate will grow at "historical" rates.

Participation rates, measured as the ratio of university or college enrolments (in first-level higher education) to the number in the 18–24-year-old group, have been increasing almost continuously since the 1950s, and quite rapidly over the last ten years. See Figure 1.2 in Chapter 1. In 2010, the university participation rate was about 30 percent and the college rate slightly above 15 percent, for total higher education participation of about 45 percent. The Ontario system can be described as near-universal higher education. By this measure, there would seem to be lots of room for participation rates to continue growing. After all, the "participation rate" is 45 percent.

Much of the work of HEQCO has been done in the context of forecasts of a coming boom in enrolments. The most recent study of Ontario undergraduate education projects an increase in demand for university enrolments, above 2009 levels, of between 28,000–45,000 in 2015, and of between 50,000 and 104,000 in 2025. "The higher end of the projection assumes participation rates will continue to increase as they have in recent years; the lower end assumes they will increase at half the rate in recent years" (Clark, Trick, and Van Loon 2011, 106). Even the mid-point forecast of participation rates implies the university system will have to grow by over 21 percent. Similar forecasts of the demand for college education have slightly lower growth in demand. But, the overall demand for higher education is forecast to rise by about 20 percent.

This is the consensus: there is a coming boom in enrolments because there will be a large increase in demand for higher education in Ontario over the next fifteen years.

This rethinking of higher education reaches a very different conclusion.

UNIVERSAL HIGHER EDUCATION HAS BEEN ACHIEVED

The starting point of the rethinking is to conceptualize the entire system of education using a life course or longitudinal approach, as set out in Figure 1.1 and discussed in Chapter 1. We conceptualize an individual, or a cohort of similar-aged people, as they move through the system from elementary school, to secondary school, to higher education. The data needed for this analysis are longitudinal data, a study that follows the same cohort of people through time. In longitudinal analysis, the participation rate would be defined as the share of the similar-aged cohort that participates in higher education. And this is what we intuitively think of when we speak of accessibility and the participation rate.

Unfortunately, the standard analysis does not use longitudinal data, but rather cross-sectional data, and defines participation in a peculiar way which does not really conform to our intuitive understanding. And this leads to misunderstandings of the data, as we shall see. Fortunately, there is a longitudinal study now available—the Youth in Transition Survey (YITS), conducted by Statistics Canada. Norrie and Zhao (2011) provide an overview of PSE accessibility in Ontario with particular attention to the research findings using the YITS data.

Finnie, Childs, and Wismer (2011) have used this survey in preparing a HEQCO-funded study "Access to Postsecondary Education: How Ontario Compares." They use Cohort A data from the survey (generally known as YITS-A) to study access to postsecondary education (PSE). "The YITS-A is ideal for this application, since it follows all young people born in 1984 (and thus age 15 as of December 31, 1999) through their high school years and beyond—and is rich in background data and other important determinants of access to PSE. The YITS-A are, in fact, arguably the best data of this type in the world." Finnie et al. used the 2006 cycle of YITS (cycle 4). "In this wave of the survey, the young people were 21 years of age, a point at which most had made their initial choices about entering PSE" (Finnie, Childs, and Wismer 2011, 4-5).

They found (Table 1a in their study) that when the cohort reached age 21 in Ontario, 45.5 percent had entered university and 36.4 percent had entered college or other PSE. The total PSE participation rate was a stunning 81.9 percent. The group going to college or other PSE can be split into 29.8 percent going to college and 6.6 going to other PSE.[5] Thus, rounding to whole numbers, 46 percent had accessed university and 30 percent had accessed college. The higher education participation rate was 76 percent. Universal higher education has been achieved!

As we rethink higher education in Ontario, this is the single most important fact to realize: the participation rate is now about 76 percent—46 percent at university and 30 percent at college.[6]

How could this be possible? How can this longitudinal data showing a 76 percent participation rate be reconciled with the standard analysis that showed a participation rate of about 45 percent?

The key is to recognize how the two approaches use different definitions of participation rates.

The longitudinal analysis defines the participation rate as the share of the single-age cohort (in YITS-A, they were age 15 in 1999) that have attended higher education when they reach a certain age (in this case, age 21). And I would argue that this is the intuitively appealing definition of participation and the measure we need for public policy analysis. We want to know, as individuals grow up, how many participate in higher education. This is what I would call the actual rate of participation.

This participation rate rises as the cohort gets older. Shaienks and Gluszynski (2007), using other data from YITS, find that PSE participation in Canada rises from 54 percent when the cohort is in their late teens to about 80 percent by their mid twenties. See Figure 4.2. It is quite understandable that this participation rate would increase with age. Not all people move through secondary school at the same rate; many do not enter higher education directly after secondary school, but over time more and more people from the cohort have entered higher education. Thus in longitudinal analysis, there is not a single participation rate, but rather a line of a single-age cohort's life course participation as it gets older. The line in Figure 4.2 is the life course participation a cohort of Canadians, aged 18 to 20 in 1999, as they moved through time, ending in 2005 when they were 24 to 26 years old. Note that even when the cohort was first observed when they were 18 to 20 years old, 54 percent had already attended postsecondary education.

FIGURE 4.2
Life Course Participation Line, Canada, 2005

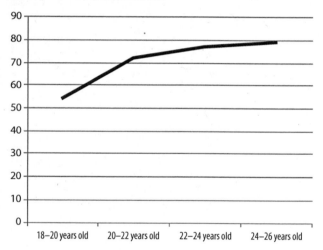

Source: Shaienks and Gluszynski (2007, 8).

The life course PSE participation line is no doubt different for different age cohorts. It would be very different for my cohort, the earliest baby boomers, aged 18 in 1965. Our line would be much lower on the graph, levelling out much below 80 percent. Over time the line of each cohort had been moving up. In this sense participation rates have been rising, until for young people today (today's 18- to 20 year olds), the life course line begins over 50 percent and will level at above 80 percent by the time they reach their midtwenties.

The standard analysis, based upon cross-sectional data, uses a different definition: the participation rate is defined as the ratio of total undergraduate university enrolments (or total college enrolments) to the number in the 18–24-year-old group. This has been the measure used since the first planning was done in the 1950s to prepare for when the baby boom generation would be finishing secondary school. We have become habituated to it, but perhaps lost sight of the fact that it does not measure participation in the intuitive, actual sense.

This usual measure of participation understates the actual participation. To illustrate, consider a numerical example. Suppose the single-age cohort had 180,000 people when it reached age 18. (This is roughly the case in Ontario today.) Suppose half of the cohort went directly to university, completed a degree in four years, and went out to work. Suppose further that all the younger single-age cohorts coming along also had 180,000 people, and also 50 percent went to university and completed in four years. The university would admit 90,000 students each year and would have total enrolments of 90,000 x 4 = 360,000 students. Assuming all single-age cohorts are the same size, the 18–24 group would have 180,000 x 7 = 1,260,000 people. In this steady state example, the participation rate measured in the standard way would be 360,000 / 1,260,000 = 28.5 percent. Yet, we know that 50 percent of all people completed a university degree. Repeating the above approach, let us suppose that 100 percent of students attended and completed university. The usual measure of the participation rate, measured as the ratio of total enrolments to the size of the 18–24 group, would be 57 percent—although the actual rate is 100 percent.

Now let us return to thinking about what lies ahead for Ontario. How many places do we need in our higher education system?

Figure 4.1 has presented the demographic data regarding the 18–21-year-old group. This group is projected to decline in size by 8.6 percent by 2021.

The cumulative participation rate of today's young people leaving high school is already about 75 percent by the time they reach their early twenties. It cannot go much higher, given the diversity of aptitudes and interests. And it would be problematic if it went much higher because there will be at least 25 percent of jobs that do not require higher education.

If participation rates cannot go higher, or even if they rise slightly, there will be a decreasing demand for higher education over the next decade, and although it begins to rise after 2021, it will not return to current levels by 2026. This is in stark contrast to the current consensus forecast. Rather than managing a coming boom in enrolments, we will have to manage decline.

This analysis is so at odds with the forecast of a coming boom in enrolments that we should try to challenge it and cross-check it in different ways.

One cross-check is to try to correct the usual measure for its downward bias. Consider the university participation rate—the usual measure is 30 percent (Figure 1.2). The basic problem with the standard measure, as a measure of actual participation, is that it divides total enrolments (and each student attends for four years) by the population aged 18–24, a group made up of seven single-year cohorts. The simplest correction would be to divide university enrolments (and assuming all students do a four-year degree) by the population group aged 18 to 21, a group with four single-year cohorts. For 2010, the correction indicates the university participation rate to be 50 percent. This is higher than the actual participation rate of 45 percent (from the longitudinal YITS data). This correction overstates the actual university participation rate because total university enrolments include not just those from the Ontario cohorts, but also out of province and international students attending Ontario universities; also many students attend both a university and a college. Nonetheless, this correction to the cross-sectional data strongly supports the conclusion that university participation is 45 percent, not the 30 percent as usually measured. (A similar correction could be done for college participation.)

Another cross-check is to look at the number of students admitted to Ontario universities directly from secondary school. These data are available from the Ontario Universities Application Centre (OUAC). In 2009, universities admitted about 70,000 students into first-year directly from secondary school (OUAC 2012). The 18-year-old age cohort was about 180,000. This implies that 39 percent of the arriving cohort goes on to university immediately after high school. Of course, as the cohort gets older, its university participation will increase. This is consistent with the YITS finding that university participation at age 21 will reach 45 percent, and contradicts the "standard" measure of university participation as 30 percent.

Another approach to asking whether there will be a coming boom in enrolments would be to ask explicitly what participation rate would be needed to generate the forecast 20 percent growth in the demand for higher education. The current rate is 76 percent. Participation would have to rise about 8 percent just to offset the demographic decline, and another 20 percent to generate the growth. Participation would have to rise by 28 percent. It would have to move to 76 x 1.28—to about 100 percent. This is not credible.

These cross-checks confirm that universal higher education has been achieved—participation rates are very high, about 76 percent by the time people are in their early twenties.[7]

But to complete the cross-checks, there is a puzzle to deal with. If we don't need any more places, how can this be squared with the fact that every year there are more applicants to university than are accepted, and that universities continue to grow and are bulging at the seams? The first key is to recognize that there has always been, and likely always will be, excess demand (applications higher than acceptances). Ontario has been expanding its university system very rapidly, that is, the number of places has grown rapidly. Those students who are turned down for admission are turned down because their secondary school grades are below the admission cutoff, rather than because of a lack of places. Most of the excess demand is from students who do not quite have the entry qualifications. The second key is to examine university enrolments over the last twenty years. (See Figure 1.3 in Chapter 1.) As we do this, we should recall the usual analysis that individual participation rates have been increasing steadily since the 1950s. Looking at the data, enrolments were level for about ten years from 1999 to 2001. (There was still excess demand throughout this period.) They were level because the eligible age group was declining, and individual participation rates were rising enough to just offset the demographic decline. The very rapid growth in university enrolments of the 2001 to 2011 decade was because the eligible age group grew very rapidly *and* the individual participation rates were still growing. But for the years ahead, the eligible age group will be declining significantly and participation rates have likely reached their maximum and cannot continue to rise.

Immediately, we should note that the 76 percent *participation* in higher education refers to students having entered higher education. However, 76 percent have not *completed* a degree or diploma. In the Schaienks and Gluszynski (2007) study, in the cohort aged 24–26 years, among those who attended higher education, 75 percent had graduated (with some of these going on to further study), 9 percent had not graduated but were still in school, and 15 percent had dropped out. With universal higher education, the central issue is no longer access. There does, however, remain an issue of persistence and completion. How can we do better in ensuring that those who enter higher education actually persist and complete their program? Also, with such a dropout rate, the question must be confronted whether some students who have entered higher education do not really have the aptitude or interest. Also, there may be mismatches between the program chosen and the student's aptitude and interest.

To conclude, let us look at the data using a life course, or longitudinal approach. People move through the entire education system, but at different paces. And people finish at different levels, some don't complete secondary school, some finish secondary school and go out to work, and some go on to postsecondary education. By the time the age cohort reaches their midtwenties, the outcomes are established (although some do go back into the education system after that). In Ontario we have reached what I call the 10/10/80 outcome: ten percent do not finish high school; ten percent finish high school and go to work; and eighty percent attend postsecondary education. (The reader might recall the quiz in Chapter 1 about these percentages.)

Universal higher education has been achieved. Now, we need to think how higher education can be improved in a 10/10/80 world.

BUILDING AN IDEAL SYSTEM

Another way to cross-check the analysis is to return to the vision of the ideal system, with not just a 75 percent participation rate but a 75 percent *completion* rate and ask the question: how many places would we need in our system of higher education to have this ideal system?

The analysis is straightforward. The Ministry of Finance projections indicate that in 2011 there are about 178,000 18 year olds in Ontario. The number of 18 year olds declines after 2014 and is 7.5 percent below the 2011 level in 2021; by 2026, it is still 2.8 percent below. But it increases after that, and in the recent past the cohort was 180,000. For ease of analysis and presentation, and to ensure we build a generous system, let us simplify things and assume that the 18-year-old age cohorts, from 2011 to 2026 are all 180,000. The model and its calculations are presented in Table 4.1.

These cohorts move through the entire education system, and let us assume that 10 percent do not finish secondary school and 10 percent complete secondary school and go to work. The remaining 80 percent will go on to postsecondary education and complete their program. And in our vision, 75 percent go to college or university and complete their degree or diploma. (The remaining 5 percent complete an apprenticeship.) Thus, each year over the next four years, 135,000 (180,000 x 0.75) students will leave secondary school and go on to higher education. Some choose university and some choose college. How shall we divide them? Current university enrolments are almost 80 percent larger than college enrolments (Table 1.1), but this does not tell us directly how any cohort divides between the two sectors, unless we correct for the length of program in the two sectors. The Finnie, Childs, and Wismer (2011) study does give direct evidence about the divide: at age 21, 29.8 percent of the cohort had entered college and 45.5 percent had entered university. Converting these data, to relate to the 75 percent who go on to higher education in our model, implies that the divide is about 60 percent to university and 40 percent to college. Thus each year over the next four years, 81,000 students will enter university (135,000 x 0.60) and 54,000 students will enter college (135,000 x 0.40). Let us assume each university student takes a four-year degree and on average each college student takes a 2-year program. Then the university sector needs 324,000 (81,000 x 4) places and the college system needs 108,000 (54,000 x 2) places to achieve our vision: 75 percent of the population completes higher education, and this is split 45 percent with a university degree and 30 percent with a college diploma.

TABLE 4.1
Calculating the Capacity of an Ideal System of Higher Education

Cohort Aged 18	75% Complete Higher Education	45% Complete University	30% Complete College
180,000	135,000	81,000	54,000

	University System Capacity		College System Capacity	
	Year 1:	81,000	Year 1:	54,000
	Year 2:	81,000	Year 2:	54,000
	Year 3:	81,000		
	Year 4:	81,000		
	Total:	324,000	Total:	108,000

Actual FTE University System Capacity	Actual FTE College System Capacity
370,000	202,000

Source: Author's compilation.

This is the vision. You might have originally thought it was very optimistic; after all, it is a vision of 75 percent with a college or university certification. Could we possibly build a system to accommodate this vision of universal higher education? The answer is yes. And indeed, we have already built such a system. There are at present about 370,000 FTE places in the university system and 205,000 FTE places in the college system. We have already built a higher education system *significantly larger* than needed to ensure universal higher education—a 75 percent completion rate—for Ontario's young people today.[8]

It might be argued that this numerical example fails to take account of the need for spaces for older students coming back to enter the higher education system.[9] However, this is not correct. To illustrate, let us suppose a certain number of students in each cohort delayed entering university. This would reduce the spaces needed at university, but some older students return to university from cohorts that have already passed through university-eligible age; this increases the number of needed places. If the long run life course participation rate is 75 percent, and if all cohorts behave in the same manner, in steady state the places needed will be just as calculated in Table 4.1.

Of course in the ideal system, there would be places for out-of-province students and international students. And, there should be places for students who finish a university degree and go on to take a college diploma, and for students who finish a diploma and go on to earn a university degree. Fortunately, our current system is large enough to accommodate these.[10] The assumptions of Table 4.1 were deliberately chosen to generate a very expansive ideal system. For example, it was assumed all students do a four-year degree, which requires a larger system, when in fact a significant minority of students only does a three-year degree. There is lots of university space for students wanting to go from college to university. And as the calculations of Table 4.1 show, there is lots of space for students going from university to college.

Nonetheless, this discussion does highlight an important issue for thinking about the needed capacity of a higher education system. The conventional pathway model in postsecondary education, implicit in Figure 1.1, is that a student proceeds from secondary school, to either university or college, and then to the labour force. Today, PSE pathways are not so linear. "Fewer students are entering PSE programs directly from high school and students are more likely to have previous PSE experience or to attain multiple credentials than in the past" (Kerr, McCloy, and Liu 2010, 2). For example, a HEQCO-funded study of college students found that "28 percent of college graduates reported that they were continuing their education within six months of graduation. Of those continuing their education, 61 percent returned to their own college for further education, around 7 percent transferred to another CAAT and approximately 25 percent continued at an Ontario university (Kerr, McCloy, and Liu 2010, 9). Some colleges have more than 10 percent of their credentials awarded to students who have come from university (Table 1.3). It is important that a system of higher education have the capacity for such flexibility and diverse pathways. However, it is also true that public support for multiple credentials need not be open-ended. At this time, Ontario does not have a policy or target of how many places it will fund for students to achieve multiple credentials.

THE GTA PROBLEM

The consensus forecast of the demand for higher education in Ontario predicted not only an increase in total demand across the province, but also that most of the growth would be in the Greater Toronto Area (GTA). The GTA is made up of Toronto, Durham, Halton, Peel, and York. The forecast highlighted a particular problem for public policy: how can this especially large growth in demand for higher education in the GTA be met?

We all can see for ourselves, in the expanding suburbs around Toronto, that the GTA has been growing rapidly. The Ministry of Finance projects that the GTA will grow by 27 percent by 2026, compared to total provincial growth of 20 percent.

But again, for higher education planning, the important projection is of the growth of the age group who will attend higher education, rather than total population growth. The Ministry of Finance projections also project the age specific population by region. Figure 4.3 reports the projections of the 18–21-year-old group for the GTA.

Recall, as reported above, the data indicate a decline across the entire province in the 18–21-year-old group of 8.6 percent over the decade to 2021, and 4.5 percent to 2026.

The 18–21 group in the entire GTA is projected to increase very slightly by 2016 (0.7 percent) and then decline to a level 2.3 percent below 2011 in 2021. It then grows over the next years to about 6.9 percent higher in 2026. There is significant growth in the GTA in this group, but the growth is more than ten years away.

Over the next fifteen years, all of the growth is in Halton, Peel, and York. They grow continuously. The 18–21 group in Toronto and Durham will decline.

The demographic data project an increase in the size of the eligible group in the GTA by 2026. In conjunction with the large increase in participation rates forecast, the consensus forecast is for a very large increase in demand in the GTA, especially in Halton, Peel, and York. The participation rate in this region is felt likely to increase strongly because much of the growth will come from immigration from China and South Asia, and children of immigrants from these regions, when they come to Canada, have had very high participation rates.

Thus the consensus forecast predicts very large growth in demand and raises a problem for public policy: how can this increase be met when the major GTA universities—University of Toronto, York, and Ryerson—are

FIGURE 4.3

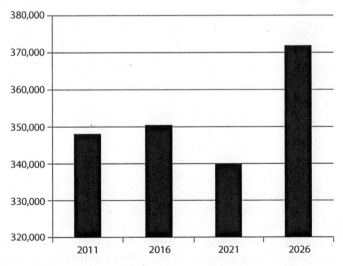

Source: Ontario Ministry of Finance (2011).

FIGURE 4.4
Rest-of-Province Population Aged 18–21

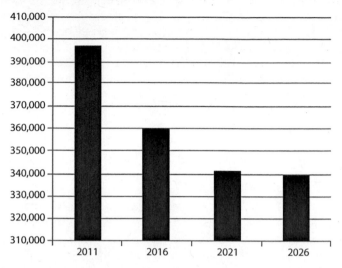

Source: Ontario Ministry of Finance (2011).

already very large. Clark, Trick, and Van Loon (2011) recommend the creation of new teaching-focused universities in the western GTA to meet this demand.

The analysis of this chapter sees the GTA situation very differently. There is a significant increase in the demographic group by 2026 (7 percent) but all of this growth is ten years away, and, as argued above, participation rates in general will not increase. They are already very high. Even with the immigration effect, the participation rates will not rise very much. Thus, the overall increase in demand will be significant, but not overwhelming, and will not occur until after 2021.

However, Ontario's existing institutions can handle the forecast increase in demand in the GTA. The worry about capacity to meet this demand focuses only on the GTA: it looks at the increase in demand there, and at the current institutional capacity *within* the GTA. The universities within the GTA include Toronto, York, and Ryerson, and also UOIT and OCAD, two relatively small institutions. It asks: can the increase in demand in the GTA be met by GTA universities? But what is a GTA university? Is it only those located within the GTA? Surely, the analysis should include those universities on the boundary of the GTA, which have traditionally drawn many of their students from the GTA. McMaster and Guelph are located just outside the western border of the GTA, and Waterloo and Laurier are very close as well. At least half of their natural catchment areas lie within the GTA, and these catchment areas are where much of the growth in demand will occur, i.e., in Halton, Peel, and York. Indeed, these close-to-the-boundary universities are all closer to the growth than University of Toronto's St. George campus, Ryerson, and University of Toronto's Scarborough campus. McMaster, Guelph, Waterloo, and Laurier should be thought of as "GTA universities" when analyzing the capacity of existing institutions to handle the growth.

There is lots of capacity in existing institutions to meet the GTA's growth in demand, when one recognizes that demand will be falling in the rest of their catchment areas and across the rest of the province.

Rather than a GTA problem, there is a rest-of-the-province problem. Outside the GTA, the 18–21-year-old group will fall significantly over the decade—14 percent by 2021. (See Figure 4.4) Managing this decline outside the GTA will be the public policy problem in higher education later in the decade.

RETHINKING ACCESS

Now that universal higher education has been achieved, we will have to rethink accessibility to higher education. This will be very difficult, and the final direction for policy is by no means clear, but some basic thoughts can be offered.

The Education Policy Institute (2008) prepared an overview of access issues for HEQCO, *Access, Persistence, and Barriers in Postsecondary Education: A Literature Review and Outline of Future Research*. It begins by noting that there are two types of access to postsecondary education (PSE): Type I and Type II. Type I relates to "how many" attend in total, as a share of the eligible group. Thus, Type I access improves as a system moves from elite, to mass, to universal higher education. Type II access relates to "who goes" to higher education. We want higher education to be accessible to all who are capable and willing, and so we want the characteristics of those who go to higher education to be unrelated to gender, family income, disability, and so on. In broad terms, we want who goes to higher education to be representative of the entire population. So, if 50 percent of the population is women, we want 50 percent of those in higher education to be women. If family income is not a barrier to higher education, we expect equal percentages of each income group to go on to higher education.

Type I and Type II access are obviously interrelated. Generally as Type I access improves, higher percentages of underrepresented groups attend higher education and so Type II access improves. (It is possible of course that as the system expands all groups increase their participation at the same rate and Type II access is unchanged.) But if Type I access does not change, it is more difficult to implement successful programs to improve Type II access. This is the situation now facing us in Ontario.

Consider the following example. Imagine that the government does not provide funding for any more places in higher education; the system will not expand because universities and colleges will admit only those students who are funded by government grants. The institutions need both the grant and the tuition to pay for providing the education. Suppose, however, that the government wanted to improve Type II access and started a program of tuition grants for students from low-income families. More low-income students might now aspire to higher education, and you might think that many more would attend higher education because the cost has gone down. But access would not change very much because more low-income students could attend only by having higher secondary school grades than those who normally attend and so displace them in the admission process. Type I access, that is, the total participation rate, is determined mainly by how many places the government funds, rather than by tuition policy or by the characteristics of the population.

In Ontario over the past fifty years, Type I has been improving significantly and so, too, Type II access has been improving. The most significant improvement in Type II access has been in the participation of women. Fifty years ago, there were more men than women in first-level higher education. Today this has been overcome, and indeed, there are more women than men. Also as the system has expanded, students from lower income backgrounds have become better represented. Type II access, across a range of characteristics, improved significantly when the college system was established. It was widely recognized that as Type I access improved, there would be a need to diversify the programs available and in particular to introduce more vocationally oriented programs in higher education. Overall, this improvement in accessibility is a great success story in the narrative of Ontario's higher education. This great improvement in Type II access has been made possible by the improvement in Type I access, i.e., the fact that the government has steadily increased the number of funded places.

But now universal higher education has been achieved; individual life course PSE participation rates have reached over 80 percent. There can be no more improvement in Type I access. And we should recall that the future economy likely will not need any more than 70 percent of population with a PSE qualification. How then can we think about and improve Type II access?

As we rethink access further, let us start with a picture about Type II access in Ontario to today. Who attends PSE today and what do we know about the barriers to higher education?

The YITS-A data give us the best picture. Table 4.2 reports PSE access in Ontario at age 21 by family income (Finnie, Childs, and Wismer 2011, Table 1a).

As already noted, 81.9 percent of students had accessed PSE: 36.4 percent to college/other and 45.5 percent to university. This is Type I access. But within this group, who is going to PSE?

Overall, females have higher rates than males—88.2 percent compared to 75.7 percent. And, the split between college/other and university is very different. Women attend university at much high rates than men, and men attend colleges/other at somewhat higher rates than women.

Overall, participation in PSE increases with family income, rising from 72.4 percent among students from the lowest income group to 92.9 percent for the highest income group. And, the split between colleges/other and university is very different by income group. Participation in college/other generally declines with family income and participation in university increases with family income.

The YITS is a unique data set, offering not only data on participation, gender, and family income, but also on high school grades and other in-dictors of academic aptitude and preparation. Access rates by high school grades are also reported in Table 4.2. Not surprisingly, high school grades are a powerful predictor of overall PSE participation and particularly of university participation. Among those with grades below 70 percent, 58.2 percent attend PSE compared to 98.3 percent among those with grades above 90 percent. Admission to university in Ontario requires a high school average of about 70 percent, or very high 60s. This is confirmed in the YITS data: only 7.5 percent of those with averages below 70 attend university while 88.5 percent of those with averages 90 percent and above attend university. The most important "barrier" to university access is high school grades.

TABLE 4.2
Rates of Access to PSE By Family Income and High School Grades

	% University	% College/Other
All	45.5	36.4
Family Income		
$5,000 to $25,000	38.7	33.7
$25,000 to $50,000	34.2	40.9
$50,000 to $75,000	42.7	36.7
$75,000 to $100,000	47.8	36.5
$100,000 and up	61.9	31.0
High School Overall Grade		
Under 70%	7.5	50.5
70% to 79%	33.3	48.7
80% to 89%	73.4	20.4
90% to 100%	88.5	9.8

Source: Finnie, Childs, and Wismer (2011), Table 1a.

This is the basic picture of Type II access today. There will have to be a difficult rethinking of access when we recognize that overall PSE participation has reached the 80 percent maximum. Suppose we thought that the "target" overall access was 80 percent, with 35 percent attending college/other and 45 percent attending university. Presumably equality of access, as we have usually thought about it, would imply that this pattern would be the same for women and men and also by income class. But, as a look at Table 4.2 shows, there are currently groups with access above these targets. Are we to call this overrepresentation? If we are to significantly increase participation from lower income groups at university, this would imply a decline in participation in higher income groups. These will be extremely difficult issues to grapple with. There is some evidence, discussed in Chapter 5, that at present there is a minority of students now at university who are adrift with neither the interest nor the aptitude for academic work. As we rethink about access, there will be a need to think about re-shifting who goes to university.

There is now a significant body of research analyzing access (further confirmed by studies using the YITS data). This analysis is pointing to a significant change in our understanding of the barriers to higher education. Traditionally, the focus has been on financial factors: family income, tuition, and student assistance. And public policy to address access concerns focused on the higher education sector, especially on tuition and assistance policies. Finnie, Childs, and Wismer (2011, 3) summarize the rethinking about access. "We now know, for example, that access appears to be much more strongly related to parental education and other 'sociocultural' factors than to family income and other financial factors. We have also learned that academic preparation for PSE, as represented by high school grades ... is another important predictor of who will go to college and university and who will not. These various influences are probably interconnected, rooted in the family and start early in a young person's life, well before the final years of high school, when they ultimately make their PSE choices." This research implies that the barriers are more cultural than financial and that new initiatives to deal with access to higher education will not be higher education polices, but rather policies at the elementary and secondary levels.

Also, the existing system of colleges and universities is large and spread across the regions of the province. The greatest improvements to access would not likely come from expanding this system, but rather by providing new pathways, alternative pathways, to higher education. The most important of these would be an open university/open college (discussed and recommended in Chapter 2).

And it is not just access; there are other important changes to how we think about first-level higher education. Our focus will shift from *access* to higher education to *persistence* in higher education and *completion* of diploma and degree programs. We have got people there, but there are still issues of completion.

HOW HIGH COULD PARTICIPATION RATES GO?

Central to the debate about whether to expand Ontario's higher education system is the question of participation rates and whether they will continue to increase. Some groups are underrepresented in higher education and so, it is argued, participation should rise as they join. Also, permeating the debate about participation is the sense that the economy continues to change and that more jobs in the future will require a PSE qualification than today. There is a strong sense that participation rates can keep rising and that there will be labour force demand for the graduates.

This question of participation rates can be explored in two ways: through the lens of access and through the lens of the demand for graduates.

Let us first consider the lens of access. As noted above, as a rough approximation, Ontario is in a 10/10/80 world; that is, 10 percent of students do not finish high school, 10 percent finish high school but go no further, and 80 percent go on to some form of PSE (about 45 percent university, 30 percent college, and 5 percent an apprenticeship).

In order for higher education participation to increase, more students must finish high school. We could not have moved up to our current very high participation rates in higher education without significant improvements in the graduation rates from secondary school. And indeed the data confirm that there has been significant improvement in graduation rates since 1991, so that in 2009–2010 in Ontario, 91 percent of the population, aged 20 to 24 years old, were high school graduates (and a further 1.8 percent were still in school). Inevitably a certain percentage of the cohort, perhaps due to aptitude, or health, or interest, will not finish high school. The percentage who do not complete high school is already less than ten and can't go too much lower.

And by similar arguments about aptitude, health, and interest, it is reasonable to conclude that the 10 percent who finish high school can be reduced, but not by too much.

We should recognize that there are many paths to holding a good job and being a full member of the community and not all paths require higher education. Many entrepreneurs take these paths; many artists, actors, musicians, and writers take the path of learning by doing, of practice, practice, practice; many high performance athletes, having spent their years until their late twenties focused on athletics, go on to successful careers without higher education, and many young people enter a family business directly from high school. The school of hard knocks is often a good teacher and still has a place in an open democratic society with a twenty-first century economy.

Can the high school dropout rate be reduced below 10 percent, and can the share finishing with just high school be reduced below 10 percent? Such changes take time and likely require significant programming changes at the high school level and cultural change in the broader community. But let us assume that the rates can be reduced to 6 and 6.

This means PSE participation could be increased from the current 80 to 88 percent. How should this be distributed compared to the current 45 percent at university, 30 percent at college, and 5 percent in apprenticeship?

Should all this increase be in universities and colleges? Reflection suggests that the aptitudes and interests of this new participation would lean more toward apprenticeships than higher education. And much of the labour market forecasting suggests that this is where there is the greatest unmet labour demand. Let us say that half of the increased participation enters apprenticeships, moving the share from 5 to 9 percent.

Overall, this analysis using the longitudinal access lens suggests higher education participation could increase a few percentage points—from 80 to 84 percent.

What about the labour market demand? Does the labour market require a still increasing number of graduates with higher education and therefore call for increasing participation rates?

Drewes (2010) surveys the evidence for Ontario, based largely upon the National Graduates Surveys from 1986 to 2005 that report on income, unemployment, and a self-assessed sense of over qualification for the job, two years after graduation. If labour supply had risen faster than labour demand, there should be evidence of a falling wage premium for higher education, rising unemployment among graduates, and increasing over qualification. None of these were true. Only the unemployment data pointed in a slightly different direction. "Unemployment rates among the province's graduates, two years after graduation, fell relative to the unemployment rates of other young Ontario workers from the 1986 to the 1991 cohort but then rose during the rest of the period. It is difficult to reconcile this with growing earnings premia to higher education over the same period (Drewes 2010).

There was some evidence of a mismatch by field between the jobs available and the graduates. Particularly among university graduates there are persistent differences in earnings by field and these have increased. Engineering, mathematics and computer science fields showed the greatest increases in relative earnings, suggesting demand is growing faster than the supply of graduates.

The labour market data support participation rates as high as they are today.

But there are some signs that the labour market could not sustain significantly higher participation rates.

Certainly the newspapers and television have been filled with stories on unemployed graduates and of high youth unemployment. Such stories should not be ignored, but they are anecdotes rather than analysis. We would do well to remember that youth unemployment was much higher after the last recessions in the early 1980s and early 1990s, only to fall significantly as the economy expanded. And what we see today is the result of a recession, slow recovery, and older workers remaining in their jobs because of worries about their income in retirement. In thinking about the desired capacity of the system of higher education, we need to think about the medium term.

The most significant indication that the labour market will not need much higher participation is that even the forecasts which indicate a very high demand for higher education graduates do not suggest that more than 80 percent of jobs will require a higher education credential.

Another sign is that there is considerable variation in the incomes earned by both college graduates and bachelor's degree holders. The analysis above showing a strong wage premium for college and university graduates dealt with the average return. The National Graduates Survey (Class of 2005) showed that 25 percent of college graduates had earnings not much higher than high school graduates, and 25 percent of university graduates had earnings at the level of the average college graduate (Statistics Canada 2009a). A high earnings premium after higher education is not a sure thing; there is considerable variability in outcome—there is considerable risk. If it can be assumed that the marginal entrant to the higher education system as it expands earns the low returns, the labour market is not paying a premium for the higher education of this student at the margin.

It is a complicated task to identify the marginal entrant to higher education as the capacity of the system expands.[11] If a student had the entry qualifications before the system expanded but chose not to apply, the expansion of the system is unlikely to lead the student to apply. The barriers to participation were not system capacity. But suppose system expansion did lead to participation, and this qualified student is regarded as the student at the margin. There is evidence that the return to higher education of this type of student at the margin (qualified students, who did not apply before, and are somehow led to participate as the system expands) is at least as high as the average return. However, if as is more likely, the student admitted at the margin through expansion is the student who had high school grades just at the cutoff for entry, then the evidence suggests a lower than average return. But, the literature is not conclusive. The basic lesson though is that in the analysis of system expansion, one should look at the labour market returns of the student at the margin, not the average return.

Another sign comes from data on all individuals between ages 25 and 64 who had employment earnings. Among OECD countries, Canada has the highest share with a higher education qualification, but in 2006 Canada also has the highest percentage of college- and university-educated workers who earn less than half the national median employment income (Statistics Canada 2009b). In Canada, 23 percent of college-educated workers and 18 percent of university-educated workers earn less than half the median income. There are many hypotheses to explain these international comparisons and no answers are yet available, but could it be a sign that Canada is "producing too many college and university graduates for the labour market to absorb? Or, is Canada not producing the right mix of postsecondary graduates?" (Statistics Canada 2009b).

A recent paper by Canadian economists using US data, *The great reversal in the demand for skill and cognitive tasks*, (Beaudry, Green, and Sand 2013) concludes: "many researchers have documented a strong, ongoing increase in the demand for skills in the decades leading up to 2000. In this paper, we document a decline in demand in the years since 2000, even as the supply of high education workers continues to grow. We go on to show that, in response to this demand reversal, high-skilled workers have moved down the occupational ladder and have begun to perform jobs traditionally performed by lower-skilled workers." And they write provocatively: "having a BA is less about obtaining access to high paying managerial and technology jobs and more about beating out less educated workers for the barista or clerical job." Their work deals only with the US, but should be a caution for our thinking about Ontario.[12]

Thus, the labour demand analysis offers some signs that participation rates (the supply of graduates) cannot go much higher and still sustain the income premium for higher education.

Both the access lens and the labour market lens suggest participation rates cannot and should not go much higher. Certainly the likely increase in participation will not overcome the demographic decline. The system is large enough.

In all the push to expand higher education, the question of how to design the educational system to best assist those who will hold jobs not requiring higher education has been pushed aside. This deserves more attention. Beaudry, Green, and Sand (2013) found that in the US high-skilled workers have been pushing low-skilled workers even further down the occupational ladder and, to some degree, out of the labour force altogether.

SHIFT THE FOCUS OF POLICY AWAY FROM EXPANSION

We can conclude this chapter as it began:

> The narrative of higher education in Ontario since the mid-1960s has been of expansion—adding new institutions and expanding existing ones—using the same basic structures. The core principle in designing the system was to provide a place in first-level higher education for every qualified student who wished to attend. The postwar expansion of Ontario's higher education

system is often described as moving from elite, to mass, to near-universal higher education. But, it is said, the desired goal of universal higher education has not yet been achieved.

But now in fact, after the huge expansion of the last fifteen years, universal higher education has been achieved. We do not need more spaces in our colleges and universities.

This is a wonderful achievement that should be a cause for celebration and a source of pride.

However, with this achievement, the focus of higher education policy will have to shift. And, this will not be easy. We all recognize that higher education is and should remain a top priority; we have become accustomed to addressing this priority by expanding the number of places. We must now shift away from expansion toward rethinking, toward assessing and reforming our existing institutions and programs.

NOTES

1. Trow (2005) reflects on the transitions from elite to mass higher education, and from mass higher education to universal higher education, in modern societies.
2. An example of such studies is Miner (2010).
3. The picture is not significantly different if the projections were for the 18–19-year-old group or for the 18–24-year-old group.
4. We should also note, as we look to the past five years and see a growth in enrolments and become tempted to conclude that this will continue, that the past five years saw the 18–21-year-old group grow by 6.5 percent. This was the baby boom echo in the system. But in the future, this group will be getting smaller.
5. This split assumes the split is the same as Shaienks and Gluszynski (2007) for Ontario.
6. There is an additional 6 percent undertaking an apprenticeship, for a total PSE participation of 82 percent.
7. In a HEQCO study, Norrie and Lin (2009, 14) survey the evidence on postsecondary participation and attainment and reach a broadly similar conclusion: "In sum, it is reasonable to expect that 70 percent of Ontarians aged 20 to 24 in 2006 will earn at least one credential in postsecondary education."
8. This analysis, comparing capacity needed for the ideal system of 75 percent completion with the capacity of the actual system, is another cross-check and again confirms that participation rates must be at least 75 percent.
9. In 2007, only 60 percent of Canadian university students were between the ages of 18–21 (Statistics Canada 2010b). Current total university enrolments include a large number of students who have either delayed entering university after high school or have entered the work force and returned to university.
10. It is not necessary to assume that all students complete their program within the four years (or two years in college). It may take longer. But provided that

they do complete and that the time patterns of passage to completion are steady, the calculation of capacity would be the same.

11. See Clark (2012) for a discussion of some of the issues and literature.

12. The authors are exploring whether Canada's labour demand shifts are similar. Their preliminary analysis suggests the Ontario situation, although not western Canada, is similar to the US.

Chapter 5

RETHINKING BACCALAUREATE EDUCATION

Over the postwar period, the overriding question in the design of Ontario's higher education system has been: how many places do we need in first-level higher education? Chapter 4 concluded that, after the expansion of the last fifteen years, the system is now large enough. The focus of policy can now shift. Key questions will be: are we achieving the learning outcomes desired in our programs, do we have the right mix of degree and diploma programs to meet future needs of our diverse student body, and do we have the right differentiation of our existing institutions to deliver the desired mix of programs?

This chapter considers only baccalaureate education, and mainly baccalaureate education at universities—although with an important section on bachelor's degrees at colleges—in part because of the experience and expertise of the author, but also because there is vastly more analysis and writing about undergraduate education than about college diploma education. Such an imbalance is both troubling and revealing. College education has not received that attention it deserves. It can be safely recommended, as we rethink higher education in Ontario, that more analysis and assessment of college diploma education is needed.

So first let us ask: how well are we doing in providing undergraduate education in Ontario?

One way to start this analysis is to think about the purposes of an undergraduate education, recalling the discussion of Chapter 1. The broad purposes of an undergraduate education are:

- to acquire knowledge and certain broad competencies (e.g., critical thinking, writing);

Rethinking Higher Education: Participation, Research, and Differentiation, G. Fallis. Kingston: School of Policy Studies, Queen's University. © 2013 The School of Policy Studies, Queen's University at Kingston. All rights reserved.

- to prepare for employment and career; and
- to prepare for membership in the community, especially for citizenship.

The first sections of this chapter examine the evidence regarding these basic purposes and ask: how well are we doing?

Another way to explore how well we are doing is to examine the writing about undergraduate education, most of which is critical as it turns out, and then to identify key themes of the critique. The remainder of the chapter looks at nine themes of criticism. The first is a criticism that runs throughout almost all the literature, regardless of the issue: undergraduate education is a low priority in universities, overwhelmed by the importance and prestige of research. The next three are criticisms of how we finance undergraduate education. The remaining themes offer critical assessments of how well we are doing, with the last three arguing the need for new degree programs, that is, the need for more diversity in the programs available to Ontario students.[1] A summary of the themes is:

- undergraduate education is a low priority;
- underfunding;
- tuition and student debt are too high;
- fiscally unsustainable;
- disengaged students;
- low commitment to improving teaching and learning;
- more career-oriented bachelor's degrees at colleges;
- more liberal education programs at universities; and
- more honours programs at universities for high-ability, high-engagement students.

Armed with this analysis, we can better consider whether some redesign of the system of higher education is needed and what form it might take. As we do this, I would urge the reader to keep two points in mind. The first is that *all Ontario universities are primarily undergraduate universities*, in the sense that the great majority of their students are undergraduates, and indeed, the majority of Ontario's undergraduates attend what are labelled doctoral/research universities. Ontario students will only be well served if changes to undergraduate education occur at *all* universities. The second is that most writing about undergraduate education tends to be critical, as that astute and wry observer Clark Kerr noted, it tends to view the past with pride and the future with alarm, so "beware the doomsayers" (Kerr 2001, 212). I call it the "grumpy elder syndrome"—much of the writing about higher education is done by elders of the academic community, who can be grumpy sometimes about the current state of affairs. We must not lose sight of the enormous accomplishments of Ontario's system of undergraduate education, and understand that the past was unlikely as wonderful as we recall.

ACHIEVING THE PURPOSES OF UNDERGRADUATE EDUCATION

The purposes of an undergraduate education, at the broadest level, are to acquire knowledge, to prepare for employment and career, and to prepare for membership in the community, especially for citizenship in a democracy. How well are we achieving these purposes? As we try to answer this question for each of the broad purposes, we should disaggregate our analysis into several parts. This first is to ask how the purpose can be articulated in more detail. The second is to ask what are the curriculum and pedagogy used to achieve these purposes. And third, what is the method of assessment used to determine how well the purposes have been achieved.

The undergraduate degree programs at Ontario universities are based in individual academic disciplines—for example one can obtain a Bachelor of Arts in English or history or economics, or one can obtain a Bachelor of Science in biology or chemistry or mathematics. And indeed the university is organized on this basis, first into faculties and then into departments. These disciplinary departments are responsible for designing their degree program. The faculty of arts (in many universities this is separated into a faculty of humanities and a faculty of social science) is divided into departments, and the department of English is responsible for the English degree and so on. The faculty of science is divided into departments, and the biology department is responsible for the biology degree and so on.[2] Students refer to this focus of their degree as their major; when asked what they are studying, they will reply English, history, economics, biology or whatever is their focus. There are some interdisciplinary degrees that cross departments, and students can do a double major or major-minor program, but even here the focus is "disciplinary" knowledge, broadly construed.

Most universities require that students take a certain number of courses outside their major, but the overwhelming concern and emphasis in designing the undergraduate degree is upon the courses that make up the major. The curriculum in each department is designed to introduce the students to that discipline, and to move the student to an increasing level of familiarity and sophistication in that discipline. They learn the main theories and methodologies of that discipline, and usually are required to gain some knowledge of the major subspecialties. It is regarded as important to make students aware of the current research in the discipline and to prepare them to read the academic literature. Professors often say that the purpose of the teaching is to learn "to think like a historian" or "to think like a biologist." Careful attention is paid, in designing the courses and course sequences of the curriculum to offer a track that will prepare the student for graduate school in that discipline.

How well are Ontario universities doing in the teaching and learning of this disciplinary knowledge? I believe the answer is: quite well.

The curriculum is designed with this purpose in mind. The assessments through tutorials, labs, tests, essays, problem sets, and exams are all designed to assess this knowledge. In most departments, professors teach the upper level courses most closely related to their subspecialty and to their research. (For example, the English course on the Victorian novel will be taught by someone who specializes in nineteenth century English literature, or the economics course in international trade will taught by a trade theorist.) This close connection between the course and the intellectual passions of the professor promotes good teaching, and ensures that the undergraduates are taught by people able to discuss the current findings and controversies of the discipline. Most professors care deeply about the students in their department and about introducing students to their discipline.

All degree programs—the degree in English, in history, in economics, in biology, and so on—are reviewed every seven or eight years. These reviews are conducted under the Institutional Quality Assurance Process (IQAP) adopted by each university (discussed in Chapter 3). The professors, students, and staff in the department prepare a critically reflective self-study, reviewers from other universities come to campus, and drawing upon the self-study and the site visit, the external reviewers write an assessment of the degree program. Recommendations from the external reviewers for improvement must be responded to by the department, and the Senate of the university (or its committees) is responsible for ensuring proper follow-up and implementation. Having participated in these reviews at my own university, and been an external auditor of the reviews at other universities, I can assert that this quality assurance process is thorough and rigorous. It is focused on the curriculum, the teaching, and the learning of this disciplinary knowledge. The reviews of most degree programs are very positive.

We do not hear complaints from employers that Ontario graduates have not learned English literature or history, or economics, or biology. The world's most selective graduate schools regularly admit students from Ontario undergraduate programs, as do the leading law schools, medical schools, and business schools. Our top graduates are very good indeed. And likely they are as good as they have ever been, or even better than before.

The university has an elaborate assessment system designed to evaluate the learning outcomes related to disciplinary knowledge. Students are assigned a grade in each course and the average grade over all courses is computed—a student may graduate with an "A" average, or a "B" average and so on. If the grades are numerical scores, the average final score is their grade point average, the GPA. There is a great diversity of results in terms of the learning outcomes of disciplinary knowledge: some students (with high final GPAs) have achieved the learning outcomes at a sophisticated level, others (with medium GPAs) have a solid under-standing, and others (with low GPAs) have only achieved the learning outcomes in a modest way. It all seems rather obvious. The main point to recognize is that there is a great difference among students in terms of their learning disciplinary knowledge through their undergraduate degree studies—some learn a great deal and others not so much.

Some critics of our current practices argue that a whole new assessment system is needed to examine learning outcomes. I would disagree. Our current practices do a pretty good job. Those institutions that are seeking students with excellent disciplinary learning outcomes—such as graduate schools, professional schools like law schools or medical schools, and many selective employers—rely very heavily on the GPA in their admission and hiring processes.[3] When employers say that they cannot tell much about a student when they see they have a BA or a BSc, I would reply: look at the GPA (and the full transcript with the grade achieved on each course), just like the law schools or the graduate schools do. It will tell you a lot.

There are, however, many complaints about what students have learned through an undergraduate education. But, the complaints tend not to relate to disciplinary knowledge. Rather, the complaints relate to knowledge more broadly conceived. For example, criticism is often heard in Ontario regarding students' abilities to write clearly and coherently.

Perhaps most worrying of all is research about undergraduate learning recently reported in the United States, particularly in a book *Academically Adrift: Limited Learning on College Campuses* (Arum and Roksa 2011). Universities have always focused upon disciplinary knowledge, but universities have asserted that disciplinary learning also develops broad competencies in critical thinking, analytical reasoning, problem solving, and writing. Over the last decade, an instrument has been developed for explicitly testing these broad competencies—the Collegiate Learning Assessment.

The Collegiate Learning Assessment (CLA) consists of three open-ended, as opposed to multiple-choice, assessment components: a performance task and two analytical writing tasks (i.e., to make an argument and to break an argument). According to the developers, the CLA was designed to assess "core outcomes espoused by all of higher education—critical thinking, analytical reasoning, problem solving, and writing." ... rather than testing for *specific content knowledge* gained in particular courses or majors, the intent was to assess "the collective and cumulative result of what takes place or does not take place over four to six years of undergraduate education in and out of the classroom." (Arum and Roksa 2011, 21)

To give readers some context, let us look at the performance task in the CLA.[4] The task allows students ninety minutes to respond in written form to a set of background documents. Here is an example, related to crime reduction. "Jamie Eager is a candidate who is opposing Pat Stone for reelection. Eager critiques the mayor's solution to reducing crime by increasing the number of police officers. Eager proposes that the city support a drug education program for addicts because, according to Eager, addicts are the major source of the city's crime problem. Students are [again] provided with a set of documents including newspaper articles, crime and drug statistics, research briefs, and internal administrative memos. The CLA requires that students should specifically address the following: Mayor Pat Stone asks you to do two things: (1) evaluate the validity of Eager's proposal and (2) assess the validity of Eager's criticism of the mayor's plan to increase police officers" (Arum and Roksa 2011, 22). Such a performance task is given at the beginning of undergraduate study, after two years, and at the end.

The results of the CLA are alarming. "With a large sample of 2,300 students, we observe no statistically significant gains in critical thinking, complex reasoning, and writing for at least 45 percent of the students in our study. An astounding proportion of students are progressing through higher education today without measurable gains in general skills as assessed by the CLA. While they may be acquiring subject-specific knowledge or greater self-awareness on their journeys through college, many students are not improving their skills in critical thinking, complex reasoning, and writing" (Arum and Roksa 2011, 36), although of course, there are many students who are making great improvements.

There are great differences among students in their core competencies on arrival at university (just as there are great differences in their high school average grades). Another alarming finding of the research in the United States is that some minority groups (and students whose parents did not attend higher education) arrive with lower core competencies— but the differences among groups are not reduced, and even widen in some cases, through the years of undergraduate study.

Would we find the same results in Ontario? Most professors teaching large undergraduate classes in large departments would say "of course." But, we have not done the assessment. This is doubly worrying. First, many Ontario undergraduates are likely achieving no improvement in these core competencies through their undergraduate education. Second, Ontario has not set up a system to assess whether these core competencies have improved. Fortunately, although belatedly, Ontario universities have begun to investigate the CLA. The test will be piloted in a compacted timeframe by HEQCO with a dozen or more Ontario universities and colleges across a range of disciplines.[5]

A new focus on learning outcomes and the assessment of improvements in general competencies is a vital part of rethinking undergraduate education in Ontario. And just as in the assessment of disciplinary knowledge, this work should recognize that there will be great differentiation among students in their learning outcomes, and in the improvements in their outcomes during undergraduate study.

The second broad purpose of undergraduate education is to prepare for employment and career. How well are Ontario universities doing on this task?

There are several ways to approach this question. One approach would be to ask: do Ontario graduates have the knowledge and skills required in the labour market? This could be addressed by comparing the qualifications sought by employers with the qualifications of the graduates. Hard evidence is difficult to obtain, although concerns are sometimes expressed by employers that graduates are weak in writing and communications skills and in "people" skills such as the ability to work in teams. Addressing this question is confounded by the more frequently heard concerns that universities are not graduating enough people in the science, engineering, and technology fields.

Universities, while recognizing their responsibility to help students prepare for employment, are rightly troubled by some of these questions. It surely is not the responsibility of universities to try to match the number of graduates in certain fields with labour market demands,[6] or indeed to match the total number of graduates with total labour market demand.

Most analyses of this purpose of undergraduate education have taken a very broad approach: the analyses examine the actual labour market outcomes of graduates—their employment rates and their incomes. Also, many analyses try to measure whether graduates have obtained jobs that match their qualifications.

It was precisely to assess this purpose of an undergraduate education that Ontario universities were required to survey the graduates of their undergraduate programs every year, as part of gathering certain key performance indicators (KPIs). (See Chapter 3 for discussion.) The most recent results are for the survey of 2009 graduates (COU 2012a). Six months after graduation their employment rate was 87.5 percent. Two years after graduation the employment rate was 93.1 percent; 82.3 percent of graduates employed full-time considered their work either "closely" or "somewhat related" to their university education, and the average annual income was $49,151. The employment rates vary somewhat by program of study, but not as much as one would expect, and some of the results do not conform to the common understanding. For example, agricultural and biological sciences have below average employment rates. Incomes by programs of study vary much more, and mostly in the expected ways.

For example, humanities, and fine and applied arts, have incomes well below the average, while dentistry, optometry, and pharmacy are well above average.

Nonetheless, there are some concerns. Since 2003, according to the KPIs, the two-year employment rate has dropped from 96.8 percent to 93.1 percent; the skills match has dropped from 85.2 percent to 82.3 percent; and two-year post-graduation annual incomes have been roughly constant (i.e., falling in real terms). No doubt the recession and slow recovery in Ontario are part of the answer, but it may be that there is a longer trend of the supply of graduates beginning to grow faster than the demand for graduates or that there is a growing mismatch between the skills of graduates and the skills sought by the labour market. The six month employment rate dropped sharply from 94.1 percent in 2006 to 87.5 percent in 2009, suggesting graduates were having increasing difficulty making the transition to the labour market.

The evidence on labour market outcomes was also examined in Chapter 4; there the issue was whether the labour market evidence supported the need to expand the system. The broad pattern using data to 2005 was that university graduates had a significant wage premium over high school and college graduates, they had lower unemployment, and there was no evidence of increasing over qualification (Drewes 2010). But, the evidence showing that graduates do well in the labour market relates to the "average" graduate. As discussed in the previous chapter, there is considerable variation in the labour market outcomes of graduates—success in the labour market is far from certain. And, there is a study from the United States that concludes the supply of graduates is now rising more rapidly than the demand. Although a US study, it raises a warning flag for Ontario. A recent study has found substantial variation in the labour market outcomes of graduates in Canada, comparing the 1986 and 2006 Census surveys. "Real incomes of fully employed males with a university degree who earn more than the minimum wage exhibit an increase 22.9 percent over this twenty year period. By 2006, however, the income distribution had become much more skewed with the emergence of two new categories: income superstars, as well as a substantial proportion of respondents who have substantially lower incomes than the corresponding 1986 cohort. Having an advanced degree is also not uniformly beneficial; some types have actually suffered from too much schooling" (McIntosh 2013).

This variability must be an important part of assessing how well we are doing. We should examine not just the labour market success of average students, but the labour market success of students who do less well academically. Perhaps the students with poor academic outcomes are doing poorly in the labour market. Unfortunately we do not have the data to conduct such an examination. But, we must consider whether there are some students currently in university programs who would be better served by another type of higher education program.

Part of rethinking undergraduate education must be to confront these fundamental questions: what are the labour market outcomes of the students admitted at the margin, and what are the labour market outcomes of the students who are disengaged during their undergraduate study? Again, our analysis must move from consideration of the average student to consideration of the differentiation among students.

The third broad purpose of undergraduate education is to prepare the student for membership in the community, particularly for citizenship in a democracy. This purpose has always been considered a necessary part of a proper "liberal education."

It is striking how little we know about how well we are doing on this third purpose, despite how often it is highlighted in general statements—at convocation addresses for example—about why go to university and what it has prepared you for. The purpose is clear. But the curriculum is not designed to fulfill this purpose; the curriculum is designed for disciplinary learning. The assessment of students is focused on disciplinary learning. And the external assessment of degree programs does not consider this purpose at all.

Derek Bok, former president of Harvard University and an astute observer of American higher education recently published a book, *Our Underacheiving Colleges: A Candid Look at How Much Students Learn and Why They Could Be Learning More* (Bok 2006). He summarized the purposes of an undergraduate education: undergraduate education should develop the ability to communicate, critical thinking, and moral reasoning; it should prepare students to be citizens, to live with diversity, and to live in a more global society. It should encourage a breadth of interests. And he found American universities wanting. The situation in Ontario is the same.

The lack of discussion and analysis of the third purpose of an undergraduate degree is caused by many factors, the two most important being the increasing emphasis on the degree as simply a necessary credential for employment and the designing of the degree to achieve mastery (or at least understanding) of a specific academic discipline/major. Ontario universities offer disciplinary degrees, not liberal education. The lack of liberal education programs in Ontario universities is discussed at greater length in a separate section below.

GIVE UNDERGRADUATE EDUCATION A HIGHER PRIORITY

Throughout the literature about undergraduate education, there is a persistent worry that undergraduate education is not receiving the priority and attention it deserves. There are many voices speaking of this worry, mine included (Fallis 2007). Pocklington and Tupper make it the focus of their critique of Canadian universities. "Modern Canadian universities wrongly and seriously devalue the education of undergraduates. ... Universities must establish undergraduate teaching as their first priority. Undergraduate teaching must be recognized and valued for what it is: a complex and important activity that demands broad reading, disciplined thought, and great effort" (Pocklington and Tupper 2002, 6-8).

The past twenty years have not been good to undergraduate education; within the funding available, both research and graduate education have done much better. This is despite the fact that total real revenue per student (grants plus tuition) has been remarkably constant over the last twenty years (Clark et al. 2009, 83). Real revenue is calculated by deflating nominal revenue by the consumer price index (CPI). The problem for universities is not that real total revenue is falling, but rather that costs, particularly compensation costs, have been rising faster than the CPI. Costs have been rising at about two to three percentage point above the CPI. This partly explains rising student-faculty ratios and increasing class sizes at the undergraduate level. But, there are other contributing factors. Universities have chosen to increase the share of spending on non-classroom activities such as administration, student services, computing and information technology, marketing, and communications. In addition, the indirect costs of research have risen as the total sponsored research income has risen, but not all the indirect costs are covered by the federal program. As research income has grown, money has been taken from the classroom to pay the indirect costs. Also, the number of classes taught by full-time faculty members has declined at the undergraduate level because faculty have shifted more of their workload to research.

Similar concerns are expressed in the United States. For example, Frank Rhodes, president of Cornell University wrote: "I believe it is time to state clearly and firmly that, while research and teaching both contribute to the strength and vitality of the U.S. research university, it is undergraduate teaching and learning that is the central task" (Rhodes 1994, 180-1). Clark Kerr, who has been one of the most astute observers of American universities, noted: "recent changes in the American university have done them [undergraduate students] little good—lower teaching loads for faculty, larger classes, the use of substitute teachers for regular faculty, the choice of faculty members based on research accomplishment rather than instructional capacity, the fragmentation of knowledge into endless subdivisions" (Kerr 2001, 77-8). Disappointment at the continuing failure to pay more attention to undergraduate education runs as a lament through Clark Kerr's forty years of observations of American universities.

The explanations for this low priority to undergraduate education are many, but given that similar problems exist across Canada and in the United States, the explanation cannot be found exclusively in Ontario's circumstances. In my judgment, the many explanations can be distilled to three: the greater prestige of research compared to teaching, the greater commitment to disciplinary education compared to liberal education, and the disengagement compact between students and professors. Each will be discussed below.

But whatever the explanations, the first conclusion in rethinking undergraduate education is that undergraduate education should be given higher priority and greater attention.

FUNDING UNDERGRADUATE EDUCATION

The next three themes of criticism relate to the funding of undergraduate education, and perhaps not surprisingly, they emphasize different aspects of current funding and reach different conclusions.

The first theme is that undergraduate education is underfunded. This criticism comes from the university presidents and from the Council of Ontario universities. They point out that Ontario has the 8th or 9th lowest government operating grant per student of all the Canadian provinces and overall has the lowest amount of government spending, per capita, devoted to postsecondary education. Furthermore, Ontario universities have 38 percent less revenue per student compared to peer, publicly supported, American universities (COU 2008, 51). The most significant results of this underfunding over that last fifteen years have been a rising student-faculty ratio and increasing class sizes. Both are proxy indicators of academic quality, and both point to declining quality. The universities need more funds—both from higher government operating grants per student and from tuition fees.

The second theme is that tuition is too high and that student debt is too high. This criticism comes from students and from the student organizations. They point out that tuition fees have risen rapidly over the last fifteen years; that as real government grants per student fell, tuition fees rose, forcing students to pay a higher share of total costs; and that average student debt has been rising, now standing at about $25,000 on graduation. The high fees, it is argued, have reduced the accessibility of higher education for those from lower income families. Tuition should be lowered and student assistance should comprise more grants and fewer loans.

The third theme is that the current model of funding is unsustainable. This criticism has come from Clark et al. (2009) and Clark, Trick, and Van Loon (2011). They point out that Ontario has used the most expensive type of postsecondary institution. "Ontario appears to be unique among jurisdictions of comparable size and rates of participation in baccalaureate programs relying exclusively upon a system of publicly supported, research-focused universities for the provision of baccalaureate education" (Clark et al. 2009, 2). They argue that such an expensive model cannot be used to fund the needed growth in places because of the restraint on government expenditure in the years ahead. There needs to be a new type of university established, teaching-focused, that can provide undergraduate education at lower cost (and, it is argued, that can provide more student-centred, innovative programs, thus allowing Ontario to offer a greater diversity of programs to meet the needs of its diverse student population).

The government, no doubt, is frustrated by this cacophony about financing because Ontario government expenditures on postsecondary education over the last decade have risen at 8.2 percent per year—faster even than health, which rose at 7.1 percent per year, the expenditure area usually thought of as rising most rapidly and squeezing out other areas.

There is truth in all of the perspectives: each contains factually correct statements. The issue is to ensure all of the facts are considered before making judgments.

COU is correct that real government grants per student have fallen, but it is also true that total real revenue per student (grants plus tuition) has been remarkably constant over the last twenty years (Clark et al. 2009, 83). Real revenue is calculated by deflating nominal revenue by the consumer price index (CPI). The problem for universities is not that real total revenue is falling, but rather that costs, particularly compensation costs, have been rising faster than the CPI. Also, universities have chosen to allocate resources to non-classroom priorities such as communications, information technology, and the indirect costs of research.

The students are correct about rising tuition fees, but they have ignored the huge increase in student support over the last twenty years. Also, some of the tuition increase is just to match inflation. The proper calculation of tuition must recognize the value of tax credits available under the personal income tax system, that have been improved over the years. Usher and Duncan (2008) found that since 1999–2000, in Canada, "once tuition is adjusted for inflation and tax credits, … it is no higher now than it was eight years ago (Usher and Duncan 2008, 5). In Ontario net real tuition rose only 2 percent over this period. And this does not account for the increase in student assistance; factoring this in, Ontario's real net tuition has likely fallen since 1999–2000. This is even truer since the introduction of the 30 percent tuition rebate. The statements about student debt are misleading: average student debt may be $25,000, but this is the average among students who graduate with debt. About 45 percent of university students graduate without debt. Finally, there is no evidence that the tuition/assistance policies in Ontario have reduced the access of those from low-income families to universities—the proportion of that group attending has risen (although still below the proportion from high income families).

The current Ontario model of providing undergraduate education through research-teaching universities is "expensive" in a certain sense, but one must be careful to understand the calculation. Following Clark,

Trick, and Van Loon (2011), suppose a typical full-time faculty member at a current research-teaching university has a salary and benefits of $120,000 per year and teaches four, one-semester courses per year, and a full-time faculty member at a new teaching-only type university has the same salary/benefits of $120,000 per year, but teaches eight, one-semester courses per year. Our current model is expensive—it costs $30,000 per course compared to $15,000 per course.

However, this calculation places no value of the research done by the faculty members at the research-teaching universities. Roughly, for such professors, half their responsibilities relate to teaching (including the service connected to teaching) and half their responsibilities relate to research (including the service related to research). If we assume only half their salary is for teaching, then the cost per course is $15,000, exactly the same as the teaching-only university.

Furthermore, at our research-teaching universities much of the teaching is done by graduate students and part-time faculty members. They receive much less per course, about $7,500. (This is roughly accurate, although actually somewhat high, but was chosen also to make calculations easier.) Thus our current research-teaching model, that combines some "expensive teaching" and some lower cost teaching, is not as expensive as it might first appear. Our current model is not to have all teaching done by full-time faculty teaching four, one-semester courses per year; rather the model is to have some teaching done by full-time faculty and some by part-time faculty; and to have the responsibility for the design of the curriculum resting with those in the research-teaching stream. This has the great benefit that the curriculum is shaped by the research-teaching culture—a benefit that would be lost in teaching-only universities.

The real issue in our current funding model, I believe, is that it has led our universities to rely too much on graduate student and part-time teaching. Some estimates are that about 50 percent of undergraduate instruction (including tutorials, lab supervision, and marking) is done by this group. At many universities, there is a group of part-time faculty members who are hired year after year, on a course-by-course basis, yet they teach a full load of courses year after year. For all intents and purposes they are full-time, but are hired and paid on a part-time basis. This is an inappropriate and unstable labour relationship—causing huge problems across universities in Ontario and indeed across North America. But, one could say that the problem is that our current model is "inexpensive"—a cheap way to provide undergraduate education because it relies so much on low-cost, part-time instructors. One remedy would be to create more full-time, teaching-only positions in current universities—but this will be more expensive than our current model.

And the government is correct that it has increased funding to universities at a very rapid rate over the last fifteen years. But most of this increase has been to finance an expansion of the system; the funding per student has been relatively stable, declining slightly in recent years.

Ontario's grant per student is about $5,800 per student in arts and $8,500 per student in science; tuition plus ancillary fees is about $6,000. Total revenue per student thus ranges from $11,800 in arts to $14,500 in science. This is at the lower end, benchmarking against comparable jurisdictions, although not far off the funding at publicly supported universities in Australia and England. However, it is highly unlikely that Ontario funding per student will increase significantly over the next few years.

All discussion of funding must now take place in the current political and budgetary context of Ontario: expenditure restraint is the order of the day. The 2012 Ontario budget allows a 1.9 percent annual increase on postsecondary spending. This is far below the 8.2 percent of the last decade. And a reasonable forecast is that even the 1.9 percent increase in spending will not be possible.

This book offers no original analysis of the funding of undergraduate education. What I can offer is a judgment based upon experience of Ontario and other jurisdictions, and upon reading the literature. In my judgment, Ontario's funding strikes a sound balance between government grant, tuition, and student assistance. The total funding per student is modest, although comparable to many jurisdictions. During the period of restraint, we should avoid radical changes and try for stability. Ontario would be very ill-served by freezing tuition as is sometimes proposed.

But the most fundamental thing to recognize about the financing of undergraduate education is that the quality of undergraduate education is already compromised. Restraint should not be allowed to erode quality any further. The student-faculty ratio and class sizes should not go any higher. The burden of restraint should fall on compensation and on non-classroom expenditures, not on faculty-student ratios and undergraduate class sizes.

DISENGAGED STUDENTS

In my judgment, the most pressing problem in undergraduate education today is student disengagement. And it is a problem we refuse to confront.

The plain truth is that there is a significant minority of students who are disengaged from their studies—they are academically adrift. They arrive unprepared for the detailed reading and abstract analytical thinking required of academic work, are only marginally interested in the substance of their degree program, and do not devote the time needed to their studies.

The context of disengagement is framed and driven by several phenomena: lack of preparation in high school, expansion of the overall university system so that the students admitted at the margin are less prepared, increasing student-faculty ratios and increasing class sizes, and universities placing a lower priority on undergraduate education compared to graduate and professional education and research. If these phenomena hadn't been operating over many years (and in the universities over many jurisdictions), we would call it a perfect storm.

Various aspects of this criticism and various aspects of explanation are found in many writers, but diagnosis and explanation have been most fully explored in a book about Canadian universities: *Ivory Tower Blues: A University System in Crisis* (Côté and Allahar 2007) with further elaboration in a follow-up book: *Lowering Higher Education* (Côté and Allahar 2011). Recently, a body of evidence from studies in the United States was brought together in the book *Academically Adrift: Limited Learning on College Campuses* (Arum and Roksa 2011). Although the data are American[7], the work has attracted much attention in Ontario, because the US situation resonates with professors teaching at Ontario universities: it seems to describe what is happening here.

It has always been the case that many students spend more time on the social and extracurricular life than on the academic life. However, "there is emerging empirical evidence that college students' academic effort has dramatically declined in recent years" (Arum and Roksa 2011, 3). Babcock and Marks (2011) examined individual-level surveys of student time use from the 1920s to today and found that "full-time college students through the early 1960s spent roughly forty hours per week on academic pursuits (i.e., combined studying and class time); at which point a steady decline ensued throughout the following decades. Today, full-time college students on average report spending only twenty-seven hours per week on academic pursuits. …Average time studying per week fell from twenty-five hours per week in 1961 to twenty hours per week in 1981 and thirteen hours per week in 2003" (Arum and Roksa 2011, 3).

Unfortunately, we do not have data systematically collected over time about the hours of study by Ontario students. Côté and Allahar (2011) undertook their own research project and provide some recent Canadian data on hours of study taken from the National Survey of Student Engagement (NSSE).

The National Survey of Student Engagement is a US-designed survey that has been modified for use in Canada that asks students dozens of questions about how they spend their time in and out of the classroom. The NSSE results are brought together as the benchmarks of effective educational practice, created by NSSE to compare performance across all universities. These benchmarks focus on five key areas: level of academic challenge, active and collaborative learning, student-faculty interaction, enriching educational experience, and supportive campus environment. Since 2006, the Canadian NSSE has been administered at all Ontario universities and the results are reported on their websites as part of their quality assurance and accountability system. But unfortunately, these reports deal only with the aggregate benchmarks and do not include the hours of study by students. Perhaps we would rather not know.

The most current Canadian data on student engagement measured by hours of study are deeply troubling.

To give proper context, it is worth quoting Côté and Allahar (2011, 132) at length[8] on how they measured student engagement.

> The most common effort-based measure of engagement (which we will simply call "course engagement") is a single question asking students how many hours per week they spend outside of classes on all aspects of class preparation and course completion ("Hours per 7-day week spent preparing for class [studying, reading, writing, doing homework or lab work, analyzing data, rehearsing, and other academic activities].") ... Consistent with other characterizations of course engagement levels, we classify those reporting 10 hours or less as "disengaged," while those reporting 11–25 hours are considered "partially engaged." Those putting in more than 25 hours are coded as "engaged."

> One logic behind this classification system comes from the "two-hour rule"—namely, that students should put in two hours of effort for every one hour in class in order to fully engage themselves.[9] With most courses having three hours of class time per week, students should put in about six hours per class. Accordingly, with a full load of five courses, they should spend some twenty-six or more hours per week engaged *out of class* in their courses.

> A more commonsensical logic behind this classification is that the total amount of time spent by full-time students should amount to a full-time job, such that class hours plus study hours approximate forty hours per week. If an institution is requiring less of its students, it is enabling disengagement; if students put in less than this amount of time, they are squandering the opportunity to benefit fully from the transformative potential of the university experience.

By this measure how engaged are Canadian university students? Côté and Allahar found about 35 percent are disengaged. And only 15 percent are engaged. And in the middle, 50 percent are partially engaged.

At least anecdotally among professors, there is much collaboration of these survey findings. Further, many professors report that students are much less likely today to come by their office for help or discussion. The contact through email has increased sharply, but most of the email questions are not about the substance of the material but about administrative matters: when is the test, what did we cover in class yesterday because I missed class? And class attendance has declined especially in large lecture courses. It begins with near full attendance as the term begins, but after a few weeks it declines, and midway through term it often falls below 60 percent, even for good teachers.

I want to emphasize that disengagement is not about students' abilities: they are capable of university study. But the problem is a significant minority (as high as 35 percent using the NSSE data) are uninterested and unwilling to put in the hours. And this applies across all Canadian universities: medical doctoral, comprehensive and mainly undergraduate. This significant minority affects the entire class. In our universities today, especially in many of the degree programs in the arts and sciences, we pool high-engagement students together with partially engaged students and with disengaged students. They are mixed together in the same classes. Professors struggle to present the material to benefit all students, but inevitably it is pitched to the middle. And out of a sincere desire to reach out to those who seem to be having difficulty, it is more often than not pitched to the lower middle. This is as much to blame for the declining quality of undergraduate education as budget cuts and rising class sizes.

Côté and Allahar (2011, 77-8) evoke all too well what is happening in our classrooms. "Imagine trying to teach large numbers of students—into the hundreds in many classes—how to interpret a highly abstract economic or sociological theory, or grasp the mechanics of a difficult statistical method, knowing that most will not read in advance of the class, and instead walk into the classroom knowing little about the topic at hand. You can spoon-feed these unprepared students by giving them the material from the readings point by point, or you can entertain them with witty stories and various theatrics, two strategies that net the teachers who use them high points on teacher evaluations. In either case, students are exposed to only a fraction of the material that should be learned if they are to become proficient in the subject, and thus able to critically analyze the material."

These books about student disengagement are part polemic, part scholarly analysis, and part *cri de coeur*. They come from the lived experience of senior professors at major (and highly ranked) research-teaching universities who have been deeply engaged with undergraduate education in large departments. As Pocklington and Tupper note in their comment on methodology, "the major books on universities invariably rest on careful reading, long observation of universities in action, and personal experience within universities" (Pocklington and Tupper 2002, 14). My own judgment rests on the same foundation, and is strongly informed by my experience teaching economics in a large department at a large university. Too often the reports about student disengagement are ignored as the complaints from grumpy elders. Certainly the senior administration of our universities don't want to talk about it, nor do the officials in the Ministry of Training Colleges and Universities. But my advice would be: if you want to understand how Ontario universities are doing in undergraduate education, listen to the people who are actually teaching the classes.

Just as worrying as the students' lack of focus and declining effort is the fact that this has had little impact on their academic grades, failure rates, or time to completion.

"Students' ability to navigate academic course requirements with such modest levels of individual investment and cognitive effort points to a second set of social actors responsible for the growing concern over undergraduate education: the college professoriate. If one is to cast aspersions on student cultures that exist on college campuses today, one would do well to focus equal attention on the faculty cultures and orientation that have flourished in US higher education" (Arum and Roksa 2011, 5).

Most professors try to be conscientious undergraduate teachers. They care about their students, especially the majors in their departments, and among them especially the engaged students. These students can get a very good education. But the commitment to undergraduate teaching is under pressures from several forces. Many professors become discouraged by the disengagement of their students. Also, many become discouraged by the grinding budget cuts, increasing class sizes, and the increasing bureaucratization of teaching a large class. Also, the faculty culture has been shifting because of the increasing priority and prestige attached to research accomplishment, and all the reward systems both material and symbolic seem to favour research over teaching.

The teaching and learning in our undergraduate classes is being shaped by both changes in students and changes in professors. Together, in the metaphor of George Kuh, they have struck a disengagement compact. He describes it as:

> "I'll leave you alone if you leave me alone." That is, I won't make you work too hard (read a lot, write a lot) so that I won't have to grade as many papers or explain why you are not performing well. The existence of this bargain is suggested by the fact that at a relatively low level of effort, many students get decent grades—B's and sometimes better. There seems to be a breakdown in the responsibility for learning—on the part of faculty members who allow students to get by with far less than maximum effort, and on the part of students who are not taking full advantage of the resources institutions provide. (Kuh 2003)

The power of Kuh's metaphor is twofold. It identifies student disengagement as the issue, but just as important, it recognizes that it is a compact between two parties: students and professors. Both will need to become more engaged.

Recent writing about student engagement and hours of study have found that there are significant variations across the sciences, social sciences and humanities. For example, data from the University of California Undergraduate Experiences Survey (UCUES) in 2008 showed mean hours of study, in and out of class, ranged from 24.4 in the humanities to 32 in engineering. Social sciences closely resembled the humanities (Brint and Cantwell 2011, 6). There were also significant differences across disciplines. And of course, there was differentiation across students. In my own informal canvassing of colleagues about disengagement, it seems that it is most serious in the basic sciences, social sciences, and humanities, and in the "popular" disciplines—for example, biology, or economics, political science, sociology, or English and history. These departments tend to have a large number of majors (as well as many students who take their courses as options with another major), very large classes in first and second year, and high student-faculty ratios. They also have many students who chose that major without any particularly strong interest in that discipline. In contrast, smaller limited-entry programs, especially the professional programs, tend to have fewer disengagement problems. The students have obviously chosen the program out of real interest; the educational program is evidently connected to future employment; the students know one another more, often moving together year by year, and the professors know the students and their progress over the years much better. Unfortunately, the programs with greater disengagement problems are the popular large programs, and where the majority of the undergraduates are enrolled.

The writing on the disengagement compact, unfortunately, is better at characterizing the situation, and at exploring its causes, than it is at offering concrete, feasible, reforms. Nonetheless, any rethinking of undergraduate education will have to come to terms with the disengagement compact.

The disengagement of the professoriate is both easier to diagnose and to address. Much of the disengagement is due to the greater prestige for research accomplishment. If undergraduate education is given a higher priority and with the commitment of the senior administration, re-engagement is possible. Also, new commitments to curricular and pedagogical innovation, discussed in the next section, will help.

The disengagement of the student will be harder to address. Part of the difficulty is that we are reluctant to talk about it. But any thoughtful analysis of how we are doing in undergraduate education will have to recognize the reality that a substantial minority of students are disengaged. It forces us to acknowledge that there are many students who do not really need to be, or want to be, at university.

There is considerable evidence that student engagement increases when students see a close connection between their studies and their future, particularly their future employment and career. Student engagement at universities is much higher in the professional programs (and fine arts programs) than the basic arts and science programs. And it is much higher among those who want to go on to graduate school or professional schools like law or medicine, because for these next steps a high level of accomplishment in undergraduate study is necessary. Many undergraduates see their university degree as simply a credential; the substantive learning and their grades do not matter much. Many also plan to go on to further study before entering the labour force. I have recently polled my students about this and 75–80 percent plan further study, especially at a faculty of education or a college; they clearly recognize their need for some career-oriented higher education. (They are naive—nowhere near 75 percent will go on—but this is the plan.)

This student orientation, as well as many other forces well discussed in Côté and Allahar (2011), has contributed to mission drift at the university and to an overlay of what they call "pseudo-vocationalism" in many arts and science programs.

My conclusion is that many (though not all) disengaged students would be much more interested and much better off with a more career-oriented bachelor's degree. They have been persuaded of the benefits of higher education and of a bachelor's degree, but do not have the preparation, interest, or willingness to work at an academically-oriented degree.

IMPROVING TEACHING AND LEARNING

In the literature about undergraduate education, there has been a recurring criticism that too little is done to improve teaching and learning. The criticism is particularly directed at professors and their failure to innovate: they deliver their lectures in the same old way, teaching as they were taught many years before, standing at the front lecturing while students listen and take notes.

This theme of criticism was acknowledged, and given official voice, at a major AUCC workshop on undergraduate education, held in Halifax, March 2011, which led to the follow-up report, *The Revitalization of Undergraduate Education in Canada* (AUCC 2011b). "There are some within the university enterprise who feel that Canada's universities collectively have lost their way. Their concern is that our institutions are not devoting sufficient attention to what is arguably their central role: offering a quality teaching and learning environment to their undergraduate students. Robert Campbell, president of Mount Allison University, captured that sentiment in a recent address: 'We all feel and know that the character of the undergraduate experience has deteriorated in our lifetimes, especially so in the last decades. And we know in our heart of hearts that this experience can and should be much better'" (AUCC 2011b, 2). AUCC now seeks to develop a "new narrative" regarding higher education, with undergraduate education as one of its priorities.

Two of the lead organizers of the workshop, Patrick Deane, president of McMaster University, and Pierre Zundel, president of the University of Sudbury, wrote an essay for the January 2011 issue of *University Affairs* magazine entitled "It's time to transform undergraduate education." In it they claimed, "What is required is a radical re-conceptualizing of the teaching and learning process, where the goal becomes 'helping students learn' rather than 'teaching.' We need to lift ourselves above the instructor-instructed dialectic, and above that equally factitious binary of teaching and research" (Zundel and Deane [2011] as quoted in AUCC, 2011b, 2). However, rather revealingly, the call to improve undergraduate education makes no mention of student disengagement.

This literature that calls for new initiatives to improve teaching and learning takes two approaches to reform.

The first is to gather up and publicize successful initiatives for improving teaching and learning. For example, the *Revitalization Report* offers eight examples from across Canada. An initiative at Laval University to establish fifty chairs (professorships) committed to improving undergraduate teaching and learning is particularly bold. Numerous other collections of successful initiatives are available; there is no shortage of good ideas being implemented.

The second approach is to emphasize the research into teaching and learning that is being done, and to build upon this research. HEQCO sponsored a collection of essays about what this research can tell us about teaching and learning: *Taking Stock: Research on Teaching and Learning in Higher Education* (Christensen Hughes and Mighty 2010). An exemplar of this research-driven innovation is the Carl Wieman Science Education Initiative at the University of British Columbia.

> Under way since 2007, the $12 million project has encouraged the adoption of evidence-based teaching practice, treating the teaching of science as a scientific process itself. Departments are encouraged to establish what students should learn, measure what they are actually learning, adapt teaching practice and curriculum—including the use of technology and research findings—to achieve the desired learning outcomes, and disseminate and adopt those approaches that work. Guiding the change is cognitive research that shows true expertise comes from extended mental grappling with problems rather than from attempts to insert facts into student's heads. That's where interactive engagement practices come in, such as the use of clicker questions, in-class small group discussion and problem solving, as well as other activities. Online pre-reading of assignments and quizzes, as well as pre- and post-testing help instructors to closely gauge how well students are grasping concepts and where they need help. (AUCC 2011b, 21)

There is a third approach to improving teaching and learning, not seen much in Ontario, but followed in many other jurisdictions, and that is one which emphasizes accountability and testing. Universities should be held accountable for student learning, learning outcomes should be regularly tested, the test results should be publicly reported, and consequences should follow from the test results—both initiatives to improve where it is needed and resources flowing to support success.

It is much beyond the scope of this book to offer an analysis and assessment of proposals to improve teaching and learning. There are many books that do this—the *Taking Stock* volume is a good example. But a number of observations can be offered.

The first may seem pessimistic, but history leaves us with a glass-half-full, glass-half-empty picture: there is no shortage of successful initiatives, there is much excellent research about what works in teaching and learning, all universities have centres devoted to improving teaching and learning, and all professors are hired, tenured, and promoted using, as one of the criteria, their record as teachers. Yet, little changes overall: the criticism remains that undergraduate teaching has a lower priority and prestige than research and that successful innovations have not been "scaled up" to change the overall approach. Steven Brint in a thoughtful essay on the US experience: "The Academic Devolution? Movements to Reform Teaching and Learning in US Colleges and Universities, 1985–2010" identifies two major reform movements over these years, but concludes there remains "continuing low levels of student effort and limited learning in college" (Brint 2009, 1). The disengagement compact has not been broken, neither in the United States nor in Ontario.

My own view is that there are three keys to understanding why so little has changed and therefore to formulating reforms proposals.

The first is that professors are, and will remain, committed to the research ideal and will define themselves by discipline and look to their peers. This implies that initiatives to improve teaching and learning should be discipline based—let us get the biology department to assess best practices in biology—rather than the current university-wide approach of creating centres to promote innovation in teaching and learning across the university. The Laval initiative is a good discipline-based example. Leadership on teaching and learning from academic leaders in the discipline is crucial, as in the Wieman initiative. The disciplinary associations (e.g., the Canadian Economics Association, or the Canadian Historical Association) should be key allies in the reform movement across universities. The years in a doctoral program are hugely formative in a professor's life; doctoral programs need to put more emphasis upon teaching and learning in their discipline.

The second is that students must be part of the analysis, and in a more candid way than currently. Much if not most of the literature and initiatives suggest that if professors do more to innovate, better learning will occur. But student disengagement goes much deeper than this. The declining hours of study are not simply caused by poor teaching practices or a lack of response to how today's students learn. Until we confront and better understand this disengagement from the entire academic enterprise, we will achieve little change across the university system. And students themselves need to become more involved with the issues of teaching and learning. In Ontario, student organizations generally have given priority to improving accessibility and to lowering tuition. They have neither acknowledged student disengagement nor offered analysis to understand it.

And third, we cannot escape the funding question. Undergraduate education in Ontario means high student-faculty ratios and large classes. And if we are honest with ourselves, most reform costs more—in faculty time to deliver the courses and in other complementary enhancements, especially the promising enhancements possible with new information and communications technologies. Successful system-wide innovation to improve teaching and learning will require more money.

No survey of current writing about undergraduate teaching and learning would be complete without some comment on the possibilities of online education. My own opinion is that the possibilities have been extravagantly over-hyped, most especially the possibilities of MOOCs—massive open online courses. Much of the hype comes from commentators, anxious to spot the next great disruptive transformation caused by new information technologies, but who have never taught an undergraduate course. Nor do they have any historical sense of the impact of past "new" technologies on teaching and learning—most obviously the impact of television in the 1960s and the impact of the internet and desktop computing in the 1990s. Especially naive is the claim that new technologies will allow the "flipped classroom"—students can watch the lectures online given by the top professors before class and then actual class time can be given over to discussion and deeper exploration of the material. (Both television and the internet/desktop were going to do just this.) The professor is no longer the "sage on the stage" but becomes the "guide on the side." What such claims fail to realize is that professors have been trying to "flip the classroom" for decades—that is, get the students to read the material in advance. The problem is most students don't read in advance, and as noted above the time spent out of class reading the material has been going down.[10] Much more thoughtful assessments of the possibilities of new technologies are available from those who have been working on the possibilities of new technologies for many years. (See for example, Daniel [2012]. Sir John Daniel was vice-chancellor of The Open University in the UK and president of the Commonwealth of Learning, a Commonwealth agency devoted to using technology to expand the scale and scope of learning.)

My sense is that new technologies are very suited to improving on distance education, hence the massive take-up of MOOCs in the developing world, well-suited to short courses for professional upgrading, and well-suited to learning small modules of material. But there will be evolutionary change, not revolutionary change, in the regular undergraduate classroom. There is strong evidence that mixed mode teaching, or blended learning, that combines the new technologies with traditional on campus instruction, is much better than traditional instruction alone, especially for large classes. However, such blended learning is more expensive to deliver than what we are doing now.[11]

Now, let us turn to the last three items on the list of criticisms of under-graduate education indentified in the literature; these deal with the lack of certain types of degree program. It is argued that Ontario, given the great diversity of ability, interests, and aspirations of students, would benefit from a greater diversity of programs. Each criticism is import-ant and well worth careful consideration, although it should be noted that there are relatively few such criticisms. On the whole, universities have been quite responsive and innovative in developing new degree programs, as disciplines develop new themes and as new interdisciplin-ary configurations emerge. At larger universities, several new degree programs are approved every year (not to mention significant changes in existing degree programs). Especially when a new program is successful at one university, others have been quite nimble in initiating analogous programs. Nonetheless, gaps have been regularly identified.

CAREER-ORIENTED BACHELOR'S DEGREES

Although it is a great simplification, programs in first-level higher educa-tion lie along a continuum between two poles: at one pole are academic-ally oriented bachelor's degree programs of the sort offered by Ontario universities in the core arts and sciences, and at the other pole are voca-tionally oriented diplomas of the sort offered by Ontario's colleges. These two poles are also characterized by whether they emphasize theoretical or applied knowledge: degrees emphasize theoretical knowledge while diplomas emphasize applied knowledge. The middle territory of this continuum is often called polytechnic education. Although the term "polytechnic education" is used in the literature and by some Canadian institutions, it is not well understood in Canada.

The term polytechnic education is by its nature ambiguous and hard to define; it is used in different ways in different countries. Jones and Skolnik (2009) provide an extensive analysis of polytechnic education and polytechnic institutions in Ontario and in other jurisdictions. Here, I will follow their summary of Canadian usage, and use the term to mean higher education with certain characteristics. Polytechnic education: "is (a) employment- or career-focused; (b) involves a blend of theoretical and applied learning; and (c) is at a fairly high level of study, i.e., that of a baccalaureate or close to a baccalaureate." To this list, I add another characteristic sometimes included in Canadian usage: polytechnic educa-tion (d) recognizes the salience of the core arts and sciences and situates the career-oriented education within them to provide global and social context. I would summarize this definition of polytechnic education to mean career-oriented bachelor's education. It is often recommended that Ontario would benefit from more polytechnic degree programs and I would re-word this recommendation to say that Ontario would benefit from more career-oriented bachelor's education.

By this definition, the Ontario system of higher education does provide opportunities for polytechnic education. Two institutions in the university sector, Ryerson and UOIT, provide polytechnic education, although both, especially Ryerson, are evolving by adding degree programs of the traditional university sort. And in the college sector, the ITALs provide polytechnic education through their four-year applied bachelor's degrees. Also, many students in Ontario create a polytechnic education program for themselves by combining a college diploma and a university degree.

One recurring question in the analysis of Ontario higher education is whether we should further differentiate our system and establish designated polytechnic institutions. Many other jurisdictions/countries have polytechnic institutions as part of their system of higher education.

In 1989, Dr. Stuart Smith prepared a report on polytechnic education as part of a review of the mandates on the CAATs. Smith (1989) concluded there *was* a need for more polytechnic programs, but recommended against the idea of some of the colleges becoming polytechnics. His primary recommendation was for "a government agency to promote joint programs between colleges and universities through a mix of exhortation, technical advice, modest financial incentives, and most important of all government giving strong indication of its commitment to such programming" (as summarized by Jones and Skolnik). Jones and Skolnik (2009) did their own investigation and similarly did not find a need to establish polytechnic institutions.

In 2009, the minister of Training, Colleges and Universities, asked HEQCO to provide advice on this matter. HEQCO (2009) chose to "advise the minister not to designate any colleges as a polytechnic at this time, but instead investigate ways to encourage existing universities and colleges, individually and collaboratively, to expand their commitment to providing high-quality education that combines theoretical and applied learning and that is directed at meeting current and future labour market needs."

There is a strong consensus that the Ontario system would benefit from more program diversity—more polytechnic education—more bachelor's level applied degrees, more and improved college/university collaborations to better allow the mix of theoretical and applied learning. There is a great demand for more experiential education and co-op programs (Sattler and Peters 2012). This increased diversity would better serve the diverse student needs. It would help students transition to the labour market, and would lead some disengaged students to choose such programs rather than the academic bachelor's degree. My reading of the evidence supports this consensus.

I believe that one of the most important areas for innovation and increased program diversity in Ontario's higher education is the development of more career-oriented bachelor's-level education. One of the fundamental purposes of first-level higher education is to prepare students for the labour market. We need to do better in preparing our students to make the transition to the labour market. The question is: how should more career-oriented bachelor's education be provided?

Clearly, some should be provided through combining bachelor's degrees at universities with graduate certificates at colleges. Some colleges have over 10 percent of their programming in graduate certificates (Table 1.3) and have the experience and know-how to expand in this area. However, this has become more difficult and costly for students because many universities have discontinued their three-year degrees to focus on four-year degrees. And our students deserve better than to have to cobble together programs at two separate institutions to achieve their desired educational goals. There do exist excellent examples, such as the Guelph-Humber two-plus-two programs, of well-integrated collaborations that do not require more than four years of study, and these should be encouraged.

However, if the expansion is to be achieved through more university-college collaborations, such a recommendation must confront a real problem. Virtually every study of these issues of the last twenty years has called for better collaboration between colleges and universities, and this has been the stated goal of government. Yet, although there is considerable collaboration and some excellent initiatives, there has not been a significant change. The approach recommended by Smith (1989) has not worked. This is both the result of government funding policy and of the institutional behaviour of colleges and universities. Government funding in each sector is based on enrolments in each institution with no special funding for collaborative programs, and both colleges and universities have not found it in their interest, given their own objectives, to develop significantly more collaborations, despite the clear indication that government wanted this to happen. In order for things to change, there will first need to be a more realistic characterization of the institutional objectives and institutional decision making of colleges and universities, and in this light, a revised funding formula devised.

I believe that the greater need is for expansion of stand-alone career-oriented bachelor's degrees. The colleges now have some history of providing these programs and they are becoming recognized as high-quality programs. The colleges already provide vocationally oriented courses and also academic courses in the general arts and sciences. Stand-alone degrees do not require the complexities of college-university collaborations. Such degrees could have a two-plus-two structure: two years of academic study and two years of applied study (or indeed, a two-plus-one, or a one-plus-two). These career-oriented degrees would serve the needs of students better, especially some of the disengaged students who would move from the traditional arts and science degrees, and also serve the needs of the labour market better. The policy question is whether these should be delivered by universities or colleges. The analysis of Chapter 2 regarding the rationale for institutional differentiation argued that institutions with a focused mandate are more efficient, deliver better quality programs, and are more likely to innovate. The colleges have a mandate to provide career-oriented education and are best placed to deliver the new bachelor's degrees. Universities could stop their drift into pseudo-vocationalism.[12]

Skolnik (2012) examined the Canadian and international experience of having the non-university sector award baccalaureate degrees—many jurisdictions have moved in this direction—and recommended that Ontario needs a more diversified range of bachelor's degrees and that the colleges be allowed to expand their offerings. He recognizes that some have criticized such expansion because it "blurs the distinction between colleges and universities and results in duplication of programs between colleges and universities." But, he argues, there is a flaw in this criticism. "It focuses on only one of the many institutional characteristics—type of academic credential awarded—that have differentiated colleges from universities. It ignores the plethora of ways in which colleges are differentiated from universities, such as: the occupational focus of college programs and the fact that they are almost always in different subjects than any university program; the more applied approach to learning in college programs; the difference in clientele served by colleges and universities; and the more teaching oriented environment of the colleges" (Skolnik 2012, 3).

Virtually every country has a university sector and a "non-university" sector as part of their system of higher education, with the non-university sector offering vocationally oriented education. In many countries, these institutions can offer bachelor's degrees and their bachelor's degrees are a substantial portion of all baccalaureates awarded, for example the *fachhochschulen* in Germany (now allowed, in English, to be called Universities of Applied Sciences), the Institutes of Technology in Ireland, and the *hogescholen* in the Netherlands. These countries have similar advanced economies to Ontario, similar commitments to access and equality of opportunity, and have been successful in preparing young people for careers.

Ontario colleges can now offer four-year degrees, after approval by the Postsecondary Education Quality Assessment Board (PEQAB). The crucial question is whether the colleges should be allowed to offer career-oriented three-year degrees and to have these degrees developed from existing three-year diploma/certificate programs. And then there is the question of whether PEQAB should be the approval body for these degrees or should a new college-specific degree approval process be established. Colleges Ontario (2011b) in their submission to MTCU, *A New Vision for*

Higher Education in Ontario, asked that colleges be allowed to expand their degree programming, particularly into such three-year degrees, and that there be a new college-specific approval process. The Expert Panel that examined the strategic mandate submissions of colleges and universities noted that many colleges wanted to expand their degree programming, but offered no recommendation (HEQCO 2013).

My own reading of the evidence is that colleges should be given the authority to offer career-oriented, three-year, bachelor's degrees based upon a substantial revision of their current three-year diplomas and that a new approval process be established. These new degrees will require a careful articulation of the desired learning outcomes, and the curriculum and pedagogy to achieve them. This expansion of career-oriented bachelor's degrees would be a truly major transformation of our higher education system. A prudent additional recommendation would be that MTCU should ask that HEQCO examine the evidence both in Canada and other jurisdictions, consult with colleges and universities, and offer advice on the selection and design of three-year applied degrees and the best means to approve them.

Colleges may now obtain the designation of Institute of Technology and Advanced Learning (ITAL) which allows them to offer up to 15 percent of their programming in bachelor's degree programs (the limit for other colleges is 5 percent). There are now 5 ITALS in Ontario—Conestoga, George Brown, Humber, Seneca, and Sheridan College. This differentiation has raised some concern that it would lead the ITALs to pay less attention to their core mandate of providing diplomas and the in-class instruction for apprenticeships. And it remains a concern. However, this must be balanced against the need for more career-oriented bachelor's programs and the recognition that the basic college mandate means they are the best place to deliver them.

All colleges should remain primarily oriented to providing diplomas and in-class instruction for apprenticeships. But a group of colleges—the ITAL group (perhaps expanded) would be the logical starting point—should be given the mandate to expand their bachelor's degrees, including three-year degrees, up to 30 percent of their total programming. Some ITALs have the open aspiration to transition into universities. This would be a mistake. What Ontario needs is a more differentiated college system, with each component having a clear (and limited) mandate, but the college sector should retain its unequivocal focus on career-oriented education. Ontario does not need a slow evolution of certain colleges into universities.

LIBERAL EDUCATION PROGRAMS

If we were to ask university presidents, or university leaders, or many parents, about the purposes of an undergraduate education, they would talk about more than acquiring disciplinary knowledge and preparing for employment and career; they would talk also about the purposes articulated by Derek Bok, cited above. They might say: the purposes are to cultivate "intellectual creativity, autonomy, and resilience; critical thinking; a combination of intellectual breadth and specialized knowledge; the comprehension and tolerance of diverse ideas and experiences; informed participation in community life; and effective communication skills." These purposes are often described as a liberal education. The preceding quotation is Paul Axelrod's description of a liberal education in his book, *Values in Conflict: The University, the Marketplace, and the Trials of Liberal Education* (Axelrod 2002). Many writers in Canada, like Axelrod and me (Fallis 2007), and in the United States like Martha Nussbaum in her books, *Cultivating Humanity: A Classical Defense of Reform in Liberal Education* (Nussbaum 1997) and *Not for Profit: Why Democracy Needs the Humanities* (Nussbaum 2010) have decried the fact the undergraduate education at our universities is no longer a liberal education.

This was not always the case. Through most of history, undergraduate education was intended to be a liberal education, although there was no single conception of what it meant to be liberally educated. Ideals of liberal learning go back to the rich diversity of ancient Greek and Roman thought. Over time, the ideals have evolved and intertwined often in contradictory ways, but certain themes recur that are of particular relevance to today. A liberal education involves both breadth and depth; it should not solely be preparation for a job or to gain mastery of one discipline. And as Cardinal John Henry Newman famously wrote in *The Idea of a University*: if "a practical end must be assigned to a University course, I say it is that of training good members of society" (Newman, in Turner, ed. 1996, 125). To be a good member of society means learning moral reasoning, codes of conduct, and to be a citizen in a democracy. A liberal education has always had a particular focus on preparation for citizenship.

It is one thing to articulate the purposes of a liberal education; it is another to articulate the curriculum that will achieve them. There has been over time much diversity in the curriculum to achieve a liberal education, but there has always been a special priority for the humanities, particularly philosophy, history, and literature. Part of the concern about the lack of emphasis on liberal education is a concern about the marginalization of the humanities.

When students arrive at the university today, we tell them they can embark on a liberal education. But they cannot. What they will find are degree programs based in individual academic disciplines. They will not find degree programs designed to achieve the purposes of a liberal education.

If one looks at degree programs in Ontario, and there is a remarkable similarity across all degree programs and all universities, we find little or no discussion of moral reasoning, codes of conduct, or preparation for citizenship; and the humanities have no special place in the curriculum. The experience of the last decade, when the procedure for reviewing undergraduate degree programs was revised, is very revealing. The Ontario Council of Academic Vice-Presidents (OCAV) mandated that all universities should specify their "undergraduate degree level expectations." What is it that students should have achieved when they are awarded a bachelor's degree? OCAV prepared a set of guidelines that were endorsed by COU and universities have followed them exactly. The flavour of these degree level expectations can be easily conveyed by quoting some of them. The honours bachelor's degree "is awarded to students who have demonstrated: (a) a developed knowledge and critical understanding of the key concepts, methodologies, advances, theoretical approaches and assumptions in a discipline overall, as well as in a specialized area of a discipline; (b) a developed understanding of many of the major fields in a discipline, including, where appropriate, from an interdisciplinary perspective, and how the fields may intersect with fields in related disciplines; (c) a developed ability to: i) gather, review, evaluate and interpret information; and ii) compare the merits of alternative hypotheses or creative options, relevant to one or more of the major fields in a discipline; and (d) a developed, detailed knowledge of and experience in research in an area of the discipline" (Quality Council 2011, Appendix 1). In the guidelines, there is no mention of moral reasoning, codes of conduct, or of citizenship; there is no need to study the humanities. The current Ontario degree level expectations relate entirely to disciplinary education, not to liberal education. The lack of differentiation across universities is remarkable. All have adopted the OCAV guidelines. The guidelines state that they should be regarded as a threshold framework. "In articulating its statement of degree level expectations, each institution is free to use language that reflects its own mission, ethos, values, and culture." None have chosen to make a liberal education part of their degree level expectations.[13]

There are two main explanations for the decline of liberal education. One, advanced by authors such as Axelrod, is that political and economic pressures—broadly summarized as the demands of the marketplace—are redefining and reshaping the functions of higher learning. The space that the university provides for the life of the mind is shrinking. "In the eyes of many, economic performance, not intellectual enlightenment, is the university's preeminent raison d'etre" (Axelrod 2002, 4). Governments value research that has commercial application. Students and their parents see an undergraduate degree as a credential necessary for a good job. Most of these forces come from outside the university. The other explanation, advanced by authors like me, argues that the specialization of knowledge, the organization of the university according to disciplines, and the preeminence of the research ideal have privileged disciplinary education over liberal education. Further, the university no longer wants to take on the teaching of moral reasoning, after the bitter controversies surrounding the old humanities curriculum that was based on reading the works of "dead, white, European males." The criticism of the old curriculum is widely accepted, but no other humanities curriculum has replaced it. Most of these forces come from inside the university. No doubt, both explanations are at work.

The lack of commitment to liberal education in Ontario universities, and lack even of substantive discussion about liberal learning appropriate for the twenty-first century, is puzzling given the vigour around this theme in the United States, where so often we look for models. In the United States, one of the major coalitions of colleges and universities, the American Association of Colleges and Universities (AAC&U) has as its raison d'etre "the quality, vitality, and public standing of undergraduate liberal education. Its members are committed to extending the advantages of a liberal education to all students, regardless of academic specialization or intended career. Founded in 1915, AAC&U now comprises more than 1,250 member institutions—including accredited public and private colleges, community colleges, and universities of every type and size." Its mission "is to make the aims of liberal learning a vigorous and constant influence on institutional purpose and educational practice in higher education" (retrieved from the AAC&U website 2012). Always a source of research and advocacy, in 2005 the AAC&U launched a major decade-long initiative, Liberal Education and America's Promise (LEAP). One of its major reports, *College Learning for the New Global Century* took on the question of "what contemporary college graduates need to know and be able to do" (AAC&U 2007, 7). They identified the essential learning outcomes that included among others—"knowledge of human cultures and the physical and natural worlds, through study in the sciences and mathematics, social sciences, humanities, histories, languages and the arts; [as well as] personal and social responsibility, including civic knowledge and engagement—local and global, intercultural knowledge and competence, ethical reasoning and action, and foundations and skills for lifelong learning, anchored through active involvement with diverse communities and real-world challenges" (AAC&U 2007, 3). The contrast with Ontario's degree-level expectations is stark.

A related movement in the United States works to enhance the civic engagement of universities, the curriculum, and students. It too has a vigorous national organization: Campus Compact, founded in 1985 by the presidents of Brown, Georgetown, and Stanford universities and the president of the Education Commission of the United States. Now, "Campus Compact is a national coalition of almost 1,200 college and university presidents—representing some 6 million students—who are committed to fulfilling the civic purposes of higher education. As the only national higher education association dedicated solely to campus-based civic engagement, Campus Compact promotes public and community service that develops students' citizenship skills, helps campuses forge effective community partnerships, and provides resources and training for faculty seeking to integrate civic and community-based learning into the curriculum" (retrieved from the Campus Compact website 2012).

And these movements now are gathering strength in Europe. There is now an International Consortium for Higher Education, Civic Responsibility, and Democracy, combining the AAC&U and the Council of Europe (among others). It was "established to bring together national institutions of higher education to promote education for democracy as a central mission of higher education around the world" (retrieved from the International Consortium website 2012). In 2006, the Council of Europe adopted the Strasbourg Declaration on The Responsibility of Higher Education for a Democratic Culture: Citizenship, Human Rights, and Sustainability. Another international organization is the Talloires Network. A 2005 conference "gave rise to the Talloires Declaration on the Civic Roles and Social Responsibilities of Higher Education. All signatories of the Declaration have committed their institutions to creating a framework enlarging, supporting, and rewarding good practice in civic engagement and social responsibility. They have agreed to apply academic standards of excellence to community engagement and encourage education for active citizenship at all levels" (retrieved from the Talloires Network website 2012).

Although a few Ontario universities have joined in these international consortia (Carleton University and the University of Guelph have joined the Talloires Network), the issues of liberal education, civic engagement, and the university's responsibility to democracy have had virtually no visibility in Ontario's discussions about undergraduate education. Neither the degree level expectations work nor the work of HEQCO has addressed the issue of liberal education within the undergraduate degree. There is a glaring gap in the degree offerings at Ontario universities; greater diversity in programs, and making available liberal education programs, would enhance Ontario's system and serve the students well.

There are several approaches to making more options for liberal education available to Ontario students.

However much one might personally feel that a bachelor's degree with a broad curriculum, strong in the humanities, designed to achieve the purposes of a liberal education is the ideal degree, it cannot be advocated as the only degree in a system of mass university education. A few very small liberal arts colleges in the United States, St. John's College, Annapolis, is the famous example, do offer a single curriculum to all students. The St. John's College curriculum is based upon the Great Books Program, developed at the University of Chicago. Students read and discuss books from the western canon of philosophical, religious, historical, mathematical, scientific, and literary works. But it's a small college, and students can choose to attend that college if this liberal education suits them. Ontario has no such small universities, although any one university could offer a liberal arts degree as one option along with all the disciplinary degrees. It is something of a puzzle why no Ontario university has done this. The forces of isomorphism are strong indeed. I believe in part it is because of the structure of the university itself, being organized into faculties and departments on the basis of disciplines. Professors have come out of graduate programs organized by discipline, are recruited by discipline, and are appointed to a faculty and department. Liberal arts degrees would require that the professors be drawn from many faculties and departments to create courses especially designed for the liberal arts degree.[14] This is very cumbersome and difficult given the university's structure. But, it is not impossible.

Most degrees from Ontario universities are honours degrees—in principle, designed to be taken over four years, two semesters each year, with five courses per semester.[15] The entire degree is 40 one-semester courses. The majority of the courses are in the major (or the double major or the interdisciplinary focus). Science degrees tend to have a higher share in the major than humanities or social science degrees. Given this structure, liberal learning can be enhanced in two ways.

One way would be to scrutinize the courses in the major, asserting that the purpose of the major is to provide both a disciplinary and a liberal education. The courses in the major would not just introduce the students to the discipline and deepen their understanding, but would also explore the limits of this knowledge and how it relates to other branches of knowledge. The departmental curriculum would point not just to graduate school, but also to life after university. Each discipline could explore the future role of graduates as citizens; for example, the biology curriculum would ask students to think of their role as citizen/ biologist, or the history curriculum would ask students to think about their role as citizen/historian. Unfortunately, Ontario's guidelines for reviewing undergraduate degree programs do not raise such issues. Our quality assurance process, that all universities must comply with, is a force for isomorphism.

Again, the US experience offers thoughtful examples of how this might be done. In each discipline, these discussions are taking place. For example, in 2006 the Teagle foundation awarded grants to investigate the role of majors from six different academic disciplines in promoting undergraduate liberal education. My own discipline, economics, was included which led to a book *Educating Economists: The Teagle Discussion on Re-evaluating the Undergraduate Major* (Colander and McGoldrick 2009) that collected the reflections and debate among some of America's leading economists. In Ontario, this kind of analysis is not being done. It has not been on HEQCO's research agenda or on the agenda of the disciplinary associations. Perhaps, with some rethinking, it can be.

The second approach is to focus upon the minority of courses outside the major, selecting and designing these to enhance liberal education. Many Ontario universities have some loose requirement on these courses, usually what is called a "distribution requirement": all students must take at least one course from the sciences, social sciences, and the humanities. A few universities even design specific courses for this purpose; they are not simply drawn from a list of disciplinary courses. But, these requirements are not at the centre of how the entire degree is conceptualized. Revealingly, the undergraduate degree review process in Ontario is focused almost entirely on the courses in the major. The process is blind to the possibility that the courses outside the major might be conceptualized as a vital component of the degree, designed specifically to enhance liberal learning to complement the disciplinary learning. (And of course, the quality assurance process would assess this component to see whether it was achieving its purposes.)

My own advocacy in this regard (Fallis 2007, 393-414) is for the creation of a liberal education minor—a group of ten one-semester courses designed to achieve the purposes a liberal education. I believe that it is neither desirable, nor realistic, to propose that the entire degree be devoted to liberal education. The need for disciplinary knowledge, depth, and focus is incontrovertible. Nonetheless, the full 40-course undergraduate degree could be made up of a disciplinary major and a liberal education minor. However, I recognize, however much I might advocate for it, that such liberal education is not what many students would choose. And therefore, the liberal education minor would be available to students *if they so chose*, in conjunction with their major. The problem today is that we do not even make this option available.

By making the liberal education minor an option, rather than a compulsory "general education" requirement as has been the case at some universities, I believe should help mitigate the controversies that have beset attempts to design such liberal education components of the undergraduate degree when they are to be compulsory. There is no longer the need to get consensus across all professors about "what every student needs to know." Such consensus is not possible—nor desirable. Each university might have several such minors, and they need not be the same across universities. The specific content could emerge from the interests and orientations of the students and professors at each university. An ecology of experimentation would be encouraged. I could imagine that some universities might offer a minor to encourage cosmopolitan citizenship requiring a foreign language and study abroad; another might offer minors focusing upon "great issues" prospectively facing this generation; another might offer a minor based on a topic for study; my own suggestion is for a minor titled: Liberal Learning and Citizenship. The minor would be devoted to three interrelated themes: the history and development of the university, the history and development of ideas of liberal learning, and the history and development of ideas of citizenship. Like all liberal education programs, there would be an emphasis on effective communication; this would emphasize not just writing and speaking to a disciplinary academic audience (as is the emphasis in disciplinary degrees) but also writing and speaking to a general audience in the public world.[16]

HONOURS PROGRAMS FOR HIGH-ABILITY HIGH-ENGAGEMENT STUDENTS

This last criticism of the undergraduate degree programs at Ontario universities was not identified by reviewing the literature; indeed it was not mentioned in the literature—which reveals much about the discourse around undergraduate education in Ontario. There was no mention of the lack of degree programs for high-ability students. The recognition of this gap in the degree programs available to Ontario students emerged for me, as I thought about the structure of our high school system, the design of university systems in other countries, and the disengagement compact between students and professors in Ontario today.

The high school curriculum was discussed in Chapter 1. The Ontario high school curriculum has three tracks, with considerable overlap and flexibility to move across tracks. One curriculum is designed for students proceeding after graduation directly into the workforce, another for those who will attend a college of applied arts and technology, and another for those who will attend university. In order to enter university, students must complete the Ontario secondary school diploma (OSSD) with courses from the academic curriculum and have achieved at least a 70 percent average (approximately) on the final six courses. Since 1980, Ontario has mandated that school boards provide special education programs for exceptional students and roughly there are two types of exceptional student provided for: the academically exceptional or "gifted" student, and the student who is exceptional due to special needs such as physical disability or learning disability. The gifted students are identified through an Identification, Placement, and Review Committee (IPRC); the criteria are a mix of high-ability, high-academic achievement, and high-engagement, both in and out of the classroom.

Thus, the Ontario high school system has long provided programs for the high-ability, high-engagement student, within an overall structure that provides highly differentiated programs to meet the needs of the highly differentiated student body. But, curiously, our university system does not provide programs for high-ability, high-engagement students, except in the most indirect manner. Along this axis of difference, university programs are less differentiated than high school programs. Ontario used to have true honours programs that attracted high-ability high-engagement students. These were a special type of four-year degree when many degrees were three-year degrees. However, with the shift to almost all degrees being four-year degrees, the true honours programs disappeared.

Suppose we were to pose the question: could a student graduating from high school in Ontario (perhaps coming out of the gifted program at high school) find degree programs that would bring together high-ability, high-engagement students? The peer-group effects among students in a degree program are very strong, and so this option would be attractive to high-ability, high-engagement students. The answer would be that it depends on what you want to study. If you want to enter a business program, you will find that the business programs are very selective and bring together high-ability, high-engagement students. The high school grade cut-off for entry is very high. The same holds true for education programs and many fine arts programs, particularly those with a studio component. But suppose you wanted to study history, or biology, or psychology. Here you will find degree programs open to all students who have met the cut-off for entry into the faculty offering the degree. You will not be able to find a history, or biology, or psychology degree program that is highly selective in terms of entry. When you attend classes, even through to fourth year, you will find students with a range of abilities and engagement—and the curriculum, teaching, and assessment are pitched accordingly. This is a curious paradox indeed. In Ontario, we have evolved highly selective degree programs in the vocationally/professionally oriented fields, but not in the core science, social science, and humanities programs.

This is not true in most other countries, even with high participation rates in a publicly supported system. Certainly it is not true in the United States, England, or Australia. In these countries, both due to policy choice and to the circumstances of their history, the university system is much more differentiated than Ontario's. These countries, like Canada, began the twentieth century with a small number of universities, and what has come to be called "elite" higher education. It was elite in the sense of a small percentage of the age group attended (the quality of education was likely very uneven and many of the programs not very demanding on average, although to be top of the class was very demanding indeed). As the countries moved to mass and then near universal higher education, these universities grew, but did not take up a large share of the overall growth. They remained elite and over time became more and more selective, choosing high-ability, high-engagement students. In parts of the US, in addition, some state systems were designed to have a group of universities that could be highly selective at the undergraduate level, even as the whole system moved to mass higher education. The famous example is California— one group of universities was designed to take the top 12.5 percent of high school graduates. The University of California at Berkeley, and at San Diego, and so on, are very selective at the undergraduate level.

(These same universities award all the doctorates in the system and so are also very selective in terms of professorial appointments.) Similarly for example, the University of Michigan or the University of Wisconsin is very selective at the undergraduate level.[17]

Ontario's system, both due to policy and to the circumstances of history, has not evolved this way. Like these other countries, we began from elite higher education; but in the move to mass higher education, a much higher share of the growth occurred at the older elite universities. University of Toronto is the striking example—and very atypical by international standards. It is now our leading centre for doctoral education and research, but also by far our largest centre of undergraduate education. Across its three campuses, it does not play the role of providing highly selective degree programs that such a university would play in other countries. Indeed across all universities of the Ontario system, especially in the social sciences and humanities, the high school grades needed for entry do not vary much, not nearly as much as in other countries. And as a result, we find some high-ability, high-engagement students looking to the United States or England for their undergraduate degrees.

Clearly, Ontario could not be restructured easily to have a group of universities significantly more selective at the undergraduate level. But, there are other means to remedy this gap in the degree programs available in Ontario. Here the experience and discussions in the Netherlands are instructive.

The Netherlands shares many characteristics with Ontario. It has about the same per capita income, a mixed economy, and a strong tradition of egalitarianism in educational matters (indeed even stronger than in Ontario). It has a binary higher education system, predominantly publicly supported: there is the vocationally-oriented *hogenscholen-sector* (or the universities of professional education, as they now prefer to call themselves) and the university sector. Universities offer most of the master's education, all the doctoral education, and have much the larger mandate for research. (*Hogenscholen* have a limited mandate in applied research.) There has always been a commitment to two "equal but different" sectors. Unlike Ontario, however, there has been over the last fifteen years an active discussion about "excellence" in undergraduate education and how the university sector might provide degree programs for high-ability, high-engagement students. The Dutch realized and acknowledged that some things had been lost in the move from elite to mass university education. An aptly titled paper "Excellence in Dutch Higher Education: Handle with Care" discusses the developments. I quote extensively from it, to let the Dutch (with a stronger egalitarian tradition than ours) speak for themselves. "The minister used the metaphor of a *high plain with peaks* to illustrate that the overall quality of Dutch higher education should be high for all students but that the talented and gifted elite should be provided with excellent programs that would bring them to a top-quality level" (Kaiser and Vossensteyn 2009, 172). Such language has not been part of the Ontario discourse. There have been two main responses in the Dutch university system to the excellence challenge.

> Most universities offer special programs or courses for highly gifted, talented and motivated students. ...These special programs or courses flourish under a wide variety of names. Honors programs, honors courses, plus-programs, excellence tracks, specialization options, and master classes are the labels most frequently used. Despite the variety of labels, these programs have a lot in common. They are organized as an add-on to the regular bachelor's program but taking the special program does not require obtaining additional credits. Participants in the programs are selected (on academic or motivational criteria from the students in the regular program) and classes are organized in a small group setting in which interaction between teacher and students is an important element. (Kaiser and Vossensteyn 2009, 174)

> In 1998 a new response to the excellence challenge emerged. In Utrecht the first *University College* was established. The university college is the "honors college" of the University of Utrecht. With this very selective school at the undergraduate level, the university wanted to make a stand against the large scale and anonymous education that (according to its founding fathers) dominated Dutch universities. New entrants (around 200 annually) are selected on motivation, international orientation and intellectual capacity. They work in small group, tutored by excellent teachers and all live on campus.

> Courses at the Colleges are challenging and demanding. The programs, all taught in English, carry a higher study load than standard undergraduate bachelor programs. Students must be highly motivated and are expected to work hard. So far the honors colleges are considered to be a success story; student demand exceeds the number of places available and the colleges are often referred to as an effective route to excellence. (Kaiser and Vossensteyn 2007, 177)

The contrast between Ontario and the Netherlands is striking. The Dutch have had an open discussion about programs for high-ability, high-engagement students and have implemented differentiated degree programs across the system, which nonetheless remains strongly egalitarian. Ontario has had no such open discussion and had little differentiation of degree programs, although honours programs and honours colleges could be easily introduced. There is a gap in the programs available to Ontario students: overall, Ontario students would be well served by the introduction of honours programs and honours colleges at our universities.

NOTES

1. Each of the themes is associated with the discourse of several, often many, authors. The following discussion of each theme cites one or two key sources.
2. Some faculties are not divided into departments, for example often business schools are not, but the fact that the undergraduate degree has a disciplinary focus still applies.
3. The GPA is not the sole criterion, but a high GPA is a necessary condition to be among the group who will be evaluated according to a wider set of criteria.
4. The CLA has its share of critics; the criticisms are presented and discussed in Arum and Roksa (2011).
5. HEQCO is also joining in a large international project, the Assessment of Higher Education Learning Outcomes (AHELO), being led by the OECD. Ontario's participation will focus on civil engineering degree programs.
6. And attempts by the government to provide extra funds for degree programs needed by the labour market have often had problems. The number of graduates expanded but all too soon there were more graduates than jobs. This was the case after expansion in computer science, nursing, and education.
7. It should be noted that in the US literature, the term "college" is usually used the way the term "university" is used in Canada.
8. The following three paragraphs are from Côté and Allahar (2011, 132).
9. Often when professors decide upon the assigned readings for each week (to be read before class, theoretically) they use the two-hour rule. There is an interesting reciprocity in the two-hour rule. In my own discussions with the best professors teaching undergraduate classes, they report that it takes two-hours of preparation for every hour in class (including developing the syllabus, preparing for class, seeing students, responding to emails, setting assignments, and marking).
10. New technologies actually require more out-of-class work than traditional instruction. Although the lectures are available online (and are watched before class), the students still have to read the syllabus. The outside-of-class time required for the truly flipped classroom is even greater with new technologies. Many commentators seem to forget that MOOCs still have a syllabus of readings.
11. The great dream is that online courses will reduce the cost of undergraduate education. It remains a dream. High-quality MOOCs are very expensive.
12. Colleges (Colleges Ontario 2012) have asked to be able to offer four-year honours degrees, and it seems that such degrees might be in the basic arts and sciences. Just as universities should halt their drift into pseudo-vocationalism, colleges should retain their focus on career-oriented education and should not be allowed to offer bachelor's degrees in the arts and sciences.
13. Indeed, none have departed in a significant way from the guidelines.
14. A properly designed liberal arts degree would not use the courses in each department that have been created to form the disciplinary degree.
15. Many students do not take a full load of courses each term and take longer than four years to complete their program. Also, many departments have two-semester courses. But the principles of the design of the degree are the same.

16. Several reviewers of Fallis (2007) felt, given its strong advocacy of liberal education and critique of the current situation, that the proposal for a liberal education minor was rather a damp squib. Alas, at most universities such squibs are too radically outside the norm to even conceive.

17. Most countries as they move to mass higher education, consider the role of elite institutions in a mass system. See Palfreyman and Tapper (2009): *Structuring Mass Higher Education: The Role of Elite Institutions.* But this has not been the case in Ontario.

Chapter 6

GRADUATE EDUCATION AND PROFESSIONAL EDUCATION

The focus in designing Ontario's system of higher education has been to provide increasing numbers of places in first-level higher education. But now, given that universal higher education has been achieved, more attention should shift to the analysis of graduate education and professional education. In Ontario, this upper-level higher education has developed in a somewhat ad hoc manner, layered on top of the structure built to deliver first-level higher education. An essential part of rethinking higher education in Ontario is to examine graduate education and professional education and to ask whether we have the best system in place for the years ahead.

The policy logic of first-level and upper-level higher education are very different.

First-level higher education has been built upon the fundamental principle that there should be a place for every qualified student who wishes to attend. Accessibility is paramount and the aspiration is to achieve universal higher education. In Ontario's binary system, this has meant that universities and colleges of applied arts and technology have been located in all regions of the province, that the different institutions in each sector are funded on the same basis, and that the different institutions in each sector offer a comprehensive range of quite similar programs of quite similar quality.

In contrast, upper-level higher education has a very different logic. Upper-level higher education requires a bachelor's degree for entry and it is assumed that the great majority of those who complete a bachelor's degree will not go on to upper-level higher education, either to graduate school or to professional school. For example, in 2008, Ontario universities awarded about 80,500 bachelor's degrees, compared to 14,500

Rethinking Higher Education: Participation, Research, and Differentiation, G. Fallis. Kingston: School of Policy Studies, Queen's University. © 2013 The School of Policy Studies, Queen's University at Kingston. All rights reserved.

master's degrees and 2,100 doctorates. Roughly, one in five graduating undergraduates goes on to a master's, and only one in six graduating master's students goes on to a doctorate. There will need to be far fewer upper-level places than first-level places in the system. Furthermore, these upper-level degrees are very focused, requiring study at an advanced level, and aim to recruit only the most accomplished students. Given that each upper-level degree program needs to have a critical mass of students, there will be a limited number of graduate degree programs and professional schools. Because of this very different policy logic, the questions for public policy regarding upper-level higher education are different: the first policy question is the same—how many places should there be—then the questions change: how many programs to have, how large should they be, and at which universities should they be located.

The issue of how many places is particularly important because upper-level education is much more expensive than undergraduate education. Upper-level education is provided through smaller classes and there is much more commitment of faculty time to student supervision, especially at the doctoral level. Upper-level education requires more library, computing, and information technology resources per student, and in the sciences better labs and equipment per student. In recognition of this higher cost, it receives more government support per student than undergraduate education. The MTCU operating grant in 2010-11 per master of arts student is $12,800 and per master of science student is $18,200 (compared to undergraduate of $5,800 and $8,500 respectively) and the operating grant per doctoral student is $29,000. Operating grants for professional programs like medicine and dentistry are $24,200 (Clark, Trick, and Van Loon 2011, 109). Upper-level higher education also receives more of the university's funds per student for financial assistance. Many graduate students receive tuition waivers and many doctoral students receive a very substantial financial support package.[1]

The policy logic of upper-level education then raises a fundamental question regarding system design: given that there will be a limited number of programs in each field, should all universities be able to offer master's degrees and doctoral degrees? Or should the system be differentiated as universities that offer bachelor's degrees, universities that offer bachelor's degrees through to master's degrees, and universities that offer bachelor's degrees, master's degrees and doctoral degrees?

The key policy issues around graduate education and professional education are quite similar in principle but are rather different in detail, so will be considered separately. Let us first consider graduate education.

HOW MANY PLACES?

Like first-level higher education, the starting policy question for graduate education is how many places should the government fund? And the main issues in the analysis are also the same. How large is the eligible group? How will their participation rate change? And what is the labour market demand for the graduates? But there are differences compared to the undergraduate analysis.

The eligible group is not based upon demography, but upon the number of bachelor's degrees awarded. And the eligible group is only the most accomplished of these graduates. In first-level higher education, a government funded place will almost always be filled[2]; but in upper-level education, it is not uncommon that a graduate program will not be able to meet its admission target—there were simply not enough highly accomplished applicants (other graduate programs are competing for these top students, perhaps with higher levels of financial assistance).[3]

The participation rate is difficult to forecast, but it has been trending upward for a long time, just as for first-level education.

Because there is no thought of universal education, because graduate school is costly for the government, for the university, and for the student in terms of income foregone, and because graduate programs are focused in a particular field, there is more emphasis on labour market demand in the discussions of graduate education. The question is often heard: should we be expanding graduate programs when there are no jobs for people in their field? But labour market demand in a field is notoriously difficult to forecast; indeed, many forecasts have proven to be quite wrong. Nonetheless, there is much more discussion of labour market issues, and on a field-by-field basis.

And in upper-level higher education, there is also the question of how many master's level places are needed and how many doctoral places are needed. In the case of master's programs, there is often the further issue of "applied" master's programs versus traditional programs.

A particular labour market question arises in the case of doctoral programs. Although only about one quarter to one third of doctoral graduates go on to become professors at a university, doctoral education is very oriented toward that end. On several occasions over the last twenty years, it has been predicted that there would be a large number of retirements among university professors and therefore that there would be a large demand for new doctorates. Unfortunately, on each occasion, the retirements occurred, but the restraints of university finances meant that many of the retirements were not replaced, and the demand for new doctorates was much below forecast. In recent years, we have again heard predictions about the coming wave of retirements, but university funding remains just as restrictive and will likely become tighter over the years ahead. In graduate programs today, there is recognition that most students will not become professors and that the programs should consider how the curriculum and requirements might be changed to better prepare students for non-university jobs.

Overall, there seems to be labour market demand for the upper-level graduates of Ontario universities. They have lower unemployment rates than those with bachelor's degrees and earn an income premium.

A recent examination of the number of upper-level places needed in Ontario's universities began in 2003. The undergraduate level was being expanded to accommodate the double cohort, the growing 18–21-year-old group, and rising participation rates. The number of bachelor's degrees awarded was rising and so the group eligible for graduate education would be growing. Much of the analysis and planning for undergraduate expansion was being done by a joint government-COU Working Group on University Capacity. The working group recognized that graduate expansion would follow undergraduate expansion, and so established a Task Force on Future Requirements for Graduate Education in Ontario. The task force asserted: "Employer demand for holders of master's and doctoral degrees exceeds the Canadian supply of graduates with these degrees, and this demand is growing. In response, the number of students available and wishing to meet that demand, by pursuing graduate education and earning advanced degrees, is also growing" (COU 2003, 1). The task force developed a projection of probable demand by estimating two components: the expanding number of eligible bachelor's degree graduates and the increasing participation rate. "The projected demand for graduate education in Ontario increases from approximately 11,200 master's intakes in 2002–03 to 22,000 in 2013–14; and from approximately 2,300 PhD intakes in 2002–03 to 4,700 in 2013–14. If this demand were responded to by matching increases in capacity, the graduate enrolment in Ontario universities would effectively double from 34,000 to 65,000 full-time equivalents over that period" (COU 2003, 1).

At about the same time, the Government of Ontario established the Task Force on Competitiveness, Productivity and Economic Progress with a mandate to conduct research on issues that would increase Ontario's competitiveness, productivity, and capacity for innovation. In its first annual report, *Closing the Prosperity Gap*, the task force identified postsecondary education as an important contributor to innovation and productivity. Ontario compared favourably to the United States in terms of investment in primary and secondary education and in postsecondary colleges. "At the university level, the pattern begins to change, and investment per student dips dramatically below US levels. While Ontario leads slightly in number of bachelor's degrees conferred per 1,000 population, the US leads dramatically at the master's level. Our US peer group continues the investment farther along the higher education spectrum than does Ontario, especially at the level of "terminal master's"—the final degree for the vast majority of its holders before they enter the economy to enhance productivity. The US also outproduces Ontario in conferring PhDs, though by a substantially lower margin" (Task Force on Competitiveness

2002, 33). It attributed some of Ontario's gap in productivity compared to the US to Ontario's underinvestment in graduate education.

These analyses were endorsed by the Rae Review, recommending that "the government should move to double the number of graduate students in Ontario to approximately 60,000 over ten years. To start the process, government should immediately establish a separate funding envelope for university graduate enrolment, providing full funding for planned growth in graduate studies. ... Funding under this initiative would be made available on a proposal basis, rather than by distribution formula. To be eligible for a share, a university would have to demonstrate that its proposal for graduate expansion advances its mission and plays to its areas of strength. It would have to demonstrate that the necessary capacity and supports are in place to sustain the expansion and provide a quality educational experience to graduate students" (Rae 2005, 87).

The McGuinty government's *Reaching Higher* plan for postsecondary education took up these recommendations announcing an expansion of graduate education by 12,000 full-time students by 2007–2008 and 14,000 students by 2009–2010. Due to fiscal challenges, the last stage of *Reaching Higher* was phased in over three years and completed in 2011–2012. The new graduate spaces were divided into separate allocations for master's places and doctoral places, and were allocated on a proposal basis as recommended by the Rae Review. Not surprisingly, as most universities wanted to grow at the graduate level as part of their strategic plan, the number of places requested by universities exceeded what the government was willing to fund. Considerable lobbying and jockeying followed until the available places were allocated to each university. As of 2011, 9,308 FTEs had been allocated at the master's level and 3,941 at the PhD level (Ontario. MTCU 2011). The allocations to each university are reported in Table 6.1 later in the chapter.

Thus, the first decade of the new millennium saw the Ontario university system grow enormously. Not only did it grow over 50 percent at the undergraduate level, but it grew by an even greater percentage at the graduate level. This was the largest expansion of graduate education in Ontario's history.

It is hard to determine whether this expansion was "enough" or "too much." Many universities had difficulty reaching their master's and PhD targets, both overall and in specific programs, although some universities exceeded their targets. Sometimes they would fall short at the master's level, but exceed at the PhD level. The ministry is now working with institutions to facilitate reassignment of allocations by level. Unfortunately, there has been little analysis, certainly almost no publicly available analysis, of the results of this massive expansion of graduate education.

The tenth annual report of the Task Force on Competitiveness, Productivity and Economic Progress, *Prospects for Ontario's Prosperity: A look back and a look ahead,* reported that the gap between Ontario and the United States in master's degrees per 1,000 of population had widened (Task Force on Competitiveness 2011, 37). And if one were to follow the methodology used by the Council of Ontario Universities task force in 2003, examining the growing number of bachelor's graduates and the upward trend in participation, the projections would see a further increase in demand.

Perhaps following this analysis, in July 2011, the government announced a commitment to a further 6,000 graduate spaces by 2015–2016.[4] COU (2012b) in its *Position paper on Graduate Education in Ontario* welcomed this expansion and recommended even more growth.

On balance, the projections of increased demand for graduate education over the next ten years are likely sound. However, given the very uneven success in meeting the allocations over the past five years—uneven success by university, by master's versus doctoral level, and by field—a pause to carefully calibrate the needs, by university and by program is in order. There is no need to push immediately for this graduate growth.

The first step in rethinking upper-level higher education is to pause in the planned growth and take the opportunity to properly assess the very rapid expansion over the last decade.

I would argue that this pause is warranted regardless of any government funding restraint. However, the argument is even stronger given the budget constraint. (See further discussion in the Epilogue.) If government expenditures are to increase at 1.5 percent per year on universities, expanding graduate education by 6,000 places by 2015–2016 will eat up most of the increase and require cuts in other areas of university activities, including undergraduate education. This surely is not the best outcome; the top priority during restraint should be to protect undergraduate education.

HOW MANY PROGRAMS AND AT WHICH UNIVERSITIES?

Given the number of places to be funded in graduate education, the questions then become: how many programs should there be in each field, how large should each program be, and at which universities?

Chapter 1 described the Ontario system of higher education and examined how universities were differentiated currently with respect to graduate education (Table 1.5), noting how the system could be classified using the Statistics Canada classification system into medical-doctoral, comprehensive, primarily undergraduate universities, and special purpose universities. Chapter 2 considered the Carnegie classification system and, following that approach, showed that Ontario universities could be divided into two groups: doctoral/research universities and master's/ bachelor's universities.

Using the total number of graduate students as the measure, every Ontario university had some graduate education in 2009, with the exception of Algoma, the very small, special purpose, university. There were quite significant differences in the amount of graduate education, with University of Toronto having the largest by a considerable margin, but even several of the primarily undergraduate universities had quite a large number of master's students, notably Ryerson, Laurier, and Brock. There was more significant differentiation at the doctoral level. Three universities had none and the remaining primarily undergraduate universities had quite low levels; 96 percent of the doctoral students were at the medical-doctoral and comprehensive universities.

In thinking about graduate education, there is a crucial distinction to be made between master's programs and doctoral programs. Master's programs last one or two years and are largely based upon course work (although some require a major research paper or thesis). Doctoral programs last four to six years and are based on a combination of course work and the dissertation—a major piece of independent research. The aspiration is that the work of the dissertation would be of sufficient originality and quality to warrant publication in the academic literature. Thus, doctoral education is both training to become a researcher and a period of working on original research.

Many countries refer to doctoral programs as "research degrees" and count the time of doctoral students on their work as part of the research activity at the university. In addition, the time of the professors spent on supervising doctoral students is also counted as part of the research activity of the university, just as the time spent on supervising a research team funded under a research grant is counted as part of the research activity. This is the approach used by the OECD when it asks countries to report the amount of research done in the university sector: the work on the dissertation and the supervision of the doctoral students are counted as part of total research in a country (OECD 2002).

Thus, doctoral education is far more connected to the research mission of the university than is master's education (or undergraduate education).

This connection is recognized in the classification systems of universities. When classification systems of universities are developed, the main categories are usually based upon the degrees awarded—only bachelor's degrees, bachelor's and master's degrees, and bachelor's through to doctoral degrees. Those universities awarding through to the doctoral degrees are then further divided into those that are particularly intensely involved with doctoral education and with research. This doctoral intensity is measured by the number of doctorates awarded annually and by the number of fields where doctorates are awarded. The research intensity is usually measured by the value of research grants and contracts secured by the university. Universities with a particularly intense commitment to doctoral education and research are called doctoral/research universities.[5]

This raises the central policy question for differentiation in the Ontario university system. All universities will award bachelor's degrees, and likely all will award master's degrees. But should all universities award doctoral degrees? After all, there will be a limited number of programs in each discipline—there will be far fewer programs than the total number of universities. The key policy design question is whether it is better to have all universities engaged in doctoral programming, with many universities having relatively few programs, or should a subgroup of universities be given the mandate for doctoral programming? Will concentrating doctoral programs in certain universities lead to higher quality doctoral programs? Given the close connections between doctoral education and research, we cannot properly and fully answer these questions without also examining the research mission of the university. The research mission is analyzed in Chapters 7 and 8, and therefore this question of system differentiation will not be fully analyzed until Chapter 9. However looking ahead, in Chapter 9 it is recommended that Ontario universities should be divided into two groups: doctoral/research universities and master's/bachelor's universities.

Many jurisdictions differentiate their universities into those that can offer degrees all the way to the doctorate and those that can offer only bachelor's and master's degrees. California's higher education system is the quintessential example: made up of the University of California, the California State Colleges (now the California State University system), and California Community Colleges system. Only the University of California can offer doctoral degrees. The California State Universities can offer bachelor's and master's degrees. Obviously, this was never part of the design of Ontario's system. But nevertheless it was frequently talked about and sometimes proposed by official studies.

Planning for expansion at the graduate level began in the 1960s not long after the actual expansion had begun to accommodate the baby boom at the undergraduate level. The Committee of Presidents of the Universities of Ontario (CPUO)[6] accorded graduate planning a high priority, recognizing the growing demand for professors to staff the expanding university system and the growing demand for people with advanced degrees from outside the university. "CPUO recognized that the high cost of graduate programming placed heavy responsibilities on the universities to plan carefully and to coordinate their efforts" (Monahan 2004, 29). In 1964, the deans of graduate studies began to meet as the Advisory Committee on Graduate Studies, which soon became the permanent body, the Ontario Council on Graduate Studies.

In 1965, CPUO commissioned a study of graduate education in Ontario headed by John Spinks, president of the University of Saskatchewan. "The report of the commission, the first major initiative in Ontario system planning, was keenly anticipated. When it came, it produced a shock. Nothing if not forthright, it described a province with fourteen fully chartered, autonomous universities free to declare their own objectives and to develop programs without regard or reference to their neighbours or to the needs of the province" (Monahan 2004, 29). The Spinks Commission argued that there needed to be a strong coordinating agency to plan and oversee the development of graduate education. But it went much beyond this. It recommended the establishment of a University of Ontario, an Ontario Universities Research Council, and a strong central coordinating agency. No doubt, the commission had been influenced by the California Master Plan for higher education.

The Ontario universities rejected the recommendation unanimously. And thereafter, although there have been several attempts, Ontario universities successfully resisted any initiative to differentiate universities by the amount of graduate programming offered, or even by the amount of doctoral programming offered.

Following the rejection of the main recommendation of the Spinks Commission for a University of Ontario and a strong central coordinating body for graduate programming, the presidents were anxious to show their commitment to greater planning and coordination. "The new Ontario Council of Graduate Studies (OCGS) agreed with the view of the Spinks Commission that all Ontario universities should move toward the development of honours and master's programs in the central academic disciplines (though not necessarily all of them) and that doctoral programs ought to be restricted to a smaller list of institutions where adequate funds and facilities are available. It was also agreed that the province should equip itself with an authorization procedure for doctoral programs. So too did CPUO. OCGS then developed a procedure for the peer evaluation of graduate programs—the appraisals process" (Monahan 2004, 31). By 1969, all Ontario universities agreed to submit all new graduate programs to the Appraisals Committee of OCGS for assessment as to their academic quality.

The appraisals process was not intended to be a vehicle for system-wide planning of graduate education—the focus of the assessment was academic quality. OCGS resisted any attempt to connect the process with the availability of funding, or with the decision of what programs might be funded out of a limited budget. A different process was developed for system-wide planning—the discipline assessment process. The chair of CPUO declared "this may well be the most important business the universities have attempted together," acknowledging that "the process of co-operation would not be painless and would require all universities to pass self-denying ordinances and curb their aspirations in some directions" (Principal Corry of Queen's University as quoted in Monahan 2004, 33).

A discipline assessment process was the correct and logical way to approach system-wide graduate planning. The graduate programs in a discipline, both master's and doctoral, would be assessed together, at the same time. The demand for graduates in that discipline could be examined and the relative strengths of the programs, across all universities, could be evaluated including whether each program had sufficient critical mass to provide a high quality graduate student experience. There could then be recommendations to expand or contract the overall level of programming in that discipline in the province, and there could be recommendations to expand or contract the intake at each university. And perhaps, as some expanded, others would have to be closed down.

Despite acknowledging the need for system-wide planning at the graduate level, progress was very slow in establishing the discipline assessment process. Impatient with the delays, the government placed an embargo of the approval of new graduate programs in 1970. And when discipline assessments were completed, the results were very controversial.

The first major attempt at system-wide planning dealt with engineering, and went beyond graduate education, to include a comprehensive examination of all engineering education. In 1969, a special commission was struck, with the approval of the university presidents, the deans of engineering and the government. The 1970s were a time of slowing economic growth and pressure on government budgets, both reinforcing the need for careful planning of the system. The commission was chaired by Philip Lapp, an engineer from the private sector with experience on university boards, and its report was titled *Ring of Iron*. The core conclusion of the report was that there needed to be a comprehensively planned system of engineering education, limiting the number of engineering schools and setting enrolment quotas for bachelor's, master's and doctoral programs at each university. Total enrolments were to be set by the demand for engineering graduates; and the enrolment quotas at each institution were to be based upon quality assessments, the need for critical mass in each program, and the reasonable balance between undergraduate and graduate education at each university.

The Lapp report asked all the right questions and identified the right issues to be addressed in system-wide planning by discipline. Unfortunately, the answers were not popular. *Ring of Iron* concluded that the system had enough capacity until at least 1975 and that no new engineering school be established until at least 1980. It recommended reducing the size of the largest schools (Toronto and Waterloo) in order to let the smaller schools expand, and recommended cancellation of a two-year program at Laurentian University. Most controversially, it concluded that existing graduate programs would produce too many graduates and that there needed to be a reduction of 17 percent. The

Council of Ontario Universities did not endorse the report and most of its tough recommendations were delayed or ignored.

The discipline appraisals similarly asked the right questions, but again, the answers were not well received. The appraisals sometimes offered unexpectedly harsh judgments. For example, the chemistry appraisal found five programs to be academically substandard and recommended they be discontinued. Often, the academic assessment was based upon a judgment regarding the critical size of a program needed to ensure quality—a highly controversial proposition. Also, forecasts of labour market demands were controversial. Few of the difficult recommendations of the discipline assessment process were implemented and by the end of the 1970s it had been largely abandoned as a means to planning graduate education across the province.

But nothing took its place. Ontario ducked the tough questions. However, they need to be addressed. This reinforces the conclusion that further growth of graduate education be postponed until the recent huge expansion has been properly assessed.

This experience of attempts at system-wide graduate planning by discipline in Ontario offers a number of lessons. The first is that although, in principle, the questions to be addressed are clear, in practice the analysis is very controversial. One should ask: what will be the demand for graduates of these programs? But labour market forecasts are notoriously inaccurate and many graduates find rewarding work outside their notional field. One should ask: what is the critical mass of faculty members and students needed to provide a high quality program? Some will set the level quite high, especially the larger universities citing as evidence the large graduate programs in leading universities in other countries; others will set the level quite low, especially the smaller universities, choosing to look at the evidence related to each specific proposal for a new program. And one should ask, beyond the decisions about each discipline: should the Ontario system be differentiated by those universities that offer degrees all the way to the doctorate with those that offer only bachelor's and master's degrees. This question has hovered in the background but never been directly addressed since the Spinks Commission in 1966.

The other lesson is that all universities, regardless of their current focus or being classified as primarily undergraduate, want to expand at the graduate level and will resist any initiative to limit their scope to expand. The forces of isomorphism are very strong—universities all aspire to the same model—they model themselves after universities that they perceive to be successful: the great doctoral research universities of the world.[7] Faculty members have this model as well as the senior administration. The Council of Ontario Universities is the collective voice of Ontario universities, and adopts positions by "consensus" among the very different institutions. Although some larger universities might favour differentiation according to doctoral programming, this will not be a consensus position, and will not be recommended by COU. Edward Monahan, writing a history of the Council of Ontario Universities from 1962 to 2000, aptly titled it: *Collective Autonomy* (Monahan 2004). Any initiative for differentiation will have to come from outside COU.

During the experience of the 1970s, there was a buffer body between government and COU called the Ontario Council on University Affairs (OCUA). It was responsible for analyzing system-wide issues and providing advice to the minister on university affairs. OCUA was the source of much of the pressure to undertake system-wide graduate planning, but was ultimately unsuccessful. Today, there is no buffer between COU (the universities collectively) and the government. The only locus for an initiative to examine graduate education across the province and to consider differentiating universities according to the amount of graduate education is government itself.

THE RECENT GRADUATE EXPANSION

Graduate education at Ontario universities has expanded very rapidly over the past fifteen years, just as undergraduate education has done. After a period of level enrolments during the early and mid 1990s, graduate enrolments began to increase. In the decade from 1998 to 2008, master's enrolments rose almost 60 percent and doctoral enrolments rose over 70 percent (CAGS 2006 and 2012).

This growth began well before the Rae Review and the *Reaching Higher* plan, but these gave more formal expression to the plans for growth from 2005 onwards.

The *Reaching Higher* plan provided operating funds[8] for expansion of master's education and doctoral education, in total about 13,250 FTEs over 2004–2005. This was a major expansion, conceptualized at one time, and offered a rare opportunity to differentiate the universities of the Ontario system. Broadly speaking, there are two approaches that could have been taken to differentiation during this expansion.

The first is the approach explored during the 1970s, from the Spinks Commission onwards. All universities would offer bachelor's degrees and master's degrees, but doctoral programs would only be offered by a smaller group of universities. After this two-part differentiation, universities could differentiate themselves by the specific degree programs offered. But especially at the master's level, all universities would offer degrees across the core arts and sciences. The development of degree programs would be constrained by an overall plan for graduate education by discipline—the overall plan would determine the number of places for each discipline (at the master's and doctoral level), the size and number of programs, and at which universities the programs would be located.

The second approach allows all universities to offer degrees at all levels. Each university would develop its own strategic plan for graduate development. The available new places would be allocated under a proposal process: each university would submit proposals, showing how they were consistent with their strategic plan, and that they had the resources to provide the programs (assuming the new government money) at good quality. Differentiation would emerge out of the planning process at each university.

The second approach was followed under the *Reaching Higher* plan, as recommended by the Rae Review. Under such a proposal process, there would need to be some criteria provided by the government to be used to select from among all the proposals. Under the *Reaching Higher* allocation process, these criteria were never made especially clear, although there was a declared preference for applied programs especially in the STEM disciplines (science, technology, engineering and mathematics).

The results of the *Reaching Higher* allocation process are presented in Table 6.1, showing the FTE allocation by university and the percentage increase over 2003 enrolments. The patterns are complex, resulting both from the strategic planning at each university and the government's selection of proposals. However, overall, using the measure of the amount of graduate education and the number of degrees offered, the Ontario university system became less differentiated as a result of the *Reaching Higher* allocations.

Two of the three universities that offered no graduate education in 2004—UOIT and OCAD—began to offer graduate degrees. If we consider the Statistics Canada classification into doctoral/research universities (the medical-doctoral and comprehensive groups) and primarily undergraduate universities, there was no clear preference for expanding graduate education at the doctoral/research universities. Indeed, the primarily undergraduate universities tended to receive above average growth allocations in doctoral education. This was part of their strategic plan and the government decision supported it. Among the primarily undergraduate universities, Ryerson had the greatest increase in graduate education, truly transformative, reflecting both its aspirations and perhaps the government's preference for applied programs. Among the doctoral/research universities, some had below average allocations at the master's level, likely reflecting their own strategic plans. At the doctoral level, some doctoral/research universities—Western and McMaster—expanded at well above the average rate; while some—Queen's, Carleton, and Windsor—received allocations well below the average. The University of Toronto, that has the largest graduate programming at both the master's and doctoral levels by a considerable margin, received below average allocations at both levels; it relative dominance was diminished.[9]

TABLE 6.1
Reaching Higher Graduate Allocations

	Doctoral Students 2008	Doctoral Allocation	Percentage Increase	Master's Students 2008	Master's Allocation	Percentage Increase
Toronto	5,514	1,103	18	8,367	1,709	20
York	1,689	379	22	4,089	760	19
Western	1,677	557	33	3,180	620	19
Waterloo	1,530	373	24	2,373	822	35
Ottawa	1,443	379	26	3,516	1,018	29
McMaster	1,233	458	37	2,076	688	33
Queen's	1,170	157	13	2,367	645	27
Carleton	927	113	12	2,475	459	19
Guelph	789	141	18	1,584	421	27
Windsor	360	30	8	1,278	199	16
Ryerson	198	143	72	1,767	972	55
Laurier	162	37	23	1,188	222	19
Trent	105	20	19	282	97	34
Laurentian	96	71	71	603	79	13
Brock	90	18	20	1,326	164	12
Lakehead	75	44	59	549	217	40
Nipissing	—	—	—	300	51	17
UOIT	—	8	—	159	149	94
OCAD	—	—	—	24	16	67
Algoma	—	—	—	—	—	—
Entire System	**17,058**	**3,941**	**23**	**37,503**	**9,308**	**25**

Sources: Graduate enrolments (CAGS 2012); Reaching Higher allocations (Ontario. MTCU 2011).

A large number of new graduate programs were established under the *Reaching Higher* funding and existing programs were expanded. Enrolments in three broad fields of study increased very rapidly—in health, parks, recreation and fitness; in architecture, engineering, and related technologies; and in visual and performing arts and communication technologies—and in two others the growth was well above average growth—in mathematics, computer and information sciences; and in social and behavioral sciences and law. Physics and life sciences grew at the average; while humanities and business, management, and public administration were well below average. (See Wiggers, Lennon, and Frank 2011 for greater detail.) From these enrolment data, it is difficult to discern whether graduate education shifted significantly into applied programs, especially in the STEM disciplines. With the establishment of new degree programs, the universities in Ontario may have become more differentiated in terms of the topics of the degree programs offered, but the available data do not allow this to be investigated.

One is left with the conclusion that the recent expansion of graduate education has reduced the differentiation among Ontario universities.

PROFESSIONAL EDUCATION

Chapter 1 documented the differentiation of Ontario universities, according to professional education, focusing on medical schools and law schools.

The incorporation of upper-level professional programs into a system of higher education confronts the same two basic questions as the incorporation of graduate education. The first is how many programs are needed? There are always fewer programs needed than there are universities. And so the second question becomes: at which university should the program be located? As the questions are answered, universities become differentiated according to their professional programs.

Let us use the example of medical schools to explore these questions. The answers come in part from history. Medical schools have been part of universities since the nineteenth century and thus medical schools tend to be at the older universities—Toronto, Queen's, Ottawa, Western, and McMaster. The overall system, as it moved to mass and to near-universal higher education, grew far faster than the need for medical doctors. And therefore, many newer universities do not have medical schools. It is a complex and politically fraught question to specify how many medical places are needed in the system. Many years ago, the number of places was cut back, as a way of trying to control health expenditures, but not long after, there seemed to be too few doctors, especially family practitioners, and the worry became that people did not have direct access to this primary care. About ten years ago, Ontario decided that it needed more places—but where to put a new school? York University wants to have a medical school, but most existing medical schools favour increasing the number of places by expanding existing schools, often through satellite campuses. Ontario decided to expand existing medical schools, let them establish satellite locations, and that a new medical school should go in the North. The North has trouble attracting and retaining doctors, and the government believed that a school in the North would be more likely to graduate doctors who wished to remain and practice there.

The six law schools in Ontario are at Toronto, Ottawa, Western, Queen's, York, and Windsor. Again, most, but not all, are at the old universities, and as the university system grew far faster than the need for lawyers, most newer universities do not have a law school. Following the pattern of choosing the North for a new medical school, Ontario announced a new law school at Lakehead University to open in 2013.

The other upper-level professional programs have many fewer programs: dentistry (Toronto, Western), optometry (Waterloo), pharmacy (Toronto, Waterloo), occupational therapy (Toronto, Queen's, McMaster, Western), and physiotherapy (McMaster, Queen's, Toronto, Western), physician's assistant (Toronto), primary health care nurse practitioner (Lakehead, McMaster, Queen's, Windsor), speech-language pathology/

audiology (Toronto, Western), and veterinary medicine (Guelph). Most of these programs are in health-related areas and tend to be at universities with a medical school. There clearly is a cluster of programs that grow up around a medical school; part of the reason why a medical school is such a defining feature of a university.

Although the questions to be addressed in professional education are the same as in graduate education, the government has taken a very different approach. For professional education, there has been strong central control of the number of universities able to offer the professional programs, whatever the strategic aspirations of individual universities. No doubt, this is partly due to the fact that the professional associations (made up of the practicing professionals) are very involved with university programs and do not wish to see the total number of places expanded. Also, professional programs are very expensive and so the government looks very carefully before expanding the number of programs (although, doctoral programs are just as expensive and the government has exercised much less control).

Overall, the Ontario system remains quite differentiated by professional education, especially by law schools and by medical schools (and the cluster of related medical professional programs).

LOOKING AHEAD

The experience of the growth of graduate education in recent years and the attempts at system-wide planning leaves several dilemmas.

The government has indicated that it is interested in exploring greater differentiation across universities. HEQCO has advocated greater differentiation (Weingarten and Deller 2010) and the Drummond Report (Commission on the Reform of Ontario's Public Services 2012) has as well. Yet, one of the most widely used means to differentiate universities, by the degrees offered and by the relative emphasis on doctoral education, has been abandoned or ignored. The government seems to have no desire or political will to differentiate the system on this basis.

The recent experience demonstrated clearly that all universities, even and perhaps most of all the primarily undergraduate universities, want to expand at the graduate level. It is a high strategic priority. COU (2012b) recommends that graduate expansion should benefit all universities and that funding for spaces should be fungible across master's and doctoral programs. This is troubling because, as Chapter 5 examining undergraduate education pointed out, a pervasive concern is that undergraduate education is a low priority and does not receive the attention and resources it needs. If we allow universities to make their own strategic plans with a high priority to graduate education and research and if we retain the strong deference to institutional autonomy, how can undergraduate education become a higher priority?

As noted earlier in this chapter, graduate education and research are closely connected and a proper analysis of differentiation cannot be conducted without examining research. The research analysis follows in the next two chapters. Among other things, the research analysis explores the issues of international competition and rankings of universities and raises the policy question of how Ontario universities compare to world-leading universities. And with such comparisons, the question arises whether Ontario wishes within its system of universities to have one (or several) world-leading universities or at least to have world-leading centres of research at its universities.

In the development of graduate education in Ontario, the issues of international competition and international benchmarking have been notably absent. Does Ontario wish to have graduate programs that are comparable to the best in the world? Does Ontario wish to have doctoral programs that will attract top international students? These questions, regrettably, have not been part of the discourse as graduate education expanded over recent years. But if Ontario aspires to have world-leading research centres, it must aspire to have world-leading doctoral programs.

NOTES

1. Financial support for graduate students usually also includes money received for helping to provide undergraduate education; for example, being a teaching assistant, marker/grader, tutorial leader, or lab assistant. This money is payment for doing a job; it is an employment relationship and should not be considered to be the same as financial assistance. The university would have to pay this money anyway to provide undergraduate education, if not to graduate students, then to part-time faculty.
2. There have been occasions when universities, especially in the North, have not met their enrolment targets. With the decline in the 18–21-year-old group, this will be more common.
3. Another difference in defining the eligible group is that graduate programs are more likely to recruit students from other provinces and from other countries.
4. This graduate expansion was to be included within the commitment to expand the system by 60,000 places (Ontario. MTCU 2011).
5. These classification systems were discussed in Chapter 2 and are discussed again in the context of research in Chapters 7 and 8.
6. The Committee of Presidents of the Universities of Ontario was the precursor to the Council of Ontario Universities.
7. See the discussion of isomorphism and the conjectures of DiMaggio and Powell (1983) in Chapter 3.
8. Capital grants were also provided.
9. Using a different database, Wiggers, Lennon, and Frank (2011) reports patterns similar to those identified in this paragraph.

Chapter 7

THE NEW RESEARCH AGENDA

Ontario's system of higher education has two basic missions: teaching and research.

Previous chapters have examined the teaching mission, at both the undergraduate and graduate levels, and asked whether we have the best system for the years ahead. The focus of these next two chapters is to analyze the research mission and to ask whether we have the higher education system best designed to support research. Because the research mission is at present the responsibility of the university sector, the discussion will be mainly about universities. However, the colleges have an important emerging role in applied research and this will be analysed as well.

The research mission is deeply imbedded in the university, and indeed I, like most scholars of higher education, would argue that a necessary characteristic of a university is that its professors have the responsibility both to teach and to conduct research.[1] The academic freedom that professors enjoy, and the institutional autonomy that universities enjoy, are both justified in large measure as necessary to ensure that the research mission can be best fulfilled. The pursuit of new knowledge and the critical reflection upon existing knowledge—tasks that society values and is willing to support through government funding—are best undertaken, rather paradoxically, in autonomous institutions whose professors have academic freedom.[2]

FROM THE POSTWAR MODEL TO THE NEW RESEARCH AGENDA

It was not, of course, always the case that professors both teach and conduct research. It was only in the late nineteenth century and early twentieth century that research became a responsibility of professors at universities in England and the United States. It was at this same time that graduate education was added to universities. This bringing together of undergraduate education, graduate education, and research in one institution defines the modern university. In Canada, graduate education did not become very significant until the early postwar period and it was not until then that research began to be considered a significant responsibility of all professors.

The involvement of Canadian governments with research began with the establishment of the National Research Council (NRC) in 1916. The government's strategy at this time was to support research in this national institution, rather than in universities. The NRC offered advice to government on science and technology, funded fellowships at Canadian universities, and conducted its own research, principally industrial and applied research. During the Second World War, the NRC expanded significantly, working on diverse projects from weapons and synthetic fuels, to food packaging and medicines. After the war, it began to support universities more extensively and established the principle that its external grants would match its internal budget. Gradually however, the strategy of the government shifted toward supporting research at universities. Three separate agencies were established to award research grants to universities (and hospital research centres). The Medical Research Council (MRC) was founded in 1966, and the Natural Sciences and Engineering Research Council (NSERC) was formed in 1978; both functions had previously existed as committees of the National Research Council. The Canada Council (for the encouragement of the arts, letters, humanities and social sciences) had been established in 1957, following the recommendations of the Massey Commission. In 1978, the Social Sciences and Humanities Research Council (SSHRC) was spun off as a separate entity.[3] These three agencies are now often referred to as the "national granting councils" or the "tri-councils."

In the postwar model, most of the external funding for university research in Ontario came from the national granting councils—the Medical Research Council,[4] the Natural Sciences and Engineering Research Council, and the Social Sciences and Humanities Research Council. Each council had many programs, but the core program of all councils made grants to support research, without restriction as to topic. Researchers would submit applications which were judged by academic peers in that field on the basis of the academic merit of the project and the track record of the applicant. Often, these grants are said to support basic, curiosity-driven, research. Certainly many such grants support basic research—that is, research seeking fundamental understanding with no special concern for its applicability. But many of these grants support very applied research—for example a psychology professor might be supported to examine the causes of adolescent bullying and to evaluate possible government programs to reduce bullying, or a biology professor might be supported to analyze the epigenetic mechanisms causing a certain type of cancer and to investigate the genetic markers that might lead to its early detection. Many professors, indeed I would conjecture most professors, are interested in basic research, but have a strong interest in its applicability as well.

The main point about these core programs of the granting councils is not that they only supported basic research; it is rather that they accepted the proposals on topics submitted by the applicants and the proposals were peer reviewed using academic criteria. The grants were not targeted at any topic; and the selection criteria were not biased in favour of applied work, indeed they were likely biased toward basic research because academic criteria usually rank basic research findings more highly. Furthermore, strong support was available across all the disciplines: of science, medicine, engineering, the humanities, and the social sciences. Available funding per discipline varied considerably, but the intent and the practice was to offer strong support to all disciplines through the curiosity-based programs of the three granting councils.

Across the three councils, these core programs had another important feature: the grants provided funds to support graduate students who would work on the research project. Particularly in the NSERC and MRC disciplines, the hiring of graduate students is necessary to conduct the research, and this involvement is an important part of their graduate training. Across all fields, the council grants provide an important component of the financial support available to graduate students while they complete their degrees. The tri-council grants thus support both research itself and the training of the next generation of advanced researchers.

University research was also supported by the operating funds of universities, which came from provincial government operating grants and tuition fees. It was these operating funds that financed the hiring of professors who had the responsibility, and therefore the time, to do research. Operating funds also helped to finance the libraries, labs, and computer systems needed for the research. (Of course, these libraries, labs, and computer systems are also needed for the teaching mission of universities.)

This, then, was the postwar model of support for research: professors were hired to do both teaching and research, and the professors could apply to the three national granting councils to obtain further support for their research. Only universities had the mandate for research. The core programs of the councils supported curiosity-based research, without restriction as to topic, allocated on the basis of academic criteria as assessed by peers in the field of research.

This postwar research model introduces an important new dimension in understanding how governments in Canada shape higher education. The previous chapters of the book have emphasized the role of the provincial government in shaping and financing the higher education system. And the provincial government is pre-eminent; recognizing that education is a provincial responsibility under the constitution. The provincial governments establish the institutions and provide the operating grants. But, the federal government has always had an important, though indirect, role in financing the operations of higher education institutions. Since the 1960s when provincial higher education systems began to expand, the federal government has provided transfer payments to help with the costs of higher education; this support is now part of the Canada Social Transfer. The design and operation of the higher education systems were provincial responsibilities and this federal support was quite indirect and carried no conditions. However, the federal government does directly shape the system with respect to research through the national granting councils.

Beginning in the 1990s, on top of this postwar model was layered a suite of new programs, revealing a new research agenda. And again, the federal government was the leader.

The role of research at Ontario universities had grown continuously over the postwar period, but the truly transforming change to the university's research mission came in the mid 1990s, as Canada struggled to respond to the turbulence of globalization and rapid technological change.

Economic globalization is a defining characteristic of our age: there is greater economic interconnection—greater mobility of goods, services, capital, people, and ideas. Since the late 1980s, there has been a great transformation in how economies are organized and how they connect to one another. Many countries—across Eastern Europe and the former Soviet Union, and across the developing world most especially China and India—shifted from heavily managed economies, relying on planned investment and state ownership, with state-regulated prices and high tariffs, to a more market-oriented and outward-looking system. Many developing countries, particularly China and India, but also Brazil and Indonesia, are growing rapidly; the goods and services they produce now compete with those produced in the developed world.

Also, our age is a period of extraordinarily rapid technological change; most notably in computing, communication, and information technologies. Many of these technological changes in computing and communications made possible and sped up the processes of globalization. Technological change in other fields—genetics and biomedical sciences, in materials science and nanotechnology—may be similarly transforming.

In this era of globalization and rapid technological change, most developed countries, and indeed many developing countries, believe that their future economic prosperity will depend upon creativity, research, and innovation. This is not to say that the traditional factors crucial to economic well-being—access to raw materials, abundant sources of energy, a sound financial system, transportation infrastructure, high levels of investment, a skilled workforce—are no longer important. These remain. But to the list, and near the top of the list, has been added the need for new knowledge: new ideas and new ways of doing things. In this new economy, countries need two things: (i) highly skilled, creative *people* and (ii) *research* generating new knowledge, new ideas, and new ways of doing things.

And of course, universities supply both.

Over the last fifteen years, governments have funded new places to allow a more than 50 percent increase in university enrolments, an extraordinary expansion. But, the new commitments to university research have been much greater. Government support of university research has grown at an astonishing rate: the federal government's funding for university research rose by four times, and the Ontario funding tripled. Just when the teaching activities of the universities were expanding rapidly, the research activities were expanding as well, and at an even more rapid rate. This great expansion of research support is one of the most fundamental forces shaping universities today.

But the important change was not just the increase in support through the usual channels. The budgets of the granting councils did increase significantly over the last fifteen years, but the great expansion of support for university research occurred through a suite of new initiatives at both the federal and provincial levels. These initiatives were supported explicitly because of the applications the new knowledge would bring, most especially because of the contributions to the economy. The new research funds were targeted at topics and disciplines, especially in science, technology, engineering, and medicine, that were thought most likely to yield economic benefits. There was a particular emphasis on research in medicine and biomedical science that offered the double promise of improvements in health and economic benefit. Under the new research agenda, the research findings should be commercialized. And furthermore the university should take on a new explicit responsibility: to encourage and manage the application and commercialization of its research. It is no longer sufficient for universities to presume that academic research will eventually yield benefits to society; now universities must actively work to see that it happens.

This agenda is a radical change. One study, *Capitalizing Knowledge: New Intersections of Industry and Academia*, argues it is so radical as to constitute an academic revolution. "The academic revolution of the late nineteenth and early twentieth centuries introduced the research mission into an institution hitherto devoted to the conservation and transmission of knowledge. ... Building upon the first revolution, the second academic revolution is the translation of research findings into intellectual property, a marketable commodity, and economic development" (Etzkowitz and Webster 1998, 21).

The emergence of this new research agenda in Canada was been eloquently set out in three Killam Lectures given by former university presidents in 2000, 2001, and 2003. The Killam Lectures are endowed by one of the largest benefactions to Canadian higher education through the estates of Izaak Walton Killam and Dorothy Brooks Killam. Mrs. Killam's will stated: "My purpose in establishing the Killam Trusts is to help in building of Canada's future by encouraging advanced study. Thereby I hope, in some measure to increase the scientific and scholastic attainments of Canadians, to develop and expand the work of Canadian universities, and to promote sympathetic understanding between Canadians and peoples of other countries" (Killam Trusts 2012). The Killam Lecture is delivered annually at the conference of the Canadian Association of Graduate Studies; the objective of the lecture is to stimulate support for university research.

The 2000 lecture was given by Robert Prichard president emeritus of the University of Toronto. Prichard set out the broad patterns of federal support for universities and how they evolved over the postwar period, paying particular attention to the shifting strategies and tensions in federal-provincial relations and the role of federal-provincial transfers; education was a provincial responsibility but the federal government has always been the leader in supporting research. In the mid 1990s, the federal approach changed, shifting away from transfer payments and from the granting councils.

> The new federal approach had a different centre of gravity: research, in-novation, ideas, productivity and growth. The concerns of the new global economy took centre stage: Canada's disappointing record of productivity growth compared to the United States, Canada's relative underinvestment of research and development, the loss of highly skilled personnel to the United States, the growing importance of intellectual capital and intel-lectual property, and the growing pressures of the knowledge economy all demanded attention.

> These concerns led to a new policy consensus: that the pre-eminent federal concern with respect to higher education should be research and innovation and that major new investments were required if Canada were to compete successfully in the global economy. And beginning with the federal budget in February, 1997, the government committed significant new resources to this agenda. (Prichard 2000, 20)

The 2001 lecture, delivered by John Evans, also president emeritus of the University of Toronto was titled: "Higher Education in the Higher Education Economy: Towards a Public Research Contract." He focused upon the economy and the role of university research, declaring that "we live now live in a world in which the organized ability to create and commercialize new ideas is the crucial determinant of economic success" (Evans 2001, 8). The thesis of his analysis was that the increase in support for university research was on fundamentally new terms, what he called the Public Research Contract. "The Contract is between governments and universities. It involves longer-term commitments by both parties. For government it is a much higher level of investment than previously provided to Canadian universities for their traditional role in the creation and transmission of knowledge. For universities the commitment is to economic and social return on public investment, and particularly jobs and wealth created in Canada. It entails new levels accountability to perform at international standards of excellence, to use efficiently substantial public funds, and to promote commercialization of the resulting intellectual property" (Evans 2001, 10).

The 2002 lecture, delivered by Martha Piper, president of the University of British Columbia, was titled: "Building Civil Society: A New Role for the Human Sciences." She offered a critique of the new agenda: believing that the focus on the economy and the increase in support for research in medicine, science and engineering, while appropriate and laudable, are inadequate and incomplete. She argued that we must think not only of the economy but also of civil society which she defined "as a vigorous citizenry engaged in the culture and politics of a free society. In this definition, the key agent of influence and change is neither the government nor the corporation, but rather the individual, acting alone or with others to strengthen civic life. In turn, how individuals think about themselves and others, the values they espouse and enact, become the essential features of a civil society" (Piper 2002, 11). The economic innovation sought in the new research agenda, she goes on to assert, requires a vigorous civil society as a pre-condition. She advocates for increased support for research through SSHRC: that will enable individuals to better understand themselves, that will assist in defining both our Canadian identity and our role as global citizens, and that informs the creation of public policy and develops the social programs on which our civil society is built.

These three Killam lectures set out the new research agenda, its history and rationale, and the new social contract. The new agenda involved significant growth in federal support with a long term commitment in exchange for the university's commitment to work to commercialize and apply the results and to ensure the research was at international standards of excellence. Thus the new agenda changed the discourse in two fundamental ways: it emphasized the applications of research and it emphasized research excellence.

The new research agenda moves away from what has been called the "linear model" of university-industry relations. The linear model is widely associated with the famous report of Vannevar Bush to the US government, *Science—The Endless Frontier*, which set the pattern for government support of university research in the postwar period.[5]

The linear model makes a sharp distinction between basic (or pure) research and applied research. For Bush (1945), "basic research is performed without thought of practical ends." Its defining characteristic is its contribution to "general knowledge and an understanding of nature and its laws." Furthermore, Bush saw an inescapable tension between basic and applied research: "applied research invariably drives out pure." Bush also declared that the dynamism of technological change comes from basic research. "Basic research is the pacemaker of technological progress." There is a linear sequence originating from basic research, which then stimulates applied research, which leads to development research, and finally to new products or processes. The linear paradigm is completed by a second proposition. Bush believed the university is the place for basic research. The industrial lab is the place for applied research. And the two must not be confused.

The linear model shaped government policies in Canada, just as in the United States. Most academics, both accept the paradigm as an accurate description of scientific and technological progress, and believe the paradigm should govern all scientific research, and indeed all university research—the university should focus upon basic research not applied research. It should steer well clear of commercial interests.

This acceptance by academics is understandable. The paradigm is consistent with core ideals of the university. The paradigm resonates with the ancient ideals of critical, independent thought. The university is a place of liberal learning, without regard for application. The university is an autonomous institution, therefore maintaining distance from business is appropriate. Academic freedom is justified by the theory that knowledge is best advanced when disinterested researchers are free to follow where their curiosity might lead. Again, the maintenance of distance from the economy is vital.

However, no matter how strongly espoused and how consonant with university ideals, this paradigm is not the complete picture of the role of the university and its connection to economic life. The early Scottish universities, the English universities of the later nineteenth and twentieth century, and the US land grant universities saw that contributing to economic development was a vital part of their mission. Much university research has always been very applied and responsive to the needs of industry and this mission has coexisted with the university's commitment to seek knowledge for its own sake. Professors act as consultants to companies, just as they do to governments and civil society organizations. Professors have usually owned the intellectual property rights to their written work, for example when they write textbooks. Students are trained in applied professional programs both because they seek an education which will prepare them for a career and because the economy needs skilled professionals. And these close connections between industry and the university have not overwhelmed the university's core ideals; indeed they are a necessary part of the university's service to society. But, even with greater historical awareness of university-industry connections, it is clear the postwar paradigm is being changed. The university and industry are in much closer partnership and in a new form.

An insightful perspective on the new agenda is provided by Donald Stokes in his book, *Pasteur's Quadrant: Basic Science and Technological Innovation*. He argues we have been trapped by an over-simplified dichotomy between basic research and applied research, which was at the centre of the postwar social contract. Stokes argues that the linear model is not an accurate or complete representation of how scientific knowledge has advanced through history. In fact much scientific work is motivated by the *simultaneous* desire to improve our basic understanding *and* to find usable knowledge. He cites the example of Pasteur who was intensely interested *both* in discovering the basic laws of nature *and* in the application of this basic knowledge. Stokes replaces the linear model with a quadrant model. In his quadrant model, scientific research can be characterized by how it is inspired: is it inspired by the quest for fundamental understanding at a high level or low level, or is it inspired by considerations of use at a high level or low level? In one quadrant research is motivated by the quest for fundamental understanding at a high level, and at a low level by considerations of use, what he calls Bohr's quadrant, "in view of how clearly Niels Bohr's quest for a model of atomic structure was a pure voyage of discovery, however much his ideas later remade the world. This category represents the research ideal of the natural philosophers, institutionalized in the pure science of the Germans in the nineteenth century and of the Americans in the twentieth, and includes Bush's concept of 'basic research.'" Another category of research is inspired by concerns with application at a high level, and at low level by concerns about fundamental understanding, which he calls Edison's quadrant, "in view of how strictly this brilliant inventor kept his co-workers at Menlo Park, in the first industrial research laboratory in America, from pursuing the deeper scientific implications of what they were discovering in their headlong rush toward commercially profitable electric lighting" (Stokes 1997, 73). A third category of research is motivated *both* by the high-level desire to discover nature's laws and by the high-level desire to apply this knowledge in a specific task: Pasteur's quadrant.

The new research agenda supports research in Pasteur's quadrant.

In order to think properly about whether we have the best system to support research for the years ahead, it is important to understand the programs of this new research agenda, in some detail, at both the federal and provincial level. It is important to see how they have evolved and the language used in their presentation and operation. This discourse is revealing of current government priorities with respect to university research. These programs will be examined in subsequent sections. And with this examination, it becomes clear that colleges have begun to participate in the research mission of higher education.

However, first let us examine how to measure the research expenditure at universities.

MEASURIZNG UNIVERSITY-BASED RESEARCH EXPENDITURE

The importance of research in the university's activities is manifest.

The duties of a professor are teaching, research, and service. Today in Ontario, the rough norm is that time should be allocated 40 percent to research, 40 percent to teaching, and the balance of 20 percent to service to the university, the academic community, and to society (Clark et al. 2009, 11).

Although their responsibilities are both to teach and to conduct research, when professors are hired, their potential as researchers is given more weight than their potential as teachers. Indeed during their doctoral programs, the necessary qualification to become a professor, most of the time is spent preparing to do advanced research and the dissertation is a piece of original research of sufficient quality (it is hoped) to warrant publication. Very little time in doctoral programs is spent preparing people to become university teachers. When professors are considered for tenure and for promotion, both teaching and research are assessed, but research accomplishment is given greater weight. Among their peers, a professor's research accomplishments are more highly valued than their teaching accomplishments.

When universities present themselves to the world, through their websites, the speeches of their presidents, their fundraising campaigns, and their submissions to government, universities tout the quality of the education provided, the accomplishments of their graduates, but most of all they celebrate the accomplishments of their researchers and the contributions of their work to society.

One measure of the importance of research at the university would be to examine the share of research expenditure in Total Operating Expenditure (TOE). As noted in Chapter 4, universities report their revenues and expenditures using the framework of fund accounting (CAUBO 2009). Total Operating Expenditure can be defined as expenditure under the general operating fund, the special purpose and trust fund, and the sponsored research fund. Expenditures under the capital fund, the ancillary fund, and the endowment fund have been excluded.

Total research expenditure includes expenditure under the sponsored research fund, the value of faculty time spent on research (that will be a percentage of faculty salaries), and a portion of the indirect costs of the university (for example libraries, computing, buildings, laboratories, human resources, finance, etc.) that should be assigned to the research mission rather than the teaching mission. To sum up, total research expenditure is:

- Sponsored research expenditure (roughly equal to sponsored research income)
- The value of faculty time spent on research (a proportion of faculty salaries)
- Indirect costs of supporting research.[6]

This method of defining TOE and of calculating total research expenditure follows Statistics Canada's method when it calculates research and experimental development (R&D) expenditure in Canada (Statistics Canada 2010a). In order to estimate the amount of faculty time spent on research, Statistics Canada commissioned a faculty time use survey in 2001. The faculty research time coefficients are presented in Table 7.1. These coefficients vary by academic discipline and by university size, in contrast to the single coefficient—0.40—assumed by Clark et al. (2009). It is likely that in reality the balance of time devoted to research does vary by type of university and by discipline of study. But it is also true that the fundamental thrust over the postwar period, over all types of institutions and all disciplines, has been to increase the share of professors' time devoted to research. A simple assumption of 40 percent is likely quite reasonable for today.[7]

Applying the Statistics Canada methodology to data on all Ontario universities in 2007/08, we find that sponsored research expenditure was 26.1 percent of Total Operating Expenditure. The 40 percent of faculty salaries was 10.3 percent of Total Operating Expenditure. The (uncompensated) indirect costs were calculated to be 6.3 percent of TOE. (See Statistics Canada 2010a for the methodology.) In total, research expenditure is 41 percent of Total Operating Expenditure of Ontario universities.[8]

TABLE 7.1
Fraction of Faculty Time Spent on Research, 2000

	Small Universities	Medium Universities	Large Universities
Natural Sciences and Engineering			
Agricultural and biological sciences	0.30	0.40	0.45
Engineering and applied sciences	0.35	0.35	0.40
Mathematics and physical sciences	0.30	0.35	0.45
Health sciences	0.30	0.40	0.45
Social Sciences and Humanities			
Education	0.20	0.25	0.25
Fine arts	0.20	0.20	0.20
Humanities	0.25	0.25	0.30
Social sciences	0.25	0.30	0.35

Source: Statistics Canada (2010a).

We should pause for a moment here to recognize how this approach to defining operating expenditure differs from the usual (with apologies to those who find accounting mind numbing). Most discussions of university operating expenditures look only at expenditures under the general operating fund, and often go on to look at the share of operating expenditures that are covered by provincial grants versus tuition fees. A recent example of this approach and analysis is the Rae Review (Rae 2005, 103). While appropriate and useful for some purposes, the usual approach ignores research expenditure in the operations of the university. The usual approach subtly, and perhaps inadvertently, examines only the teaching function of the university and ignores the research function. The better approach for a study such as this, which examines both the teaching and research functions together, is to define Total Operating Expenditure following the Statistics Canada approach.[9] Thus, as a rough summary, research expenditure is more than 40 percent of Total Operating Expenditure.

With the new research agenda, research has become a major part of university activities. Assigning all the costs of running the university to either teaching or research, we can say that 60 percent of expenditure is for teaching and 40 percent for research. Unfortunately, the Ministry of Training, Colleges and Universities has focused only on the teaching component.

These calculations draw out that the province, through its operating grants (although they are a function of enrolments), actually supports research because the operating grants pay for faculty salaries and some of the indirect costs of research.[10] All too often this is ignored. Provincial policy toward universities has focused almost exclusively on undergraduate education: on issues of access and enrolment expansion, on how expansion should be funded, and on tuition policy and student assistance. The policy discussion has not properly recognized that provincial operating grants support research.

THE NATIONAL INNOVATION SYSTEM

Much of the new research agenda emerged out of a new way of thinking about the economy.

The concept of a "national innovation system" developed in the 1990s as economic analysts struggled to understand the policies that might ensure economic growth in a time of globalization and rapid technological change. What could enhance economic performance in the knowledge-based economies of today? The key was innovation.

The Conference Board of Canada (2007), in its assessment of Canada's innovation system, defines innovation as: "a process through which economic and social value is extracted from knowledge—through the creation, diffusion and transformation of knowledge to produce new or significantly improve products or processes that are put to use by society." The nature and benefits of innovation are expansively conceived. "Innovation is a means to an end—the end being our continued well-being and high quality of life." However, the actual analysis of national innovation systems usually proceeds within a much narrower conception: innovation is a process through which knowledge yields a new product or process which has commercial value, and the benefits of innovation are economic growth and an increase in per capita GDP.

What determines the level of innovation in an economy?

A traditional starting point in the study of national innovation is to measure expenditure on research and experimental development (R&D) within the country. But the study of innovation requires more than just examining R&D expenditures. The concept of a national innovation system emphasizes the role of *institutions*. The crucial institutions in the innovation system are of three types: businesses, universities, and governments. Each has their role and each interacts with the others. The concept of a national innovation system involves not just new knowledge (R&D) and the three types institutions, but also creative and skilled *people*—and most important the interactions and flows of knowledge and people among institutions.[11]

A country's innovation system includes not just the institutions and people engaged in research and the process from discovery, to development, through to commercial application; the innovation system of a nation also includes many other components—from the country's competition policy, trade agreements, foreign investment rules, and tax policy, to its financial system and venture capital markets, its intellectual property and patent laws, and indeed even its entrepreneurial spirit.

There are many approaches to the analysis of national innovation systems; for example, firm-level innovation analyses that study the interactions and flows within an industry, and cluster analyses that study interactions and flows within a city-region.[12]

The iconic model of innovation in a city-region is Silicon Valley that emerged around Stanford University in Palo Alto, California. It all began with the vision of Fred Terman, professor, then dean of engineering, and then provost at Stanford. Originally, he was concerned with the lack of employment opportunities for Stanford graduates and that the best students had to go east for truly challenging jobs. His response was twofold. He encouraged high tech firms to locate in the Stanford Industrial Park, especially companies that were complementary to the research done by Stanford faculty members. And he encouraged his students to become involved with local industry, to visit industrial labs, to offer consulting services, to invest in companies, and even to start their own companies. He also encouraged firms from the Stanford Industrial Park to become involved at the university. Co-ventures with university researchers and firms were encouraged; industrial researchers taught courses at the university. All these were part of the Silicon Valley model.

There have been many attempts to analyze what makes Silicon Valley so successful; one of the most analytical is a collection of papers, *Understanding Silicon Valley: The Anatomy of an Entrepreneurial Region*. Identification of "the crucial ingredients of Silicon Valley—a strong research university with close links to industry, entrepreneurial corporate and academic cultures, aggressive venture capital markets, supportive government institutions, a pleasant climate, a technology park"—is relatively easy (Leslie 2000, 48), although using the recipe elsewhere is rather more difficult. Other crucial ingredients are indentified. Labour flexibility—moving from job to job, moving around among university, government, and the private sector—is a means for ideas to circulate in an ecology of innovation. Venture capitalists and lawyers are key actors, speeding the spread of new ideas. And it is a very different picture of a university than we usually see. "They do more than teach students. They actively encourage their faculty to take what they know and start companies. They also encourage faculty to contribute their talents to established companies in the area as consultants. ... [But], the flow of knowledge doesn't just go from inside to out. Knowledge also moves in from the rest of the region. Indeed, some of the most highly attended classes at Stanford are those taught by, or include lectures by, key figures in the Valley, carrying what they know back to the school" (Brown 2000, xiii-xv).

The Silicon Valley experience has inspired much of the change in government thinking about support for university research. Ontario has its own initiative to apply the lessons—the MaRS discovery district, at College Street and University Avenue, in Toronto. Originally started to commercialize publicly funded medical research, it now works as well in information technology, engineering, and social innovation. The MaRS buildings bring together university researchers, businesses, lawyers, venture capital funds, investment bankers, and government officials to nurture the development of new ideas, new products and services, and new companies.

To examine Silicon Valley or the MaRS district is to examine the national innovation system made concrete at the city-region level. But, the most widely used approach to examining national innovation systems begins by looking at the country as a whole. One component of this examination, most relevant for the purposes of this chapter on university research, looks at research and experimental development (R&D) expenditure in the country. How much research is being done in the country and who is doing it? First, gross R&D expenditure in the country by all sectors

(GERD) is documented, and then it is separated into R&D expenditure by businesses (BERD), universities (HERD)[13], and governments (GOVERD). Table 7.2 and Table 7.3 provide this perspective on Canada's innovation system and compare us to a few other countries. These data are reported to OECD by each country and then published in *Main Science and Technology Indicators* (OECD various years).

The basic patterns of Canada's innovation system are well known. There is a significant amount of R&D done in Canada, in absolute dollars. We are a major player—the seventh largest centre of R&D among the OECD countries. But as a share of GDP, Canada's R&D commitment is modest. We devote only 1.87 percent of GDP, below the OECD average of 2.35, and well below leaders such as Sweden that devotes 3.9 percent. Most countries have set a target of at least 2 percent of GDP; the European Commission, in creating the European Research Area, has set a target of 3 percent. Canada is committed to raising its total R&D, but our aspirations are below many countries.

It is well known that Canada stands out in the low share of total R&D done by the business sector. Business conducts only 52 percent of Canadian R&D, compared to the OECD average of 68 percent. In Sweden, the share is 75 percent. The relatively low level of R&D conducted by Canadian business has long been recognized as a problem in Canada's innovation system, but it remains stubbornly low despite many programs intended to encourage business R&D.

The part of the picture that is less well known is that Canada stands out in the very high share of total R&D done by the university sector. In Canada, 38 percent of our R&D is done by the university sector, compared to the OECD average of 18 percent. And Canada spends the highest share of GDP on university R&D of any OECD country.[14]

University-based research is exceptionally important in Canada's national innovation system.

TABLE 7.2
Research and Experimental Development Expenditure (R&D) by Sector

Country	GERD* $Million PPP	% Performed by Business	% Performed by Higher Education	% Performed by Government
Australia	18,755	61	24	12
Canada	23,991	51	38	10
Netherlands	12,273	47	40	13
United Kingdom	40,384	62	27	9
United States	398,194	73	13	11

*GERD = Gross R&D Expenditure.

Source: OECD (2011).

TABLE 7.3
**Research and Experimental Development Expenditure (R&D) by Sector as
Percentage of GDP**

Country	GERD as % of GDP	BERD as % of GDP	HERD as % of GDP	GOVERD as % of GDP
Australia	2.21	1.35	0.54	0.27
Canada	1.87	0.99	0.68	0.19
Netherlands	1.76	0.88	0.67	0.21
United Kingdom	1.77	1.10	0.47	0.16
United States	2.79	2.02	0.36	0.30

GERD = Gross R&D Expenditure; BERD = Business R&D Expenditure; HERD = Higher Education R&D Expenditure; GOVERD = Government R&D Expenditure.

Source: OECD (2011).

FEDERAL SUPPORT FOR UNIVERSITY RESEARCH

Before examining the federal programs of the new research agenda and to provide a larger perspective, the sources of all sponsored research income for Ontario universities in 2007/08 are presented in Table 7.4. Almost half (46 percent) of the research income comes from the federal government, mainly from the granting councils and the new agenda initiatives of the last fifteen years. The balance comes from a diversity of sources, in particular grants and contracts from the province (14.5 percent), from the business sector (15.9 percent), and from the non-profit sector (15.3 percent).

As we think about the design of Ontario's system of universities, the most important thing to note in this distribution of sources is that the federal government supplies by far the largest amount of research income—the provincial government contributes only 14.5 percent of re-search revenue.[15] Therefore, we have the provincial level of government responsible for designing the university system and the federal level dominant in shaping the research endeavour.[16]

The main sources of federal support for university research are pre-sented in Table 7.5, taken from the AUCC report *Momentum: the 2008 report on university research and knowledge mobilization* (AUCC 2008, 14). The data (which cover all of Canada, not just Ontario) tell the remarkable story of the decade from 1997/98 to 2007/08.

At the beginning of the decade, virtually all of the federal support for university research came from the three granting councils: CIHR, NSERC, and SSHRC.[17]

NSERC had the largest budget by a considerable margin, followed by CIHR, and then SSHRC. SSHRC received only 12.5 percent of the tri-council funding, despite the fact that SSHRC faculty members are about

55 percent of total faculty, and the fact that about 60 percent of students are in SSHRC disciplines (HSSFC 2008). This imbalance in the shares to each council reflects in part the greater costs of doing research in NSERC and CIHR fields, but also in part reflects how much research society wishes to support in these three broad domains.

The main story of the next decade is the enormous growth of federal support for university research—it grew fourfold! This main story can be subdivided into two separate stories.

The first is that the budgets of all three of the granting councils were expanded: SSHRC's was doubled, NSERC's grew 77 percent, and CIHR's was tripled. Each granting council moved some of its funding toward targeted research, but given the large overall increase, the money available for basic, curiosity-driven research increased significantly. During this decade, the total number of full-time faculty members across Canada rose by 30 percent and thus the funding available per faculty member, across all granting councils, rose enormously (something we academics seldom admit, or indeed, are even aware of).

TABLE 7.4
Sponsored Research Income of Ontario Universities, 2007–2008
($ thousands)

	Amount	Percentage
Federal Grants and Contracts		
SSHRC	83,721	
NSERC	270,180	
CIHR	293,180	
CFI	185,741	
CRCs	85,821	
Other federal	203,179	
Total federal	**1,135,736**	**46.4%**
Provincial Grants and Contracts	354,268	14.5%
Business Grants and Contracts	387,079	15.9%
Nonprofit Grants and Contracts	373,862	15.3%
Total sponsored research income	**2,426,217**	

Source: CAUBO (2009).

The second story is the new research agenda—the initiation of large programs outside the granting councils. The four most important were the Canada Foundation for Innovation, the Canada Research Chairs program, the Indirect Costs program, and a group of programs bringing together university researchers and business to conduct research in designated priority areas and commercialize the results. Some observers would characterize a fifth component of the new agenda: the enormous commitment to health and medical research, in part through the tripling of the CIHR budget but also through the high priority to health and medical research in many of the new initiatives.

The various programs of the new research agenda are described below, citing heavily from websites and documents in order to draw out and emphasize the new language that was being used to describe and justify research.

TABLE 7.5
Main Federal Funding Mechanisms for University Research
($ millions)

	1997–1998	1998–1999	1999–2000	2000–2001	2001–2002	2002–2003	2003–2004	2004–2005	2005–2006	2006–2007	2007–2008
Granting Councils											
SSHRC	87	87	108	116	121	135	155	169	180	178	179
NSERC	395	450	491	494	489	525	579	620	651	661	698
CIHR	215	246	275	339	449	528	574	614	650	680	725
Tri-agency Programs											
Canada Graduate Scholarships							23	52	83	104	116
Canada Research Chairs				13	59	103	146	188	222	247	258
Centres of Excellence for Commercialization											163
Indirect Costs Program					200		225	245	260	300	315
Networks of Centres of Excellence	35	46	64	75	75	74	74	75	79	80	80
Canada Foundation for Innovation		27	114	183	231	325	349	263	427	355	298
Genome Canada				2	43	60	83	82	90	85	92
Total	733	856	1,052	1,222	1,668	1,750	2,208	2,308	2,641	2,690	2,924

Source: AUCC (2008).

The Canada Foundation for Innovation (CFI) funds research infrastructure: "research infrastructure consists of the state-of-the-art equipment, buildings, laboratories, and databases required to conduct research." "The CFI normally funds up to 40 percent of a project's infrastructure costs which are invested in partnership with eligible institutions and their funding partners from the public, private, and voluntary sectors who provide the remainder." Usually, the Province of Ontario would match the federal 40 percent, leaving 20 percent to be raised from private sector or non-profit partners. "Created by the Government of Canada in 1997, the Canada Foundation for Innovation strives to build our nation's capacity to undertake world-class research and technology development to benefit Canadians. Thanks to CFI investment in state-of-the-art facilities and equipment, universities, colleges, research hospitals and non-profit research institutions are attracting and retaining the world's top talent, training the next generation of researchers, supporting private-sector innovation and creating high-quality jobs that strengthen Canada's position in today's knowledge economy" (from the CFI website, CFI 2012). Rather than funding the operating costs of a specific research project like the granting councils, CFI provides federal funding for infrastructure—building, equipment, laboratories—for major research initiatives. Because it focused on larger, world-class, research programs, the CFI funds flowed to the larger, more research-intensive universities. The CFI funds were restricted to infrastructure in the fields of health, environment, science, and engineering, although later a few social science and humanities projects were funded.

The Canada Research Chairs (CRC) program directly funds new faculty positions for outstanding scholars. "The Canada Research Chairs program stands at the centre of a national strategy to make Canada one of the world's top countries in research and development. In 2000, the Government of Canada created a permanent program to establish 2,000 research professorships—Canada Research Chairs—in eligible degree-granting institutions across the country. The Canada Research Chairs program invests $300 million per year to attract and retain some of the world's most accomplished and promising minds" (from the CRC website, CRC 2013). Never before had the federal government directly funded faculty positions. And together with the CFI, never before had there been such an emphasis on excellence—world-class excellence.

The CRCs were first divided into an SSHRC pool (20 percent), an NSERC pool (45 percent), and a CIHR pool (35 percent). Then, each pool was allocated to universities according to their share of total grants from that council (a three-year average); thus the CRCs were awarded to larger, more research-intensive universities, whose faculty members had been securing tri-council grants.[18] The distribution of CRCs to Ontario universities was reported in Table 1.6 in Chapter 1. Over 90 percent of the chairs in Ontario went to nine (of Ontario's twenty) universities.

Both the CFI and the CRC programs were intended to be strategic rather than across-the-board. Universities had to prepare plans to show their research strengths and the strategic directions they wished to pursue, and then demonstrate how the CFI money and CRCs would lever the existing strengths and enable a major leap forward in the quality of the work. The hope was that these programs would help (or force) universities to choose their strategic priorities. Also, the hope was that the university strategic research plans could be aggregated to give a picture of research across the country. Neither hope was particularly realized.

A third new major source of federal research support was the Indirect Costs program. Universities had long argued that the tri-council research grants did not cover all the costs of the work—with the unfortunate result that success in securing research grants meant that indirect costs would go up, forcing the universities to take money from other purposes, including undergraduate education. The federal government finally acknowledged the problem and began to cover a portion of the indirect costs, allocating funds to universities in proportion to the allocation of tri-council grants. So, again, the new money flowed to the larger, more research-intensive universities.

The fourth group of programs represents a strategy for the support of university research in targeted areas and for the commercialization of the research findings. Usually, the programs first establish a non-profit corporation—creating an entity neither within government, the university, or business, but whose members are university researchers, businesses, and governments. The non-profit corporation becomes the centre of a network, combining researchers from many universities, around a targeted area of research. The federal government provides about 30–40 percent of the funds, the rest must be provided by the other members or partners. Within its targeted field, the network develops its own programs, supporting research and its commercialization.

The first such program was the Networks of Centres of Excellence (NCE). The NCE "fosters multi-disciplinary, multi-sectoral partnerships between academia, industry, government and not-for-profit organizations. It supports academic research, the commercialization of products and ideas, and the development of significant Canadian business advantages. The partnerships that this initiative cultivates result in ideas that are transformed into economic and social benefits for all Canadians. The Networks of Centres of Excellence (NCE) program leads the world in research areas as diverse as disease prevention, diagnosis and treatment, natural resource management and information technology and provides opportunities for Canadian researchers and students to work with receptor communities to accelerate the creation and application of knowledge" (from the NCE website, NCE 2012).

A special case of this strategy was "Genome Canada—a not-for-profit organization established in February 2000—given a mandate by the

Government of Canada to develop and implement a national strategy for supporting large-scale genomics and proteomics research projects, for the benefit of all Canadians." Its priorities are: "Connecting ideas and people across public and private sectors to find new uses and applications for genomics; investing in large-scale science and technology to fuel innovation; and translating discoveries into applications to maximize impact across all sectors" (from Genome Canada website, Genome Canada 2012).

The focus in this strategy on application and commercialization was increased when "in 2007, the Government of Canada invested $285 million over five years to create the Centres of Excellence for Commercialization and Research (CECR) program. This innovative model creates centres to advance research and facilitate commercialization of technologies, products and services within the four priority areas identified in the federal Science and Technology (S&T) Strategy. The four areas are: Environment; Natural Resources and Energy; Health and Life Sciences; and Information and Communications Technologies. The currently active CECRs focus on biotechnology, digital media, drug research and development, energy efficiency, personalized medicine, green chemistry, cancer treatment, ocean observatories, and prostate cancer research, as well as many other areas. Building on the success of the original Networks of Centres of Excellence program which funds research, the CECR program supports the operating expenses of a centre, and the commercialization of such research. The CECR program helps bridge the gap between innovation and commercialization, allowing new products and technologies to go to market more easily" (from the CERC website, CERC 2012).

The focus has been pushed still further with a small new program: Business-Led Networks of Centres of Excellence program (BL-NCE). "These networks are an amalgamation of the original NCE program's academic perspectives and the eagerness of the private sector to solve specific problems. They are headed by industrial consortia, and help to increase private sector investments in Canadian research, support training of skilled researchers, and accelerate the timeline involved in transferring ideas from the laboratory into products and services in the marketplace" (from the BL-NCE website, BL-NCE 2012). This program even allows tri-council funds to support research within industrial laboratories.[19]

Together, these federal initiatives had great implications for university research in Ontario.

Foremost, these federal initiatives made it unambiguously clear that the rationale behind government support for university-based research had shifted. This was the new Public Research Contract identified by John Evans in his Killam Lecture (Evans 2001). In the past, it was always supposed that although new knowledge was valuable for its own sake, this new knowledge should *eventually* lead to improvements in the well-being of society—economic, social, and cultural well-being. And overall, the driving direction of the research should come from the curiosity of the researchers and the academic review process of the granting councils. The new research agenda makes clear the primary rationale for supporting research was to contribute to economic well-being. The academic review process would still be important but governments would set the broad directions for research. And the university could not simply presume that *eventually* the results would benefit society; rather the university should directly facilitate the commercialization or application of the research. A short summary of the new federal rationale for supporting academic research would be: to support the academic research enterprise within the national innovation system.

Equally important, the initiatives introduced a discourse of excellence and international comparisons into the discussion of research: the programs seek to attract and retain the very best scholars and to support world-class work.

The funds did not flow in proportion to enrolments. In the case of CRCs, the chairs were allocated to each university on the basis of past success in receiving competitively awarded council grants. Most of the other programs awarded funds through a competitive process, adjudicated by leading scholars from across Canada and often from across the world. Excellence was to be achieved by competitive allocation of funds.

And, although the budget of each granting council rose, most of the new funds were targeted at specific fields, with the great majority of the new funds supporting work in science, medicine, engineering, and technology rather than the humanities and social sciences.

Together these initiatives provided a powerful thrust toward differentiation among universities on the basis of research.

The thinking behind the expanded support for university-based research was made clear through the development of "Canada's Innovation Strategy" announced by the Liberal government of Jean Chrétien in 2001. The strategy was presented in two papers, whose titles speak for themselves: *Achieving Excellence: Investing in People, Knowledge and Opportunity* (Canada, 2002a) and *Knowledge Matters: Skills and Learning for Canadians* (Canada 2002b). These had been preceded by the report of the Expert Panel on the Commercialization of University Research: *Public Investments in University Research: Reaping the Benefits* (Advisory Council on Science and Technology 1999). A lead recommendation was: "In order for researchers to qualify for federal research funding and universities to qualify for commercialization support, universities (and their affiliated research hospitals and research centres) should be required to adopt policies consistent with the principles set out below: Universities (and their affiliated organizations) must recognize the importance of research-based innovation as a mainstream activity by identifying "innovation" as their fourth mission, in addition to teaching, research, and community service; alternatively they might explicitly identify innovation as an element of the three missions." This report defined innovation as: "the process of bringing new goods and services to market, or the result of that process" (Advisory Council on Science and Technology 1999).

Nonetheless, despite this new focus on the economic rationale for supporting university research and the desire for partnerships with the private sector and for commercialization of the results, the federal research initiatives were developed with a strong sense of the university and its research mission: the major initiatives funded university research infrastructure, they funded faculty positions, and they covered the universities' indirect costs of research. The professors who were supported were leaders in their field, using traditional academic criteria, and the research that was done was published in the leading academic journals. No doubt, this is because of the long federal role in university research through the granting councils. In contrast, as we shall see, Ontario also expanded research funding, but the expansion was not rooted in a strong sense of the university and its research mission.

The next component of Canada's Innovation Strategy was a study by the Council of Canadian Academies.[20] The mandate of the Council is "to perform independent, expert assessments of the science that is relevant to public policy issues. Here 'science' is interpreted broadly to encompass any knowledge-generating discipline, including the natural, social and health sciences, engineering and the humanities. The council's assessments are performed by independent panels of qualified experts from Canada and abroad" (Council of Canadian Academies 2006, iv). The Council of Canadian Academies was asked to address a number of questions by the Ministry of Industry about science and technology (S&T) in Canada. Their report: *The State of Science & Technology in Canada* analyzed the strength of science and technology in Canada, identifying those areas where Canada is currently strong in comparison with other economically advanced countries, and areas where we are believed to be getting stronger. Their assessment was based on two approaches: a survey of informed opinion (in government, universities, the private sector, and in the council academies) about S&T in Canada, and an analysis of the published research of Canadians in academic journals using bibliometric techniques. The latter was a radical new approach: this was the first time the quality of academic publications was used in selecting priority areas in innovation policy.

The report identified four broad areas of strength and these have been adopted by the federal government as areas for strategic focus:

- Natural resources and energy[21]
- Information and communications technologies
- Health and related life sciences
- Environmental sciences and technologies.

The new research initiatives were largely begun under the Liberal government of Jean Chrétien. But, they have continued under the Conservative government of Stephen Harper (elected in February 2006), based on the same analysis of the global economy and what needs to be done for Canada to prosper. The approach of "Canada's new government" was set out with the release of its plan: *Advantage Canada: Building a Strong Economy for Canadians* (Canada 2006). Under the heading of "Investing for Sustainable Growth," the government said it would maintain Canada's leadership in the G7 for public sector research and maximize its value by focusing on excellence and increased linkages with the private sector. This report was soon followed by the more detailed plan: *Mobilizing Science and Technology to Canada's Advantage* (Canada 2007). It retained the same focus on the innovation system[22] (of which universities are a part), the same focus on talented, skilled and creative people, the same focus on world-class research excellence, and the same focus on commercialization of research through university-business-government partnerships. The four priority research areas were retained.

The Liberal-initiated programs of the new research agenda were retained by the Harper Conservative government and their funding improved year by year. And further initiatives were added, most importantly the Canada Excellence Research Chairs (CERC) program. Launched in 2008, CERC "supports Canadian universities in their efforts to build on Canada's growing reputation as a global leader in research and innovation. The program awards world-renowned researchers and their teams up to $10 million over seven years to establish ambitious research programs at Canadian universities. These awards are among the most prestigious and generous available globally" (CERC 2012). The program is an initiative of the three national granting councils—CIHR, NSERC, and SSHRC—and administered by the Canada Research Chairs secretariat. The program is part of the government's science and technology strategy and the research must be in the four priority research areas. Eighteen CERCs were awarded and the 2011 federal budget announced funding for ten more chairs.

Even after the financial crisis and recession of 2009, the commitment to university research was maintained. The 2009 budget focused on fiscal stimulus, much of which was to be spending on infrastructure. The budget had a special section on "knowledge infrastructure" and committed "up to $2 billion to support deferred maintenance and repair projects at post-secondary institutions. Preference will be given to projects at universities that can improve the quality of research and development at the institution. Projects at colleges will strengthen their ability to deliver advanced knowledge and skills training." Also, funds were increased for the Canada Foundation for Innovation (Canada. Ministry of Finance 2009).

As the stimulus was wound down, and the focus shifted to creating economic growth and jobs through innovation, the commitment to university research continued. Budget 2010 contained new commitments to research infrastructure and advanced research of $61 million as well as $175 million in programs for knowledge transfer and commercialization (Canada. Ministry of Finance 2010, Table 3.3.1). Budget 2011 provided $120 million towards Canada's digital economic strategy, $131 million for advanced research including increases to the granting councils, ten new Canada Excellence Research Chairs, and $65 million to Genome Canada (Canada. Ministry of Finance 2011, table 4.3.1).

It is only with the budget of 2012, with its focus on expenditure restraint, that federal support for research was cut back, but only slightly. And the focus on university research as a central component of economic strategy continued. One chapter of the budget was titled: Supporting Entrepreneurs, Innovators and World-Class Research (Canada. Ministry of Finance 2012, Chapter 3.1). This focus continued in the 2013 budget, with a chapter titled: Investing in World-Class Research and Innovation (Canada. Ministry of Finance 2013, Chapter 3.4).

Thus the federal commitment to university-based research has grown enormously over the past twenty years and remains strong. The commitment does not depend upon the party in power. This commitment has remained strong because the diagnosis of what is required for Canada to prosper in a global, knowledge-based, economy—the emphasis on the national innovation system, the importance of talented people, and the importance of university research at a world-class level—has remained over the past twenty years. Indeed, there is a broad and long lasting consensus among developed countries on the diagnosis. The OECD has made it a focus of its economic analysis since the mid 1990s. A recent book *National Innovation and the Academic Research Enterprise: Public Policy in Global Perspective* concluded: "governments in OECD countries have come to believe that higher education is an engine of economic development and that the effective steering of the Academic Research Enterprise (ARE) is a critical means of improving national innovation" (Dill and Van Vught, eds. 2010, ix).

In Canada however, there are worries that despite huge federal commitments over many years, Canada still lags in business and commercially oriented R&D and lags in the translation of research into actual new products and processes.[23] In 2010, the government commissioned an expert panel to review federal support to research and development and their report *Innovation Canada: A Call to Action* (Jenkins Report) (Canada. Industry Canada 2011) made a number of recommendations taken up in Budget 2013. Although none of the major recommendations were directed at universities, the implication for universities was clear: the priority should not be to increase support for research at universities; rather the priority should be to translate this research into commercial applications. This has been a theme of the new research agenda for the past few years and will certainly continue. There will be increasing pressure on universities to demonstrate that research has contributed to economic growth.

PROVINCIAL SUPPORT FOR UNIVERSITY RESEARCH

Of course, the province always supported university research, but until the mid 1990s, the province's support for university research was mainly indirect—the operating grants supported the payment of faculty salaries and the indirect costs of research. It was the federal government, through the three granting councils, that directly supported and thus shaped the research endeavour at universities. When the province began to support university research directly, it did not follow the granting council model; rather, all the provincial programs conformed to the principles of the new research agenda.

Prior to the 1990s, there was one major Ontario initiative with a direct influence on university research—this was the Ontario Centres of Excellence program, begun in 1987. Each centre is a consortium of university-based researchers, industry leaders, and government officials committed to bridging the gap between basic science and the successful application of science and technology in profitable new businesses. Each centre had its own specialty developed around four key functional areas: investing in research, investing in people, moving technology into the marketplace, and building the infrastructure for innovation in Ontario. Ontario was an early leader in Canada with this approach; the federal government began its Networks of Centres of Excellence program a few years later.

Four centres were established. Their self-description is revealing. "Communications and Information Technology Ontario (CITO) worked to foster critical links between the industry/business community and academic research in information technology, telecommunications and digital media sectors. The Centre for Research in Earth and Space Technology (CRESTech) focused on investing in multidisciplinary col-laborative research and development in clean air and energy, clean water, sustainable agriculture, sustainable infrastructure, and niche technolo-gies within Ontario's environmental, resource management and space sectors. Materials and Manufacturing Ontario (MMO) took the lead in developing new knowledge and technology relevant to needs, now and in the future, of Ontario's materials and manufacturing industry. And Photonics Research Ontario (PRO) focused its research and development efforts on photonics—the generation, transmission, storage and detec-tion of light—and biomedicine, seeking a competitive edge for Ontario's industrial sector in the generation and harnessing of light and other forms of radiant energy" (Ontario Centres of Excellence 2012).

The Centres of Excellence both sponsor faculty research projects (in conjunction with government and industry partners) and support graduate students. The Centres of Excellence program was rooted first and foremost in a vision of the innovation system of Ontario, not in a vision of the university system and its research function. The program was managed by the ministry responsible for economic development, not the ministry responsible for higher education. Ever since, this has been Ontario's approach when it directly supports university research.

The severe recession of the early 1990s, and the years of fiscal restraint that followed, put many longer term policy questions on hold; the provincial focus was expenditure control and deficit reduction. However, economic growth was strong in the late nineties, fiscal balance was restored, and longer term planning was taken up again. This was when the great expansion of the university system was planned, first to accommodate the double cohort, and then the baby boom echo. It was at this time that Ontario began planning for a twenty-first century economy, with a report prepared by the Ontario Jobs and Investment Board (OJIB): *A Road Map to Prosperity: An Economic Plan for Jobs in the 21st Century*, in March 1999. This was the roadmap of Mike Harris' Conservative government for Ontario's economic future. The report identified five strategic goals: knowledge and skills for prosperity, innovation culture, strong global orientation, building on our industry and regional strengths, and a favourable investment climate. Each strategic goal was accompanied by an implementation strategy and performance measures to track progress toward the goals (Ontario Jobs Investment Board 1999, 8).

The OJIB report was followed nine months later by a companion study: *Growing Ontario's Innovation System: The Strategic Role of University Research* written by Heather Munroe-Blum, then vice-president for research at University of Toronto, with James Duderstadt, former president of the University of Michigan, and Sir Graeme Davies, vice-chancellor of the University of Glasgow (Munroe-Blum 1999a).

At the time of the Munroe-Blum report, three major provincial programs of research support had just been established, in addition to the Centres of Excellence: the Ontario Research Development Challenge Fund (ORDCF); the Ontario Innovation Trust (OIT); the Premier's Research Excellence Awards (PREA). Together with the Centres of Excellence, these were the major programs of the Conservative government's innovation strategy.

ORDCF was created in 1997 to support leading edge, innovative and industrially relevant university and hospital research, in partnership with private sector businesses. Like many of these initiatives, ORDCF sought to support world leading research. In a letter to potential applicants, Cal Stiller, chairman of the ORDCF Board wrote: "The vision should be clear and ambitious." The fund was directed toward "building, improving and enhancing your research capacity. In assessing excellence, we include the level, quality and achievement in the education and 'track record' of young recruited faculty, and the scientific publications, citations and competed-for grant awards of established researchers. The Fund is designed only to support the excellent."[24]

OIT, established in 1999, was a trust created by the Ontario government to help fund research infrastructure at Ontario's universities, research hospitals, colleges and research institutes. OIT functioned much like CFI and was used as the vehicle for provincial contributions to CFI grants won by Ontario researchers and to complement the large research projects under ORDCF.

PREA awarded money to gifted researchers to help them attract talented graduate students, post-doctoral fellows, or research associates to their research teams. PREAs were typically $100,000 awards that must be matched on a 2:1 basis with funds from a research institute or private sector funding partner.

These programs had not been going long and were not analyzed or assessed in the Munroe-Blum report.[25] (The federal tri-council programs were discussed extensively, reflecting the pre-eminent federal role in research support). Overall, the Munroe-Blum report set out the new framework for the analysis of economic growth and innovation and the role of universities that has governed Ontario policy since and was to become federal policy at about the same time. The key feature was an emphasis on the innovation system, made up of government, business, and the universities. "At the root of regional innovation is a set of six conditions: (1) An emphasis on excellence, competition, distinctive advantage and global profile and networks; (2) talented educated people who share a culture of entrepreneurship; (3) Accessible, high quality university research; (4) high-quality information infrastructure and connectedness; (5) An ample supply of risk capital; (6) Effective public policies" (Munroe-Blum 1999a, 14).

Ontario was an early leader in addressing the problems of the indirect costs of research. It was recognized that the operating grant, although tied to enrolments, did cover the bulk of research overheads, but nonetheless, a special envelope—the Research Overheads/Infrastructure (ROIE)—was established to help cover the indirect costs of federal grants. This became part of the basic operating funding from the Ministry of Training, Colleges, and Universities. It is distributed to universities in proportion to their share of grants from the three national granting councils: MRC (later CIHR), NSERC, and SSHRC. While some help, the ROIE funds have not kept pace with the growth in funds from the granting councils. Then, in 2000, the province established the Research Performance Fund (RPF) to cover the indirect costs of provincially funded research. If the provincial grant carries no overheads, the coverage through RPF is 40 percent; if some are covered RPF provides the difference up to 40 percent.

These research programs expanded over the next few years, so that by 2001–2002, the Science and Technology Program of the Ministry of

Energy, Science and Technology was spending over $135 million per year (Table 7.6). The provincial commitments continued to grow significantly over the next ten years—the province had an important role in the new research agenda.

In 2005, the new Liberal government sought to give its role in the new research agenda a higher profile and priority, by creating the Ministry of Research and Innovation (MRI), and by making the premier its first minister. The desire to rebrand the endeavour arose not just because there was a new government and because it was a high priority, but also because the auditor general, in the 2003 report, had been very critical of the Science and Technology Program. "Since the inception of the Ontario Research and Development Challenge Fund, the ministry has announced more than a dozen new science and technology transfer programs, some of which target highly specific areas of research. These program commitments range from $10 million to more than $1 billion. But the announcement of new programs did not result from executing a comprehensive plan or from systematically assessing long-term provincial needs. ... The Ministry's science and technology activities need an overall strategic plan to set parameters and consistent policies for existing programs and to guide the development of new programs" (Office of the Auditor General of Ontario 2003).

One of the tasks of the new Ministry of Research and Innovation was to prepare an overall strategic plan for Ontario. It was a long time in preparation, being released in 2008: *Seizing Global Opportunities: Ontario's Innovation Agenda*. The hallmarks of Ontario's innovation agenda were:

- Excellence. "The innovation agenda is built on an ongoing commitment to excellence in world-class, peer-reviewed, basic and applied research."
- Commercialization. "Attention will also focus on extracting value from investments in public research through commercialization."
- Partnerships. "The innovation agenda, through government programs like the Next Generation of Jobs Fund, supports industry-academia partnership investments in areas where Ontario is or will be indentified as a global leader."
- Strategic focus. "Initial areas of focus include the bio-economy and clean technologies; advanced health technologies; pharmaceutical research and manufacturing; and digital media and information and communications technologies" (Ontario. Ministry of Research and Innovation 2008).

Like the federal government, the Province of Ontario made health and biological science research a high priority with a number of targeted commercialization initiatives; Ontario has made a very large commitment to cancer research whose programs have been gathered into the Ontario Institute for Cancer Research (OICR) that now receives over $80 million annually.

Ontario did not have a program to endow new faculty positions like the CRCs, but in 2005 it did create the Ontario Research Chairs program to fund eight positions in key areas of public policy: postsecondary education policy and measurement, environmental policy and renewable energy, health policy and system design, biomarkers in disease management, urban policy—crime or transportation, educational achievement and at-risk students, economics and cross cultural studies, and bioethics. There is also a Human Health Resources Chair, funded by the Ministry of Health and Long-term Care.

TABLE 7.6
Main Provincial Funding Mechanisms for University Research, 2001–2002 (dollars)

Ministry of Energy, Science and Technology	
Science and Technology Program	
Ontario Centres of Excellence	32,300,000
Ontario Research and Development Challenge Fund	48,400,000
Ontario Research Performance Fund	29,700,000
Premier's Research Excellence Awards	10,700,000
Ontario Cancer Research Network	4,755,000
Telecommunications Access Partnerships	3,975,000
Interactive Digital Media Small Business Growth Fund	3,070,000
Total	**135,150,000***

* Includes other smaller programs not listed.
Source: Ontario. Ministry of Finance (2001).

Overall, the provincial Liberal's innovation agenda was very like the provincial Conservative's innovation agenda that preceded it. But this was not very surprising. At the same time in Ottawa, the broad thrust of the new Conservative government was the same as the Liberal government that preceded it. And the core strategy at both levels was very similar: excellence, commercialization, partnerships, and strategic focus.

The provincial programs continued to grow, so that by 2011–2012, the Research and Innovation program of MRI was to spend $350 million (Table 7.7) (Ontario. Ministry of Finance 2011a). As the strategy evolved, the programs previously listed under the Science and Technology Program were divided into two categories: Innovation and Commercialization, and Science and Research.

TABLE 7.7
Main Provincial Funding Mechanisms for University Research, 2011–2012
(dollars)

Ministry of Research and Innovation	
Innovation and Commercialization	
Business Ecosystem Support Fund	12,340,000
Bio-economy	6,285,000
Commercialization and Innovation Network Support	58,300,000
Innovation Demonstration Fund	16,900,000
Biopharmaceutical Investment Program	3,346,000
Ontario Emerging Technologies Fund	41,934,000
Ontario Life Sciences Commercialization Strategy	9,500,000
	155,056,000*
Science and Research	
Ontario Brain Institute	6,590,000
Ontario Institute for Cancer Research	84,000,000
Ontario Research Fund	86,473,500
Perimeter Institute	5,000,000
Research Talent Programs	3,661,000
	195,857,500*
Overall total	**350,913,500**

* Includes other smaller programs not listed.
Source: Ontario. Ministry of Finance (2011a).

It seems likely that Ontario's commitment to the new research agenda will remain strong, although like all government spending will be subject to expenditure restraint.

The greater problem is structural. Ontario does not seem to have achieved a stable structure for its programs. Until 2005, the research and innovation agenda was the responsibility of the Science and Technology Division of the Ministry of Enterprise, Opportunity and Innovation (MEOI); the agenda became the mandate of the newly established Ministry of Research and Innovation (MRI) from 2005 to 2011, but in 2011, MRI ceased to be a standalone ministry and became a part of the Ministry of Economic Development and Innovation. And most important throughout this entire period, there was little connection between provincial policy on research and innovation and provincial policy on higher education. The two were delivered by different ministries; both were undergoing massive expansions, but there is little evidence of coordination or recognition that research expansion and enrolment expansion were going on in the same institutions.

FEDERAL AND PROVINCIAL SUPPORT FOR APPLIED RESEARCH AT THE COLLEGES

Throughout most of the postwar period, neither the federal nor provincial[26] governments were much engaged with the colleges regarding research; indeed, research was not part of their mandate except insofar as it was implicit in their mandate to contribute to the economic and social development of their region. However, this has changed with the new research agenda and the focus on the national innovation system. Ontario colleges were given authority to conduct applied research in 2002. And clearly, colleges have always been a significant part of the innovation system as institutions of higher education; their highly trained graduates are important in the knowledge-based economy.

Many countries, especially those that have their non-university sector award bachelor's degrees, such as Germany with its *fachhochschulen*, and the Netherlands with its *hogescholen*, have such institutions also conduct applied research. And Germany and the Netherlands seem especially successful in translating research into economic application.

The college role in the new research agenda began to take shape in the early 2000s. In 2002 the Association of Canadian Community Colleges conducted a survey of applied research among its members for Industry Canada's Policy Branch, which led to the report: *Innovation at Colleges and Institutes* (ACCC 2005). At about the same time, NSERC senior management visited nineteen colleges across the country "to learn more about the form, nature, and scope of applied research that is being carried out in Canadian colleges" (NSERC 2007). These surveys indicated a modest overall level of research—a 2004 report from the colleges stated about 2 percent of full-time faculty engaged in applied research and about 20 percent hold research-based master's or doctoral degrees (ACAATO 2004)—but revealed many examples of sophisticated projects and successful college-industry collaborations.

Following NSERC's cross-Canada investigation, the federal government, through NSERC, established a pilot program in 2004, the College and Community Innovation (CCI) program as a component of the new research agenda. And after a review (NSERC 2007), it was made permanent in 2008. The CCI program now offers six types of grants to colleges and institutes of technology to support applied research and to enhance collaborations between colleges and companies (NSERC 2013). The March 2011 federal budget made further major commitments to applied research at colleges. It proposed $80 million in new funding over three years through the Industrial Research Assistance Program to help small and medium-sized businesses accelerate their adoption of key information and communications technologies through collaboration and projects with colleges. It proposed 30 new Industrial Research Chairs at colleges ($5 million per year) and an allocation of $12 million over five years for the Ideas to Innovation program to support joint college-university commercialization projects (Canada. Ministry of Finance 2011).

The 2013 budget increased support for this research, one of the few areas to actually increase its funding during a time of expenditure restraint. "Colleges and polytechnics play an important role in helping small and medium-sized enterprises bring new technologies, products and processes to the marketplace. [As indicated above], the Economic Action Plan 2013 includes an additional $12 million annually for the College and Community Innovation Program (CCIP) starting in 2013–14, increasing the budget to $50 million per year. CCIP supports collaboration between colleges and industry on research and development projects that focus on company needs, helping firms to become more innovative and productive. To further encourage the contribution of the colleges to the innovation system, the granting councils will also extend eligibility for their undergraduate industrial internships and scholarships to students enrolled in bachelor degree programs in colleges and polytechnics" (Canada. Ministry of Finance 2013).

Amidst this increasing research role for all colleges, in 2003, a small group of particularly research-intensive colleges came together to form Polytechnics Canada, representing itself as "a national alliance of Canada's leading research-intensive, publicly-funded colleges and institutes of technology" (Polytechnics Canada 2010). Of the ten current members, six are Ontario colleges: Conestoga, Sheridan, Humber, George Brown, Seneca, and Algonquin.

At the provincial level, the Ontario Ministry of Research and Innovation included colleges along with universities as key academic institutions in Ontario's Innovation Strategy, and colleges are now eligible to apply under many of Ontario's programs. Ontario encourages the colleges to work with businesses in their region on applied research projects.

In 2006, Colleges Ontario established the Colleges Ontario Network for Industry Innovation (CONII) as an applied research and development network—based at ten of Ontario's leading postsecondary institutions—aimed at "helping small- and medium-sized enterprises solve their technical problems, adapting new technologies for the marketplace, and developing new or improved products and processes. Ontario's Ministry of Research and Innovation provided $3.5M over three years to give Ontario-based small and medium-sized enterprises (SMEs) increased access to the expertise of Ontario's top researchers, and to the sophisticated equipment and research tools that existed within the member colleges" (CONII 2013).

"In 2009, Ontario announced a further 3-year, $10.2 million dollar contribution to CONII. This enabled the expansion of the network from 10 to 20 colleges, and has created a province-wide network dedicated to connecting Ontario business to the applied research and commercialization expertise across the Ontario college system. All 20 CONII-member colleges have an Industry Innovation Centre on their campus, which serves as the point of contact for the business community to the college applied research system. IIC staff assist by connecting business and community organizations with college expertise in order to foster economic development and innovation" (CONII 2013).

Colleges Ontario, in their paper *A New Vision for Higher Education in Ontario*, recommends an increased role in applied research (Colleges Ontario 2011b, 14). The Report of the Expert Panel to Assess the Strategic Mandate Agreement Submissions, *Quality: Shifting the Focus*, reported on the NSERC funds awarded to college faculty in 2010–2011. Four colleges had received over $1 million (HEQCO 2013, 21).

There is not yet a comprehensive picture of the role of colleges in research. The annual publication of Re$earch Infosource (2012) regularly includes a section on college research, but does not report total sponsored research income at each institution. HEQCO (2013, 21) reported on NSERC grants at colleges, but such grants are only a portion of total research income. And the CCI program does offer opportunity for SSHRC and CIHR to support college-based applied research. Whatever its current dimensions, it is clear that the college role is growing as part of the new research agenda.

CRITICISMS OF THE NEW RESEARCH AGENDA

We can begin rethinking our system of supporting university research by looking at the literature. What have analysts been writing about the new research agenda? Perhaps we can identify concerns and criticisms of the current approach and suggestions for improvement or reform. There are a number of criticisms.

Some writers argue that the whole approach of linking university-based research to the innovation system is deeply misguided; part of a neo-liberal, business-oriented agenda. They believe the approach has compromised the core principle of university autonomy, corrupting the university, taking it away from its commitment to free inquiry. They urge outright rejection of the agenda and a return to a time (that never really existed) when all research support flowed through the granting councils and was awarded on the basis of the academic merit of the project and of the proposer. They argue for public support, but it is to be justified because knowledge is valuable for its own sake. Cardinal Newman stated it famously: "knowledge is, not merely a means to something beyond it, or the preliminary of certain arts into which it naturally resolves, but an end sufficient to rest in and to pursue for its own sake" (Newman in Turner 1996, 78).

A second theme of criticism is somewhat similar, but less rejectionist; the analysis less tied to a larger criticism of neo-liberalism, and more accepting of the premise that a legitimate rationale for government support might be to encourage economically useful innovation. It too starts from the belief in the autonomous university committed to free inquiry, but argues that the new research agenda misunderstands the research process and how university research can best contribute to the economy. It argues that the current approach is too targeted, too applied, too orientated to immediate commercial usefulness. The true source of innovation in the long term, it is argued, comes from basic research, driven by the curiosity of the professor and not by thoughts of how it could be applied in the economy. Thus good science policy (and good economic policy) is compatible with the core values of the university. This criticism calls for a shift away from support for innovation-linked applied research and back toward curiosity-driven basic research.

A third critique accepts that research must demonstrate its value to society but worries that the new agenda marginalizes research in the social sciences, humanities, and fine arts—not recognizing its potential contribution to economic, social, and cultural well-being. Well articulated by Martha Piper in her Killam Lecture (Piper 2002) and by the leadership of the Social Sciences and Humanities Research Council (SSHRC), this view calls for more support for "knowledge mobilization" programs in the social sciences and humanities.

The place of the SSHRC fields in the new research agenda is sometimes ambiguous. Often the reports will acknowledge the importance of SSHRC work. For example at the provincial level, the Munroe-Blum report indentified one characteristic of effective public policy, which was that it "directed sufficient public investment into basic university research and into the range of scholarly fields and disciplines" (Munroe-Blum 1999a, 14). Ontario's Innovation Agenda states: "the arts, humanities and social sciences are essential components of a creative, knowledge-based economy. ... Ontario's innovation strategy recognizes the role of the arts, humanities and culture in fueling creativity and innovation, and encourages partnerships across disciplines to advance economic and social goals" (Ontario. Ministry of Research and Innovation 2008). The Council of Canadian Academies, in its assessment of science and technology in Canada, interpreted "science" broadly "to encompass any knowledge generating discipline, including the natural, social and health sciences, engineering and the humanities" (Council of Canadian Academies 2006). And, there have been some notable initiatives in the SSHRC areas. In 1999, SSHRC established the Community University Research Alliances (CURA) program linking university researchers and outside institutions, emphasizing joint definition of problems and issues, knowledge co-production, and eventual knowledge mobilization to address social problems. Building on several other programs, SSHRC in 2009 adopted a knowledge mobilization strategy and made knowledge mobilization a core objective of SSHRC. At the provincial level, a recent example is the announcement that the Ontario Centres of Excellence will establish a Social Innovation Program: the program "brings together not-for-profit organizations (NPOs) and social enterprises (SEs) with industry partners to collaborate on projects that lead to the development of new products and services that address tough social and environmental challenges (Ontario Centres of Excellence 2012). The MaRS district in Toronto now has a social innovation component.

There does seem to be a strengthening of the roles of SSHRC knowledge mobilization and social innovation within the new research agenda. Nonetheless, there is no question that the overall priority in the huge expansion of support for university research is science, medicine, engineering, and technology.

Within this third critique, there is a subtheme sharper in its criticism. The problem is not that the potential contribution of social sciences and humanities research to addressing economic and social problems has been overlooked; rather the problem is that much research in social science and humanities cannot be, and should not be, fitted into the innovation framework. Such research has different, but equally valuable, purposes. Consider two examples: one from the social sciences and the other from the humanities.

Many, perhaps most, social scientists see themselves as objective, neutral scientists documenting and analyzing social phenomena. Yet, as Thomas Bottomore, a British sociologist wrote in his book, *Critics of Society*, "it is difficult to separate entirely social science and social criticism. ... Even the most disinterested and objective description when it deals with certain aspects of social life implies or encourages a critical view. To depict faithfully and clearly, though dispassionately, gross inequalities, oppression, misery and suffering, is already a kind of criticism or an incitement to it. To point to the causes may also be to show how they can be removed, and by whom. Thus whether they will or not, the social sciences, social criticism and social reform have proceeded hand in hand" (Bottomore 1968, 15). This is clearly evident in the research not only in social sciences such as political science and sociology, but also in professional fields such law and education. Such social criticism is an essential responsibility of the research university in a democratic society, however uneasy it makes the university's sponsors in government and business,[27] or however uneasy it makes university presidents.

And what is the societal contribution of research in the humanities? David Dyzenhaus wryly and wisely observed in a paper, "The Case for Public Investment in the Humanities," that "knowledge for knowledge's sake is not only an inadequate slogan to combat an even more unrelenting utilitarian campaign than Newman faced; it is also inadequate for reasons that go beyond the expedience of the moment. For it might be right that if the Humanities are not useful, there is no reason for the public to invest in them. At most, they should be preserved in the great private universities of the United States of America—a luxury for those institutions which can fund useless inquiry from private pockets" (Dyzenhaus 2005, 165).

But most research in the humanities cannot be fitted into the innovation-linked approach, even if extended to include knowledge mobilization. Dyzenhaus' case for humanities research is presented as a reflection
on the argument of the famous American judge, Billings Learned Hand:

> I dare hope why it might now begin to be clearer why I am arguing that an
> education which includes the "humanities" is essential to political wisdom.
> By "humanities" I especially mean history; but close behind history and
> of almost, if not quite equal importance are letters, poetry, philosophy, the
> plastic arts, and music. Most of the issues that mankind sets out to settle,
> it never does settle. They are not solved because ... they are incapable of
> solution properly speaking, being concerned with incommensurables. At
> any rate, even if that be not always true, the opposing parties seldom do
> agree upon a solution; and the dispute fades into the past unsolved, though
> perhaps it may be renewed as history, and fought over again. It disappears
> because it is replaced by some compromise that, although not wholly
> acceptable to either side, offers a tolerable substitute for victory; and he
> who would find the substitute needs an endowment as rich as possible in
> experience, an experience which makes the heart generous and provides
> the mind with an understanding of the hearts of others. (Learned Hand as
> quoted in Dyzenhaus 2005)

This endowment is built by reading in the humanities and by the
research surrounding them. Justice Hand was writing about the proper
preparation to be a lawyer or judge, but it is also preparation to be a
citizen. And Dyzenhaus argues that such humane citizens are a public
good, the resources of a civilized society, and whose presence is necessary in a society where we can pursue our self-interest, and indeed, is
necessary in a society with a vigorous culture of innovation.[28]

There is merit, I believe, in each of these critiques; but I also believe
that the problems are often overstated.

It is impossible to escape entirely the instrumental justification for
university research. Certainly, the value of knowledge for its own sake
must be recognized and always be a starting point. Cardinal Newman's
position must always be part of our conception of a university But, I
would argue that we should not seek to escape entirely from instrumental
justifications. Research at our universities is publicly supported: directly
through research grants and contracts from the granting councils and
government departments, and indirectly through government operating
grants that support faculty salaries and the indirect costs of research. In
a democratic society, the government must justify and explain, to the
citizens, the purposes and outcomes of its expenditures.

The budgets of the three granting councils have been increased significantly, faster than the number of faculty members, and despite each
council shifting toward supporting more applied research, the available

funds per faculty member for curiosity-based research have increased. The underlying support for academically driven research across all disciplines remains strong. And we should remember that the foundation of support for university research—operating grants to fund the faculty positions across all disciplines with time for research and their indirect costs—continues. Of course, there has been much greater growth of research funds linked to innovation and to knowledge mobilization. But it is entirely appropriate that our democratically elected governments should consider how much research to support, in what broad fields, and toward what purposes. For example when new societal issues arise, research to analyze the problems can be chosen as a priority, whether the issue be AIDS, climate change, or economic growth. In a democracy it is entirely appropriate to "politicize" these decisions; the real problem arises when the selection of projects is based upon political criteria rather than scientific criteria. On the whole, we do not have this problem. In both the federal and provincial programs, however targeted are their purposes, the selection of projects is based upon academic criteria.

And much of the criticism focuses too much on the stated purposes of the research funding and not enough on what research is actually being done and published. The actual research being done can be seen by examining the curriculum vitae (CV) of a professor. I call this the "CV Test." If we look at the CVs of scientists supported under the current innovation-linked approach—those with CFI grants, or who hold Canada Research Chairs, or who are supported by one of the Centres of Excellence—we find that these leading academics are publishing basic research in leading academic journals. Indeed, probably more basic research is being published now, after the huge expansion of innovation-linked funding, than was published thirty years ago when support came only from the granting councils. Or if we look at another criticism, if we were to look at the CVs of our sociologists, or political scientists, or our law professors, or our education professors, we would find much research with a socially critical edge, and again there is probably more socially critical research published now than thirty years ago.

These critiques do not seem to me to require wholesale redesign of the system of supporting university research.

Although perhaps a more devastating critique is beginning to emerge: the new research agenda has not yielded much improvement in Canada's innovation record.

Geiger and Sá (2008) provide a measured analysis of the new research agenda in several countries and warn against promising—or expecting—too much. In 2009, the Council of Canadian Academies published a report of its Expert Panel on Business Innovation: *Innovation and Business Strategy: Why Canada Falls Short* (Council of Canadian Academies 2009). The title speaks for itself. The OECD's Economic Survey of Canada (2012) notes that Canada has implemented most of the "desiderata" for improvements in productivity: a sound macro framework, free trade, deregulation of most sectors and labour markets, low corporate taxes and tax incentives for research and development, a strong university sector and high attainment rates, and support for university research and for business-university partnerships. Yet, "the pay-off in terms of business innovation and productivity growth has not been large" (OECD 2012, 8). It is fair to say that Canada has still not solved its "productivity puzzle."

Today, both federal and provincial governments face difficult choices as they try to restrain government expenditure. The programs of support to business, which include the programs of the new research agenda, are coming under increasingly critical scrutiny: what results have been achieved by these expenditures? If government cuts fall heavily on these programs, university research will suffer.

NOTES

1. While the majority of professors have the responsibility both to teach and to do research, there are some professors, especially part-time or limited-term professors, who only have teaching responsibilities.
2. See Fallis (2007) for a more thorough discussion of the nature of the modern university and its social contract with the society that supports it.
3. The Canada Council for the Arts continues and supports individual professional artists (some of whom are at universities) and arts organizations.
4. The MRC became the Canadian Institutes for Health Research (CIHR) in 2000.
5. For a more extensive discussion of the linear model and the transition to the new research agenda, see Fallis (2007) from which the following has been drawn.
6. The federal government now has a program to pay for some of the indirect costs of research. This would be included in sponsored research income and deducted from total indirect costs to avoid double counting.
7. Jones et al. (2012) present data of the weekly hours of work of Canadian academics devoted to teaching, research, and service during teaching terms and non-teaching terms.
8. There is considerable variation across universities, due mainly to the variation in sponsored research income.
9. It should be noted that this calculation of research expenditure includes the faculty salaries and indirect costs associated with research of all professors, including those in the humanities. This measure of humanities research is included in the calculation of Research and Development Expenditure in the Higher Education Sector (HERD), discussed in the next section, dealing with the national innovation system. Somewhat paradoxically, although humanities research is not associated usually with innovation that can lead to economic growth, this measure is included in a country's total R&D expenditure.
10. Insofar as tuition fees help pay for the 40 percent of faculty salaries and for indirect costs, tuition fees also support research.

11. For a more detailed discussion of the roles of university, government, and business in the national innovation system, see Fallis (2007) from which the following is drawn.

12. OECD (1997) provides a good overview of national innovation system analyses.

13. HERD actually stands for Higher Education Research and Development, but most countries including Canada include only universities in this sector.

14. There are problems of comparability in how each country measures higher education R&D, but nonetheless, Canada would still have a very high share. See AUCC (2008, 18-19).

15. Although, as was discussed in the previous section, provincial grants pay for the time spent on research through professors' salaries and some of the indirect costs of research.

16. Also noteworthy, despite the often-heard worry that universities have had to seek funding from the private sector and have become beholden to it, only about 16 percent of research revenue comes from businesses; almost the same amount comes from the non-profit sector.

17. The Medical Research Council (MRC) became the Canadian Institutes of Health Research (CIHR) in 2000.

18. There was a small separate allocation for smaller universities.

19. Federal policy continued its evolution in this direction in 2013, as the government announced a transformation of the National Research Council (NRC) into an industry-focused research and technology organization.

20. The Council operates at arm's length from government. It is made up of three member academies whose members are selected for their distinguished academic contributions and contributions to Canadian society: the Royal Society of Canada: The Academy of the Arts, Sciences and Humanities of Canada, the Canadian Society of Engineering, and the Canadian Academy of Health Sciences.

21. The government broadened the title of the first area of focus from "natural resources" to "natural resources and energy."

22. The new government established the Science, Technology and Innovation Council (STIC) reporting to the minister of Industry. STIC produced a major assessment of Canada's innovation system: *State of the Nation 2008: Canada's Science, Technology and Innovation System* (Science, Technology and Innovation Council 2009).

23. In 2007, the Council of Canadian Academies was asked to examine business innovation in Canada and produced an expert panel report: *Innovation and Business Strategy: Why Canada Falls Short* (Council of Canadian Academies 2009).

24. As quoted on the University of Ottawa website, retrieved 15 February 2012.

25. For further descriptions of the programs, and other smaller programs, see Munroe-Blum (1999b, 13-17).

26. The Munroe-Blum report (Munroe-Blum, 1999a and b) on research and innovation in Ontario did not consider the applied research at colleges.

27. For a more extensive discussion of the role of the university in democratic society, see *Multiversities, Ideas, and Democracy* (Fallis, 2007).

28. Martha Nussbaum makes an analogous argument in *Not for Profit: Why Democracy Needs the Humanities* (Nussbaum 2010).

Chapter 8

RETHINKING UNIVERSITY RESEARCH

The research mission is a vital part of our higher education system—the previous chapter calculated that research expenditure was 40 percent of the university's total operating expenditure (TOE). Yet if we ask—when Ontario designed and built its higher education system—what has been Ontario's policy with respect to research? We have to pause and ponder, and then we realize that Ontario didn't really have a policy. Ontario developed its higher education system as a binary system of universities and colleges, designed primarily to provide first-level higher education. Universities had a research mandate and colleges did not (at least as a formal part of their mandate). All universities had the same research mandate and were funded on the same basis. And recently there was an emerging role for colleges in applied research. Beyond this, there was no policy on research. It is not so much that we need to *rethink* Ontario's system of supporting research, as it is that we need to *start thinking* about how to design the system for supporting research.

It is the university sector that has had the explicit mandate for research and therefore the chapter deals with universities. At the end of the next chapter, there is a small, but important, section dealing with colleges, which recommends that a subset of colleges be given an enhanced mandate for applied research.

RESEARCH AND THE DESIGN OF THE UNIVERSITY SYSTEM

Ontario's system of universities has been designed around the provision of undergraduate education and around the principle that there should be a place for every qualified student who wished to attend. Universities were located in all regions of the province, each providing comprehensive undergraduate degree programming and each funded on the same basis to ensure roughly similar quality. The research mission has been layered on top of this design. Given the needs at the undergraduate level, new universities were created and individual universities expanded. This meant more professors were hired, and given their joint responsibilities for teaching and research, more research was done. The professors were hired across all fields in order to provide comprehensive undergraduate degree programming, and so the research was comprehensive across all fields. The professors also applied for research grants, especially from the national granting councils, and so more research could be supported. The costs for faculty time on research and most of the indirect costs of research were covered from the general operating fund, that is, from the operating grant (and tuition) which is a function of enrolment. The university-based research endeavour in Ontario has been largely driven by the expansion of the system at the undergraduate level and by the availability of federal research funds. Provincial policy for the design of the university system has had little to say explicitly about the research mission of universities.

Consider the two major examinations of Ontario's system of higher education over the last twenty years: the Smith Commission (Ontario. Ministry of Education and Training 1996) and the Rae Review (Rae 2005). It is worth quoting the mandate of each because these mandates are very revealing of the thrust of higher education policy in Ontario.

The mandate given the Smith Commission (Advisory Panel on Future Directions for Postsecondary Education) was:

- to recommend the most appropriate sharing of costs among students, the private sector, and the government, and ways in which this might best be achieved;
- to identify ways to promote and support co-operation between colleges and universities, and between them and the secondary school system in order to meet the changing needs of students;
- to provide advice on what needs to be done to meet the expected levels of demand for postsecondary education, both with reference to existing public institutions and existing or proposed private institutions. (Ontario. Ministry of Education and Training 1996, 1)

The mandate given the Rae Review (the Postsecondary Review) was to advise on strategies to improve higher education by providing recommendations on:

- the design of a publicly funded postsecondary system offering services in both official languages that promotes:
  > recognized excellence in curricular activities to build the skilled workforce and promising scholars of the future;

> an integrated and articulated system that meets the diverse learn-
ing needs of Ontarians through the most cost-effective design;

• funding models(s) that:
> link provincial funding to government objectives for postsecond-
ary education, including the objectives of better workers for better
jobs in an innovative economy and an accessible, affordable and
quality system;
> establish an appropriate sharing of the costs of postsecondary
education among the government, students and the private sector;
> identify an effective student assistance program that promotes
increased access to postsecondary education. (Rae 2005, 1)

Neither mandate mentions research.

The report of the Smith Commission, nonetheless, recognized that
universities are places of both teaching and research (perhaps because
the commission was headed by David Smith, a distinguished academic
who had just stepped down as principal of Queen's University). The
report recommended that the Government of Ontario increase its funding of research overheads and that Ontario develop a research policy. It
also recommended that all professors be assessed with respect to their
teaching and research, that the province permit the emergence of differentiation of universities, and that the performance of all institutions
be assessed against standards for the full range of institutions including
"research-intensive institutions competing internationally." However,
although research is discussed, the mandate did not directly ask for such
a discussion and the bulk of the report is devoted to issues surrounding
the provision of first-level higher education.[1]

The report of the Rae Review, adhering more closely to its mandate,
contains very little analysis of research—its title is revealing: *Ontario: A
Leader in Learning.* (There was no one with senior university administrative experience on the Advisory Panel). There is mention that "education,
research and innovation lie at the heart of our economy," and that we
need "government and institutions that are unwaveringly committed to
excellence in teaching and research." It does say that Ontario "needs to be
clearer on its support for research and innovation" and Recommendation
25 reads: "Research Priorities: Establish a Council, reporting to the
Premier, to advise on and co-ordinate research priorities, and allocate
provincial funding in line with these priorities and in partnership, where
appropriate with federal funding agencies" (Rae 2005, 34). But these are
the only mentions of research in a 106 page report; the report is entirely
driven by how to provide and fund places at the undergraduate and
graduate level; by issues of access, tuition policy, and student assistance;
by issues of quality assurance; and by issues of governance and account-

ability. Whether Ontario has the best system of supporting university research is simply not addressed.

The follow-on from the Rae Review has a similar focus and similarly is absent any analysis and scrutiny of university research. The Ontario Budget 2005 announced *Reaching Higher: The McGuinty Government Plan for Postsecondary Education* (Ontario. Ministry of Finance 2005, 10-18). *Reaching Higher* funded a dramatic expansion of both first-level and upper-level education, through a $6.2 billion cumulative investment by 2009/10. "This is a historic, multi-year investment in postsecondary education—the largest in 40 years" (Ontario. Ministry of Finance 2005, 11). The budget rhetoric was not overblown; it was accurate—Ontario made a historic commitment to expanding the higher education sector; the equal of the expansion to accommodate the baby boom. It was during this time that both federal and provincial support for research was rapidly expanding. Yet, in the entire *Reaching Higher* framework, there is no analysis of the research function of universities.

The budget also announced the creation of a new arm's length Higher Education Quality Council of Ontario (HEQCO) that would take "a lead role in supporting quality improvement in postsecondary education. The Council would undertake research on indicators and outcomes, advise on system-wide results, and report on system performance" (Ontario. Ministry of Finance 2005, 16). HEQCO has focused its work on accessibility, educational quality, and accountability, but it has chosen not to examine the research activities of universities. Rather puzzlingly, HEQCO has also been asked to examine the "system design" and whether greater differentiation of universities would be desirable—all without building a body of analysis about university-based research.

The two most recent exercises to reform the Ontario system, the MTCU discussion paper *Strengthening Ontario's Centres of Creativity, Innovation and Knowledge* (Ontario. MTCU 2012) and the call for each institution to submit a Strategic Mandate Agreement *Quality: Shifting the Focus. A Report from the Expert Panel to Assess the Strategic Mandate Submissions* (HEQCO 2013b) had almost nothing to say about research.

Just as the Ontario policy on the design of the university system has had little to say about the research mission of universities, so too the provincial programs that support university research have had little to say about the design of the university system. Chapter 7 outlined these provincial programs supporting university research. They were all developed for the innovation agenda and delivered by ministries other than the ministry responsible for universities and colleges. First, they were delivered by the Ministry of Energy Science and Technology, then by the Ministry of Enterprise, Opportunity and Innovation, next by the Ministry of Economic Development and Trade, then by the Ministry of Research and Innovation, and recently folded back into the Ministry of Economic Development and Innovation. Throughout, there has been a curious disconnect between these innovation-linked programs and the provincial strategy on higher education.

Even when the major reviews of postsecondary education did make recommendations regarding research—when the Smith Commission recommended that Ontario develop a research policy or when the Rae Review recommended that the province needs to be clearer on its support for research and that it should establish a council reporting to the premier to advise on and co-ordinate research priorities—these recommendations were not followed.

Ontario policies have been incomplete and disconnected. We cannot develop a higher education policy for the years ahead, and we cannot think carefully about system design and differentiation, unless *both* the teaching mission and the research mission are included. The first step, and highest priority, in rethinking research is to integrate the research mission explicitly into provincial higher education policies. The research mandate of the system must be part of the purview of the Ministry of Training, Colleges and Universities.

Putting the research mission into higher education policy will require many changes and a change in perspective at the provincial level. But what is most important, provincial policy on university research should begin with the proper foundation.

THE PROPER FOUNDATION

The research mission is integral to the university; it is part of what defines a university. And the teaching by those engaged in the research enterprise is part of the character of university-level education, including undergraduate education. The majority of professors at any university and all universities should be responsible for both teaching and research. The research mission is carried out in universities that have autonomy, in which academic policy is the responsibility of the Senate, and in which professors have academic freedom.[2]

The ongoing operating funding for a university should be recognized to be supporting both the teaching mission and the research mission.[3] The fundamental purposes of this research are several: the synthesis of existing knowledge, the critical reflection on existing knowledge, and the search for new understanding and new knowledge. Its deepest purpose is knowledge for its own sake, although it presumes that knowledge will eventually be of general social benefit. This research must be supported across all the disciplines of inquiry at the university. The research is curiosity driven—it can be basic or applied, it can be socially critical or analytically objective, it can contribute to the economy, to the culture, or it can contribute to the political wisdom of the citizens. But it does not begin from concern with application.

The support to the research mission from the ongoing operating funds is complemented by curiosity-driven grants from the national research councils, judged according to the academic merits of the proposed project.

This is the foundation of the research mission of the university system.

I should emphasize that this foundation is not the entire research mission by any means; it is simply the foundation. But, the new research agenda—emphasizing economic innovation, knowledge mobilization, and social innovation—is an addition to, not a substitute for, this foundation.

The Smith Commission was followed up by a discussion paper, prepared by David Smith for the Ministry of Education and Training (then responsible for universities and colleges), titled: *Framework for a Research Policy for Ontario* (Smith 1997). This paper provides much insightful and wise analysis and is an excellent, and still timely, starting point for bringing the research mission into Ontario higher education policy. "Ontario should make clear in public statements that a strong research performance is a policy objective with a shared responsibility for its achievement." This was Smith's (1997) first of twelve key characteristics of a research policy for Ontario.

The public commitment to the research mission should also involve a clear articulation of the social contract for research—a social contract with two parts: the first governing the proper foundation and the second governing the new research agenda. In the first part, the government commits to funding research for all professors through operating grants, the research can be on topics that the professor finds most worthy of attention, and the professors promise that the research will be performed well and honestly and published for the general use of all. In the second part of the social contract, outlined by John Evans in his Killam Lecture, the government commits to additional research support, on topics that the government deems most worthy of attention, and the professors again promise that the research will be performed well and honestly and published for the general use of all, but they also undertake, together with the university, to work to see the results applied. The new research agenda remains controversial and misunderstood in many quarters at the university. A full discussion of this two-part social contract is needed if research is to be fully integrated into higher education policy.

At a more operational level, certain changes in perspective are needed. It should be recognized that the ongoing operating funds for universities—for the teaching and research missions—come from three sources. Ongoing operating funds come from provincial operating grants, from tuition fees, and from sponsored research income, especially the federal research programs. At present, operating funds are seen as coming from government grants and tuition.

There needs to be more careful analysis of how resources are allocated to the teaching mission, the research mission, and the indirect costs of each. This may lead to some radical changes in perspective. At present, operating funds are seen as coming from grants and tuition; tuition represents about 40 percent of such operating funding and so the conclusion is drawn that students pay 40 percent of the costs of their education. But the grants and tuition also pay for the time of professors devoted to research and many of the indirect costs of research. If we looked only at the direct costs of teaching (professors' time and the time of all the graduate students and part-time faculty engaged in teaching, running seminars and labs etc.) plus the indirect costs of teaching (a share of the library, computing, building, and administrative costs, students services and students assistance costs), we would find that students pay more than 40 percent of the costs of their education.

"A research policy for Ontario should include steps to establish ongoing relationships with the development of research policies at the national level" (Smith 1997). Ontario has much experience with the innovation agenda and is relatively well connected to federal initiatives here, but Ontario has no programs connected to the curiosity-driven foundation. The innovation agenda is most engaged with the NSERC and CIHR disciplines. The innovation agenda is much less connected to the SSHRC disciplines and therefore Ontario has less experience in these areas and less connection with federal programs. It will require special care to ensure that with the integration of the research mission into Ontario's higher education policy "an appropriate balance of research activity across the spectrum of intellectual inquiry [is] maintained" (Smith 1997).

As the Ontario programs that support university research evolved over the last ten years, they were taken from the "economic development" ministry and placed in the new Ministry of Research and Innovation (MRI). As these programs expanded, MRI divided them into streams for policy planning purposes: one headed "Innovation and Commercialization" and the other headed "Science and Research." In the expenditure estimates of 2010–2011, programs for Innovation and Commercialization were allocated $151,752,500, and programs for Science and Research were allocated $197,294,200. (See Table 7.7.) All these programs in both streams have now been folded back into the "economic development" ministry, the Ministry of Economic Development and Innovation. To integrate the research mission into higher education policy, a good first step would be to assign responsibility for the Science and Research programs to the Ministry of Training, Colleges and Universities.

RAISING SOME DIFFICULT QUESTIONS

One of the main reasons why the research mission has not been integrated into Ontario higher education policy is that the federal level has historically supported research through the granting councils and the provincial level has focused on access, undergraduate education, and the teaching mission. In many countries, the same level of government is responsible for both and there is much better integration of the teaching mission and the research mission in higher education policy. With integration, however, some fundamental questions tend to get raised and addressed. Three are paramount. Should all professors devote the same share of their workload to research? How should research be evaluated? Should universities be differentiated according to their relative focus on research? Many jurisdictions have addressed these questions; Ontario has not.

If we are to rethink research, and integrate the research mission into higher education policy, Ontario will have to address these three questions.

THE RESEARCH RESPONSIBILITIES OF PROFESSORS

Professors have three categories of responsibility: teaching, research, and service. The norm that has emerged over the last fifteen years in Ontario is that the professor's time should be divided as 40 percent on teaching, 40 percent on research, and 20 percent on service. Of course, the actual division of time will vary by professor, and likely also varies in a relatively predictable way by size/type of university and by discipline, as the survey by Statistics Canada showed (Table 7.1). Nonetheless, the 40/40/20 norm is now considered the best summary of the state of things in Ontario (Clark et al. 2009, 11).

Although the professor has responsibilities in three areas—teaching, research, and service—in only *one* area, teaching, does the employer (usually the dean) formally assign tasks. In simple terms, the professor is assigned a certain number of courses to teach each year—in academic parlance, this is the teaching load. And even this formal assignment of teaching responsibilities by the employer takes place within a framework of collegial self governance. If we define a course as operating for one term, the norm today in Ontario is that a professor is assigned two courses to teach in the fall term (September to December) and two courses to teach in the winter term (January to April); that is, a 2+2 teaching load.[4] The summer term (May to August) is for research and preparation for teaching the next year.

A professor is formally assigned only their teaching load—the balance of time across all their activities is not formally assigned. The professor operates in some ways like a professional in the wider society—governed by the norms and expectations of their colleagues, but largely responsible themselves for deciding upon their tasks and how to best use their time.

There is controversy, and I believe some misunderstanding particularly outside the university, about the time required to prepare and deliver an undergraduate university course, including meeting with students after class, often supervising teaching assistants, setting tests, essays, problem sets, and exams, and completing the marking. The standard class meets for three hours per week. My own experience, and confirmed by an admittedly informal survey of colleagues who are regarded as both conscientious teachers and active researchers, is that over the term about two hours of preparation/seeing students/course administration/ marking time is required for every hour of in-class time. This would be for experienced mid-career professors, giving a course they have taught before. (For young professors starting out, preparing courses for the first time, much more time is required.) Thus a one-term course meeting three hours per week in class requires six hours of other time per week. The two courses thus require about eighteen hours of time per week.

Using this measure of teaching time, and assuming roughly one day per week of research during the fall and winter terms, one day per week of service during these terms, and the summer term largely for research, one arrives at the 40/40/20 allocation of time across the year for a professor. (Regular holiday time, of say four to five weeks, is taken mainly during the summer term.)

Under most collective agreements (or faculty association agreements) there is a strong commitment to an equitable allocation of workload, which translates into an equitable allocation of teaching load. There is a strong presumption that all professors should have the same teaching load. Nonetheless, certain variations are commonly recognized. Young professors on first appointment often have a lower teaching load, recognizing their need to become established in research and the extra burden of preparing new courses. Most positions with heavy administrative responsibilities, for example the chair of a department, allow the person to have a reduced teaching load; senior administrative positions such as deans, vice-presidents, or presidents usually have no teaching responsibilities. Some research grants provide funds so that the grant-holder can "buy-out" some teaching responsibilities,[5] reducing their teaching load to allow more time for research. Some endowed professorships provide for a lower teaching load. Many universities provide a lower teaching load for their Canada Research Chairs (CRCs).

But save these exceptions, the norm is for all professors to have the same teaching load. And this implies that all professors have the same time for research.

Should we design our university system to have all professors following the 40/40/20 norm? Should there be variations within a university and/ or between universities? Common sense would suggest that it might be better to have professors doing different amounts of teaching and research depending upon their strengths.

Some professors will be better teachers, and some will be better researchers. Surely, it would be sensible to have them allocate their time differently, while still recognizing that all professors should both teach and do research.

And perhaps, the share of time devoted to research should vary over a career. Most professors are hired, tenured, and promoted at the same university and remain there throughout their career. There is always uncertainty about what they will achieve as researchers at the time of their appointment. Some few will not realize their potential, not be granted tenure, and leave the university. Another few will flourish and become leaders in their field; and most make steady sustained contributions. Still others will achieve modestly and plateau, perhaps becoming less energetic and committed researchers. A fair-minded observer might say becoming "less energetic and committed" would be better described as "becoming more balanced." To achieve and sustain research publication at the top of one's field requires an all-consuming passion, often at the expense of other dimensions of one's life. To invoke a cliché, to be a top researcher is a 24/7 commitment. Be that as it may, a common sense look at this framework of an academic career would suggest that after a professor is hired, goes through the probationary period, and is tenured (given a permanent position), there should be procedures to vary the amount of time each professor allocates to research. Presumably, those whose research is proving most fruitful and contributing most to the field should continue with a 40/40/20 pattern. Others would shift more of their time into teaching.

And these questions are posed against the history of teaching loads at Ontario universities. Forty years ago, most professors had 3+3 teaching loads and many had 3+2 loads. Yet today the norm is 2+2. Should all professors in the university system have moved to lower and lower teaching loads? Is this the best possible research policy for Ontario?

Very often, the move to lower teaching loads has been justified by the fact that the supervision of doctoral students is very time consuming and yet is not "credited" in the teaching load calculation; the move to lower loads is just realization of this other form of teaching. However, at many universities, and in many departments, most professors do not have doctoral students, yet their teaching loads have been reduced as well.

The other justification for lower teaching loads is that society has asked that universities contribute more through research. Yet society's request (backed by funding through the new research agenda) is to have more contribution to the innovation agenda and the knowledge mobilization agenda. The research of many professors does not fit this agenda, yet their teaching loads have been reduced to allow more time for research.

These declining teaching loads are the result of the collective negotiations at universities. On the whole, professors would prefer to have a higher share of their workload devoted to research. And it turns out that most boards of governors and senior administrations have had the same view. So powerful is prestige of research accomplishment, both parties to the negotiations—the employer and the employee—have felt it is in the university's interest to have the faculty members devote a larger share of their time to research.

Most jurisdictions do not have external policies to require differences in teaching loads between professors within universities. However, most jurisdictions, either through the evolution of their university system or by conscious design, have different types of universities—and teaching loads differ between types of university. Ontario does not have different types of university, and so, roughly all professors have the same teaching/research norms.[6]

If the government wanted more variation in teaching loads across universities and between professors, we must understand that change will be extraordinarily difficult.

Suppose the government wished to have more variation in teaching loads within universities. The university president or the dean could not simply assign higher teaching loads to certain professors because this would not be allowed under the collective agreement. In the short run, it could only be achieved by the government directly overriding the collective agreements at universities. The opposition from the faculty and the labour movement would be vehement. And the Supreme Court would likely declare it unconstitutional. But what should be even more worrying, such micro-management, such intrusion into internal decisions of university governance, would disrupt the entire social contract between government and universities built up over the years precisely to allow universities to do their job well. The only reasonable route to change within universities would be for government funding of universities to change in ways that would provide incentives for both parties—the board of governors and the faculty union/association—to negotiate a change in the way teaching loads are assigned.

In order to have teaching loads differ across universities there would need to be a partitioning of universities into groups, likely two groups. The two groups would have different missions, different funding arrangements, and different accountability requirements.

Over the years, the question of teaching loads, and the allocation of time between teaching and research, was almost never mentioned in the dialogue about the university system in Ontario; perhaps in part because research was so little a part of discussions about system design. The issue of teaching loads at Ontario universities is now very much part of discussions because of the clear-eyed analysis of one group of policy writers, Clark et al. (2009) and Clark, Trick, and Van Loon (2011). They have made the recommendation, provocative to many, that Ontario should create a new type of university: a teaching-oriented university, whose professors would have 4+4 teaching loads and little or no research responsibility, save research about pedagogy. Their recommendation arose perhaps in part because they recognized the difficulty of changing teaching loads within universities and the difficulty of dividing the existing universities into two groups to eventually force a difference in teaching loads between the groups. Instead, they recommend two groups: one with all the twenty existing universities and the other with the three new teaching-oriented campuses.

The usefulness of their recommendation relies, of course, on there being a need to expand the system with three new campuses. In Chapter 4, my analysis concludes that there is not a need for three new campuses. Therefore, to me, their recommendation is moot. Nonetheless, I would oppose it on the grounds that all universities should have both teaching and research responsibilities, although the balance between the two would differ between universities and between professors.[7]

Nonetheless, the teaching-research balance is now part of the discussion—as it should be. Ontario will have to confront the question. Should teaching loads differ within universities, and across universities, more than at present? I would argue: yes, they should. And because universities and their faculty members will not make such changes themselves, this will require a change in government policy. The real question is how to design such a government policy.

EVALUATION OF ACADEMIC RESEARCH

The second difficult question is: how should university research be evaluated?

As we rethink the research mission at our universities, it is important to ask: how well are we doing? Just as we asked what is the quality of undergraduate education provided at our universities, we should ask what is the quality of the research being conducted at our universities? This question is especially important because the explicit intent of the new research agenda was to support "excellent" research. The work was to be "world class," a judgment that would be sustained by international comparisons. This desire to support excellence is evident in the expanded programs at both the federal and provincial level discussed in Chapter 7.

To what extent is the research conducted at Ontario universities evaluated?

In a certain fundamental sense, all published research is evaluated and is being constantly appraised.

After a piece of research is completed, it is written up and submitted for publication: either to the editors of an academic journal for publication as an article, to the editor of a book for inclusion as a chapter, or to the editors of an academic press for publication as a book or monograph. On receiving the submission, the editor sends it to scholars/experts in the field of the research for assessment, a process called "peer review." These reviewers (or referees as they are often called) write an assessment of the work: the criterion for judgment is the contribution to knowledge and understanding in the discipline/field of the work. It is being judged by others who work in the author's field—by peers. Sometimes the editor of a book will do the assessment of a proposed chapter (being expert in the field). The reviewers/referees write a report on the submission, often suggesting clarifications, extensions, or revisions. The referees are of course looking at the soundness/correctness of the analysis and the clarity of argumentation and presentation, but they are also looking for originality and depth of analysis. Some work makes a major contribution to knowledge and understanding in the field (this is quite rare), most makes a modest contribution, and some makes a minor contribution. Sometimes the referees recommend rejection of the submission, not because it is incorrect, but because the contribution is too minor to warrant publication. After the author receives the referees' reports, the author discusses them with the editor to decide what further work needs to be done, and usually makes revisions. The editor receives the revised work and makes the final decision about whether to publish. This peer review process is the fundamental assessment mechanism in all academic research.

Peer review is an important evaluation system governing academic research. But, if we are honest with ourselves, professors have to admit that there is much peer-reviewed research published that is not of very high quality. The number of outlets, especially online journals, has expanded enormously and many of the articles published in some journals can only be generously described as of "modest" quality. This is handled in the academic community through the recognition that some journals publish higher quality work than others. The reviewers for these leading journals recognize this, and in their reviewing, they ask themselves the question: is this paper of sufficiently high quality and such a contribution to general understanding in the field that it warrants publication in the leading journal. Certainly some relatively weak work gets published in leading journals, and what proves to be very important work gets published in medium quality journals (it is very seldom what is later judged as top quality contributions are published in the marginal journals). But overall, there is a rough consensus about the "ranking" of the journals. I must emphasize that there is only a rough consensus and also emphasize that the way to determine the best quality outlets varies a great deal by field. (For example, some very small fields will have excellent work published in what to the outsider would appear to be an obscure monograph series.) But nonetheless, there is a rough quality assessment process operating through where the work was published.

Research is also assessed, albeit indirectly, before the work is done, through the granting process. All the research support programs, whether those of the granting councils or the more recent innovation-linked programs, are competitive. There are far more proposals for support than there are funds available. Each program has its own criteria for choosing, but all share three fundamental characteristics: the assessment involves

228 RETHINKING HIGHER EDUCATION

peers (experts in the field), the academic quality/promise of the work is assessed, and the track record of the proposers is part of the assessment.

And the assessment does not end with a peer-reviewed publication. Once published, the assessment is constant and ongoing by others working in the field. Others researchers may find it especially helpful, and draw upon it, citing it in their own published work. The number of citations is often taken as an indicator of quality. Some works may be included on the reading lists of graduate courses, where the next generation of advanced researchers is being educated. But the published work may be criticized, challenged, and even contradicted by subsequent published work (a paper that is criticized is also cited). This is the ongoing dynamic of research—constant sifting, challenging, assessing, setting aside and retaining. Much peer-reviewed published work is soon irrelevant in the ongoing dynamic and some never receives more than the odd citation. And some published work, even in the leading journals, will eventually be proven to be irrelevant or even quite wrong. The final assessment takes a long time, and of course, such is the nature of research; no assessment is truly final. Tomorrow may bring a new challenge, a new perspective.

Some research by professors is not published through journals, chapters, books, or monographs, but is disseminated in other ways. Research can be presented through conference presentations, government reports, working papers, reports to business or non-profit groups, and increasingly today over the internet. Most of this work is not peer reviewed, but once disseminated, it enters the same ongoing shifting and assessment processes as peer-reviewed publications. The research disseminated in these alternative ways may be intended to serve other purposes—for example, it may be intended to change public policy—but one judgment, if authored by a university professor, is always the academic judgment: does it contribute to knowledge and understanding in the field?

Also, research assessment is integral to the career progress of a professor. The entire body of published work of each professor is carefully evaluated at two stages in his or her career. The career of a professor is divided into three stages. The first stage is after appointment into what is often called a "tenure-stream" position, and the professor holds the rank of assistant professor.[8] As an assistant professor in the tenure stream, the position is provisional, not a permanent appointment; it is only made permanent—that is, the professor is granted tenure—after a period of five or six years, and after an assessment of the professor's work to date: the teaching, the research, and the service (and to some extent also the promise shown in these areas for the future). If the work in all three domains is assessed highly, the professor is granted tenure and promoted to associate professor. Sometime later, usually about eight to twelve years later, the entire work—the teaching, research, and service—of the associate professor is assessed again, when he or she is considered for promotion to full professor.

Consider when professors are being considered for tenure and promotion to associate professor. Their research, teaching, and service are assessed. The research assessment begins with the curriculum vitae (CV) prepared by each professor: all published research, in all forms, is listed. The assessment focuses upon publications in peer-reviewed media, although research disseminated in other ways will also be assessed. Then, the peer-reviewed publications are sent to a group of leading scholars in the candidate's field. These scholars write an assessment of the entire body of work: its originality, depth, and contributions to the discipline/field. The assessment letters are qualitative, but many also include quantitative bibliometric data, discussing the number of articles/chapters/books published, the quality of the journals and academic presses that have published the research, and how and where the work has been cited. Many universities complement the referees' letters with their own bibliometric analysis of the body of research. The assessment also considers honours and awards received by the candidate because of his or her research: perhaps having a paper named "best article" in a journal—many disciplines/fields have prizes for the best book published—or being elected a fellow of the society in the candidate's discipline. And the assessment usually also considers the research grants received to support the work, as a proxy for research accomplishment. Of course, fields of research differ greatly in the availability and need for research grants, and so the record of securing grants plays a very different role in research assessment across disciplines and fields.

The tenure and promotion process is the gold standard of research assessment: (i) it is comprehensive, considering all research although focusing on peer-reviewed publications; (ii) the body of work is assessed by leading scholars; (iii) there is bibliometric assessment of the number of publications, quality of journals/presses, and citations; (iv) there is consideration of honours and awards; and (v) there is assessment of the grants secured to support the research.

Finally, in most, although by no means all universities, there is research assessment through an annual report required of each professor documenting his or her teaching, service, and research, both ongoing and completed. The professor's record on teaching, service, and most importantly on research is linked to merit/performance pay. Because characteristic (ii) of the gold standard assessment method used in promotion and tenure—the body of work is assessed by leading scholars—is so time consuming and expensive, the annual research assessment does not use external peer review. Rather, it uses easily available quantitative measures, generally looking only at the numbers of articles, chapters, books and monographs published, where they are published, honours and awards, and grants received.

Thus in Ontario, there is ongoing research assessment of the work of every professor: when he or she submits a work for publication; when

considered for tenure and promotion to associate professor, and for promotion to full professor; when submitting a proposal for a grant; and for
most professors, during their annual performance review. And their work
is subject to the dynamic ongoing assessment of their field.

But in Ontario there is very little assessment of research at the level
of the overall system, at the level of each university, or at the level of
a department in a university. (When a graduate program is assessed,
there is some assessment of the published research of the participating
members to ensure they are capable of teaching in the program and of
supervising doctoral students.) In Chapter 1, where universities were
characterized according to research there were no data presented, even
on the number of publications by university, let alone on the quality of
the published research. The only data to assess research were data on
grants and other research income. And as was clear from the discussion,
the data on grants and research income are only proxies and very poor
proxies in many fields, especially the SSHRC fields.

Discussions about how and why to assess university research, and
the development of research documentation and assessment systems,
have been going on in most countries across the world for over twenty
years[9]. These discussions have been explicit and formal and have engaged both governments and universities together; the discussions
have shaped policy and programs. Most jurisdictions have some form
of reporting of research output and assessment at their universities as
part of the accountability framework. And many jurisdictions tie government research money to performance in research. (See, for example,
a survey published over twelve years ago of the international experience, "University Research Evaluation and Funding: An International
Comparison" [Geuna and Martin 2001]). Ontario (and indeed all of
Canada) is an anomaly. Ontario has had no such discussions about how
to assess university research.

I believe that it is unacceptable that the public support for university
research not be accompanied by research assessment to see how well we
are doing. The Smith Commission (1996) called for research assessment.
The Ministry of Research and Innovation's *Strategic Plan* (2006) called for
measuring results, including academic indictors relating to publications,
comparing Ontario against competing jurisdictions, both within Canada
and internationally.

Ontario needs to follow up. Ontario should implement a research
documentation and assessment system.

I would argue that, as a minimum first step, the CV of each professor,
listing his or her publications, should be a public document. This would
be helpful to students and represent basic accountability to the public
who support the research.[10]

A RESEARCH ASSESSMENT FRAMEWORK

The development of research assessment systems in other countries has been controversial. Some argue the systems are inherently flawed, neither fully documenting the research nor properly assessing it, especially because the quality of the work can only be established over the long term; it is argued the bibliometric assessment processes are weak in the SSHRC fields, especially the humanities. Others argue that the assessment exercises have set in motion destructive competition between individuals and universities, that universities "game" the system to make themselves look better, and overall that the assessment exercises actually inhibit good work. Still others argue that the exercises are clumsy and expensive, reveal little that is not already known, and therefore are a waste of resources—too costly for the benefits. One might argue that Ontario has been wise, sparing ourselves these problems. After all, as was discussed in the previous section, the research of professors is subject to ongoing assessment through long-established academic processes.

I disagree with these arguments. True, there are many problems with system-wide research assessment. But, any institution that is publicly supported has a fundamental responsibility to report on its activities, on how they are being assessed, and on the processes used to achieve improvements. This applies to teaching, and it applies to research. We do a fairly good job of assessing our degree programs; it is time to get started on analogous processes to assess our research.

Ontario can learn from the international experience. In some countries the exercise has been terribly controversial—for example, the Research Assessment Exercise (RAE) in England; in other countries like Australia and Denmark, research documentation and assessment have been developed over the years and are now considered a normal part of the system. Certainly, designing and implementing a sound system will take some time, and the development should be a joint exercise of government and the universities. But we should get started.[11]

A basic conceptual framework[12] for thinking comprehensively about university research is set out in Figure 8.1. The framework is made up of three components, and each could be the subject of an evaluation.

The first component is the research institutions and processes. Within this component, one would examine how many universities there are, how they are organized and differentiated; one would examine the inputs to research such as faculty time, libraries, labs, computer systems, and research grants; one would examine public policies regarding research and how grants and contracts are allocated; one would examine how universities allocate resources to research and the mechanisms of evaluation within these institutions; and one would examine the role of competition between universities and the competition for faculty members.

The second component is the "output," the research that is published and disseminated. Within this component one would examine the number of articles, chapters, books, and monographs published, the conference presentations, book reviews, government reports, and so on. Also, one could evaluate the means of dissemination—academic journals and presses, conferences, the Internet—to see whether the publications could be more effectively circulated.

The third component is the impact of the research; the impact assessment is separated into two separate streams. One examines the academic contributions of the work—what is its contribution to knowledge and understanding in the field? The other examines the contribution to society of the work—how does it contribute to the economy, to medical treatments and health, to public policy, or to civil society and democracy? Each stream of assessment is very difficult to do; fair-minded people will disagree about whether the assessments have asked the right questions and disagree about whether the measures used are appropriate; and inevitably the assessments will be incomplete. But is it vital that each—the academic-contribution assessment and the social-contribution assessment—be undertaken. In the long run, those who support the research endeavour will require it.

I would argue that Ontario's research assessment framework should have two parts. The first would document the amount of research published (the middle component in Figure 8.1). This should not be difficult. Australia, for example, has had this for years. The second part would provide an academic assessment of this published research (one stream of the third component in Figure 8.1). This is more difficult, but most jurisdictions have some type of academic assessment. The academic assessment cannot have the five characteristics of the gold standard; usually the systems rely heavily on bibliometric information and some involve peer assessments. Not only would this system improve the accountability of our universities, it would also be a great benefit to students, especially graduate students, as they choose which university to attend.

Social-contribution assessment is vitally important, but too complex to be done on a system-wide basis. It must rely more on case studies. But certainly, it is getting underway: the government is beginning to ask whether the huge expansion of support under the new research agenda is actually contributing to the economy.

The research assessment system should not be designed and operated by government. Rather it should be developed jointly by government and the universities. A good model for how to approach this issue is the model used for assessing undergraduate degree and graduate degree programs. These assessment systems were designed by universities themselves under the guidance of the Ontario Council of Academic Vice-Presidents (OCAV)—anticipating the government's and the general public's desire for such assessment. Unfortunately, OCAV has not been so prescient on research assessment.

FIGURE 8.1
University Research Framework

Research Institutions and Processes

- Universities
- Granting councils
- University and research funding
- Faculty salaries and teaching load

Research Output

- Number of publications
- Dissemination

Assessment of Impact/Contribution

ACADEMIC CONTRIBUTION	SOCIETAL CONTRIBUTION
• Synthesis	• Economy
• Critique	• Health
• New knowledge/understanding	• Public policy
	• Culture
	• Democracy

Source: Author's compilation.

A sound approach would be for the government to ask, through the university presidents, that OCAV develop and implement a system of research reporting and assessment. The assessment should report on the university system as a whole, on each university, and on disciplines within each university. This system should be open and transparent, comparing the research at Ontario universities against international standards.

It is especially important that the universities themselves support the research assessment exercise and are involved in its design. If not, others will soon do it for them. The government might do it itself. Or private businesses will do it (because there is a demand for it). In fact, private business has been doing it in Canada for many years.

Re$earch Infosource Inc. annually publishes league tables of "Canada's Top 50 Research Universities" (Re$earch Infosource, various years). Unfortunately, their approach uses only sponsored research income as a "measure" of research. (The ranking of Ontario universities by sponsored research income was presented in Table 1.6.) This measure heavily favours universities with medical schools and is very biased against humanities and social sciences research. Sponsored research income is the most widely used indicator of research at universities, simply because the data were easily available, but it is probably the weakest indictor. It has no measure of the actual publications and no measure of the quality and impact of the publications.

However recently, new indicators have been developed, measuring the number of publications and their impact.[13] Another private firm—Higher Education Strategy Associates (HESA)—together with Stoakley-Dudley Consultants, an executive search firm, developed a database of almost all Canadian professors, their publications, and the number of citations of each publication. The list of professors was taken from the websites of each university (almost 50,000 professors) and the publications and citations searched using the Google Scholar database. All of this is public domain information. HESA then created a proprietary database—H-index Benchmarking of Academic Research (HiBAR). First, the raw data on professors, publications, and citations was manually and extensively checked, particularly to remove incorrect attributions caused by similar names. Then the H-index of each professor was calculated. The Hirsch-index (H-index) has become a widely used metric to assess a professor's publications. The H-index is defined as the largest possible number n for which n of a researcher's publications have been cited at least n times. It values therefore a large number of papers that have been highly cited. The HiBAR database is itself an extraordinary undertaking, entirely without precedent in the Canadian higher education landscape. The HiBAR database has more information about individual professors at each university than the universities have themselves. Then, HESA went on to make an innovation; path breaking even among the world's research assessment databases. It has always been recognized that the publication cultures differ widely by discipline. For example, in some fields of science or medicine, researchers publish many papers, papers have multiple authors, and average-quality papers receive many citations; whereas in other disciplines, especially in the humanities, researchers publish books rather than articles, there are fewer multiple-authored papers, and any single item receives far fewer citations. HESA addressed this by generating field-normalized H-indexes. First, the discipline of each professor was identified (using the national granting council list of disciplines); then the average H-index for Canadian professors in that discipline was calculated. A professor's field-normalized H-index was calculated as their H-index divided by the average H-index of Canadian professors in that field. Therefore, a professor who had an H-index of 10 in a field with an average H-index of 10 would have a normalized index of 1.0. (For full discussion see Jarvey, Usher and McElroy (2012) and Jarvey and Usher (2012). HiBAR looks only at NSERC and SSHRC disciplines because in the CIHR/medical domain, it proved too problematic to identify the professors at each university, distinguishing them from researchers at affiliated hospitals.)

Jarvey and Usher (2012) have used the HiBAR database to assess "the research strength" of each Canadian university in the NSERC and in the SSHRC fields, and published their results.[14] These research assessments are presented in Table 8.1 and include all Ontario universities. These will be used again in Chapter 9 in the context of analysis of how universities might be differentiated based upon consideration both of research strength and doctoral education.

TABLE 8.1
Research Strength by University
Average Field-Normalized H-index Score

Universities	SSHRC Average Field-Normalized H-index	Universities	NSERC Average Field-Normalized H-index
Toronto	1.546	Toronto	1.425
Queen's	1.533	Waterloo	1.257
McMaster	1.364	Ottawa	1.254
York	1.331	York	1.208
Guelph	1.320	Queen's	1.200
Waterloo	1.289	McMaster	1.197
Trent	1.238	Trent	1.160
Carleton	1.162	Western	0.996
Western	1.016	Guelph	0.868
UOIT	0.980	Carleton	0.823
Windsor	0.964	Windsor	0.795
Wilfrid Laurier	0.945	Laurentian	0.663
Ottawa*	0.845	Wilfrid Laurier	0.633
Brock	0.829	Lakehead	0.591
Ryerson	0.724	UOIT	0.576
Lakehead	0.651	Ryerson	0.493
Laurentian	0.560	Brock	0.300
Nipissing	0.387		
OCAD	0.189		

*Rank likely affected by language of publication.
Source: Jarvey and Usher (2012).

The Centre for Science and Technology Studies (CWTS) of Leiden University publishes (online) assessments of research at universities, also based on publications and citations. The Leiden rankings use a different database—the Web of Science database (see detail below) rather than Google Scholar—and different metrics than the H-index to measure research strength. The Leiden database can be used to calculate different metrics; the metric presented here is PP(top 10%). It measures the proportion of the publications of a university that, compared with other publications in the same field and in the same year, belong to the top 10

percent most frequently cited. CWTS regards "the PP(top 10%) indicator as the most important impact indictor of the Leiden ranking." The
Leiden rankings can be used to rank the published research at Canadian
universities in five broad fields: biomedical and health sciences, life and
earth sciences, mathematics and computer sciences, natural sciences and
engineering, and social sciences and humanities (Leiden 2013). Table 8.2
presents the rankings for Ontario universities. The Leiden analysis covers
only five hundred large universities worldwide and reports on only eight
Ontario universities. The Leiden research assessments will also be used
in the next chapter's analysis of university differentiation.

TABLE 8.2
Research Strength by University
Leiden PP(top 10%) Indicator

	PP(top 10%) All Fields	PP(top 10%) Rank CIHR Fields	PP(top 10%) Rank NSERC Fields	PP(top 10%) Rank SSHRC Fields
Toronto	13.3	1	1	2
Ottawa	11.1	3	2	6
McMaster	10.8	2	7	4
Waterloo	10.5	8	3	7
York	10.1	4	4	3
Queen's	9.5	6	5	5
Guelph	9.3	7	6	8
Western	9.0	5	8	1

Source: Leiden (2013). The PP(top 10%) indicator in the NSERC fields was calculated as the
average of the indicators in the Life and Earth Sciences, Mathematics and Computer Science,
and Natural Sciences and Engineering. The CIHR indicator was PP(top 10%) in Biomedical and
Health Sciences; the SSHRC indicator was PP(top 10%) in Social Sciences and Humanities.

Thus, we now do have assessments of the published research at
Ontario universities and these assessments can be separated into the
CIHR, NSERC, and SSHRC fields. These indicators create quite a different picture of research intensity/research strength than the sponsored
research income indicator.

The top eight Ontario universities by sponsored research income are
Toronto, McMaster, Ottawa, Western, Queen's, Guelph, Waterloo, and
York. (See Table 1.6). These are the same universities reported in the Leiden
rankings. But the measures of research impact have some significant
differences in ordering. Toronto is still the clear leader by the indicators
in Table 8.1 and 8.2. But York moves from eighth in research income to
fourth on measures of research impact. Western is fourth by income but
much lower by research impact. And overall, the direct research assessments show much less difference between universities than sponsored
research income.

If we look only at Table 8.1 that offers NSERC and SSHRC assessments for all universities using the field-normalized H-index, we see eight of the top nine universities to be the same top eight by research income. But, the H-index does identify research excellence in small universities. Trent does strikingly well in both SSHRC and NSERC research, and is within the top eight by these indicators.

Clearly, with these new indicators, the landscape is changing at an extraordinarily rapid rate. Unfortunately, Ontario has done little research documentation and assessment to date. The HEQCO consultation paper—*Performance Indicators for the Public Postsecondary System in Ontario* (HEQCO 2013a)—made only the most tentative move in this direction. Among thirteen proposed indicators, only one related to research and that was to measure Ontario's share of tri-council funding.

However, with the will, an effective system of research documentation and assessment, suited to Ontario universities, could be quickly developed. This should be a top priority in rethinking research.

RESEARCH ASSESSMENT: WORLD UNIVERSITY RANKINGS

No discussion of research assessment would be complete without a discussion of world university rankings—the most controversial research assessments are those that are imbedded in world university rankings. Let me begin by stating that I believe we *should* ask: how do our universities *as research institutions* compare with other universities around the world? This question is seldom asked when we design the system of higher education in Ontario (or Canada), despite the priority to world class work in the recent expansion of support for university research. Also I believe that Ontario (and Canada) would be well served to have some research universities that are among the best in the world. If this seems unrealistic, this aspiration might alternatively be phrased using the words of the Smith Commission (1996): Ontario would be well served to have some "research-intensive institutions that are competing internationally."

Before turning to how we might assess Ontario's universities and their place in the world, I want to reiterate a theme that has run throughout the book.

The university has many missions, not just to conduct research. Its mission is also to provide education, especially undergraduate education. We should be reminded that most of the leading research universities of the world—just like Ontario universities—have more undergraduate students than graduate students. The university has a mission to contribute to the economic, political, and cultural life of our society. It has a role in a democracy as independent analyst, critic, and conscience—a countervailing power to government and business. A university must be judged according to how it fulfills all of these missions, not just research.

Nonetheless, let us focus on the research mission: how are we to judge the research at a university? As academics, the main criterion will be the quantity and quality of the research published by its professors. We judge the quality of research by its contribution to knowledge: by its originality, depth, and influence on the discipline or a field within the discipline. We believe these assessments should be made by peers, by scholars in the field.

Certain world university rankings, and the rankings that will be of interest to this chapter, are based *only on the research at universities*, not on the teaching and other activities. And the research assessments in the rankings are academic-contribution assessments; they are not social-contribution assessments. Thus, the rankings only include one of the two streams of a proper assessment of research impact (Figure 8.1).

Ideally, to assess the research at a university we would apply the gold standard used in tenure and promotion (with its five components articulated above) to *all* the work published by *all* the professors. The assessment would have to be done on a discipline-by-discipline basis. Then to see a university's place in the world, we would compare this gold-standard assessment with a similar assessment of other leading research universities.

However, this ideal is unattainable. Nonetheless, I do not believe we should ignore the question of how Ontario universities rank in the world as research institutions. We should approach the question as scholars: thoughtfully, rigorously, and mindful of what the data can and cannot tell us.

The possibility of large scale research assessment exercises arose with the establishment of the Institute for Scientific Information (ISI), founded by Eugene Garfield in 1960. ISI first provided a print-based indexing service, most importantly the Science Citation Index (SCI), the Social Science Citation Index (SSCI), and the Arts and Humanities Citation Index (AHCI). (Science is defined to include medicine, mathematics, and engineering.) The creation of these citation indices begins with *a list of journals to be monitored*. Having selected the list, each article published in each journal is recorded, along with the author(s) of the article, the institutional affiliation of each author, and all the articles cited in the original article.

In 1992, ISI was acquired by what is now Thomson Reuters. The unit is now called Thomson Scientific. Thomson Scientific has created the Web of Science, an enormous database, now digital rather than print-based. In 2009, the Web of Science monitored over 10,000 journals. The Web of Science includes within it the Science Citation Index Expanded (monitoring over 7,100 journals), the Social Science Citation Index (monitoring over 2,100 journals), and the Arts and Humanities Index (monitoring over 1,200 journals).

The Web of Science therefore allows one to count the number of articles published by professors at a given university (since the affiliation of each

The curriculum vitae (CV) of each professor should be a public document.

Ontario, through the Ontario Council of Academic Vive-presidents (OCAV), should develop and implement a research documentation and assessment system.

NOTES

1. The Smith Commission was followed by a discussion paper, also prepared by David Smith, *Framework for a Research Policy for Ontario* (Smith 1997), but its recommendations were not taken up. This paper is discussed later in this chapter.
2. This reinforces the argument, made in Chapter 5, that it would be a mistake to establish teaching-only universities in Ontario.
3. There may be, as in many countries, separate funding envelopes for teaching and for research, but the ongoing funding for the research responsibilities of all professors must be assured.
4. Although this is the norm, in some universities and some departments, there is a 3+2 teaching load.
5. The funds permit a part-time instructor to be hired in their stead.
6. Historically in Ontario, professors at the larger, more research-intensive, universities had lower teaching loads. However, over the past thirty years, the teaching loads have become more similar across universities.
7. An equally clear-eyed look at attempts to create teaching-oriented universities in other jurisdictions would conclude that it would take about two to four years for the new teaching-focused campuses to begin lobbying the government for a change in their mission and funding to allow more research by their professors.
8. Many professors at universities do not hold tenure-stream positions and are hired for a limited number of years or hired each year to teach a certain number of courses.
9. For examples of recent discussion in Europe, see Boulton (2010) and the League of European Research Universities (2012).
10. I would argue that all forms of research support and consulting should also be reported on this public CV. There have been many concerns about conflict-of-interest and conflict-of-commitment regarding university research. The starting point to addressing these concerns is transparency about support and other work.
11. There is a large literature about research assessment systems, with a section of the literature paying particular attention to the difficulties of assessment in the humanities and social sciences. Some excellent survey papers have been prepared in Canada. See, for example, ab Iorwerth (2005) and Archambault and Gagné (2004).
12. I have tried to avoid the input/production/output language, drawn from an analogy to industrial production, often used to set out a research framework.
13. Chant and Gibson (2002) provided bibliometrically based assessment of research at Canadian universities.

14. The database could easily be used to produce assessments by discipline, by university.

15. For example, the European Reference Index for the Humanities being developed by the European Research Council, www.esf.org/erih. Google Scholar has much better coverage in the humanities and social sciences.

16. Waltman et al. (2012) provide a detailed report on the Leiden methodology with a comparison to the Shanghai and THE approaches.

17. However much one may dislike university rankings, these rankings have helped University of Toronto to demonstrate its excellence in research by comparing it to universities around the world.

18. For example, looking at my own field—economics—one will find many papers discussing research assessment and departmental rankings. So too, for example, in the history literature, the physics literature, and so on, you will find such papers.

Chapter 9

FURTHER DIFFERENTIATION OF
THE BINARY SYSTEM

Since the 1960s, Ontario has had a binary system of higher education—universities and colleges of applied arts and technology (CAATs). Each sector has a distinct mandate: the college sector offers first-level higher education; the university sector offers both first-level and upper-level higher education, and the university sector has a mandate for research. There is a separate policy framework for each sector: operating grants are different, tuition is different, and the governance, quality assurance, and accountability structures are different. Within each sector, the institutions are funded on same basis and operate under the same policy framework.

Thus, the institutions of higher education in Ontario are differentiated as two groups. The differentiation arises because of the mandate given by government to each sector, supported by the separate policy framework for each sector. Within each sector, there is differentiation among institutions, but particularly in the university sector, universities have tended to become more similar over time through their own institutional decision making because they have shared the same vision of what they would like to be.

A central question, as we rethink higher education for the decades ahead, is whether Ontario would be better served by a more differentiated system. In this book, it has been argued that the question cannot be addressed without a comprehensive analysis of first-level higher education, upper-level higher education, and research. These three components have now been analyzed.

Is there need for more differentiation? As with much of the book, this chapter will deal mainly with universities. At the end of the chapter, there is a short section focusing only on colleges.

Rethinking Higher Education: Participation, Research, and Differentiation, G. Fallis. Kingston: School of Policy Studies, Queen's University. © 2013 The School of Policy Studies, Queen's University at Kingston. All rights reserved.

The first conclusion, after reviewing the three components, is that the essential features of Ontario's current system of first-level higher education should be retained: a binary system of vocationally oriented colleges and academically oriented universities, a place for every qualified student who wishes to attend, geographical distribution of institutions of both sectors across the province, a comprehensive range of programming offered by each institution, and the same government funding and fees for the same activity in order that within each sector institutions provide first-level higher education of roughly similar quality. The last feature is especially crucial. Even if institutions within each sector become more differentiated, there should not be differentiation of their funding for first-level higher education. Differentiation should not be a covert vehicle for delivering first-level higher education at lower cost and a separation of the system into a better-funded elite group and another group.

A second conclusion is that all professors in the university sector should have the responsibility to teach and to conduct research. The operating funding of all universities should be recognized as supporting research of all professors across all fields. The national granting councils should offer curiosity-driven grants across all fields, awarded competitively and using academic criteria.

Any policy of differentiation should build on this sound foundation.

The conclusion to retain these essential features of our current system means that universities will not be much differentiated at the undergraduate level. And indeed, given that the great majority of their students will be undergraduates, all universities will be primarily undergraduate universities. And given that all professors both teach and conduct research, all universities will be research universities. What then could be the basis for differentiation and how might it be accomplished?

DOCTORAL/RESEARCH UNIVERSITIES

The important domain for differentiation arises in doctoral education and in the relative emphasis on research, especially the new research agenda. The logic of what will best serve Ontario in these domains is very different than the logic of what will best serve for first-level undergraduate education. Doctoral education and research should not simply evolve out of the structure designed for accessible undergraduate education. The logic for differentiation arises because of the recognition that there will be limited, as opposed to universal, activity and that it should be concentrated in nodes of critical mass and excellence. Universities with a special mandate in doctoral education and research will deliver these more efficiently, more innovatively, and they can be more clearly assessed and held accountable for achieving results at international standards. And without an explicit policy of differentiation, all universities will aspire to expand in doctoral education and in the new research agenda, without ever achieving the critical mass needed for excellence.

Doctoral education offers the clearest basis for differentiation. Ontario needs only a limited number of doctoral programs and each should have both the critical mass of students and the critical mass of faculty members needed for high-quality programs. In addition, Ontario should benchmark its doctoral programs against the best in the world and develop programs of comparable standard; a process that further emphasizes the need for focus on a small number of programs. In order to have truly strong individual doctoral programs, there needs to be a large community of similarly high-aspiration graduate programming within the university. Top quality programs, across a range of fields, are part of the necessary critical mass at one university. Within this group of doctoral universities, doctoral programming should be planned and assessed on a province-wide basis.

Similar focus in research is required if Ontario is to realize the stated goals of the research programs of the new research agenda. Throughout these programs there is an emphasis on excellence, judged against the best research in the world. All Ontario universities should be engaged in research, but there needs to be a subset of them that have particular research intensity. And again, to create a culture of high aspiration, there needs to be a critical mass of high quality research across a range of fields. And within this group of research-intensive universities, there should be province-wide planning and assessment of the new research agenda, including planning across the designated priority areas and across commercialization initiatives.

The new research agenda focuses on strategic areas for the totality of the research effort across all universities. For example, Ontario's current strategic areas of focus include the bio-economy and clean technologies, advanced health technologies, pharmaceutical research and manufacturing, and digital media and information and communications technologies. Furthermore, the programs of the new research agenda, especially the Canada Foundation for Innovation and the Canada Research Chairs program, sought to have each university develop its own strategic areas of focus. As a condition of receiving funds, each university had to file a strategic research plan. However, this province-wide strategic planning and institutional-level strategic planning have never been brought together. The research group of universities would be the place to bring them together.

The focuses of differentiation through doctoral education and through research intensity complement one another. Of all education, doctoral education is most connected to the research enterprise. Strong doctoral programs beget strong research, and strong research begets strong doctoral programs. Also, all the major professional programs of the province—law, medicine, business, and so on—would be in this group of universities.

Thus, I would argue that Ontario will be best served for the years ahead by designating a group of doctoral/research universities. Any further doctoral programs should be limited to this group of universities. The goal of provincial policy should be to increase the share of graduate education at these universities, placing restrictions on any further undergraduate expansion. This group would be the focus of province-wide planning of doctoral education and of the new research agenda.

The master's/bachelor's group of universities would offer both bachelor's degrees and master's degrees, but not doctoral programs. Further, there would be limits on the share of master's programming in total enrolments.

This further differentiation of the university system must be rooted in mandates specified by the government.

DIFFERENTIATION OF UNIVERSITIES BY ACADEMIC CULTURE

The classification of universities into a doctoral/research and a master's/bachelor's group is controversial, doubly so when it is extended to mandating such differentiation by the government. It seems to tier universities into a research-focused group and a teaching-focused group, and such is the prestige of research today that it seems to tier universities into two quality levels. And certainly in the Ontario tradition all universities have always had responsibilities to both teach and conduct research. This concern about "tiering" needs to be faced.

The most important point to reiterate is that whatever classification and mandate system is adopted, all Ontario universities are and will remain primarily undergraduate universities: the great majority of their students will be at the undergraduate level and their primary task will be undergraduate education. The second point is that all undergraduate education would still be funded on the same basis and can be provided at similar quality levels in all universities. And the third point is that all professors and all universities will be responsible for both teaching and research; the issue will be one of relative emphasis.

And in fact this relative emphasis on research already differs across universities.

Another way to think about differentiation and classification of universities comes from the work of the sociologists who have studied the culture of academic life. This work offers insights to complement the empirically based categories of the Carnegie system. It builds upon the famous work of Robert Merton who studied the way science operates and the lives of scientists. Merton used the terms science and scientists, but the analysis applies to all the activities that seek to create new knowledge, new insight, and deeper understanding—in constant dialogue with, and challenge to, existing knowledge. He called these activities "science;" in the terminology of this book, it is called "research." It is both difficult and rare to make a major contribution to knowledge and understanding, and, central to the operation of science, central to these processes that generate new knowledge, central to the research endeavour, is to grant recognition to those who make major contributions. Most research makes at best a modest contribution, and much research, even though peer-reviewed and published, will be cited rarely and will not become part of the required reading of those who come next to that same problem or field of study. Inherent in the research enterprise is stratification—of contributions, of professors, of universities, and of their departments. The research process operates with a reward system based on recognition of the extent and depth of a professor's contributions to knowledge. "Recognition for originality becomes the socially validated testimony that one has successfully lived up to the most exacting requirements of one's role as a scientist" (Merton 1973, 293).

Against this background analysis of the research enterprise, the sociologist Joseph Hermanowicz studied the lives of academic scientists to see how this stratified research enterprise fit into actual university lives and careers, and how the cultures of academic departments were created. (His work dealt with US universities.) Of course, the responsibilities of professors include not only research, but also teaching, and service to their university and communities beyond the university, and each of these has their reward system. Also, not all professors are "equally and evenly socialized to pursue recognition, that is, to pursue research careers" and many "individuals identify more strongly with non-research roles" (Hermanowicz 2009, 13-14). On the basis of interviews with scientists at various sorts of universities, and at various stages in their careers, Hermanowicz developed a characterization of three cultures and showed how it could be used to classify universities in an article: "Classifying Universities and Their Departments: A Social World Perspective" (Hermanowicz 2005).

Hermanowicz notes that professors at all four-year higher education institutions have the triumvirate of roles: research, teaching, and service. "This is fully expected, since all of the institutions form parts of a socially regularized system of higher education. What is important in the present concern is not similarities, but differences …. Thus I call attention to the premiums the respective worlds assign to these roles, most particularly to research, because this role is least constant (and therefore most different) among the institutional types.

"The elite academic world consists of those institutions that place the highest premium on research. The overriding organizational goal is to garner additional prestige through the research and scholarly achievements of a faculty. Such universities often go to lengths to attract, retain, and compete among each other for 'stars'"—stars are those academics who have made truly major contributions and are expected to continue to do so. "Most, if not all, departments in such institutions run doctoral programs, and their students are recruited from a nationally and internationally competitive pool of candidates.

"The pluralist academic world consists of those institutions that place a premium on both research and teaching. The pursuit of additional prestige through faculty research and scholarly achievement is a goal of this type of institution, but not an overriding one. Such institutions typically employ a faculty that is more variegated in its goals and its achievements. While some highly accomplished academics and sometimes even 'stars' work at this type of university, they are a decided minority. This type of university does not compete to hire 'stars,' first because they are outcompeted by elite institutions and because they may lack the resources and an organizational priority to recruit such individuals. Most departments in this type of institution confer master's and doctoral degrees, and tend to recruit students from a mixed regional and national pool of candidates.

"The communitarian world consists of those institutions that place a premium on teaching in the presence of research. Faculty in this type of institution often engage in research or scholarship ... In instances, highly accomplished researchers and scholars work in this type of institution. Teaching, however, is the overriding organizational goal, and an allegiance to that goal defines the overall collective identity—loyalty to local concerns. Some departments in this type of institution may possess master's programs, and others may possess doctoral programs in addition, but many other departments confer only undergraduate degrees. This type of institution typically recruits from a local or regional base."

Hermanowicz' classification of institutions—based on research aspirations, relative priorities, extent of doctoral education, and range of recruiting—is insightful and has the ring of reality. The basic characterization of institutions as elite—research is given particular emphasis in the presence of teaching, or pluralist—research and teaching are *either* given roughly co-equal priority emphases *or* where large factions of individuals alternatively stress one over the other, so as to create a collective hybrid, or communitarian—teaching is given particular emphasis in the presence of research, is particularly useful in considering the design of a system of higher education.

Ontario does not have any universities with an entirely elite culture. Most universities have a blend, some more elite/pluralist and others more pluralist/communitarian. Within any university, different departmental cultures will be elite, pluralist, or communitarian. With this sociological perspective on the actual system, it means that any proposal to differentiate the system according to the relative emphasis on teaching and research is not tiering by quality but rather differentiation by culture and focus. Many Ontario professors would prefer, and proudly so, that their department have a communitarian or pluralist culture, rather than an elite culture.

This proposal to differentiate Ontario universities into a doctoral/research group and into a master's/bachelor's group can be seen as designating an elite/pluralist group and a pluralist/communitarian group.

GROUPS OF DOCTORAL/RESEARCH UNIVERSITIES

In many countries over the last twenty years, and Canada is no exception, there have emerged self-indentified groups of "research-intensive" universities. They begin usually as informal associations among the presidents and vice-chancellors, but many go on to become formal organizations with a secretariat. They emerge because they share common aspirations and problems, and feel they have more in common with each other than with the other universities in the system. They share information and best practices, make submissions to governments as a collectivity, and usually seek to have the government recognize their special character and to have special funding arrangements suited to this character.

It is not always explicit what criteria are used to determine membership in the group. The focus is mainly on "research intensity" as measured by research income, but doctoral-education intensity is also used as a criterion. Chapter 3 discussed classification systems of universities, particularly the Carnegie system which begins by classifying universities by the highest degree awarded. The doctorate-granting group is then classified into subtypes according to the number of doctorates awarded and the amount of research income at the university. These self-identified groups of research universities are operating in the spirit of the Carnegie classification, selecting themselves as a top subtype within the doctorate-granting group.

The oldest of these groups is the Association of American Universities (AAU), founded by fourteen American doctorate-granting universities in 1900 to strengthen and promote American doctoral education. It now has sixty American members, admitted by invitation (and two members from Canada: University of Toronto and McGill University). The sixty American members award more than half of all doctorates and receive almost 60 percent of federal research funding in the United States (AAU 2012). The AAU includes both public and private universities.

The United States has always had a system of very differentiated universities, not because of any national plan or policy but rather because of its history with elite, richly endowed, private universities (the Ivy League of eight, old, east-coast universities being the most famous) and because of the competition among states to establish leading universities. In the US, higher education is a state responsibility, the federal role has been to support research and to provide student assistance programs.

Some states, most famously California, designed their systems of higher education into distinct sectors. As California prepared for the coming of the baby boom to higher education, it codified a three-tier system under the California Master Plan for Higher Education, adopted in 1960. The three tiers are the University of California (UC) system, the California State university system, and the California Community Colleges system. The plan laid out that the top eighth of graduating high school seniors would be guaranteed a place at one of the University of California campuses (e.g., Berkeley, UCLA, etc.), the top third would be able to enter the California State University (e.g., San Francisco State, Cal State LA, etc.), and that the community colleges (e.g., Bakersfield College, College of the Canyons, etc.) would accept all applications. Only the University of California universities could award doctorates. By the mid 1960s, the University of California had nine campuses (a tenth, UC Merced was added in 2005). This three-tier system has attracted attention all over the world, especially the idea that within a public system there should be a group of doctorate-granting universities with very selective admission standards at both the undergraduate and graduate level. The UC universities have been remarkably successful, renowned around the world. Four campuses—UC Berkeley, UC Los Angles, UC San Diego, and UC San Francisco—are ranked by both the Taiwan and Shanghai rankings as among the top twenty-five universities in the world.

In the United Kingdom, the research-intensive group is known as the Russell Group, begun in 1994. Today it "represents twenty-four leading UK universities which are committed to maintaining the very best research, an outstanding teaching and learning experience, and unrivalled links with business and the public sector." The Russell Group universities received 68 percent of the income from the research councils and award 57 percent of the doctorates (Russell Group 2012).

In Australia, the group is called the Group of Eight, informally established in 1994 and formally incorporated in 1998. The Group of Eight is "a coalition of leading Australian universities, intensive in research and comprehensive in general and professional education." The Group of Eight receives about 70 percent of research income and educates over 50 percent of the doctoral students (Group of Eight 2012).

In Canada, the research-intensive group is now known as the U15; alone among the groups discussed so far remaining an informal coalition, although it has now moved to formalize itself having hired an executive director (Berkowitz 2012). It began in 1991 as the Group of Ten, or the G10; it expanded in 2006 to become the Group of Thirteen (G13), and expanded again in 2011, renamed as the U15. It describes itself as Canada's fifteen leading research universities. The six Ontario members of U15 are, in alphabetical order: McMaster University, Queen's University, University of Ottawa, University of Toronto, University of Waterloo, and University of Western Ontario (now Western University). The U15 is a self-selected group and the criteria for membership are unclear; the main criteria seem to be the presence of a medical school and sponsored research income.[1]

BENCHMARK MODEL OF A DOCTORAL/RESEARCH UNIVERSITY

Whether in discussions of classification systems, or in discussions of world university rankings, or in discussions of how best to differentiate institutions in a large national system, much is made of the special character of these universities. Defining features are certainly the high level of research income and the large number of doctorates awarded—and all of course, as we should remind ourselves, have significant numbers of undergraduate students and award many more bachelor's degrees than doctorates. They are highly selective at the undergraduate and graduate level, and highly selective in hiring faculty members and in granting tenure to faculty members.[2]

To further explore their character, two approaches were taken.

Using the average Taiwan/Shanghai 2009 ranking, I examined the top thirty universities to see if they have any distinguishing characteristics. Twenty-two of the top thirty universities come from the United States, four from England, two from Japan, and two from Canada (University of Toronto ranked eighteenth and University of British Columbia ranked thirtieth).

Among this top thirty, 87 percent have a medical school and 57 percent are public universities. Medical schools are important in these science-focused rankings because the publications by researchers in university-affiliated hospitals and medical research institutes are included as publications of the university. (A university is defined here as "public" if the government provides substantial operating funds for undergraduate education. By this definition the English, Canadian, and Japanese universities are public; only the United States has private universities.) The US private universities are a case unto themselves with their huge endowments: they average half the size of the public universities, are over 50 percent graduate students, and have very low student-faculty ratios. Although even at US private universities, most of the funding for research comes from the public sector.

The better comparators for Canada and Ontario are the public universities in the top thirty. These universities average about 30,000 students with about 33 percent of their students being graduate students.

A second approach, perhaps even more relevant to the Canadian experience, is to examine the Group of Eight in Australia and the Russell Group in the UK, countries of comparable income and traditions and commitment to higher education.

All members of the Australian Group of Eight have medical schools. They average about 38,000 students of which 34 percent are graduate students.

All but two of the members of the Russell Group have a medical school (LSE and Exeter are the exceptions). They average about 23,600 students of which 33 percent are graduate students.

The two benchmarks of research-intensive/doctorate-intensive, publicly supported, universities have a number of characteristics: they range in average size, from 23,600 to 38,000 students; about one third of their students are graduate students; and virtually all have medical schools. They are quite selective at the undergraduate level, at the graduate level, and in their hiring and tenure processes. How do Ontario's research intensive universities compare to the benchmarks?

If we examine Ontario's doctoral/research universities, identified in Chapter 1, we find that they do not conform to the benchmark model.[3]

The most striking difference, noted in Chapter 1, is that none have a very high share of their total student body in graduate education. The benchmark is 33 percent; in Ontario the average is 18 percent. Either by design, or rather more likely by inadvertence, Ontario has not developed universities with a high share of graduate students.[4] Thus, none of our universities have the intensive graduate-research character of the benchmark universities.

In terms of absolute size, two Ontario universities are much larger than the benchmark: University of Toronto and York University.

Ontario's leading research university, University of Toronto, is a striking anomaly on both counts: U of T has almost 70,000 students of which about 19 percent are graduate students. U of T is much larger and more undergraduate-focused compared to the other top public research universities in the world.

As was discussed in Chapter 5, Ontario universities do not differ significantly in their selectivity at the undergraduate level in the main disciplines of the sciences, social sciences, and humanities. Again, we are unlike the benchmark. Designing our system so that some universities are much more selective at the undergraduate level has not been the Ontario experience.

The public policy questions, then, has two parts: (i) should Ontario strive to have doctoral/research universities among the best in the world and (ii) should we try to have our leading doctoral/research universities closer to this benchmark: 30–36,000 students with one third at the graduate level? Given that these universities would have 20–24,000 undergraduates, Ontario's larger universities would have to have fewer undergraduates and therefore would become more selective at the undergraduate level than they are at present.

If the Government of Ontario, as a matter of public policy, took this benchmark as the goal, U of T is something of an elephant in the room. U of T has not been evolving toward this benchmark. From 1997 to 2007, University of Toronto added 23,000 full-time undergraduates, an increase of over 70 percent. Over the same period, it grew at the graduate level by

57 percent: U of T reduced its percentage at the graduate level. It would be impossible to attract enough high-quality graduate students for U of T to reach the 33 percent graduate benchmark, given its current 53,000 undergraduates. The benchmark structure could only be achieved with a radical restructuring of U of T.

If we can agree that Ontario should strive to have research universities comparable to the leading universities across the world, what might this imply for public policy?

One approach might be to designate a flagship university. Chapter 1 noted University of Toronto was in a group of its own in terms of sponsored research income and doctoral education. However, a jurisdiction as large and diverse as Ontario would be ill served by one flagship university, with it given pre-eminence across all disciplines. What we want to accomplish is differentiation across universities: with one group of universities being more research-intensive and doctoral-intensive, with excellent and accessible undergraduate education available across the province, with universities encouraged (and held accountable) to be excellent at what they do, and with a handful being world class in research across many disciplines and others being leaders in a few disciplines. The heart of the matter is system design, the funding formula, and accountability. It will not be accomplished by "picking winners" or granting privileges to single institutions based on past performance. What is needed is an unambiguous focus on international standards of excellence in allocating research funds within a system where universities both collaborate and compete.

ACHIEVING DIFFERENTIATION

Virtually every jurisdiction with a system of mass or universal higher education is confronting the dilemma of how to structure its system and how to differentiate its institutions. And most are asking whether a subgroup of universities should have a special role in doctoral education and research at an internationally competitive level. An overview of international developments is provided in a recent volume: *Structuring Mass Higher Education: The Role of Elite Institutions* (Palfreyman and Tapper 2009). In some countries, there has emerged, more through history than through explicit policy choice, a group of universities with special roles in doctoral education and research. Australia is an example (Marginson 2009), as is England. The United States is a mix of history and policy. In some other countries, universities have traditionally been treated in the same manner and were very similar, but over the last decade have been differentiated by explicit public policy. Here, Germany is an example. In Germany, the tradition of undifferentiated universities was so exceptionally strong that the opening up of differentiation discussions was referred to as "the breaking of a taboo" (Kehm and Pasternack 2009, 113).

Ontario has also had an exceptionally strong tradition of undifferentiated universities. But, it is time to break the taboo.

The Ontario government has not tried to restrict the domain of any university; rather it has allowed each to pursue its own strategic direction. And over the last fifteen years, there has been less discussion in official policy circles about system differentiation than during the 1970s and 1980s. The expansion of graduate education since the mid 1990s illustrates this clearly: universities expanded at the graduate level, provided that they could show that the expansion was consistent with their strategic plan and that they had the resources to provide programs of good quality. Because the government was to provide full operating funding for graduate expansion, and some capital funding, the adequacy of resources was not much of an issue. The strategic plans of all universities called for aggressive graduate expansion and all were able to do this. There was little attempt to design a system-wide strategy for graduate expansion. The universities themselves, through their collective voice, the Council of Ontario Universities, have always resisted any formal differentiation of universities.[5]

Nonetheless, the question of university differentiation has reappeared in policy discussions. In July 2010, the deputy minister of Training, Colleges, and Universities asked the Higher Education Quality Council of Ontario (HEQCO) to explore "whether a more strongly differentiated set of universities would help improve the overall performance and sustainability of the system, and help Ontario compete internationally ... [and] ... how to operationalize a differentiation policy, should government be interested in pursuing this as a strategic objective" (Weingarten and Deller 2010, 6).

HEQCO submitted its report, *The Benefits of Greater Differentiation of Ontario's University Sector,* in December 2010 (Weingarten and Deller 2010). The report acknowledged that Ontario universities are already "somewhat differentiated" but argued that there would be many benefits to increasing the differentiation of Ontario's system. The report recommended that the move to a more differentiated system begin with each university submitting to MTCU a mission statement including its desired enrolment targets and mix, the priority areas of teaching and research, new programs planned, and particular university strengths. The MTCU would review the mission statements to ensure that they are "credible and reasonable" and that "the sum of the individual mission statements add up to the required contribution of the university sector to public goals" (Weingarten and Deller 2010, 17). After review and perhaps revision, MTCU would sign a MYAA with each university, including an articulation of performance indicators that would be used to assess the university's progress towards agreed-upon goals. Funding would be linked to performance.

The Council of Ontario Universities responded to the HEQCO report with its own policy paper: *Differentiation in Ontario Universities* (COU 2011b). COU argued that the current system was already "highly differentiated" and that it supported "ongoing development of a postsecondary sector that rewards competitive innovation." COU set out as a fundamental principle: "Differentiation should start from each university's unique aspirations and strategic plan. Universities' plans will be built on their particular strengths and developed through collegial governance. The province's approach to differentiation should not categorize universities or arbitrarily limit these aspirations" (COU 2011b, 3). Differentiation would be achieved by new funding: there would be a new differentiation grant awarded proportionally to each university. Any discussion of performance indicators, or of linking funding to such indicators, was conspicuous by its absence.

This book has taken up this differentiation discussion and comes to different recommendations.

As discussed in Chapter 2, differentiation can arise in two ways: it can result from differences in mandate and it can result from institutional choice. Both the HEQCO and COU approaches emphasize the second, albeit with government policy steering the institutional choices. My analysis is that differentiation will require the government to specify the mandates. The first step would be to identify and limit where doctoral education can be offered.

Could such further differentiation be accomplished using the processes outlined by HEQCO and COU? I do not believe so. Both begin too much from the strategic plans and aspiration of each university. Neither has a strong system-wide vision. A strong system-wide vision can only come from the government. To achieve this differentiation will require a much stronger government vision than in the past. It will require a vision that acknowledges there will be a limited number of doctoral programs, that judges research against the best in the world, and that recognizes the importance of critical mass and institutional culture.

And perhaps most importantly, neither the HEQCO nor COU analysis acknowledges the powerful forces of isomorphism in the university sector. Yes, individual universities have their locales, their histories and their individual strategic plans, but in many fundamental ways all universities have similar aspirations. Particularly in recent years in Ontario, all universities have placed a high priority on expanding at the graduate level and expanding their research endeavours. Without government imposed limitations, universities, through their own decision making, will continue to become more similar.

The first step in establishing this differentiated system in Ontario would be to formalize these limitations on doctoral enrolment patterns through agreements between the government and each university. In recent years in Ontario these agreements have had different names. First, they were called Multi-Year Accountability Agreements (MYAAs); then they were called Strategic Mandate Agreements (SMAs). To emphasize that my recommended approach is different and that these agreements must place a limitation on the mandates of institutions, I shall call these Mandate and Accountability Agreements (MAAs).

IDENTIFYING ONTARIO'S DOCTORAL/RESEARCH UNIVERSITIES

The crucial question of course becomes: which universities should belong to each group?

There is no easy answer. If the doctoral/research group is too small, competition is lost (although there is competition from across Canada and the world). And competition, more than performance indicators and accountability agreements, is what drives improvement. Also if the designated group is too small, we risk complacency among the group and might miss the vigour and vision of a young university evolving into a major graduate and research centre. For example, if the group had been selected twenty years ago, Waterloo might not have been included, but it certainly belongs today. And we also need to ensure that the group includes the major centers of doctoral education and research across all the disciplines, across the CIHR, NSERC, and SSHRC domains. This argues against using a medical school as a necessary characteristic.

The logical basis for establishing the two groups is to examine the data on doctoral programming and research; those universities that already have significant doctoral programming and significant research would be in the doctoral/research group. The data for doctoral programming are presented in Chapter 1, Table 1.5 and for research in Table 1.6. Of course, the problem will be to define "significant" doctoral programming and "significant" research.

One obvious way to designate the doctoral/research group would be to make them the six Ontario universities that are members of the U15: Toronto, Western, Waterloo, Ottawa, McMaster, and Queen's. These universities are the top six in terms of doctorates awarded 2007–2009 in Ontario (and are listed in this order in the previous sentence). They are also the top six universities in terms of Canada Research Chairs. (Although the U15 universities are a self-selected group, the selection in Ontario does identify the top six universities using these criteria.) Using the six U15 universities would have the advantage of having the national association and the provincial association consistent, and presumably therefore more consistent in the federal/provincial activities. However, it is unlikely all provinces would follow this same approach: if each province engaged in a similar differentiation of their universities, it is unlikely their U15 universities would be the only ones selected.[6]

But there is a bigger problem with using the U15 universities: while it includes Ontario's major centres in the CIHR domain, it does not include all major centres in the SSHRC and NSERC domains.

It does not include York, which is a major centre of social sciences and humanities doctoral education and research in Ontario. York awards the second most doctorates in the SSHRC fields of Ontario universities. A good indicator of the quality of doctoral students is the number of Canada Graduate Scholarships (CGS-doctoral) awarded by SSHRC to students at that university. Here, York ranks second in the province. It has the second highest number of SSHRC CRCs. York also has a top-ranked law school and business school, as well as fine arts faculty. These are all components of the SSHRC domain. There is a powerful argument for York's inclusion in order that the Ontario doctoral/research group contains the major universities across the CIHR, NSERC, and SSHRC fields.[7] Furthermore, considering all fields, York has the third largest number of doctoral students in Ontario and awarded over four hundred doctorates during 2007–2009. York's inclusion is also strongly supported by the research quality indicators of Chapter 8 in Table 8.1 and 8.2. York is ranked fourth in Ontario using the normalized H-index for both SSHRC and NSERC domains and is ranked third using the Leiden PP(top 10%) indicator in the SSHRC domain and fifth across all domains.

Also, a strong argument can be made for the inclusion of Guelph, as a major NSERC centre: it has more external research income than Waterloo, and more NSERC CRCs than Ottawa, and the same number as Western. Guelph students receive more NSERC CGS-doctoral fellowships than at Ottawa. Further, although its doctoral programming is slightly smaller than the U15 universities, it already has over eight hundred doctoral students and awarded over three hundred doctorates in 2007–2009.

This larger group of eight universities, the U15 with York and Guelph, would be defined as awarding more than three hundred doctorates over three years, having over thirty CRCs, and having over $60 million in annual external research income.

A still larger group, adding those with considerable doctoral programming and research income, would include Carleton and Windsor. This group of ten would then include all the medical-doctoral and comprehensive universities of the Statistics Canada (*Maclean's*) classification system. This group would be defined as awarding more than one hundred doctorates over three years, having over fourteen CRCs, and having over $25 million in annual external research income.

If Ontario were to design from scratch a university system differentiated as doctoral/research universities and master's/bachelor's universities, the doctoral-research group would likely number about five or six. However, a policy of differentiation for the next twenty years must begin from the enrolment patterns that already exist. A realistic and pragmatic recommendation would be that the doctoral/research group be made up of ten universities, defined as above. This determination has a number of advantages. It corresponds to the longstanding distinction between, on the one hand, the medical-doctoral and comprehensive universities, and on the other hand the primarily undergraduate and special purpose universities. These two groups already exist and are recognized. The differentiation policy would at the outset merely put restrictions on future enrolment patterns, most importantly restricting new doctoral programs to the doctoral/research group and also putting limits on their undergraduate enrolments. This group of ten also has the advantage of ensuring wide distribution of the universities across the regions of the province. And finally, the definitional characteristics of the group are quite distinct and no university of the master's/bachelor's group could meet the definition over the next five or ten years.

The first step, as noted, is to identify the two groups and establish the enrolment limits in the MAAs. This should begin to alter the strategic planning in each group and also should break some of the pressures of isomorphism in the system. Simply digesting this differentiation regime and altering strategic plans will take some time, but moving in this direction is a fundamental part of rethinking higher education in Ontario.

Over time, a robust differentiation regime will require differences in funding arrangements, governance, and accountability between the two groups. It is premature to specify these in any detail, but some directions can be suggested. As has been already stated, the funding for undergraduate and master's students should be the same across the two groups.

Over the coming years, the marginal increases in government funding available to each group might be allocated differently. For example, the increase to the doctoral/research group might be placed in a central fund and allocated to members of the group on a competitive basis for projects in doctoral education and/or research. The criterion for support would be the achievement of excellence at an internationally recognized level. The increase to the master's/bachelor's group would also be placed in a central fund and allocated to members on a competitive basis for projects that would improve undergraduate or master's education.

Each group would need to establish a mechanism for meeting together and some secretariat for analyzing common problems. This would require that the Council of Ontario Universities be redesigned to accommodate two subgroups.

The accountability regimes would have many similarities because both groups teach at the undergraduate and graduate level and both groups conduct research. It might be that the doctoral/research group be charged with a special role on developing the research assessment framework and the means for regularly benchmarking the research of their group against international comparators (discussed in Chapter 8). The master's/bachelor's group might have a special role in developing better means to assess the quality of undergraduate education to lead in the development of the "new narrative" around undergraduate education called for by AUCC (discussed in Chapter 5).

NEW MANDATE FOR THE ITALs

The analysis of the previous chapters has recommended two major new roles for the college sector: the expansion of bachelor's degrees and an enhanced mandate in applied research. This would be a major transformation and runs a risk that the fundamental mandate of the sector—to provide vocationally oriented diplomas and certificates and to provide the in-class instruction for apprenticeships—would be diminished. Whatever lies ahead, all colleges should continue to have this fundamental mandate. A sound approach would be to differentiate the college system as two groups, one of which would take on these new roles. The college system is already evolving this way and it should now be formalized.

The college system has been differentiating by allowing a college to take on the designation of Institute of Technology and Advanced Learning (ITAL) and increase its programming in bachelor's degrees. In Chapter 5, dealing with baccalaureate education, it was recommended that more career-oriented bachelor's degrees be created in Ontario and that this expansion should occur primarily through the ITALs, including three-year degrees developed from existing three-year diplomas. At present, ITALS can have up to 15 percent of their programming as bachelor's degrees. This should be raised to 30 percent.

Some of the colleges have been taking on a growing role in applied research, especially related to small and medium sized business in their region. Both the federal and provincial programs of the new research agenda have included a role for colleges and see them as an important part of Canada's national innovation system. A group of colleges should be given an enhanced mandate in applied research. This would require the establishment of proper administrative procedures and policies to support research, including policies on academic freedom, research ethics, and research accounting. Many colleges have these already. It would also require changes in the responsibilities of some faculty members and changes in the collective agreement making applied research part of the workload. The change will take time, requiring that some newly hired faculty have doctorates. The Ontario system has experience in this regard, making the transition to include research in the workload of some faculty members, for example at Ryerson University. And it would also require changes in the funding of the college to support the enhanced research mandate.

The increased bachelor's level programming and enhanced applied research are complementary so the two new roles should be assigned to one group. The complementarity will be especially beneficial to students, as those in the applied bachelor's degrees could gain familiarity and experience with applied research. The logical group to have the two new roles would be the ITALs, although this might be expanded to include other colleges with strong bachelor's programs and applied research, but which have not taken on the ITAL designation.

This new differentiated structure is a major transformation of the college sector, much greater than the differentiation of the university sector. It should be implemented carefully and gradually. MTCU should ask that HEQCO examine the evidence both in Canada and other jurisdictions, consult with colleges and universities, and offer advice on how to carry forward this transformation. And throughout it is vital that the college sector retain its essential character and its focus on preparing students for the labour market and on applied research in collaboration with businesses in their region. This should not be an exercise to transform certain colleges into universities.

NOTES

1. See Fallis (2013) for analysis of the criteria for membership in the U15.
2. Their faculty members usually have lower teaching loads than faculty members at other universities in their national system.
3. Chapter 1 identified a group of nine universities with significantly greater doctoral programming than other universities and a group of nine universities with significantly greater sponsored research income. The two groups were the same.
4. The University of Toronto's St. George campus is closest to the benchmark.
5. All universities are, of course, not the same. Chapter 1, describing Ontario's system of higher education, thoroughly documented the current level of differentiation.
6. For example, British Columbia has created The Research Universities Council, which includes six of its eleven public universities. Only UBC is a member of U15.
7. York is also a major SSHRC centre in Canada, certainly within the top ten. These same facts give York a strong claim to be included in the U15.

Chapter 10

CONCLUSION: POLICY DIRECTIONS AND IMPLEMENTATION

Ontario has had an extraordinary expansion of its higher education system over the last fifteen years—first-level higher education, graduate education, and research have expanded as never before in our history. Most of the advocacy and most of current Ontario government policy has pointed toward continued expansion—more places in first-level education, more places in graduate education, more support for research. But I have argued that rather than focusing on expanding higher education, we need instead to focus on rethinking higher education. Do we have the best system to meet this continuing top priority in the years ahead? Do we have the best system of first-level higher education, the best system of graduate education, and the best system for supporting research? Within the public policy discussions, some rethinking has begun, centred particularly on whether we need a more differentiated system to meet the needs of the future.

This book presents my own rethinking, drawing upon a large academic and policy literature about the issues. There are a number of specific policy proposals, but just as important, I advocate for a number of policy directions. Indeed to follow on these policy directions is more important than the specific proposals: as these policy directions are explored—by governments, by universities and colleges, by faculty, staff, and students—the specifics will emerge.

The main policy directions of the book are drawn together and summarized in this final chapter and placed within a discussion of how they might be implemented.

Rethinking Higher Education: Participation, Research, and Differentiation, G. Fallis. Kingston: School of Policy Studies, Queen's University. © 2013 The School of Policy Studies, Queen's University at Kingston. All rights reserved.

The great expansion of higher education has been made possible, at least in the decade from 1998 to 2008, by strong economic growth and growing government revenues. However, the sequence of the financial crisis in 2008, recession, deficit-financed stimulus, and halting recovery has left Ontario in a precarious position. There is a large deficit that must be eliminated in the medium term, but the medium-term prospect is for only modest economic growth. After I began writing this book, both the federal and provincial governments began to implement expenditure restraint that is planned to continue for several years until their budgets are balanced. But, the thesis of the book is that rethinking is required in any event. And we will be better able to address the fiscal challenge if we approach our rethinking inspired by the desire to have the best possible higher education system, rather than haunted by the demands for expenditure restraint. An Epilogue follows this chapter discussing higher education policy in a time of expenditure restraint.

- **Develop a stronger system-wide vision.**

As we rethink higher education, it becomes clear that change is needed. And if change is to be accomplished, a basic dilemma must be faced. The system we now have is the result of government policy that sets the broad framework, but the details—the actual programs offered and the balance between teaching and research—are set by the decisions of the individual universities and colleges. Each institution sets its strategic direction. There are differences among institutions because of these strategic choices and also because of history and location. But there are also powerful forces of isomorphism—universities in particular seek to develop in broadly similar directions. If there is to be change from the patterns of the current system, there will have to be a stronger government vision of the entire system. System-level change will not occur through the strategic choices of individual institutions. The heart of rethinking higher education is this vision of the entire system.

We should set our standards high, aspire to excellence, be outward looking, and seek to have a higher education system equal to any in the world. Sometimes in current discussion of excellence and international comparisons, the argument is made that Ontario needs some top-ranked universities, especially in light of the excellence initiatives in other countries. This is an important issue to address. Nonetheless, the crucial aspiration should be to have a *system* of higher education with all its components—from college programs to doctoral programs to research labs—that is equal to any in the world.

Apart from establishing the binary system, Ontario has never had a strategic plan for its higher education system. It is time to develop and implement one.

- **Stop the focus on expansion: universal higher education has been achieved.**

The development of higher education in Ontario has been guided by the principle that there should be a place in first-level higher education for every qualified student who wishes to attend. This should remain the guiding principle.

However, after the rapid expansion of the number of places in first-level higher education over the past fifteen years, we have achieved a huge increase in participation—by the time Ontarians have reached the age of 21, 45.5 percent have entered university and 36.4 percent have entered college or other form of postsecondary education (PSE). Furthermore, the size of the 18–21-year-old cohort will decline by 8 percent over the next ten years. We have in place a system large enough that more than 70 percent of this cohort of students will achieve a postsecondary credential. This is above the target set by government and above the forecast of the number of PSE-qualified people that the labour market will demand in years ahead. Universal higher education has been achieved—a tremendous accomplishment that should be celebrated. But, with this recognition, a radically new mindset is required in planning higher education. We must shift the focus away from expansion.

But it will not be easy. Higher education is a top priority; it was in the past and should be in the future. Governments, universities, colleges, faculty, staff, and students have grown accustomed to addressing this priority through new initiatives, new funding, and continued expansion.

- **Retain the solid foundation.**

As one begins to rethink higher education, it is important to understand the design of our existing system and appreciate its accomplishments. More differentiation for its own sake will not necessarily bring improvement.

Higher education is provided through a binary system—a university sector, offering academically oriented programs, and a college sector, offering career-oriented programs—with institutions located across the regions of the province. The institutions in each sector are quite similar, having the same mandate and being funded on the same basis, with all offering a comprehensive range in first-level programs.[1] This binary system of regionally distributed institutions offering comprehensive programming of high quality is Ontario's hallmark and the reason why we have achieved such success in access and equality of opportunity.

Universities offer bachelor's degrees in the arts and sciences, as well as in career-oriented fields such as engineering, education, and business. Colleges offer career-oriented diplomas and certificates, the in-house classes for apprenticeships, and in recent years, have begun to offer career-oriented bachelor's degrees. Universities have the sole responsibility for graduate and upper-level professional education. All universities have both undergraduate and graduate education, although in terms of student numbers, all are primarily undergraduate institutions. All universities have the mandate to conduct research, and all professors have the three responsibilities of teaching, research, and service. Colleges historically have not had a research mandate, but in recent years such a mandate is emerging.

The basic structure of Ontario's higher education is sound.

There have been several major proposals to differentiate this system further with new types of institutions: the creation of teaching-only undergraduate universities and the creation of polytechnic institutions. Neither of these would be a wise policy direction. In part, this is because the fiscal limits would not allow it. Also, this is because, in order to be successful, there would have to be many institutions of the new type that could work together to establish a recognizable, distinctive identity, preventing drift back toward the existing models of universities and colleges. But most importantly, it is because the projections of future demand for higher education do not support the need for several new institutions. Notwithstanding these arguments, neither is a wise direction, in the Ontario context, on the merits.

There is, though, one new type of institution that has been called for in Ontario that is justified on the merits.

- **Establish an open university/open college.**

All universities and colleges in Ontario offer extensive part-time instruction and provide courses online. This program diversity is vital to meeting the needs of diverse students and to meeting our accessibility goals. Building upon this base, an open university/college would be the best initiative to further improve access, particularly for adult learners and those already working who cannot travel to attend university or college. This open university/college would go beyond part-time, online courses to embody a philosophy of student-focused flexibility to meet their diverse needs. It would be based upon open admissions, 24 hour learning, and affordability.

- **Differentiate institutions within the university and the college sectors based on mandate.**

The core aspect of the new vision should be to differentiate the university sector as two groups and to differentiate the college sector as two groups. This differentiation would be accomplished by government specification of the mandate of each group. Initially, this differentiation would be implemented by Mandate and Accountability Agreements (MAAs), particularly through restrictions on the degrees offered by each institution and clarification of the research mandate. Over time, the government should implement different funding models and accountability structures for each of the four groups.

- **Differentiate universities: designate a group of doctoral/research universities.**

The analysis of what will best serve Ontario in doctoral education is very different than the logic of what will best serve for first-level undergraduate education. Ontario needs only a limited number of doctoral programs and each should have both the critical mass of students and the critical mass of faculty members needed for high-quality programs. In addition, Ontario should benchmark its doctoral programs against the best in the world and develop programs of comparable standard; a process that further emphasizes the need for focus on a small number of programs. These programs should be located at a limited number of universities. A collection of programs, across a range of fields at one university, is part of the necessary critical mass to sustain top-quality doctoral programs. Any further doctoral programs in Ontario should be limited to this group of universities. The goal of provincial policy should be to increase the share of doctoral education at these universities, placing restrictions on any further undergraduate expansion.

Similarly, the logic of what will best serve Ontario to support research is not the same as the logic for delivering first-level higher education. Research should not simply be layered upon a system designed for access to first-level higher education. All universities have, and should continue to have, a research mandate. However, one group of universities should be designated to be more research intensive. The standards for appointment and for tenure would be more demanding in terms of research accomplishment. These universities would have a special mandate and responsibility to contribute to the new research agenda—with its commitments for focus in certain broad areas, its commitments to research at world class levels, and its commitments to actively work to commercialize the research findings.

Doctoral education and research are closely interconnected; there should be one group of doctoral/research universities.

The system-level planning of nodes of excellence in doctoral education and research should be undertaken across the universities of the doctoral-research group.

- **Differentiate colleges: designate a group to expand their offerings of career-oriented bachelor's degrees and to have an enhanced mandate to conduct applied research.**

The college system has been differentiating by allowing colleges to take on the designation of Institute of Technology and Advanced Learning (ITAL) and have up to 15 percent of programming in bachelor's degrees. Also, many colleges have been taking on a role in applied research as part of the new research agenda. Several recent federal programs have been directed toward colleges and most Ontario programs allow applications from the college sector.

This evolving differentiation should be formalized. The ITALs (or a somewhat larger group should others choose to join) should be allowed to expand applied bachelor's programming, including three-year degrees, to 30 percent and should be given an enhanced mandate for applied research. The research mandate will require changes in college funding and in the agreements governing responsibilities and workload of faculty members.

Although the college system has been evolving in this direction, to formalize this group of colleges—with major changes in both the teaching and research roles—is a larger change than the formalization of a group of doctoral/research universities. The differentiation of the colleges should be implemented through a full review of the mandate of Ontario's Colleges of Applied Arts and Technology and their governance structures. MTCU should ask that HEQCO examine the evidence both in Canada and other jurisdictions, consult with colleges and universities, and offer advice.

- **Differentiate and steer the system through Mandate and Accountability Agreements.**

About seven years ago, the government established Multi-Year Accountability Agreements (MYAAs) with each university and college. About two years ago, each was invited to submit a Strategic Mandate Agreement (SMA). Such agreements represent a new way for government to steer and differentiate the system, beyond the legislation establishing the institutions and the funding of them. These agreements provide a picture of each institution and its commitments and, when aggregated, a picture of the entire system. Such agreements would be the logical first step for implementing this vision of differentiation of each sector into two groups. I shall call the agreements, Mandate and Accountability Agreements (MAAs), to distinguish them from the previous versions.

The starting point of each MAA would be the current situation: the enrolment agreements between the institution and government, in the case of universities regarding bachelor's, master's, and doctoral enrolments, and in the case of colleges regarding degrees and diplomas of various types. These enrolment patterns are a model of transparent, measurable, and auditable goals, and goals that shape internal decision making in each institution. Also, they can be aggregated to provide a picture of the entire system. As the MAAs are used to differentiate the system, the new arrangements should build upon this foundation and try as much as possible to follow a similar approach.

Using the MAAs to implement differentiation by research mandate will be new in Ontario's experience. The advice of an expert panel should be sought about how best to structure such agreements and how to hold institutions accountable for the accomplishment of their mandate.

- **Do not micromanage institutions.**

However, there are a number of concerns about the use of MAAs. The most basic is that the government might become too intrusive, attempting to micromanage the affairs of universities, and so erode the autonomy of universities too severely. The delicate balance, on which the system relies, between the university's autonomy and the government's setting of public policy priorities, could be lost. But it need not be. The Ontario government has played a smaller role in system design than practically any other jurisdiction. An increased government role in steering the system can be consistent with university autonomy.

Another concern is that accountability agreements have a seductive simplicity and appeal, but the confidence in their efficacy is not warranted. It seems rather simple and straightforward: the government and the institution set a goal, the institution is accountable for achieving that goal, and resources from the government are tied to the achievement. The institution therefore has an incentive to achieve that goal. And institutions, like individuals, respond to incentives. As a general principle, it is simple and straightforward, but the reality as implemented is often very different.

Often, the goals which are chosen are not something over which the institution has much control. Consider for example, the goal would be to have the university mount degree programs that are more closely related to the labour market and the MYAA would tie resources to the employment rate of graduates two years after graduation. This two-year employment rate is one of the current key performance indicators (KPI). However, the employment rate of graduates has much more to do with the state of the economy than with the degree programs mounted by a university. The KPI will move up and down in ways unrelated to university decisions. Or consider a goal covered under the current MYAAs. Institutions were asked to file plans to show that the increased revenue from tuition fees would be used to improve "the quality of the learning environment" (rather than to increase salaries). However, the quality of the learning environment was hard to define and to measure. Each institution reported very differently regarding the same policy goal (and salaries rose at all institutions).

The approach of MAAs can easily degenerate into Stalin-esque central planning. Higher education institutions (despite being hugely complex organizations with decentralized decision making on many issues) file reports with a single central planning authority (MTCU). The MAA reports are detailed, complex, and many of the indicators do not measure what they are intended to quantify. Junior officials in the central planning authority read the reports, but have little sense of the situation at each institution. There is an appearance of control and steering of the system, but the reality is of bureaucratic detail with little influence.

When MAAs are used to steer the system, it is important both to retain a strong measure of institutional autonomy and to ensure that there remains competition between institutions. A vital aspect of quality improvement and of innovation in the higher education system is the "culture of excellence and improvement" in each institution and the competition between them.

Rethinking higher education in Ontario requires a stronger government vision of the system as a whole; the whole cannot simply be the aggregate of individual aspirations. But the steering of the system through the MAAs should operate at a macro level, leaving considerable room for individual aspiration and autonomy. The structure of the MAA targets should be transparent, the outcomes measurable, and the reported results auditable. The power and influence of the MAAs should come as much from how they shape internal decision making as from government monitoring university activities.

- **Increase the career-oriented programming at the bachelor's level at the colleges.**

Ontario students need to be offered a greater range of degree programs. The greatest need is for more career-oriented programs at the bachelor's level. At present in the academically-oriented arts and sciences at universities, there is a significant minority of undergraduates who are disengaged from their studies. Also many arts and science graduates are having difficulty making the transition to the labour market; the variation in labour market outcomes is significant and some are not realizing significant income increases as a result of their bachelor's degrees, and some are prolonging their education by following their bachelor's degree with an applied diploma at college. These new degree programs should be offered through the colleges who have long had the mandate to offer career-oriented education; in particular these should be offered through the ITAL group, which would also have the applied research mandate. The degrees should include three-year degrees, based upon revisions and enhancement to existing three-year diplomas and certificates. The approval of the new career-oriented degrees should be handled by an expanded college-specific quality assurance agency.

- **Give higher priority to undergraduate education at universities.**
  i) **Make transparent the resources allocated to undergraduate education.**
  ii) **Maintain in real terms the resources allocated to undergraduate education.**

The past twenty years have not been good to undergraduate education, despite the enormous commitments to expanding the number of undergraduate places and despite the fact that the real revenue per student, calculated using the Consumer Price Index (CPI), has been constant. Average class sizes have risen, more instruction is being done by graduate students and part-time faculty, and student-faculty ratios have risen. The teaching loads of full-time professors have been reduced to allow more time to be spent on research; also the amount of graduate education has expanded faster than undergraduate education, with both changes resulting in full-time professors being less involved with undergraduate education. Non-classroom expenditures have taken resources from the classroom; in particular the salaries of senior administrators and professors have risen significantly, meaning fewer professors can be hired. Also resources have been shifted to cover the indirect costs of research. The prestige of research (and to some extent of graduate education) has overwhelmed undergraduate education. And all this has happened when undergraduate tuition has been rising.

This is both a serious problem and a difficult dilemma for public policy. The vast majority of students are undergraduates; undergraduate education is the primary task of universities. Yet, it has not received the support it needs. The complex interaction of government policy and institutional decision making that "governs" our system has let this happen. Governments have provided the grants and set the tuition and student assistance regime, but deferred to institutional autonomy in terms of how resources are allocated within the universities.

Universities themselves have made these decisions about how best to allocate resources. And therefore, we must presume that universities see this outcome as in their best interests, given the available money. Research, graduate education, salaries, and other expenditures outside the undergraduate classroom have had higher priority. However, if the government disagrees with these decisions and wished to change them, it might lead to micro-management of university affairs that goes far beyond anything we have had before. It could become too intrusive and seriously damage the nuanced structure of government-university interaction.

But the problem needs to be addressed.

The first step should be to require that universities be more transparent about how resources are allocated. For example, at present one cannot determine how much is spent on undergraduate education. Rather worryingly, this is not because universities choose not to publish this information; they do not even calculate it for themselves. No doubt this reflects not just the low priority of undergraduate education, but also the rather ad hoc resource allocation and budgeting processes of universities. It would not be a difficult task to calculate and publish the resources allocated to the "classroom" for undergraduate education. It would include the value of faculty time, graduate student and part-time faculty in teaching, marking and grading, giving tutorials and lab sessions and so on. All the needed expenditure data are already recorded. The Ontario group of the Canadian Association of University Business Officers (CAUBO) could easily develop protocols to ensure common reporting across institutions.

There are of course indirect costs associated with undergraduate education—libraries, admissions and student services offices, computing systems and so on, not to mention the operation of the physical plant—but it is crucial that the direct expenditures on the classroom for undergraduate education be transparent.

With such data, one could also see what share of undergraduate education, comprehensively measured, is being delivered by full-time faculty. One of the most commonly heard concerns about undergraduate education is that more and more is being delivered by part-time faculty and graduate students. Many estimates say that it is over 50 percent in the arts and sciences. Yet, we do not have the data to validate this or to document how it has changed over time. This is unacceptable. This is not just a problem in Ontario; it is a problem in most jurisdictions—a very worrying testament to the culture and budgeting of universities. A recent book looking at this issue in the United States, *Off-Track Profs: Nontenured Teachers in Higher Education* (Cross and Goldenberg 2009) begins by asking: do we know who teaches our students? And it concludes, that in the US, they don't know. Even presidents, provosts, and deans, while protesting budget problems, do not know what share of undergraduate teaching (including marking, tutorials, labs etc.) is done by non-tenured faculty. The same is true in Ontario: we do not know who is teaching our students.

Knowing the total direct expenditure on undergraduate education, one could calculate and publish the share of revenues of undergraduate-targeted revenue (i.e., from undergraduate operating grants and undergraduate tuition) that is spent on the undergraduate classroom. And we could calculate the share of undergraduate teaching being done by full-time faculty members. These could be compared across universities.

Over time, the greater transparency would assist the university in conducting its academic tasks and might lead universities to give undergraduate education a higher priority.

And for the shorter run, this calculation would provide a means to protect undergraduate education. Universities under their Mandate and Accountability Agreement should be required to calculate direct spending on undergraduate education in 2012–2013 and then commit that this direct spending not be reduced over the next four years—*in real terms*. The actual expenditures would be deflated by the rate of salary increases to full-time faculty, part-time faculty and to graduate students. This would make very clear that salary increases have put pressure on undergraduate classroom expenditures, but it would not be allowed to happen. Of course, protecting the undergraduate classroom in this way will require more restraint elsewhere, but this is exactly the intended result.

- **Increase the diversity of undergraduate programs at universities.**
  - **i) Offer liberal education programs.**
  - **ii) Offer honours programs.**

The rethinking of undergraduate education in Chapter 5 concluded that the Ontario university system needed greater program diversity. Two examples of degree programs that could be introduced to better suit the diverse needs of students were a liberal education minor, and honours programs for high-ability, high-engagement students in the arts and sciences.

Again one is confronted with a public policy dilemma. The analysis of this book has argued that such programs are needed and would be taken up by students. Yet universities have not seen fit to offer them. Why wouldn't they, if the programs would meet student needs? My conjectured explanations are several. The first is that liberal education initiatives do not fit easily into the current departmental/faculty structure of the university that arises from the commitment to specialization, disciplinary education, and the research ideal. Liberal education programs have no departmental champion. The honours programs would have departmental champions, but the egalitarian spirit has proven to be stronger than the commitment to encouraging excellence. These structures and attitudes contribute to the powerful isomorphism in university development. However, probably the main explanation is that new initiatives cost money. Our universities are not well-funded and undergraduate education is being delivered in a low-cost manner with large classes and extensive use of part-time and graduate student instructors, tutorial leaders, markers etc. Any change will need more money.

This also explains why universities have not invested much in new pedagogies or in research into how teaching and learning could be improved—investing in teaching and learning costs money.

This suggests new program initiatives will only be undertaken by universities if they receive more money tied to the initiatives. Indeed, this was exactly the response of the Council of Ontario Universities (COU) to proposals for greater institutional differentiation in its paper *Differentiation in Ontario Universities*. COU welcomed the "ongoing development of a postsecondary sector that rewards competitive innovation." COU argued for additional differentiation grants. "For these differentiation grants, each university would reach a specific agreement with MTCU for specific use of funding to support each university's differentiated mission, within provincial priorities" (COU 2011b, 4).

New initiatives could, however, be funded by requiring that universities reallocate their own resources to support them. But would this be sound public policy? Surely universities are the best judges of how to allocate resources to achieve their many responsibilities. To override this will require a strong rationale. I believe there is such a rationale.

Universities tend to act to maximize their prestige and reputation—and research achievements are most prestigious, so they will allocate resources there. Also, research has been a clear top priority of government through the innovation agenda. Furthermore, while academic culture values both good teaching and good research, the highest accolades accrue to the leading researchers. All these lead universities to squeeze undergraduate education. In addition, improvements in undergraduate education are very difficult to measure and to demonstrate. Investment in a new initiative, even if successful, may not increase its reputation. A better investment may be in advertising and branding—this is more likely to improve the university's reputation. And so, all universities invest heavily in advertising and branding. For all these reasons therefore, universities may not allocate their own resources in ways that best serve the public interest.

In any event, it is not such an intrusion for the government to ask for a specific allocation of existing money; it is really no different than government offering new money tied to a specific area.

I would propose that all universities be required, under their MAA, to allocate the revenue from increases in undergraduate tuition toward improvement in undergraduate education. This reallocation would be over and above the commitment to maintain past expenditure in real terms, discussed above. Students could therefore be assured that their extra contributions have gone to improve undergraduate education (not to increase salaries or to support other priorities).

These two new commitments under the MAA would constrain and change university budgeting and resource allocation. But the constraints have been structured to allow universities maximum flexibility as to how they will go about protecting and improving undergraduate education. This leaves open a domain for differentiation of programs across institutions—the competitive innovation that COU supports.

The universities would have to report to MTCU, and to the public, as to how the commitments under the MAA have been implemented. But the main reporting mechanism should be internal to the university—to the board of governors, senate, professors, staff, and students. Only if the entire university community is aware of the change in priorities and resource allocation, participates in how the new initiatives are designed, and monitors the implementation will real changes occur. The real power of the MAA that includes these government constraints arises not because it is a new "contract" between government and the university, but rather because the MAA commitments will change internal university deliberations and decisions. Real monitoring will only occur if there are those within the university who want to ensure that undergraduate education is protected and improved.

- **Pause the graduate growth and undertake a system-wide analysis of the expansion to date.**

Over the last fifteen years, graduate education has expanded at an even faster rate than undergraduate education, and there is likely to be increasing demand in the years ahead.

Graduate education is very expensive, requiring a much higher level of public support per student than undergraduate education. Furthermore, only a small fraction of those who achieve a bachelor's degree will go on to graduate school. The design of a system of graduate education will therefore have to confront the issues of how many graduate programs we need, how large each program should be, and at which universities they should be located. There will have to be careful analysis of the critical mass needed—in terms of the number and quality of student and the number and quality of professors—for a high-quality graduate program. Also, the designers will have to confront whether we wish to benchmark our programs against the leading universities in the world and whether we wish to have some graduate programs, especially doctoral programs, at an internationally competitive level.

Unfortunately in Ontario, expansion has occurred with little attention to these system-wide issues. We have not tried to design a system of upper-level higher education, rather we have built upon a system designed to provide undergraduate education, and allow each institution to pursue its strategic objectives. Not surprisingly, all universities have wanted to expand at the graduate level and all have been able to do so over the last fifteen years. However, after this expansion, some universities have not met their targets and some degree programs have not been able to attract enough qualified applicants.

We should undertake a system-wide analysis before any further expansion. Such an analysis cannot be led by COU because it has a consensus position that any system-wide strategy should not limit the aspirations of individual institutions. MTCU does not have the expertise to conduct such a review. The best approach would be for MTCU to charge HEQCO with the responsibility, asking it to consult widely with the universities and to draw upon international experience and expertise.

- **Establish a provincial policy regarding research at higher education institutions.**
  i)   **Make transparent the resources allocated to research at universities.**
  ii)   **Establish a system for documenting the quantity and assessing the quality of research published at universities.**
  iii) **Give ITALs an enhanced mandate for applied research.**

Research is clearly a crucial part of the mission of the university. Expenditures on research are about 40 percent of total operating expenditure. And over the last fifteen years, both the federal and provincial governments have expanded their support for research enormously. In recent years, colleges have begun applied research. Yet, curiously, the design of Ontario's system of universities has never paid much attention to the research mission. We have not asked ourselves: do we have the best system for the support of research?

The design of the Ontario system has been driven almost entirely by provision of first-level education, by ensuring that there will be a place for every qualified student who wishes to attend. The most recent commissions charged to study our postsecondary system and to make recommendations—the Smith Commission (1996) and the Rae Review (2005)—did not have a mandate to analyze research. The Higher Education Quality Council of Ontario (HEQCO) has chosen not to look at the research mission.

In Ontario, the ministry responsible for universities, the Ministry of Training, Colleges, and Universities (MTCU) looks only at the teaching mission, particularly first-level education. MTCU is responsible for the operating grants, which are based upon enrolments. Another ministry, now the Ministry of Economic Development and Innovation, provides the great majority of explicit provincial government support for research. Virtually all of this support comes as part of the new research agenda— the innovation agenda. The two ministries do not coordinate their strategies in order that Ontario could address the question of how best to support research at universities and colleges and for what purposes.

The first step in rethinking research in Ontario is to establish a provincial policy on research at higher education institutions.

Ontario's approach lacks coherence and transparency. Clearly, the operating grants of universities support the research mission as well as the teaching mission. (If there were no external research income, there would still be much research done at universities.) All professors have the responsibility to teach and to conduct research, and their salaries are supported by the operating grants. And some of the indirect costs of this research are also supported by the operating grants. Yet, this role for the operating grants is never articulated and analyzed. We should make transparent the resources devoted to research, especially at universities.

There is a glaring gap in the accountability framework for universities. Despite research being a central mission, despite the enormous increase in government support for university research, and despite this increase in support being explicitly for research at an internationally competitive level, there is no regular reporting or assessment of the research published by professors at universities. The research of each professor is assessed when he or she is hired, considered for tenure and promotion, and at some universities, considered in the annual merit pay assessment. But there is no reporting by department, by faculty, by university of the total output. The public has no means to compare the published research in discipline "x" at university "y" with the research published at another university.

Most jurisdictions have had some type of research documentation and assessment for many years.

It is often controversial, especially when the results of the assessment are used to decide upon the allocation of funding. The Research Assessment Exercise (RAE) in the United Kingdom has been notoriously controversial. But many other countries—Denmark and Australia for example—have developed their system so that today it seems a normal and sensible part of academic life.

There are several keys to developing a successful system. Most important is to recognize that the system must be developed discipline by discipline, and with the involvement of the academic community. Each discipline has its own norms of research publication and these must be accommodated if it is to be credible. A logical approach to follow would be for the provincial government to ask, through the presidents, that the Ontario Council of Academic Vice-Presidents (OCAV) develop a system of research documentation and assessment. This approach is analogous to how the system for assessing degree programs (both existing degrees and proposed new degrees) was developed in Ontario. The government wanted this assessment and quality assurance system, and OCAV developed it. The government accepted the system that OCAV developed.

The colleges have begun to take on a role in applied research, despite not having a formally funded mandate for this work. Both the federal and provincial research support programs see an increasing role for such applied research. The ITAL group of colleges should be given an enhanced mandate for applied research, and with this there should be a determination of the appropriate funding, governance, and accountability structures for this new mandate.

• **Higher education should remain a top priority.**

The past expansion of Ontario's system of higher education reflects the deep consensus that higher education is more important than ever before: to achieve our goal of equality of opportunity in a knowledge-based society, to support cultural flourishing, to support effective public policy, and to sustain economic prosperity during this era of globalization and rapid technological change. There is little doubt that higher education will be just as important in the years ahead.

We have established a first rate system of higher education. It is time to rethink this system, to build upon it, and to create the system that will best serve Ontario for the years ahead.

Looking back over the policy directions and proposals of this chapter and over the analysis of the previous chapters, several themes run throughout that should be noted in conclusion. All of these will run throughout a rethinking of higher education in Ontario.

Rethinking higher education will mean more attention to excellence: excellence in undergraduate honours programs, excellence in doctoral programs, and excellence in research. We should judge ourselves against the highest international standards. The development of our system of higher education has focused upon providing degree and certificate programs of roughly similar quality at institutions across the province. This has been very successful and is an important reason why our accessibility goals have been realized. As we rethink higher education we need to provide more diverse programs and to differentiate institutions by special areas of excellence. It is perhaps ironic that we have programs to meet the needs of gifted students in our secondary schools, but we do not have these programs in our universities. This needs to change.

Rethinking higher education will require a stronger vision of the entire system. Of course, the development of more diverse programs and institutional differentiation will continue to be driven in part by government policy and in part by the strategic decisions of individual institutions and in part by the decisions of students of which program will be their major and which institution to attend. But, if we are to realize significant change and improvement, there will have to be a stronger government role in structuring and steering the system. The stronger government role can either come from MTCU itself or from a government-appointed buffer body between the government and the higher education sector. Ontario used to have such an agency for the university sector—the Ontario Council on University Affairs (OCUA)—and during its existence, issues of system design were much more important. If there is no appetite for a new permanent body, the broad direction for the stronger system-wide vision could come from a specially appointed commission.

But the main conclusion is clear: the goal of a more differentiated system and more differentiation of programs will not be realized by the aggregation of the plans of each university. A strong system-wide vision is needed.

Then, the task is to implement it.

NOTE

1. OCAD and UOIT are slight exceptions, being more focused in their offerings.

Epilogue

HIGHER EDUCATION POLICY IN A TIME OF EXPENDITURE RESTRAINT

The decade leading to 2008 saw very significant annual growth in expenditures on higher education: to support enrolment growth in first-level education, to support enrolment growth in graduate education, and to support research, both research funded by the national granting councils and research linked to economic innovation funded under the new research agenda. Ontario's expenditure on postsecondary education had been growing at 8.2 percent per year to finance this expansion (even faster than health care). And during this expansion, the average salaries of professors and senior administrators were rising at over 5 percent per year.

The financial crisis of 2008 precipitated a global recession that hit Ontario particularly hard; from peak to trough, Ontario's real GDP fell 5 percent, causing tax revenues to fall. The province responded to the recession, in a coordinated effort of jurisdictions across the world, with fiscal stimulus (expenditure increases) to help combat the recession. The expenditure increases were financed by increased government borrowing. By 2010, economic growth had returned, but the Ontario government still had a large annual deficit, and the accumulated debt had grown significantly. Expenditure restraint and tax increases will be required to reduce the deficit and balance the budget.

The high rate of growth of expenditure on higher education cannot continue. The policy environment will be changing dramatically.

The Ontario budget of March 2011 began to express some concern and committed to balancing the budget by 2017–2018. Government revenue was forecast to grow by 3.3 percent annually over the next three years and expenditures were forecast to grow by 1.7 percent (Ontario. Ministry

Rethinking Higher Education: Participation, Research, and Differentiation, G. Fallis. Kingston: School of Policy Studies, Queen's University. © 2013 The School of Policy Studies, Queen's University at Kingston. All rights reserved.

of Finance 2011c). To limit the annual expenditure growth to 1.7 percent would, by any measure, require significant expenditure restraint. But, the budget provided few details about how it would be achieved.

To help address the problem, the government appointed the Commission on the Reform of Ontario's Public Services, chaired by Don Drummond. The Commission was to "provide advice on how to deliver the most efficient and effective public services possible" and report to the minister of Finance in time to inform the development of the 2012 budget. The Commission was to examine the way government delivers services to people, including: "programs that are no longer serving their intended purpose and could be eliminated or redesigned; areas of overlap and duplication that could be eliminated to save taxpayer dollars; and areas of value in the public sector that could provide a greater return on the investment made by taxpayers." The Commission could "not make recommendations that would increase taxes or lead to the privatization of health care or education" (Ontario. Ministry of Finance 2011b).

An election was held in October 2011 and during the campaign, none of the parties explicitly and candidly addressed Ontario's fiscal problems. Perhaps the voters did not want to deal with difficult choices—voter turnout was a record low, below 50 percent. Perhaps, everyone was awaiting the report of the Commission. The election returned a minority Liberal government.

The Commission reported in February 2012; the report is now known as the Drummond Report (Commission on the Reform of Ontario's Public Services 2012). The message was sober. It examined the 2011 budget and concluded that the announced measures would not lead to balance by 2017–2018. It wryly noted: "if there are now plans under development within the government to secure all the fiscal restraint, they have not been provided to the Commission" (Drummond Report 2012, 1). Without major changes, Ontario's debt would reach crippling levels. The report argued Ontario cannot rely on robust economic growth to bring down the deficit and that the 2011 budget was too optimistic in its forecast of the growth of the Ontario economy. The budget assumed annual growth of real GDP of 2.2 percent from 2015 to 2018; whereas the report believed a 2 percent growth was more realistic (nominal growth, on which government revenues is determined, was assumed to be 3.9 percent). To achieve a balanced budget by 2017–2018, the report recommended some "revenue measures" (despite the prohibition against recommending tax increases) and that overall program expenditures should grow at 0.8 percent per year. The priority areas of health and postsecondary education could grow slightly more—health by 2.5 percent annually and postsecondary education by 1.5 percent annually. To accommodate these priorities, most other areas would have to shrink by 2.4 percent per year.

These simple numbers about growth rates can mask the enormity of the task. Suppose expenditure can grow annually by 1 percent. And suppose that the government did not do anything new but simply wanted to continue to do what it had done in the past year. The cost of doing just what was done last year will have risen more than one percent because of salary increases and increases in the prices of all the goods and services used to deliver public services. (The report assumed an annual inflation rate of 1.9 percent.) Just to do the same thing next year, savings must be found through efficiencies. And this must be done, year after year, for five years. And this allows no new government initiatives to address new concerns. More likely services will have to be reduced year after year.

The Drummond Report recognized that postsecondary education should be a top priority, recommending a 1.5 percent annual increase in government spending. It did not make a specific recommendation on tuition, but argued that tuition freezes are "not in students' interests." It recommended that the government "keep the five percent ceiling on overall tuition increases, but let institutions adjust tuition fees for individual programs within the ceiling." It forecast that enrolments would be growing by 1.7 percent per year through to 2017–2018, which would require growth in government operating grants, and noted that the cost of continuing to do the same thing has been rising by 3 to 5 percent annually. The report stated that "post secondary enrolment in universities and colleges has grown dramatically in recent years, but there is no coherent plan that addresses the whole system" (Drummond Report 2012, 17-19).

The report is remarkably vague, indeed virtually silent, about how the expenditure restraint is to be achieved. There are vague statements about minimizing duplication of programs, and integrating administrative and back-office functions, to realize efficiencies. And "the government should work with the institutions to align bargained compensation increases with more recent settlements in the BPS" [Broader Public Sector] (Drummond Report 2012, 17-19).

The process and mandate of the Commission were widely criticized. With such a broad mandate to be carried out over a short period, the Commission did not conduct any public consultations. It did ask to meet with many groups, and they "offered great ideas for reforms in their domains" (Drummond Report 2012, 1), but the report contains no list of who was consulted. Not surprisingly, many felt shut out of the process and that there were no strong voices arguing on behalf of public services. Further, the mandate ruled out tax increases, which critics correctly argued further prejudiced the fiscal strategy toward expenditure restraint (although it should be noted no political party had called for tax increases in their platforms in the 2011 election). In response to the limited mandate of the Drummond Commission, the Public Services Foundation of Canada, a recently formed national research and advocacy organization dedicated to defending and promoting the value of high-quality public services, established the Ontario Commission on Quality Public Services and Tax Fairness and held public hearings. Its interim report, *Something to Value*, has been published (Public Services Foundation of Canada, 2012). Other critics of the Drummond Report argued that the forecast of economic growth was too pessimistic. However, recent developments make the forecasts seem, if anything, optimistic. Despite the criticisms, the Drummond Report, having clearly identified the enormous fiscal challenge, set the agenda and in terms acceptable to the government. Nonetheless, the government made clear that the report was advisory and not all the recommendations would be adopted.

The 2012 budget was tabled in March 2012 and again committed to a balanced budget by 2017–2018. But, it focused upon the medium-term to 2014–2015, and forecast annual revenue growth of 3.5 percent and program expenditure growth of 1.0 percent (slightly lower than the 2011 budget). Four program expenditure areas were deemed priorities and granted higher growth rates: health (2.1 percent), primary and secondary education (1.7 percent), postsecondary education (1.9 percent), and the children's and social services sector (2.7 percent). There were few specifics about how this expenditure restraint would be achieved, although they were many, often vague, references to compensation restraint. The really tough decisions about restraint were put off until later (Ontario. Ministry of Finance 2012).

The 2013 budget remained committed to a balanced budget by 2017–2018, but again postponed the tough decisions on expenditure restraint. To achieve the 2017–2018 target, program expenditure is forecast to increase 3 percent in the first year, 1.1 percent in the second, and then be frozen for three years. Over the next three years, postsecondary education rises at 2.0 percent annually, health rises at 2.0 percent and other areas must be cut at 4.3 percent annually (Ontario. Ministry of Finance 2013).

The task to 2017–2018 is monumental: it requires three years of frozen total spending and many years of annual 4 percent cuts in lower priority areas—not to mention holding health increases to 2 percent per year, well below population growth plus inflation.

Where does this leave higher education?

It remains a high priority and expenditure increases are planned, mainly to handle enrolment growth; although, it seems that the ambitious plan to expand the entire system, perhaps by adding new three new university campuses, has been put on hold.

However, the overall fiscal plan is unlikely to be achievable and additional restraint will be very likely everywhere, including the higher education sector.

The government has announced a new tuition framework for the next four years limiting average increases to 3 percent per year.

Considering government grants and tuition together, a reasonable assumption would be that total revenue will increase at 2 (or less) percent per year. What does this imply for higher education?

The restraint will have to be severe.

The three drivers of expenditure are enrolment increases, price increases on all the goods and services bought by universities and colleges, and salary increases. The growth across all three will have to be held to 2 percent.

Expenditure on enrolment increases is a government policy decision. The 2013 budget said the increases in expenditure were to support enrolment growth and student assistance. If the system expands as planned, it will require all of the available increase in revenue. There will not be any increased revenue to address inflation or compensation increases.

Inflation on goods and services will likely run at least 2 percent per year. The institutions of higher education have no control over these increases; they must simply pay the higher prices or buy fewer goods and services.

This leaves no room for salary increases. Both the Drummond Report and Ontario budgets recognize this, but have no detail about how compensation might be determined in this time of severe restraint.

There will have to be wrenching adjustment in compensation patterns from the past fifteen years. Average professors' salaries (*nominal* income) have been going up at about 5 percent per year (CAUT, various years). The salaries of senior administrators have been going up even faster. The higher education sector has its own 1 percent problem, just as in the private sector. The average salary of the top 1 percent of earners at universities and colleges rose 35 percent (*real* income) from 1996 to 2010. Just as in the private sector, even within the 1 percent, the greater gains are at the very top. The average salary of the top 0.1 percent of earners rose 48 percent and of the top 0.01 percent rose 66 percent (Dobrescu et al. 2013). The Ontario government has now frozen the salaries of executives for two years.

A worrisome outcome has been seen before: the salaries of existing professors (and administrators and staff) increase; to meet the budget constraint, retiring professors are not replaced and part-time faculty are hired on a course-by-course basis; class sizes go up and the student-faculty ratio goes up. The quality of education, especially undergraduate education, goes down.

Unless there is radical rethinking, this will be the outcome of the next five years.

We seem incapable of finding a mechanism to bring government, higher education institutions, faculty, staff, and students together to hammer out a higher education policy in time of expenditure restraint that does not force most of the adjustment onto the quality of first-level higher education. Everyone outside government—the colleges, the universities, the professors, the students—tries to escape the restraint for themselves and for their sector, and the government does not have the will or the mechanisms to impose the restraint in ways that protect the quality of education.

The analysis of this book argues that enrolment growth is not needed—this would leave some room for inflation and compensation increases. It also argues, and provides a means to ensure it, that expenditure restraint should not fall on the undergraduate classroom. The MAA should require that the resources allocated to undergraduate education be maintained in real terms.

There will also be restraint on the availability of research funds, bringing wrenching adjustment in this domain. Ontario research support falls into the category of "other program expenditure" and will have to shrink at more than 4 percent annually. The 2012 federal budget maintained its strong commitment to the research and innovation agenda, while returning to a balanced budget by 2016–2017. Each of the granting councils will have to find savings in 2012–2013 that will be redirected to enhance their support for industry-academic partnerships. Thereafter, their annual budgets will be cut by $30 million (for CIHR and NSERC) and $14 million (for SSHRC). These represent a one-time cut of about 3 percent.

Overall, the financial situation of higher education will change fundamentally. Expenditure and compensation restraint will be the context for rethinking higher education in the years ahead. The challenge is to manage restraint in ways that best preserve the quality of education and research.

REFERENCES

ab Iorwerth, A. 2005. *Methods of Evaluating University Research Around the World.* Working Paper. Ottawa: Department of Finance.

Advisory Council on Science and Technology (Expert Panel on the Commercialization of Research). 1999. *Public Investments in University Research: Reaping the Benefits.* Ottawa: Advisory Council on Science and Technology.

American Association of Colleges and Universities (AAC&U). 2007. *College Learning for the New Global Century.* A report of the project, Liberal education and America's Promise (LEAP). Washington: American Association of Colleges and Universities.

——. 2012. Website. Accessed 5 June 2012. http://www.aacu.org/.

American Association of Universities (AAU). 2012. Website. Accessed 14 June 2012. http://www.aau.edu/.

Archambault, E. and E.V. Gagné. 2004. *The Use of Bibliometrics in the Social Sciences and Humanities.* Science Metrix Report prepared for the Social Sciences and Humanities Research Council (SSHRC). Montreal: Science Metrix.

Arum, R. and J. Roksa. 2011. *Academically Adrift: Limited Learning on College Campuses.* Chicago: University of Chicago Press.

Association of Canadian Community Colleges. (ACCC). 2005. *Innovation at Colleges and Institutes.* Ottawa: Association of Canadian Community Colleges.

——. 2006. *Applied Research at Canadian Colleges and Institutes.* Ottawa: Association of Canadian Community Colleges.

Association of Colleges of Applied Arts and Technology Ontario (ACAATO). 2004. *Applied Research and Innovation Ontario Colleges—An Underutilized Resource.* Toronto: Association of Colleges of Applied Arts and Technology Ontario.

Association of Universities and Colleges of Canada (AUCC). 2008. *Momentum: the 2008 report on university research and knowledge mobilization.* Ottawa: Association of Universities and Colleges of Canada.

——. 2009. *Institutional Costs of Research.* Ottawa: Association of Universities and Colleges of Canada. Accessed 5 June 2012. http://www.aucc.ca/_pdf/english/reports/2009/indirect_costs_fact_sheet_e.pdf.

——. 2011a. *Statistics: Enrolment.* Accessed 30 May 2011. http://aucc.ca/publications/stats/.

——. 2011b. *The Revitalization of Undergraduate Education in Canada.* Ottawa: Association of Universities and Colleges of Canada.

Axelrod, P. 1982. *Scholars and Dollars: Politics, Economics, and the Universities of Ontario 1945–1980.* Toronto: University of Toronto Press.

———. 2002. *Values in Conflict: The University, the Marketplace, and the Trials of Liberal Education.* Montreal: McGill-Queen's University Press.

Babcock, P.S. and M. Marks. 2011. "The Falling Time Cost of College: Evidence from Half a Century of Time Use Data." *The Review of Economics and Statistics* 93 (2): 468-478.

Bates, T. 2011. *Recommendations for a new Ontario Online Institute.* Accessed 12 August 2013. http://www.tonybates.ca/2011/06/06/recommendations-for-a-new-ontario-online-institute/.

Beaudry, P., D. Green and B. Sand. 2013. *The Great Reversal in the Demand for Skill and Cognitive Tasks.* Vancouver: printed by author.

Bergan, S. 2011. *Not by Bread Alone.* Strasbourg: Council of Europe Publishing.

Berkowitz, P. 2012. "U15 Begins to Formalize its Organization." *University Affairs/Affaires universitaires.* Accessed 6 June 2013. http://www.universityaffairs.ca/u-15-begins-to-formalize-its-organization.aspx.

Birnbaum, R. 1983. *Maintaining Diversity in Higher Education.* San Francisco: Jossey-Bass.

Bok, D. 2003. *Universities in the Marketplace: The Commercialization of Higher Education.* Princeton: Princeton University Press.

———. 2006. *Our Underachieving Colleges: A Candid Look at How Much Students Learn and Why They Should Be Learning More.* Princeton: Princeton University Press.

Bottomore, T.B. 1968. *Critics of Society: Radical Thought in North America.* New York: Pantheon Books.

Boulton, G. 2010. *University Rankings: Diversity, Excellence and the European Initiative.* Advice paper, League of European Research Universities. Leuven: League of European Research Universities. Accessed 14 June 2012. http://www.leru.org/index.php/public/home/.

Bowen, H.R. 1981. "Observations on the Costs of Higher Education." *Quarterly Review of Economics and Business* 21: 47-57.

Brewer, D.J., S.M. Gates, and C.A. Goldman. 2002. *In Pursuit of Prestige: Strategy and Competition in U.S. Higher Education.* New Brunswick: Transaction Publishers.

Brint, S. 2009. *The Academic Devolution? Movements to Reform Teaching and Learning in US Colleges and Universities, 1985–2010.* Research and Occasional Paper Series: CSHE.12.09. Berkeley: Center for Studies in Higher Education, University of California, Berkeley.

Brint, S. and A.M. Cantwell. 2011. *Academic Disciplines and the Undergraduate Experience: Rethinking Bok's "Underachieving Colleges" Thesis.* Research and Occasional paper Series: CSHE.6.11. Berkeley: Center for Studies in Higher Education, University of California, Berkeley.

Brown, J.S. 2000. Foreword. In *Understanding Silicon Valley: The Anatomy of an Entrepreneurial Region,* M. Kenney, ed. Stanford: Stanford University Press.

Bush, V. 1945. *Science: The Endless Frontier.* Accessed 14 June 2012. http://www.nsf.gov/od/lpa/nsf50/vbush1945.htm.

Business-Led Networks of Centres of Excellence (BL-NCE). Website. Accessed 11 June 2012. http://www.nce-rce.gc.ca/NetworksCentres-CentresReseaux/BLNCE-RCEE_eng.asp.

Butler, L. and M.S. Visser. 2006. "Extending Citation Analysis to Non-source Items." *Scientometrics* 66 (2): 327-343.

Campus Compact. 2012. Website. Accessed 5 June 2012. http://www.compact.org/.

Canada. 2002a. *Knowledge Matters: Skills and Learning for Canadians. Canada's Innovation Strategy.* Ottawa: Government of Canada.

——. 2002b. *Achieving Excellence: Investing in People, Knowledge and Opportunity. Canada's Innovation Strategy.* Ottawa: Government of Canada.

——. 2006. *Advantage Canada: Building a Strong Economy for Canadians.* Ottawa: Government of Canada.

——. 2007. *Mobilizing Science and Technology to Canada's Advantage.* Ottawa: Government of Canada.

Canada. Industry Canada (Jenkins Report). 2011. *Innovation Canada: A Call to Action.* Review of Federal Support to Research and Development—Expert Panel Report. Ottawa: Industry Canada.

Canada. Ministry of Finance. 2009. *The Budget in Brief.* Ottawa: Ministry of Finance.

——. 2010. *The Budget in Brief.* Ottawa: Ministry of Finance.

——. 2011. *The Budget in Brief.* Ottawa: Ministry of Finance.

——. 2012. *The Budget in Brief.* Ottawa: Ministry of Finance.

——. 2013. *The Budget in Brief.* Ottawa: Ministry of Finance.

Canada Excellence Research Chairs (CERC). 2012. Website. Accessed 11 June 2012. http://www.cerc.gc.ca/hp-pa-eng.shtml.

Canada Foundation for Innovation (CFI). 2012. Website. Accessed 11 June 2012. http://www.innovation.ca/en.

Canada Research Chairs (CRC). 2013. Website. Accessed 11 June 2013. http://www.chairs-chaires.gc.ca/home-accueil-eng.aspx.

Canadian Association of Graduate Studies (CAGS). 2006. *36th Statistical Report 1992–2004.* Ottawa: Canadian Association of Graduate Studies.

——. 2012. *40th Statistical Report 2000–2009.* Ottawa: Canadian Association of Graduate Studies.

Canadian Association of University Business Officers (CAUBO). 1999. *Financial Statistics of Universities and Colleges 1997–1998.* Ottawa: author.

——. 2009. *Financial Information of Universities and Colleges 2007–2008.* Ottawa: Canadian Association of University Business Officers.

Canadian Association of University Teachers (CAUT). Various years. *CAUT Almanac of Post-Secondary Education in Canada.* Ottawa: Canadian Association of University Teachers.

Carnegie Foundation for the Advancement of Teaching. 2012. *The Carnegie Classification of Institutions of Higher Education.* Washington: Carnegie Foundation for the Advancement of Teaching. Accessed 5 June 2012. http://classifications.carnegiefoundation.org/.

Centres of Excellence for Commercialization and Research (CECR). 2012. Website. Accessed 11 June 2012. http://www.nce-rce.gc.ca/NetworksCentres-Centres-Reseaux/CECR-CECR_eng.asp.

Chant, J. and W. Gibson. 2002. "Quantity or Quality? Research at Canadian Universities." In *Renovating the Ivory Tower: Canadian Universities and the Knowledge Economy,* D. Laidler, ed. Toronto: C.D. Howe Institute.

Christensen Hughes, J., and J. Mighty. eds. 2010. *Taking Stock: Research on Teaching and Learning in Higher Education.* Montreal & Kingston: Queen's Policy Studies Series, McGill-Queen's University Press.

Clark, I.D. 2012. *Recent Research on the Benefits of University for Marginal Students: Implications for Ontario's Enrollment Planning.* Accessed 29 May 2013. http://ppgreview.ca/2012/11/29/recent-research-on-the-benefits-of-university-for-marginal-students-implications-for-ontarios-enrollment-planning/.

Clark, I.D., G. Moran, M.L. Skolnik, and D. Trick. 2009. *Academic Transformation: The Forces Shaping Higher Education in Ontario.* Montreal & Kingston: Queen's Policy Studies Series, McGill-Queen's University Press.

Clark, I.D., D. Trick, and R. Van Loon. 2011. *Academic Reform: Policy Options for Improving the Quality and Cost-Effectiveness of Undergraduate Education in Ontario.* Montreal & Kingston: Queen's Policy Studies Series, McGill-Queen's University Press.

Codling, A. and V.L. Meek. 2006. "Twelve Propositions on Diversity in Higher Education." *Higher Education Management and Policy* 18 (3): 31-54.

Colander, D. and K.M. McGoldrick, eds. 2009. *Educating Economists: The Teagle Discussion on Re-evaluating the Undergraduate Economics Major.* Cheltenham: Edward Elgar.

Colleges Ontario (CO). 2011a. *2011 Environmental Scan.* Toronto: Colleges Ontario.

——. 2011b. *A New Vision for Higher Education in Ontario.* Toronto: Colleges Ontario. Accessed 5 June 2012. http://www.chairs-chaires.gc.ca/program-programme/2008_allocations_attributions.pdf.

——. 2012. *Empowering Ontario: Transforming Higher Education in the 21st Century.* Toronto: Colleges Ontario.

Colleges Ontario Network for Industry Innovation (CONII). 2013. *History.* Toronto: author. Accessed 17 June 2013. http://www.conii.ca/about-us/history.html.

Commission on the Reform of Ontario's Public Services (Drummond Report). 2012. *Report of the Commission on the Reform of Ontario's Public Services.* Toronto: Commission on the Reform of Ontario's Public Services. Accessed 5 June 2012. http://www.fin.gov.on.ca/en/reformcommission/.

Conference Board of Canada. 2007. *How Canada Performs: A Report Card on Canada.* Ottawa: Conference Board of Canada.

Côté, J.E. and A.L. Allahar. 2007. *Ivory Tower Blues: A University System in Crisis.* Toronto: University of Toronto Press.

——. 2011. *Lowering Higher Education: The Rise of Corporate Universities and the Fall of Liberal Education.* Toronto: University of Toronto Press.

Council of Canadian Academies. 2006. *The State of Science and Technology in Canada.* Ottawa: Council of Canadian Academies.

——. 2009. *Innovation and Business Strategy: Why Canadian Business Strategy Falls Short.* The Expert Panel on Business Innovation. Ottawa: Council of Canadian Academies.

Council of Ontario Universities (COU). 2003. *Advancing Ontario's Future Through Advanced Degrees.* Report of the COU Task Force on Future Requirements for Graduate Education in Ontario. Toronto: Council of Ontario Universities.

——. 2008. *The Ontario University Sector: Overview and Issues 2007–2008.* Toronto: Council of Ontario Universities.

——. 2011a. *Applications and Enrolment.* Toronto: Council of Ontario Universities.

——. 2011b. *Differentiation in Ontario Universities.* Toronto: Council of Ontario Universities.

——. 2011c. *2010 Survey Highlights: Employment Outcomes of 2008 Graduates of Ontario University Undergraduate Programs.* Toronto: Council of Ontario Universities.

——. 2012a. *2011 Survey Highlights: Employment Outcomes of 2009 Graduates of Ontario University Undergraduate Programs.* Toronto: Council of Ontario Universities. Accessed 3 June 2013. http://cou.on.ca/publications/reports/pdfs/2011-survey-highlights---ontario-graduate-employme.

——. 2012b. *Position Paper on Graduate Education in Ontario.* Toronto: Council of Ontario Universities.

——. 2012c. *Interprovincial Comparison of University Revenue.* Toronto: Council of Ontario Universities.

——. 2012d. *A Tuition Framework to Support Access, Quality and Sustainability.* Toronto: Council of Ontario Universities.

Cross, J.G. and E.N. Goldenberg. 2009. *Off-Track Profs: Nontenured Teachers in Higher Education.* Cambridge: The MIT Press.

Daniel, J. 2012. *Making Sense of MOOCs: Musings in a Maze of Myths, Paradox, and Possibility.* Korea: printed by author.

Dill, D. and F. Van Vught, eds. 2010. *National Innovation and the Academic Research Enterprise: Public Policy in Global Perspective.* Baltimore: Johns Hopkins University Press.

DiMaggio, P.J. and W.W. Powell. 1983. "The Iron Cage Revisited: Institutional Isomorphism and Collective Rationality in Organizational Fields." *American Sociological Review* 48 (April): 147-160.

Dombrescu, V., S. Mirkovic, S. Mohsenzadeh and M.R. Veall. 2013. *Top-End Incomes and the Ontario Public Sector.* Hamilton: printed by author.

Douglass, J.A. 2010. *Re-imagining California Higher Education.* San Francisco: Center for Studies in Higher Education, University of California at Berkeley.

Drewes, T. 2010. *Postsecondary Education and the Labour Market in Ontario.* Toronto: Higher Education Quality Council of Ontario.

Dyzenhaus, D. 2005. The Case for Public Investment in the Humanities. In *Taking Public Universities Seriously,* F. Iacobucci and C. Tuohy, eds. Toronto: University of Toronto Press.

Education Policy Institute. 2008. *Access, Persistence, and Barriers to Postsecondary Education: A Literature Review and Outline of Future Research.* Toronto: Higher Education Quality Council of Ontario.

Ehrenberg, R.G. 2000. *Tuition Rising: Why College Costs So Much.* Cambridge: Harvard University Press.

Etzkowitz, H. and A. Webster. 1998. Entrepreneurial Science: The Second Academic Revolution. In *Capitalizing Knowledge: New Intersections of Industry and Academia,* H. Etzkowitz, A. Webster, and P. Healy, eds. Albany: State University of New York Press.

European Commission. 2012. *U-Map The European Classification of Higher Education Institutions.* Brussels: European Commission. Accessed 5 June 2012. http://www.u-map.eu/.

Evans, J.R. 2001. *Higher Education in the Economy: Towards a Public Contract for Research.* 2001 Killam Annual Lecture. Halifax: Trustees of the Killam Trusts.

Fallis, G. 2007. *Multiversties, Ideas, and Democracy.* Toronto: University of Toronto Press.

——. 2010. *Benchmarking Canada's University-based Research: A Missing Component of Our National Innovation System.* Toronto: printed by author.

——. 2013. *Criteria for Membership in the U15.* Toronto: printed by author.

Finnie, R., S. Childs, and A. Wismer. 2011. *Access to Postsecondary Education: How Ontario Compares.* Toronto: Higher Education Quality Council of Ontario.

Geiger, R.L. and C.M. Sá. 2008. *Tapping the Riches of Science: Universities and the Promise of Economic Growth.* Cambridge: Harvard University Press.

Genome Canada. 2012. Website. Accessed 11 June 2012. http://www.genome-canada.ca/.

Geuna, A. and B.R. Martin. 2001. *University Research Evaluation and Funding: An International Comparison.* Electronic Working paper Series, No. 71. Brighton: Science and Technology Policy Research Unit, University of Sussex.

Goldin, C. and L. Katz. 2008. *The Race between Education and Technology.* Cambridge: The Belknap Press of Harvard University Press.

Group of Eight (Go8). 2012. Website. Accessed 14 June 2012. http://www.go8.edu.au/.

Hermanowicz, J.C. 2005. "Classifying Universities and Their Departments: A Social World Perspective." *Journal of Higher Education* 76 (1): 26-55.

——. 2009. *Lives in Science: How Institutions Affect Academic Careers.* Chicago: University of Chicago Press.

Higher Education Quality Council of Ontario (HEQCO). 2009. *Report to the Minister: Polytechnics.* Letter to the minister and attached report. Toronto: Higher Education Quality Council of Ontario.

——. 2010. *Third Annual Review and Research Plan.* Toronto: Higher Education Quality Council of Ontario.

——. 2013a. *Performance Indicators: A report on where we are and where we are going.* Toronto: Higher Education Quality Council of Ontario.

——. 2013b. *Quality: Shifting the Focus. A Report from the Expert Panel to Assess the Strategic Mandate Submissions.* Toronto: Higher Education Quality Council of Ontario.

Humanities and Social Sciences Federation of Canada (HSSFC). 2008. *The Humanities and Social Sciences Federation of Canada.* Ottawa: Humanities and Social Sciences Federation of Canada.

International Consortium for Higher Education, Civic Responsibility, and Democracy (International Consortium). 2012. Website. Accessed 5 June 2012. http://www.internationalconsortium.org/.

Jarvey, P. and A. Usher. 2012. *Measuring Academic Research in Canada: Field Normalized Academic Rankings 2012.* Toronto: Higher Education Strategy Associates.

Jarvey, P., A. Usher, and L. McElroy. 2012. *Making Research Count: Analyzing Canadian Academic Publishing Cultures.* Toronto: Higher Education Strategy Associates.

Jones, G.A. 1997. Higher Education in Ontario. In *Higher Education in Canada: Different Systems, Different Perspectives,* G.A. Jones, ed. New York: Garland Publishing, Inc.

Jones, G.A., T. Shanahan, and P. Goyan. 2004. "The Academic Senate and University Governance in Canada." *The Canadian Journal of Higher Education.* (34) 2: 35-68.

Jones, G.A. and M.L. Skolnik. 2009. *Degrees of Opportunity: Broadening Student Access by Increasing Institutional Differentiation in Ontario Higher Education.* Toronto: Higher Education Quality Council of Ontario.

Jones, G.A., J. Weinrib, A.S. Metcalfe, D. Fisher, K. Rubenson, and I. Snee. 2012. "Academic Work in Canada: the Perceptions of Early-Career Academics." *Higher Education Quarterly* 66 (2): 189-206.

Kaiser, F. and H. Vossensteyn. 2009. Excellence in Dutch Higher Education: Handle with Care. In *Structuring Mass Higher Education: The Role of Elite Institutions*, D. Palfreyman and T. Tapper, eds. New York and London: Routledge.

Kehm, B.M. and P. Pasternack. 2009. The German 'Excellence Initiative' and Its Role in Restructuring the National Higher Education Landscape. In *Structuring Mass Higher Education: The Role of Elite Institutions*, D. Palfreyman and T. Tapper, eds. New York and London: Routledge.

Kerr, C. 2001. *The Uses of the University*, 5th edition. Cambridge: Harvard University Press.

Kerr, A., U. McCloy, and S. Liu. 2010. *Students Who Transfer Between Ontario Colleges and Universities*. Toronto: Higher Education Quality Council of Ontario.

Killam Trusts. 2012. Website. Accessed 11 June 2012. http://www.killamtrusts.ca/.

Kuh, G.D. 2003. "What Are We Learning about Student Engagement from NSSE." *Change* 35 (2): 24-32.

League of European Research Universities (LERU). 2012. *Research Universities and Research Assessment*. Leuven: League of European Research Universities. Accessed 12 June 2012. http://www.leru.org/index.php/public/home/.

Leiden. 2013. *CWTS Leiden Ranking*. Accessed 5 June 2013. http://www.leidenranking.com/.

Leslie, S.W. 2000. The Biggest 'Angel' of Them All: The Military and the Making of Silicon Valley. In *Understanding Silicon Valley: The Anatomy of an Entrepreneurial Region*, M. Kenney, ed. Stanford: Stanford University Press.

Maclean's. Various years. *Guide to Canadian Universities*. Toronto: *Maclean's*.

Marginson, S. 2009. The Elite Public Universities in Australia. In *Structuring Mass Higher Education: The Role of Elite Institutions*, D. Palfreyman and T. Tapper, eds. New York and London: Routledge.

McDaniel, S. and P. Bernard. 2011. "Life Course as a Policy Lens: Challenges and Opportunities." *Canadian Public Policy–Analyse de politiques* 37(1): 1-13.

McIntosh, J. 2013. *The Value of a Canadian University Degree*. Montreal: printed by author.

Merton, R. 1973. Priorities in Scientific Discovery. In *The Sociology of Science: Theoretical and Empirical Investigations*. Chicago: University of Chicago Press.

Miner, R. 2010. *People Without Jobs, Jobs Without People: Ontario's Labour Market Future*. Accessed 5 June 2012. http://www.collegesontario.org/research/research_reports/people-without-jobs-jobs-without-people-final.pdf.

Monahan, E.J. 2004. *Collective Autonomy: A History of the Council of Ontario Universities 1962–2000*. Waterloo: Wilfrid Laurier University Press.

Munroe-Blum, H. 1999a. *Growing Ontario's Innovation System: The Strategic Role of University Research*. Toronto: printed by author.

———. 1999b. *Case Studies. Growing Ontario's Innovation System: The Strategic Role of University Research*. Toronto: printed by author.

Natural Sciences and Engineering Research Council (NSERC). 2007. *College and Community Innovation Pilot Program Mid-Term Review*. Ottawa: Natural Sciences and Engineering Research Council.

———. 2013. College and Community Innovation Program. Ottawa: Natural Sciences and Engineering Research Council. Accessed 17 June 2013. http://www.nserc-crsng.gc.ca/professors-professeurs/Rpp-pp/CCI-ICC_eng.asp.

Neave, G. 2000. "Diversity, differentiation and the market: the debate we never had but which we ought to have done." *Higher Education Policy* (13)1: 7-22.

Networks of Centres of Excellence (NCE). 2012. Website. Accessed 11 June 2012. http://www.nce-rce.gc.ca/index_eng.asp.

Norrie, K. and M.C. Lennon. 2011. *Tuition Fee Policy Options for Ontario*. Toronto: Higher Education Quality Council of Ontario.

Norrie, K., and S. Lin. 2009. *Postsecondary Education Attainment and Participation in Ontario*. Toronto: Higher Education Quality Council of Ontario.

Norrie, K. and H. Zhao. 2011. *An Overview of PSE Accessibility in Ontario*. Toronto: Higher Education Quality Council of Ontario.

Nussbaum, M.C. 1997. *Cultivating Humanity: A Classical Defense of Reform in Liberal Education*. Cambridge: Harvard University Press.

——. 2010. *Not For Profit: Why Democracy Needs the Humanities*. Princeton: Princeton University Press.

Office of the Auditor General of Ontario. 2003. *2003 Annual Report*. Toronto: Office of the Auditor General of Ontario.

Ontario. 2011. *Progress Report 2011: Education*. Accessed 15 September 2011. http://www.ontario.ca/en/initiatives/progressreport2011/ONT05_039131. html?openNav=education.

——. 2013. *News Release: New Tuition Framework Reduces Cap on Tuition Increases*. Toronto: Province of Ontario. Accessed 17 June 2013. http://news.ontario. ca/tcu/en/2013/03/new-tuition-framework-reduces-the-cap-on-tuition-increases.html.

Ontario. Ministry of Education. 1999. *Ontario Secondary Schools, Grades 9 to 12: Program and Diploma Requirements*. Accessed 5 June 2012. http://www.edu.gov. on.ca/eng/document/curricul/secondary/oss/oss.html.

——. 2010. *Course Codes 2010*. Accessed 5 June 2012. http://www.edu.gov.on.ca/ eng/general/list/commoncc/ccc.html.

Ontario. Ministry of Education and Training (Smith Commission). 1996. *Excellence, Accessibility, Responsibility: Report of the Advisory Panel on Future Directions for Postsecondary Education*. Toronto: Ontario. Ministry of Education and Training.

Ontario. Ministry of Finance. 2001. *Expenditure Estimates 2001–02*. Toronto: Ontario. Ministry of Finance.

——. 2005. *2005 Ontario Budget: Investing in People Strengthening Our Economy. Budget Papers*. Toronto: Ontario. Ministry of Finance.

——. 2011. *Population Projections Spring 2011*. Toronto: Ontario. Ministry of Finance.

——. 2011a. *Expenditure Estimates 2011–12*. Toronto: Ontario. Ministry of Finance.

——. 2011b. *Announcement of the Commission on the Reform of Ontario's Public Services*. Accessed 20 June 2012. http://www.fin.gov.on.ca/en/reform commission/announcement.html.

——. 2011c. *2011 Ontario Budget*. Accessed 5 November 2011.http://www.fin.gov. on.ca/en/budget/ontariobudgets/2011/ch1a.html#c1_secA_postSecondary

——. 2012. *2012 Budget: Chapter II: Section E: Ontario's Economic Outlook and Fiscal Plan*. Accessed 20 June 2012. http://www.fin.gov.on.ca./en/budget/ontario budgets/2012/ch2e.html.

——. 2013. *2013 Ontario Budget*. Accessed 20 June 2013. http://www.fin.gov. on.ca/en/budget/ontariobudgets/2013/.

Ontario. Ministry of Research and Innovation (MRI). 2008. *Seizing Global Opportunities: Ontario's Innovation Agenda*. Toronto: Ontario. Ministry of Research and Innovation.

Ontario. Ministry of Training, Colleges and Universities (MTCU). 2011. Memo from Deborah Newman, Deputy Minister, to Executive Heads of Provincially-Assisted Ontario Universities with Graduate Programs, 12 July 2011. Toronto: Ontario. Ministry of Training, Colleges and Universities.

———. 2012. *Strengthening Ontario's Centres of Creativity, Innovation and Knowledge.* Toronto: Ontario. Ministry of Training, Colleges and Universities.

Ontario Centres of Excellence. 2012. Website. Accessed 12 June 2012. http://www.mri.gov.on.ca/english/programs/OCE-Program.asp.

Ontario Jobs Investment Board (OJIB). 1999. *A Road Map to Prosperity: An Economic Plan for Jobs in the 21st Century.* Toronto: Ontario Jobs Investment Board.

OntarioLearn. 2012. *About OntarioLearn.com.* Toronto: OntarioLearn. Accessed 5 June 2012. http://www.ontariolearn.com/index.php?page=aboutus_29535.

Ontario PC Caucus. 2013. *Paths to Prosperity: Higher Learning for Better Jobs.* Toronto: Ontario PC Caucus. Accessed 16 May 2013. http://www.ontariopc.com/paths/.

Ontario Universities Application Centre (OUAC). 2011. *e-INFO.* Toronto: Ontario Universities Application Centre http://www.electronicinformation.ca.

———. 2012. *Undergraduate Application Statistics.* Toronto: Ontario Universities Application Centre. Accessed 5 June 2012. http://www.ouac.on.ca/statistics/ugrad-app-stats/.

Ontario Universities Council on Quality Assurance (Quality Council). 2011. *Quality Assurance Framework.* Toronto: Ontario Universities Council on Quality Assurance.

Organisation for Economic Co-operation and Development (OECD). 1997. *National Innovation Systems.* Paris: Organisation for Economic Co-operation and Development.

———. 2002. *Frascati Manual 2002: Proposed Standard Practice for Surveys on Research and Experimental Development.* Paris: Organisation for Economic Co-operation and Development.

———. Various years. *Main Science and Technology Indicators.* Paris: Organisation for Economic Co-operation and Development.

———. 2012. *OECD Economic Surveys: Canada.* Paris: Organisation for Economic Co-operation and Development.

Orton, L. 2009. *Statistics Canada's Definition and Classification of Postsecondary and Adult Education Providers in Canada.* Ottawa: Statistics Canada.

Palfreyman, D. and T. Tapper, eds. 2009. *Structuring Mass Higher Education: The Role of Elite Institutions.* New York and London: Routledge.

Piper, M.C. 2002. *Building a Civil Society: A New Role for the Human Sciences.* 2002 Killam Annual Lecture. Halifax: Trustees of the Killam Trusts.

Pocklington, T. and A. Tupper. 2002. *No Place to Learn: Why Universities Aren't Working.* Vancouver: UBC Press.

Polytechnics Canada. 2010. *About Polytechnics Canada.* Ottawa: Polytechnics Canada. Accessed 4 June 2012. http://www.polytechnicscanada.ca/about.

Prichard, J.R.S. 2000. *Federal Support for Higher Education and Research in Canada: The New Paradigm.* 2000 Killam Annual Lecture. Halifax: Trustees of the Killam Trusts.

Public Services Foundation of Canada. 2012. *Something to Value.* Toronto: Public Services Foundation of Canada. Accessed 25 June 2012. http://www.public-

servicesfoundation.ca / sites / publicservicesfoundation.ca / files / documents /
Something_to_Value.pdf.

Rae, B. (Rae Review). 2005. *Ontario: A Leader in Learning. Report and Recommendations*. Toronto: Ministry of Training, Colleges and Universities.

Re$earch Infosource. Various years. *Canada's Innovation Leaders*. Toronto: Re$earch Infosource. http:/ /www.researchinfosource.com / advert.shtml.

Rhodes, F.H.T. 1994. The Place of Teaching in the Research University. In *The Research University in a Time of Discontent*, J.R. Cole, E. Barber, and S.R. Graubard, eds. Baltimore: The Johns Hopkins University Press.

Russell Group. 2012. Website. Accessed 14 June 2012. http:/ /www.russellgroup. ac.uk/.

Sattler, P. and J. Peters. 2012. *Work-Integrated Learning in Ontario's Postsecondary Sector*. Toronto: Higher Education Quality Council of Ontario.

Science, Technology and Innovation Council (STIC). 2009. *State of the Nation 2008: Canada's Science, Technology and Innovation System*. Ottawa: Science, Technology and Innovation Council.

Shaienks, D. and T. Gluszynski. 2007. *Participation in Postsecondary Education: Graduates, Continuers and Drop Outs, Results from YITS Cycle 4*. Ottawa: Statistics Canada.

Skolnik, M.L. 1989. "How Academic Program Review Can Foster Intellectual Conformity and Stifle Diversity of Thought and Method." *Journal of Higher Education* (60)6: 619-643.

——. 2012. *College Baccalaureate Degrees and the Diversification of Baccalaureate Production in Ontario*. Toronto: printed by author.

Smith, D. 1997. *Framework for a Research Policy for Ontario*. Discussion paper. Toronto: Ontario Ministry of Education and Training. Accessed 12 June 2012. http:/ /www.tcu.gov.on.ca / eng / document / discussi / research.html.

Smith, S.L. 1989. *Skilled and Educated: A Solution to Ontario's Urgent Need for More Polytechnic Programs*. Paper prepared for the Vision 2000 Review of the Mandate of the Ontario Colleges of Applied Arts and Technology. Toronto: Ontario Council of Regents.

Statistics Canada. 2009a. *Graduating in Canada: Profile, Labour Market Outcomes and Student Debt of the Class of 2005*. Ottawa: Statistics Canada. Accessed 29 May 2013. http:/ / www.statcan.gc.ca / pub / 81-595-m / 81-595-m2009074-eng.htm.

——. 2009b. *College and university graduates with low earnings in Canada—Demographic and labour market characteristics*. Ottawa: Statistics Canada. Accessed 29 May 2013. http:/ /www.statcan.gc.ca / pub / 81-004-x / 2009002 / article / 10897-eng.htm.

——. 2010a. *Estimates of Research and Development Expenditures in the Higher Education Sector, 2008/2009*. Ottawa: Statistics Canada.

——. 2010b. *Trends in the Age Composition of College and University Students and Graduates*. Ottawa: Statistics Canada. Accessed 14 June 2012, http:/ /www. statcan.gc.ca / pub / 81-004-x / 2010005 / article / 11386-eng.htm.

Stokes, D.E. 1997. *Pasteur's Quadrant: Basic Science and Technological Innovation*. Washington: Brookings Institution.

Talloires Network. 2012. Website. Accessed 5 June 2012. http:/ /www.tufts.edu / talloiresnetwork /.

Task Force on Competitiveness, Productivity and Economic Progress (Task Force on Competitiveness). 2002. *Closing the Prosperity Gap*. Toronto: Task Force on Competitiveness, Productivity and Economic Progress.

——. 2011. *Prospects for Ontario's Prosperity: A look back and a look ahead*. Toronto: Task Force on Competitiveness, Productivity and Economic Progress.

Trow, M. 1973. *Problems in the Transition from Elite to Mass Higher Education*. Washington: Carnegie Commission on Higher Education.

——. 2005. *Reflections on the Transition from Elite to Mass to Universal Access: Forms and Phases of Higher Education in Modern Societies since WWII*. Berkeley: Institute of Governmental Studies, UC Berkeley.

Turner, F., ed. 1996. *The Idea of a University: John Henry Newman*. New Haven: Yale University Press.

University of Toronto. 2012. *Multi-Year Accountability Agreement Report-Back 2008– 09*. Toronto: University of Toronto. Accessed 5 June 2012. http://www.utoronto. ca/__shared/assets/MYAA_Report_Back_for_2008-20093854.pdf?method=1.

Usher, A. and P. Duncan. 2008. *Beyond Sticker Shock 2008: A Closer Look at Canadian Tuition Fees*. Toronto: Educational Policy Institute.

Waltman, L., C. Calero-Medina, J. Kosten, E. Noyons, R. Tijssen, N. van Eck, T. van Leeuwen, A. van Raan, M. Visser, and P. Woouters. 2012. "The Leiden Ranking 2011/2012: Data collection, indicators, and interpretation." *Journal of the American Society for Information Science and Technology* 63(12): 2419-2432.

Weingarten, H.P. and F. Deller. 2010. *The Benefits of Greater Differentiation of Ontario's University Sector*. Toronto: Higher Education Quality Council of Ontario.

Weisbrod, B.A., J.P. Ballou, and E.D. Asch. 2008. *Mission and Money: Understanding the University*. Cambridge: Cambridge University Press.

Wiggers, R., M.C. Lennon, and K. Frank. 2011. *Expanding Opportunities for Graduate Studies: The Recent Experience of Ontario*. Toronto: Higher Education Quality Council of Ontario.

York University. 2012. *Multi-Year Accountability Agreement Report-Back 2008–09*. Toronto: York University. Accessed 5 June 2012. http://www.yorku.ca/president/ mya/docs/YORK_2008-09_MYAA_report_back_template.pdf.

Zundel, P. and P. Deane. 2011. "It's Time to Transform Undergraduate Education." *University Affairs/Affaires universitaires* 01/11: 18-24.

INDEX

ABOUT THE AUTHOR

University Professor George Fallis is professor of economics and social science at York University, and the author of *Multiversities, Ideas, and Democracy*. He has served as chair of the department of ecnonomics, dean of the faculty of arts, and as as York's academic colleague on the Council of Ontario Universities.

Queen's Policy Studies
Recent Publications

The Queen's Policy Studies Series is dedicated to the exploration of major public policy issues that confront governments and society in Canada and other nations.

Manuscript submission. We are pleased to consider new book proposals and manuscripts. Preliminary inquiries are welcome. A subvention is normally required for the publication of an academic book. Please direct questions or proposals to the Publications Unit by email at spspress@queensu.ca, or visit our website at: www.queensu.ca/sps/books, or contact us by phone at (613) 533-2192.

Our books are available from good bookstores everywhere, including the Queen's University bookstore (http://www.campusbookstore.com/). McGill-Queen's University Press is the exclusive world representative and distributor of books in the series. A full catalogue and ordering information may be found on their web site (**http://mqup.mcgill.ca/**).

For more information about new and backlist titles from Queen's Policy Studies, visit http://www.queensu.ca/sps/books.

School of Policy Studies

Making Policy in Turbulent Times: Challenges and Prospects for Higher Education, Paul Axelrod, Roopa Desai Trilokekar, Theresa Shanahan, and Richard Wellen (eds.) 2013. ISBN 978-1-55339-332-0

Intellectual Disabilities and *Dual Diagnosis: An Interprofessional Clinical Guide for Healthcare Providers,* Bruce D. McCreary and Jessica Jones (eds.) 2013. ISBN 978-1-55339-331-3

Building More Effective Labour-Management Relationships, Richard P. Chaykowski and Robert S. Hickey (eds.) 2013. ISBN 978-1-55339-306-1

Navigationg on the Titanic: Economic Growth, Energy, and the Failure of Governance, Bryne Purchase 2013. ISBN 978-1-55339-330-6

Measuring the Value of a Postsecondary Education, Ken Norrie and Mary Catharine Lennon (eds.) 2013. ISBN 978-1-55339-325-2

Immigration, Integration, and Inclusion in Ontario Cities, Caroline Andrew, John Biles, Meyer Burstein, Victoria M. Esses, and Erin Tolley (eds.) 2012. ISBN 978-1-55339-292-7

Diverse Nations, Diverse Responses: Approaches to Social Cohesion in Immigrant Societies, Paul Spoonley and Erin Tolley (eds.) 2012. ISBN 978-1-55339-309-2

Making EI Work: Research from the Mowat Centre Employment Insurance Task Force, Keith Banting and Jon Medow (eds.) 2012. ISBN 978-1-55339-323-8

Managing Immigration and Diversity in Canada: A Transatlantic Dialogue in the New Age of Migration, Dan Rodríguez-García (ed.) 2012. ISBN 978-1-55339-289-7

International Perspectives: Integration and Inclusion, James Frideres and John Biles (eds.) 2012. ISBN 978-1-55339-317-7

Dynamic Negotiations: Teacher Labour Relations in Canadian Elementary and Secondary Education, Sara Slinn and Arthur Sweetman (eds.) 2012. ISBN 978-1-55339-304-7

Where to from Here? Keeping Medicare Sustainable, Stephen Duckett 2012. ISBN 978-1-55339-318-4

International Migration in Uncertain Times, John Nieuwenhuysen, Howard Duncan, and Stine Neerup (eds.) 2012. ISBN 978-1-55339-308-5

Life After Forty: Official Languages Policy in Canada/Après quarante ans, les politiques de langue officielle au Canada, Jack Jedwab and Rodrigue Landry (eds.) 2011. ISBN 978-1-55339-279-8

From Innovation to Transformation: Moving up the Curve in Ontario Healthcare, Hon. Elinor Caplan, Dr. Tom Bigda-Peyton, Maia MacNiven, and Sandy Sheahan 2011. ISBN 978-1-55339-315-3

Academic Reform: Policy Options for Improving the Quality and Cost-Effectiveness of Undergraduate Education in Ontario, Ian D. Clark, David Trick, and Richard Van Loon 2011. ISBN 978-1-55339-310-8

Integration and Inclusion of Newcomers and Minorities across Canada, John Biles, Meyer Burstein, James Frideres, Erin Tolley, and Robert Vineberg (eds.) 2011. ISBN 978-1-55339-290-3

A New Synthesis of Public Administration: Serving in the 21st Century, Jocelyne Bourgon, 2011. ISBN 978-1-55339-312-2 (paper) 978-1-55339-313-9 (cloth)

Recreating Canada: Essays in Honour of Paul Weiler, Randall Morck (ed.), 2011. ISBN 978-1-55339-273-6

Data Data Everywhere: Access and Accountability? Colleen M. Flood (ed.), 2011. ISBN 978-1-55339-236-1

Making the Case: Using Case Studies for Teaching and Knowledge Management in Public Administration, Andrew Graham, 2011. ISBN 978-1-55339-302-3

Centre for International and Defence Policy

Afghanistan in the Balance: Counterinsurgency, Comprehensive Approach, and Political Order, Hans-Georg Ehrhart, Sven Bernhard Gareis, and Charles Pentland (eds.), 2012. ISBN 978-1-55339-353-5

Security Operations in the 21st Century: Canadian Perspectives on the Comprehensive Approach, Michael Rostek and Peter Gizewski (eds.), 2011. ISBN 978-1-55339-351-1

Institute of Intergovernmental Relations

Canada and the Crown: Essays on Constitutional Monarchy, D. Michael Jackson and Philippe Lagassé (eds.), 2013. ISBN 978-1-55339-204-0

Paradigm Freeze: Why It Is So Hard to Reform Health-Care Policy in Canada, Harvey Lazar, John N. Lavis, Pierre-Gerlier Forest, and John Church (eds.), 2013. ISBN 978-1-55339-324-5

Canada: The State of the Federation 2010, Matthew Mendelsohn, Joshua Hjartarson, and James Pearce (eds.), 2013. ISBN 978-1-55339-200-2

The Democratic Dilemma: Reforming Canada's Supreme Court, Nadia Verrelli (ed.), 2013. ISBN 978-1-55339-203-3

The Evolving Canadian Crown, Jennifer Smith and D. Michael Jackson (eds.), 2011. ISBN 978-1-55339-202-6

The Federal Idea: Essays in Honour of Ronald L. Watts, Thomas J. Courchene, John R. Allan, Christian Leuprecht, and Nadia Verrelli (eds.), 2011. ISBN 978-1-55339-198-2 (paper) 978-1-55339-199-9 (cloth)

The Democratic Dilemma: Reforming the Canadian Senate, Jennifer Smith (ed.), 2009. ISBN 978-1-55339-190-6